MAC OS® X Leopard For Dummies®

I0572124

Top Six Things You Should Never Do

6. Never clean your monitor with Windex (or another product not designed to be used on video display). And nix on the paper towels and tissues, too — use a soft cloth (microfiber is best) if you want to avoid scratching the display.

5. Never pay attention to anyone who says that Windows is just like the Mac. Yeah, right. And Hyundai is the Asian cousin of BMW.

4. Never bump, drop, shake, wobble, dribble, drop-kick, or play catch with a hard drive (or PowerBook, iBook, MacBook, or MacBook Pro, which contain hard drives) while it's running. Don't forget: Your desktop Mac has a hard drive inside it, too.

3. Never shut off your Mac by pulling the plug. Always use the Shut Down command from the Apple menu (or press the Power button and then click the Shut Down button).

2. Never get up from your Mac without saving your work. Just before your behind leaves the chair, your fingers should be pressing ⌘+S. Make it a habit.

1. Never keep only one copy of your important documents. Make at least two backup copies and keep one of them in another location. Period.

Five Awesome Web Sites for Mac OS X Lovers

www.apple.com/support: The Apple support site and Knowledge Base are treasure troves of tech notes, software update information, troubleshooting tips, and documentation for most Apple products.

www.macintouch.com: This is the preeminent Mac news and information site, full of tips, hints, and troubleshooting information. Many users consider MacInTouch (along with MacSurfer and MacFixit) a must-read every day.

www.versiontracker.com: VersionTracker is the place to go to find freeware, shareware, and software updates for Mac OS X. If VersionTracker doesn't have it, it probably doesn't exist.

www.macminute.com: This site is where those in the know go for up-to-the-minute Mac news. Just the facts — usually in a single paragraph, with a link to more information.

www.boblevitus.com: This is the site for what is, in effect, my day job. I have a team of Mac experts ready to provide you with technical help and training via telephone, e-mail, and/or our unique Internet-enabled remote control software. We (usually) offer same-day service, and our prices are quite reasonable.

MAC OS® X Leopard For Dummies®

Cheat Sheet

Keyboard Shortcuts

Make these shortcuts second nature. All these shortcuts work in the Finder, and many of them work in other application programs, as well. See those perforations over there? That's so you can tear out this cheat sheet and memorize these shortcuts. Ready? Fold at the perforations, crease, and RIP!

Command	Keyboard Shortcut
Add Selected Item to Sidebar	⌘+T
Close All Windows	⌘+Option+W
Close Window	⌘+W
Copy	⌘+C
Cut	⌘+X
Dashboard	F12
Duplicate	⌘+D
Eject Disk	⌘+E
Empty Trash	⌘+Shift+Delete
Exposé: All Windows	F9
Exposé: Application Windows	F10
Exposé: Desktop	F11
Find	⌘+F
Get Info	⌘+I
Go to Applications Folder	⌘+Shift+A
Go to Desktop	⌘+Shift+D
Go to Home Folder	⌘+Shift+H
Help	⌘+Shift+?
Hide Current Application	⌘+H
Log Out Current User	⌘+Shift+Q
Make Alias	⌘+L

Command	Keyboard Shortcut
Minimize Window	⌘+M
Move to Trash	⌘+Delete
New Finder Window	⌘+N
New Folder	⌘+Shift+N
New Smart Folder	⌘+Option+N
Next Window	⌘+`
Open	⌘+O
Open Inspector	⌘+Option+I
Paste	⌘+V
Quick Look (at selected item)	⌘+Y
Select All	⌘+A
Show Original (of selected alias)	⌘+R
Show View Options	⌘+J
Show/Hide Dock	⌘+Option+D
Turn VoiceOver On/Off	⌘+F5
Turn Zoom On/Off	⌘+Option+8
Undo	⌘+Z
View Window as Columns	⌘+3
View Window as Icons	⌘+1
View Window as List	⌘+2

For Dummies: Bestselling Book Series for Beginners

Mac OS® X Leopard™
FOR
DUMMIES®

by Bob "Dr. Mac" LeVitus

Wiley Publishing, Inc.

Mac OS® X Leopard™ For Dummies®

Published by
Wiley Publishing, Inc.
111 River Street
Hoboken, NJ 07030-5774
www.wiley.com

WILEY

About the Author

Bob LeVitus, often referred to as "Dr. Mac," has written nearly 50 popular computer books, including *Dr. Mac: The OS X Files* and *GarageBand For Dummies* for Wiley Publishing, Inc.; *Stupid Mac Tricks* and *Dr. Macintosh* for Addison-Wesley; and *The Little iTunes Book*, 3rd Edition and *The Little iDVD Book*, 2nd Edition for Peachpit Press. His books have sold more than a million copies worldwide.

Bob has penned the popular Dr. Mac column for the Houston *Chronicle* for the past ten years and has been published in dozens of computer magazines over the past 15 years. His achievements have been documented in major media around the world. (Yes, that was him juggling a keyboard in *USA Today* a few years back!)

Bob is known for his expertise, trademark humorous style, and ability to translate techie jargon into usable and fun advice for regular folks. Bob is also a prolific public speaker, presenting more than 100 Macworld Expo training sessions in the U.S. and abroad, keynote addresses in three countries, and Macintosh training seminars in many U.S. cities. (He also won the Macworld Expo MacJeopardy World Championship three times before retiring his crown.)

Bob is considered one of the world's leading authorities on Mac OS. From 1989 to 1997, he was a contributing editor/columnist for *MacUser* magazine, writing the Help Folder, Beating the System, Personal Best, and Game Room columns at various times.

In his copious spare time, Bob heads up a team of expert technical consultants who do nothing but provide technical help and training to Mac users via telephone, e-mail, and/or our unique Internet-enabled remote control software, which allows the team to see and control your Mac no matter where in the world you may be.

If you're having problems with your Mac, you ought to give them a try. You'll find them at www.boblevitus.com or 408-627-7577.

Prior to giving his life over to computers, LeVitus spent years at Kresser/Craig/D.I.K. (a Los Angeles advertising agency and marketing consultancy) and its subsidiary, L & J Research. He holds a B.S. in Marketing from California State University.

Dedication

This book is dedicated to my wife, Lisa, who taught me almost everything I know about almost everything except computers. And to my children, Allison and Jacob, who love Macs almost as much as I love them (my kids, not my Macs).

Author's Acknowledgments

Special thanks to everyone at Apple who helped me turn this book around in record time: Keri Walker, Janette Barrios, Greg (Joz) Joswiak, and all the rest. I couldn't have done it without you.

Thanks also to super-agent Carole "Swifty-for-life" McClendon, for deal-making beyond the call of duty, again. You've been my agent for over 20 years and you're *still* a treasure.

Big-time thanks to the gang at Wiley: Bob "Is the damn thing done yet?" Woerner, Becky "Whipcracker VII" Huehls, Andy "The Big Boss Man" Cummings, Barry "Still no humorous nickname" Pruett, and my technical editor Dennis R. Cohen, who did a rocking job as always, and all the others.

Thanks also to my family and friends, for putting up with me during my all-too lengthy absences during this book's gestation. And thanks to Saccone's Pizza, Home Slice Pizza, The Iron Works BBQ, Taco Cabana, Diet Coke, and ShortStop for sustenance.

And finally, thanks to you, gentle reader, for buying this book.

Publisher's Acknowledgments

We're proud of this book; please send us your comments through our online registration form located at www.dummies.com/register/.

Some of the people who helped bring this book to market include the following:

Acquisitions, Editorial, and Media Development

Project Editor: Rebecca Huehls

Sr. Acquisitions Editor: Bob Woerner

Copy Editor: Virginia Sanders

Technical Editor: Dennis Cohen

Editorial Manager: Leah P. Cameron

Editorial Assistant: Amanda Foxworth

Sr. Editorial Assistant: Cherie Case

Cartoons: Rich Tennant
(www.the5thwave.com)

Composition Services

Project Coordinator: Lynsey Osborn

Layout and Graphics: Claudia Bell, Stacie Brooks, Carl Byers, Reuben Davis, Joyce Haughey, Barbara Moore, Melanee Prendergast

Proofreaders: John Greenough, Kathy Simpson

Indexer: Sherry Massey

Anniversary Logo Design: Richard Pacifico

Special Help:
Kate Jenkins

Publishing and Editorial for Technology Dummies

Richard Swadley, Vice President and Executive Group Publisher

Andy Cummings, Vice President and Publisher

Mary Bednarek, Executive Acquisitions Director

Mary C. Corder, Editorial Director

Publishing for Consumer Dummies

Diane Graves Steele, Vice President and Publisher

Joyce Pepple, Acquisitions Director

Composition Services

Gerry Fahey, Vice President of Production Services

Debbie Stailey, Director of Composition Services

Contents at a Glance

Table of Contents

Introduction

You made the right choice twice: Mac OS X Leopard and this book.

Take a deep breath and get ready to have a rollicking good time. That's right. This is a computer book, but it's going to be fun. What a concept! Whether you're brand spanking new to the Mac or a grizzled old Mac vet, I guarantee that discovering the ins and outs of Mac OS X Leopard will be fun and easy. Wiley, Inc. (the publisher of this book) couldn't say it on the cover if it weren't true!

About This Book

This book's roots lie with my international bestseller *Macintosh System 7.5 For Dummies,* an award-winning book so good that now-deceased Mac cloner Power Computing gave away a copy with every Mac clone it sold. *Mac OS X Leopard For Dummies* is the latest revision and has been, once again, completely updated to include all the cool new features found in Mac OS X Leopard. In other words, this edition combines all the old, familiar features of editions — but is once again expanded and updated to reflect the latest and greatest offering from Apple.

Why write a *For Dummies* book about Leopard? Well, Leopard is a big, somewhat complicated, personal-computer operating system. So I made *Mac OS X Leopard For Dummies* a not-so-big, not-very-complicated book that shows you what Leopard is all about without boring you to tears, confusing you, or poking you with sharp objects.

In fact, I think you'll be so darned comfortable that I wanted the title to be *Mac OS X Leopard Without Discomfort,* but the publishers wouldn't let me. Apparently, we *For Dummies* authors have to follow some rules, and using *Dummies* and *Mac OS X Leopard* in this book's title are among them.

And speaking of *"dummies,"* remember that it's just a word. I don't think you're dumb — quite the opposite! My second choice for this book's title was *Mac OS X Leopard For People Smart Enough to Know They Need Help with It,* but you can just imagine what Wiley thought of that. ("C'mon, that's the whole point of the name!" they insisted. "Besides, it's shorter this way.")

Anyway, the book is chock-full of information and advice, explaining everything you need to know about Mac OS X in language you can understand — along with timesaving tips, tricks, techniques, and step-by-step instructions, all served up in generous quantities.

What You Won't Find in This Book

Another rule we *For Dummies* authors must follow is that our books cannot exceed a certain number of pages. (Brevity is the soul of wit, and all that.) So I wish I could have included some things, but they didn't fit. Although I feel confident you'll find everything you need to know about Mac OS X Leopard in this book, some things bear further looking into, including these:

✔ **Information about some of the applications (programs) that come with Mac OS X Leopard**

An installation of Mac OS X Leopard includes more than 50 separate applications, mostly found in the Applications folder and the Utilities folder within it. I'd love to walk you through each one of them, but that would have required a book a whole lot bigger, heavier, and more expensive than this one.

This book is, first and foremost, about using Mac OS X, so I brief you on the small handful of bundled applications essential to using Mac OS X Leopard and keep the focus there — namely, iCal, Address Book, TextEdit, and the like, as well as important utilities you may need to know how to use someday.

For what it's worth, many books cover the applications that come with Mac OS X Leopard as well as applications commonly bundled with Leopard on a new Mac, such as iLife; the one my publisher suggested I recommend is *Mac OS X Leopard All-in-One Desk Reference For Dummies,* written by Mark L. Chambers, which is (by sheer coincidence, of course) also published by Wiley.

✔ **Information about Microsoft Office, iLife, iWork, Adobe Photoshop, Quicken, and most other third-party applications**

Okay, if all the gory details of all the bundled (read: *free*) Mac OS X Leopard applications don't fit here, I think you'll understand why digging into third-party applications that cost extra was out of the question.

✔ **Information about programming for the Mac**

This book is about *using* Mac OS X Leopard, not writing code for it. Dozens of books cover programming on the Mac, most of which are two or three times the size of this book.

For what it's worth, Dennis Cohen, my technical editor, and his brother Michael wrote a great book about Xcode 3, the development environment included with Mac OS X Leopard. It's called *The Xcode 3 Book* and, by sheer coincidence, is also published by (who else?) Wiley.

Conventions Used in This Book

To get the most out of this book, you need to know how I do things and why. Here are a few conventions I use in this book to make your life easier:

- When I want you to open an item in a menu, I write something like "Choose File⇨Open," which means, "Pull down the File menu and choose the Open command."

- Stuff you're supposed to type appears in bold type, **like this.**

- **Sometimes an entire a sentence is in boldface, as you see when I present a numbered list of steps. In those cases, I leave the bold off what you're supposed to type,** like this.

- Web addresses, programming code (not much in this book), and things that appear on-screen are shown in a special monofont typeface, `like this.`

- For keyboard shortcuts, I write something like ⌘+A, which means to hold down the ⌘ key (the one with the little pretzel and/or symbol on it) and then press the A key on the keyboard. If you see something like ⌘+Shift+A, that means to hold down the ⌘ and Shift keys while pressing the A key. Again, for absolute clarity, I never refer to the ⌘ key with the symbol. I reserve that symbol for the menu (Apple menu). For the Command key, I use only the ⌘ symbol. Got it? Very cool.

Foolish Assumptions

Although I know what happens when you make assumptions, I've made a few anyway. First, I assume that you, gentle reader, know nothing about using Mac OS X — beyond knowing what a Mac is, that you want to use OS X, that you want to understand OS X without digesting an incomprehensible technical manual, and that you made the right choice by selecting this particular book.

And so I do my best to explain each new concept in full and loving detail. Maybe that's foolish, but . . . oh well.

Oh, and I also assume that you can read. If you can't, ignore this paragraph.

How This Book Is Organized

Mac OS X Leopard For Dummies is divided into six logical parts, numbered (surprisingly enough) 1 through 6. By no fault of mine, they're numbered using those stuffy old Roman numerals, so you see I–VI where you (in my humble opinion) ought to see Arabic numbers 1–6. It's another rule that *For Dummies* authors have to follow, I think.

Anyway, it's better if you read the parts in order, but if you already know a lot — or think you know a lot — feel free to skip around and read the parts that interest you most.

Part I: Introducing Mac OS X Leopard: The Basics: This first part is very, very basic training. From the mouse to the Desktop, from menus, windows, and icons to the snazzy-but-helpful Dock, it's all here. A lot of what you need to know to navigate the depths of Mac OS X safely and sanely and perform basic tasks can be found in this part. And although old-timers might just want to skim through it, newcomers should probably read every word. Twice.

Part II: Leopard Taming (Or "Organization for Smart People"): In this part, I build on the basics of Part I and really get you revving with your Mac. Here, I cover additional topics that every Mac user needs to know, coupled with some hands-on, step-by-step instructions. The part starts with a closer look at ways you can organize your files and folders, followed by a chapter about using removable media (which means *ejectable disks* — mostly CDs and DVDs). Last, but certainly not least, is a chapter about all the Leopard applications (such as iCal, Address Book, and Mail) that help you keep your digital life organized.

Part III: Do Unto Leopard: Getting Things Done: This part is chock full of ways to do productive stuff with your Mac. In this section, you discover the Internet first — how to get it working on your Mac and what to do with it after you do. Next, you look at the digital-media side of things with chapters about music, video, games, and digital photos. Finally, you look at Leopard's built-in tools for writing — namely, TextEdit and fonts.

Part IV: Making This Leopard Your Very Own: Here, I get into the nitty-gritty underbelly of making Mac OS X Leopard work the way you want it to work. I start with the ins and outs of printing under OS X. Then I move on to somewhat more advanced topics, such as file sharing, creating and using multiple users (and why you might want to), and the lowdown on numerous Mac OS X Leopard features — Text to Speech, speech recognition, automation, and more — that can make your computing experience even more pleasant.

Part V: The Care and Feeding of Your Leopard: This part starts with a chapter about backups and security, which not only stresses the importance of backing up your data, but also shows you how to do it almost painlessly. Then I introduce you to a handful of useful utilities included with Leopard and explain when and how to use them. Finally, I tell you how to avoid most disasters, as well as what to do in the unlikely event that a major mishap does occur.

Part VI: The Part of Tens: Finally, it's The Part of Tens, which might have started life as a Letterman rip-off, although it does include heaping helpings of tips, optional software, great Mac Web sites, and hardware ideas.

Appendix: Last, but certainly not least, I cover installing Mac OS X Leopard in the appendix. The whole process has become quite easy with this version of the system software, but if you have to install Leopard yourself, it would behoove you to read this helpful appendix first.

Icons Used in This Book

Little round pictures (icons) appear off to the left side of the text throughout this book. Consider these icons miniature road signs, telling you a little something extra about the topic at hand. Here's what the different icons look like and what they all mean.

Look for Tip icons to find the juiciest morsels: shortcuts, tips, and undocumented secrets about Leopard. Try them all; impress your friends!

When you see this icon, it means that this particular morsel is something that I think you should memorize (or at least write on your shirt cuff).

Put on your propeller-beanie hat and pocket protector; these parts include the truly geeky stuff. It's certainly not required reading, but it must be interesting or informative, or I wouldn't have wasted your time with it.

Read these notes very, very, very carefully. (Did I say *very?*) Warning icons flag important information. The author and publisher won't be responsible if your Mac explodes or spews flaming parts because you ignored a Warning icon. Just kidding. Macs don't explode or spew (with the exception of a few choice PowerBook 5300s, which won't run Leopard anyway). But I got your attention, didn't I? I'll tell you once again: It is a good idea to read the Warning notes very carefully.

These icons represent my ranting or raving about something that either bugs me or makes me smile. When I'm ranting, imagine foam coming from my mouth. Rants are required to be irreverent, irrelevant, or both. I try to keep them short, more for your sake than mine.

Well, now, what could this icon possibly be about? Named by famous editorial consultant Mr. Obvious, this icon highlights all things new and different in Mac OS X Leopard.

Where to Go from Here

Go to a comfortable spot (preferably not far from a Mac) and read the book.

The first few chapters of this book are where I describe the basic everyday things that you need to understand to operate your Mac effectively. If you're new to Macs and OS X Leopard, start there.

Even though Mac OS X Leopard is way different from previous Mac operating systems, the first part of the book is so basic that if you've been using a Mac for long, you might think you know it all — and you might know most of it. But hey! Not-so-old-timers need a solid foundation. So here's my advice: Skip the stuff you know; you'll get to the better stuff faster.

I didn't write this book for myself. I wrote it for you and would love to hear how it worked for you. So please drop me a line or register your comments through the Wiley Online Registration Form located at www.dummies.com.

You can send snail mail in care of Wiley, or send e-mail to me directly at Leopard4Dummies@boblevitus.com. I appreciate your feedback, and I *try* to respond to all reasonably polite e-mail within a few days.

Did this book work for you? What did you like? What didn't you like? What questions were unanswered? Did you want to know more about something? Did you want to find out less about something? Tell me! I have received more than 100 suggestions about previous editions, most of which are incorporated here. So keep up the good work!

So what are you waiting for? Go — enjoy the book!

Part I

Introducing Mac OS X Leopard: The Basics

The 5th Wave   By Rich Tennant

"He saw your laptop and wants to know if he can check out the new OS X features."

In this part . . .

Mac OS X Leopard sports tons of new goodies and features. I get to the hot new goodies soon enough, but the standard approach is to crawl first and walk later.

In this part, you discover the most basic of basics, such as how to turn on your Mac. Next, I acquaint you with the Mac OS X Desktop, with its windows, icons, and menus (oh my)! Then you find out how to make this cat your own by customizing your work environment to suit your style. After that is a date with the Dock. And last but certainly not least, you discover some basic tasks that make life with Leopard ever so much easier.

So get comfortable, roll up your sleeves, fire up your Mac if you like, and settle down with Part I, a delightful little section I like to think of as "The Hassle-Free Way to Get Started with Mac OS X Leopard."

Chapter 1

Mac OS X Leopard 101 (Prerequisites: None)

Congratulate yourself on choosing Mac OS X, which stands for Macintosh Operating System X — that's the Roman numeral *ten,* not the letter *X* (pronounced *ten,* not *ex*). You made a smart move because you scored more than just an operating system upgrade. Mac OS X Leopard includes a plethora of new or improved features to make using your Mac easier and dozens more that help you do more work in less time.

In this chapter, I start at the very beginning and talk about Mac OS X in mostly abstract terms; then I move on to explain important information that you need to know to use Mac OS X Leopard successfully.

If you've been using Mac OS X for a while, you might find some of the information in this chapter hauntingly familiar; some features that I describe haven't changed from earlier versions of Mac OS X. But if you decide to skip this chapter because you think you have all the new stuff figured out, I assure you that you'll miss at least a couple of things that Apple didn't bother to tell you (as if you read every word in Mac OS X Help, the only user manual Apple provides, anyway!).

Tantalized? Let's rock.

If you're about to upgrade to Leopard from an earlier version of Mac OS X, I feel obliged to mention a major pitfall to avoid: One very specific misplaced click, done while installing your new OS, could erase every file on your hard drive. The appendix describes this situation in full and loving detail, and it contains other important information about installing Leopard that can make upgrading a more pleasant experience.

Gnawing to the Core of OS X

The operating system (that is, the *OS* in *Mac OS X*) is what makes a Mac a Mac. Without it, your Mac is a pile of silicon and circuits — no smarter than a toaster.

"So what does an operating system do?" you ask. Good question. The short answer is that an *operating system* controls the basic and most important functions of your computer. In the case of Mac OS X and your Mac, the operating system

- Manages memory
- Controls how windows, icons, and menus work
- Keeps track of files
- Manages networking
- Does housekeeping (No kidding!)

Other forms of software, such as word processors and Web browsers, rely on the operating system to create and maintain the environment in which that software works its magic. When you create a memo, for example, the word processor provides the tools for you to type and format the information. In the background, the operating system is the muscle for the word processor, performing crucial functions such as the following:

- Providing the mechanism for drawing and moving the on-screen window in which you write the memo
- Keeping track of a file when you save it
- Helping the word processor create drop-down menus and dialogs for you to interact with
- Communicating with other programs
- And much, much more (stuff that only geeks could care about)

So, armed with a little background in operating systems, take a gander at the next section before you do anything else with your Mac.

The Mac advantage

Most of the world's personal computers use Microsoft Windows. You're among the lucky few to have a computer with an operating system that's intuitive, easy to use, and (dare I say?) fun. If you don't believe me, try using Windows for a day or two. Go ahead. You probably won't suffer any permanent damage. In fact, you'll really begin to appreciate how good you have it. Feel free to hug your Mac. Or give it a peck on the disc-drive slot — just try not to get your tongue caught.

As someone once told me, "Claiming that the Macintosh is inferior to Windows because most people use Windows is like saying that all other restaurants serve food that's inferior to McDonald's."

We might be a minority, but Mac users have the best, most stable, most modern all-purpose operating system in the world, and here's why: UNIX — on which Mac OS X is based — is widely regarded as the best industrial-strength operating system on the planet. For now, just

know that being based on UNIX means that a Mac running OS X will crash less often than an older Mac or a Windows machine, which means less downtime. And being UNIX-based also means far fewer viruses and malicious software. But perhaps the biggest advantage OS X has is that when an application crashes, it doesn't crash your entire computer, and you don't have to restart the thing to continue working.

By the way, with the advent of Intel-powered Macs last year, you now have the ability to run Windows natively. That's right — you can now install and run Microsoft Windows on any Mac powered by an Intel processor, as described in Chapter 16.

Don't let that UNIX stuff scare you. It's there if you want it, but if you don't want it or don't care (like most of us), you'll rarely even know it's there. All you'll know is that your Mac just runs and runs and runs without crashing and crashing and crashing.

One last thing: As I mention in the introduction (I'm only repeating it in case you don't read introductions), Mac OS X Leopard comes with more than 50 applications. And although I'd love to tell you all about each and every one, I have only so many pages at my disposal. If you need more info on the programs I don't cover, may I (again) recommend *Mac OS X Leopard All-in-One Desk Reference For Dummies,* written by Mark L. Chambers, or *iLife All-in-One Desk Reference For Dummies,* written by my old friends Tony Bove and Cheryl Rhodes (both from Wiley).

A Safety Net for the Absolute Beginner (Or Any User)

In the following sections, I deal with the stuff that the manual that came with your Mac doesn't cover — or doesn't cover in nearly enough detail. If you're a first-time Macintosh user, please, *please* read this section of the book carefully — it could save your life. Okay, okay, perhaps I'm being overly dramatic. What I mean to say is that reading this section could save your *Mac*. Even if you're an experienced Mac user, you might want to read this section anyway. Chances are good that you'll see at least a few things you might have forgotten that might come in handy.

Turning the dang thing on

Okay. This is the big moment — turning on your Mac! Gaze at it longingly first and say something cheesy, such as "You're the most awesome computer I've ever known." If that doesn't turn on your Mac (and it probably won't), keep reading.

Apple, in its infinite wisdom, has manufactured Macs with power switches and buttons on every conceivable surface: on the front, side, and back of the computer itself, and even on the keyboard or monitor.

So if you don't know how to turn on your Mac, don't feel bad — just look in the manual or booklet that came with your Mac. It's at least one thing that the documentation *always* covers.

 These days, most Macs have a power-on button on the keyboard. It usually looks like the little circle thingie you see in the margin.

 Don't bother choosing Help⇨Mac Help, which opens the Help Viewer program, because it can't tell you where the switch is. Although the Help program is good for finding out a lot of things, the location of the power switch isn't among them. Of course, if you haven't found the switch and turned on the Mac, you can't access Help anyway. (D'oh!)

What you should see on startup

When you finally do turn on your Macintosh, you set in motion a sophisticated and complex series of events that culminates in the loading of Mac OS X and the appearance of the Mac OS X Desktop. After a small bit of whirring, buzzing, and flashing (meaning that the operating system is loading), OS X first tests all your hardware — slots, ports, disks, random-access memory (RAM), and so on. If everything passes, you hear a pleasing musical tone and see the tasteful gray Apple logo in the middle of your screen, along with a small spinning-pinwheel cursor somewhere on the screen. Both are shown in Figure 1-1.

Figure 1-1:
This is
what you
see when
Mac OS X
starts up.

Here are the things that might happen when you power up your Mac:

✔ **Everything is fine and dandy:** Next, you might or might not see the Mac OS X login screen, where you enter your name and password. If you do, press Return or Enter (after you type your name and password, of course), and away you go.

If you don't want to have to type your name and password every time you start or restart your Mac (or even if you do), check out Chapter 17 for the scoop on how to turn the login screen on or off.

Either way, the Desktop soon materializes before your eyes. If you haven't customized, configured, or tinkered with your Desktop, it should look pretty much like Figure 1-2. Now is a good time to take a moment for positive thoughts about the person who convinced you that you wanted a Mac. That person was right!

Figure 1-2:
The Mac
OS X
Desktop
after a
brand-
spanking-
new
installation
of OS X.

The legend of the boot

Boot this. *Boot* that. "I *booted* my Mac and...." or "Did it *boot*?" and so on. Talking about computers for long without hearing the *boot* word is nearly impossible.

But why *boot*? Why not *shoe* or *shirt* or even *shazam*?

Back in the very olden days — maybe the 1960s or a little earlier — starting up a computer required you to toggle little manual switches on the front panel, which began an internal process that loaded the operating system. The process became known as *bootstrapping* because if you toggled the right switches, the computer would "pull itself up by its bootstraps." This phrase didn't take long to transmogrify into *booting* and finally to *boot.*

Over the years, *booting* has come to mean turning on almost any computer or even a peripheral device, such as a printer. Some people also use it to refer to launching an application: "I booted Excel."

So the next time one of your gearhead friends says the *b*-word, ask whether he knows where the term comes from. Then dazzle him with the depth and breadth of your (not-quite-useful) knowledge!

✔ **Sad Mac:** If any of your hardware fails when it's tested, you might see a black or gray screen that might or might not display the dreaded Sad Mac icon (shown in the left margin) and/or hear a far less pleasing musical chord (in the key of F-minor, I believe), known by Mac aficionados as the *Chimes of Doom.*

Some older Macs played the sound of a horrible car wreck instead of the chimes, complete with crying tires and busting glass. It was exceptionally unnerving, which might be why Apple doesn't use it anymore.

The fact that something went wrong is no reflection on your prowess as a Macintosh user. Something inside your Mac is broken, and it probably needs repairs. If any of that has already happened to you, check out Chapter 19 to try to get your Mac well again.

If your computer is under warranty, dial 1-800-SOS-APPL, and a customer-service person can tell you what to do. Before you do anything, though, skip ahead to Chapter 19. It's entirely possible that one of the suggestions there can get you back on track without your having to spend even a moment on hold.

✔ **Prohibitory sign (formerly known as the flashing-question-mark disk):** Although it's unlikely that you'll ever see the Sad Mac, most users eventually encounter the prohibitory sign shown in the left margin (which replaced the flashing question-mark-on-a-disk icon and flashing folder icon back in Mac OS X Jaguar). This icon means your Mac can't find a startup disk, hard drive, network server, or CD-ROM containing a valid Macintosh operating system. See Chapter 19 for ways you can try to ease your Mac's ills.

✔ **Kernel panic:** You shouldn't see this very often, but you might occasionally see a block of text in four languages, including English. This means that your Mac has experienced a kernel panic, the most severe type of system crash. Look in Chapter 19 for a myriad of cures for all kinds of ailments, including this one.

How do you know which version of the Mac OS your computer has? Simple. Just choose About This Mac from the menu (the menu with the symbol in the upper-left corner of the menu bar). The About This Mac window pops up on your screen, as shown in Figure 1-3. The version you're running appears just below *Mac OS X* in the center of the window. Click the More Info button to launch the System Profiler application, which has much more information, including bus speed, number of processors, caches, installed memory, networking, storage devices, and much more. You can find more about this useful program in Chapter 18.

Figure 1-3:
See which version of Mac OS X you're running.

Shutting down properly

Turning off the power without shutting down your Mac properly is one of the worst things you can do to your poor Mac. Shutting down your Mac improperly can really screw up your hard drive, scramble the contents of your most important files, or both.

If a thunderstorm is rumbling nearby or you're unfortunate enough to have rolling blackouts where you live, you might *really* want to shut down your Mac. (See the next section, where I briefly discuss lightning and your Mac.)

To turn off your Mac, always use the Shut Down command on the menu (which I discuss in Chapter 4) or shut down in one of these kind-and-gentle ways:

Eternally yours . . . *now*

Mac OS X is designed so you never have to shut it down. You can configure it to sleep after a specified period of inactivity. (See Chapter 16 for more info on the Energy Saver features of OS X.) If you do so, your Mac will consume very little electricity when it's sleeping and will be ready to use just a few seconds after you awaken it (by pressing any key or clicking the mouse). On the other hand, if you're not going to be using it for a few days, you might want to shut it down anyway.

Note: If you leave your Mac on constantly and you're gone when a lightning storm or rolling blackout hits, your Mac might get wasted. So be sure you have adequate protection (say, a decent surge protector designed specifically for computers) if you decide to leave your Mac on and unattended for long periods. See the section "A few things you should definitely NOT do with your Mac," elsewhere in this chapter, for more info on lightning and your Mac. Frankly, if I plan to be away from mine for more than a day, I usually shut it down, just in case. But because OS X is designed to run 24/7, I don't shut it down at night unless it's dark and stormy.

✔ Press the Power key once and then click the Shut Down button.

✔ On keyboards that don't have a Power key, press Control+Eject instead and then click the Shut Down button that appears (or press the Return key, which does the same thing).

Of course, most Mac users have broken this rule several times without anything horrible happening — but don't be lulled into a false sense of security. Break the rules one time too many (or under the wrong circumstances), and your most important file *will* be toast. The only time you should turn off your Mac without shutting down properly is when your screen is frozen or when your system crashed and you've already tried everything else. (See Chapter 19 for what those "everything elses" are.) A really stubborn crash doesn't happen often — and less often under OS X than ever before — but when it does, turning your Mac off and then back on might be the only solution.

A few things you should definitely NOT do with your Mac

In this section, I cover the bad stuff that can happen to your computer if you do the wrong things with it. If something bad has already happened to you — I know . . . I'm beginning to sound like a broken record — see Chapter 19.

✔ **Don't unplug your Mac when it's turned on.** Very bad things can happen, such as having your operating system break. See the preceding section, where I discuss shutting down your system properly.

✔ **Don't use your Mac when lightning is near.** Here's a simple life equation for you: Mac + lightning = dead Mac. 'Nuff said. Oh, and don't place much faith in inexpensive surge protectors. A good jolt of lightning will fry the surge protector right along with your computer — as well as possibly frying your modem, printer, and anything else plugged into it. Some surge protectors can withstand most lightning strikes, but these warriors aren't the cheapies that you buy at your local computer emporium. Unplugging your Mac from the wall during electrical storms is safer and less expensive. (Don't forget to unplug your external modem, network hubs, printers, and other hardware that plugs into the wall, as well — lightning can fry them, too.)

✔ **Don't jostle, bump, shake, kick, throw, dribble, or punt your Mac, especially while it's running.** Your Mac contains a hard drive that spins at 4,200 revolutions per minute (rpm) or more. A jolt to a hard drive while it's reading or writing a file can cause the head to crash into the disk, which can render many or all files on it unrecoverable. Ouch!

✔ **Don't forget to back up your data!** If the stuff on your hard drive means anything to you, you must back it up. Not maybe. You must. Even if your most important file is your last saved game of Call of Duty 2, you still need to realize how important it is to back up your files. Fortunately, Mac OS X Leopard offers, for the very first time, an awesome backup utility called Time Machine. So I beg you: Please read Chapter 17 now and find out how to back up before something horrible happens to your valuable data!

I *strongly* recommend that you read Chapter 17 sooner rather than later — preferably before you do any significant work on your Mac. Dr. Macintosh says, "There are only two kinds of Mac users: those who have never lost data and those who will." Which kind do you want to be?

✔ **Don't kiss your monitor while wearing stuff on your lips.** For obvious reasons! Use a soft cloth and/or OmniCleanz display cleaning solution (I love the stuff, made by RadTech; www.radtech.us) to clean your display.

Point-and-click boot camp

Are you new to the Mac? Just figuring out how to move the mouse around? Now is a good time to go over some fundamental stuff that you need to know for just about everything you'll be doing on the Mac. Spend a few minutes reading this section, and soon you'll be clicking, double-clicking, pressing, and pointing all over the place. If you think you have the whole mousing thing pretty much figured out, feel free to skip this section. I'll catch you on the other side.

Still with me? Good. Now for some basic terminology:

- ✔ **Point:** Before you can click or press anything, you have to *point* to it. Place your hand on your mouse and move it so that the cursor arrow is over the object you want — like on top of an icon or a button. Then click the mouse button to select the object or double-click to run it (if it's an application or an icon that starts up an application). You point and then you click — *point and click,* in computer lingo.

- ✔ **Click:** Also called *single-click.* Use your index finger to push the mouse button all the way down and then let go so the button produces a satisfying clicking sound. (If you have one of the new optical Apple Pro mice, you push down the whole thing to click.) Use a single-click to highlight an icon, press a button, or activate a check box or window.

- ✔ **Double-click:** *Click twice* in rapid succession. With a little practice, you can perfect this technique in no time. Use a double-click to open a folder or to launch a file or application.

- ✔ **Control+click:** Hold down the Control key while single-clicking. Control+clicking is the same as right-clicking on a Windows system and displays a menu (called a *contextual menu*) where you Control+clicked. In fact, if you're blessed with a two-or-more-button mouse such as the Apple Mighty Mouse, you can right-click and avoid having to hold down the Control key.

  I use the five-button Microsoft IntelliMouse Explorer 3.0 and recommend it highly.

- ✔ **Drag:** *Dragging* something usually means you have to click it first and hold down the mouse button. Then you move the mouse on your desk or mouse pad so the cursor and whatever you select move across the screen. The combination of holding down the button and dragging the mouse is usually referred to as *click and drag.*

- ✔ **Choosing an item from a menu:** To get to Mac OS menu commands, you must first open a menu and then pick the option you want. Point at the name of the menu you want with your cursor, press the mouse button down, and then drag downward until you select the command you want. When the command is highlighted, finish selecting by letting go of the mouse button.

If you're a longtime Mac user, you probably hold down the mouse button the whole time between clicking the name of the menu and selecting the command you want. You can still do it that way, but you can also click the menu name to open it, release the mouse button, then drag down to the item you want to select, *and then click again.* In other words, OS X menus stay open for a few seconds after you click them, even if you're not holding down the mouse button. After you click a menu to open it, you can even type the first letter (or letters) of the item to select it and then execute that item with the spacebar or the Return or Enter key.

Go ahead and give it a try . . . I'll wait.

Not Just a Beatles Movie: Help and the Help Menu

One of the best features about all Macs is the excellent built-in help, and Mac OS X doesn't cheat you on that legacy: This system has online help in abundance. When you have a question about how to do something, the Mac Help Center is the first place you should visit (after this book, of course).

Clicking the Help menu reveals the Search Help field at the top of the menu and the Mac Help item, which opens the Mac Help window, as shown in Figure 1-4.

Figure 1-4: Mac Help is nothing if not helpful.

The keyboard shortcut for Help appears on the Help menu as ⌘+?, but you really need to press ⌘+Shift+? to open Help through the keyboard. Just so you know, this is the only case where you need to press Shift to make a keyboard shortcut work, but the menu where the shortcut appears doesn't actually tell you that. You can find out much more about keyboard shortcuts in Chapter 2.

To use Mac Help, simply type a word or phrase into the text field at the top right and then press Return or Enter. In a few seconds, your Mac provides you one or more articles to read, which (theoretically) are related your question. Usually. For example, if you type **menus** and press Return, you get 25 different help articles, as shown in Figure 1-5.

Now, here's a cool new feature I like to call *automatic visual help cues*. Here's how they work:

1. **Type a word or phrase in the Help menu's Search field.**

2. **Select any item that has a menu icon to its left (such as the Secure Empty Trash item in Figure 1-6).**

   The automatic visual cue — an arrow — appears, pointing at that command in the appropriate menu.

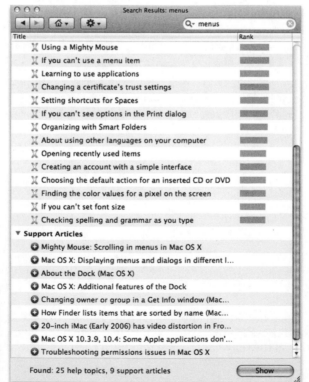

Figure 1-5: You have questions? Mac has answers.

Figure 1-6:
If you
choose an
item with a
menu icon,
an arrow
points to
that item in
context.

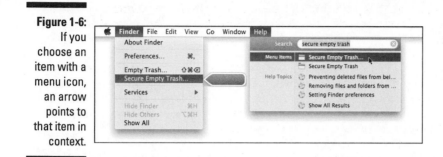

Although you don't have to be connected to the Internet to use Mac Help,
you do need an Internet connection to get the most out of it. (Chapter 9
can help you set up an Internet connection, if you don't have one.) That's
because OS X installs only certain help articles on your hard drive. If you ask
a question that those articles don't answer, Mac Help connects to Apple's
Web site and downloads the answer (assuming that you have an active
Internet connection). These answers are the "results from product support,"
denoted by a plus sign and underlined text, shown in the lower part of the
window in Figure 1-5, earlier in this chapter. Click one, and Help Viewer
retrieves the text over the Internet. Although this can sometimes be inconvenient, it's also quite smart. This way, the Help system can be updated at any
time by Apple without requiring any action from you.

Furthermore, after you've asked a question and Mac Help has grabbed the
answer from the Apple Web site, the answer remains on your hard drive forever. If you ask for it again (even at a later date), your computer won't have
to download it from the Apple Web site again.

Chapter 2

The Desktop and Windows and Menus (Oh My)!

*T*his chapter introduces important features of Mac OS X, starting with the first thing you see when you log in — the Finder and its Desktop. After a quick look around the Desktop, you get a look into two of its most useful features: windows and menus.

Windows are and have always been an integral part of Macintosh computing. Windows in the Finder (sometimes called "on the Desktop") show you the contents of the hard drive, optical drive, flash (thumb) drive, network drive, disk image, and folder icons; windows in applications do many things. The point is that windows are part of what makes your Mac a Mac; knowing how they work — and how to use them — is essential.

Menus are another quintessential part of the Macintosh experience. The latter part of this chapter starts you out with a few menu basics. As needed, I direct you to other parts of the book for greater detail.

So relax and don't worry. By the end of this chapter, you'll be ready to work with windows and menus in any application that uses them (and most applications, games excluded, do).

Touring the Finder and Its Desktop

The Finder is the program that creates the Desktop, keeps track of your files and folders, and is always running. Just about everything you do on your Mac begins and ends with the Finder. It's where you manage files, store documents, launch programs, and much more. If you ever expect to master your Mac, the first step is to master the Finder and its Desktop.

Check out the default Mac Finder and Desktop for Mac OS X Leopard in Figure 2-1.

The Finder is the center of your Mac OS experience, so before I go any further, here's a quick description of its most prominent features:

✔ **Desktop:** The Desktop is the area behind the windows and the Dock, where your hard drive icon (ordinarily) lives. The Desktop isn't a window, yet it acts like one. Like a folder window or drive window, the Desktop can contain icons. But unlike most windows, which require a bit of navigation to get to, the Desktop is a great place for things you use a lot, such as folders, applications, or particular documents.

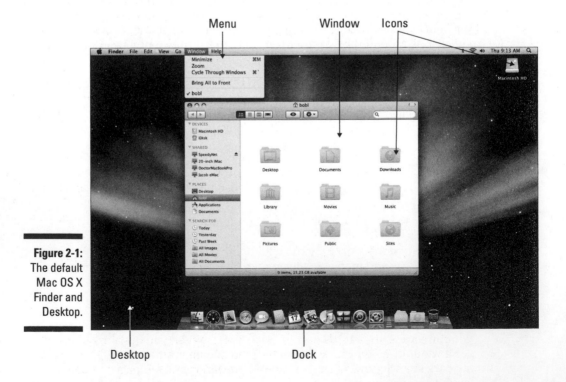

Figure 2-1:
The default
Mac OS X
Finder and
Desktop.

Some folks use the terms *Desktop* and *Finder* interchangeably to refer to the total Macintosh environment you see after you log in — the icons, windows, menus, and all that other cool stuff. Just to make things confusing, the background you see on your screen — the picture behind your hard drive icon and open windows — is also called the Desktop. In this book, I refer to the application you use when the Desktop is showing as the *Finder.* When I say *Desktop,* I'm talking about the picture background behind your windows and Dock, which you can use as a storage place for icons if you want.

✔ **Dock:** The Dock is the Finder's main navigation shortcut tool. It makes getting to frequently used icons easy, even when you have a screen full of windows. Like the Desktop, the Dock is a great place for things you use a lot, such as folders, applications, or particular documents. Besides putting your frequently used icons at your fingertips, it's almost infinitely customizable, too; read more about it in Chapter 4.

✔ **Icons:** Icons are the little pictures you see in your windows and even on your Desktop. Most icons are containers for things you work with on your Mac, such as programs and documents, which are also represented by — you guessed it — icons.

✔ **Windows:** Opening most icons (by double-clicking them) makes a window appear. Windows in the Finder show you the contents of hard drive and folder icons, and windows in applications usually show you the contents of your documents. In the sections that follow, you can find the full scoop on Leopard windows, which are very different from Mac windows in previous OS releases.

✔ **Menus:** Menus let you choose to do things, such as create new folders; duplicate files; cut, copy, or paste text; and so on. I introduce menu basics later in this chapter; you find details about working with menus for specific tasks throughout this book.

Whereas this section offers a basic introduction to the Finder and Desktop, Chapter 5 explains in detail how to navigate and manage your files in the Finder. You find out how to use the Finder toolbar, navigate folders and subfolders, and switch among views, among other things. But before you start using the Finder, it will help you to know the basics of working with windows and menus; if these Mac features are new to you, I suggest you read all of this chapter and pay special attention to Chapter 5 later.

Anatomy of a Window

Windows are a ubiquitous part of using a Mac. When you open a folder, you see a window. When you write a letter, the document that you're working on appears in a window. When you browse the Internet, Web pages appear in a window . . . and so on.

For the most part, windows are windows from program to program. You'll probably notice that some programs (Adobe Photoshop or Microsoft Word, for example) take liberties with windows by adding features (such as pop-up menus) or textual information (such as zoom percentage or file size) in the scroll bar area of a document window.

Don't let it bug you; that extra fluff is just window dressing (pun intended). Maintaining the window metaphor, many information windows display different kinds of information in different *panes,* or discrete sections.

And so, without further ado, the following list gives you a look at the main features of a typical Finder window (as shown in Figure 2-2). I discuss these features in greater detail in later sections of this chapter.

Close

Minimize

Zoom   View buttons

Quick Look/Slideshow

Window title   Action button   Hide/Show toolbar

Search field   Toolbar

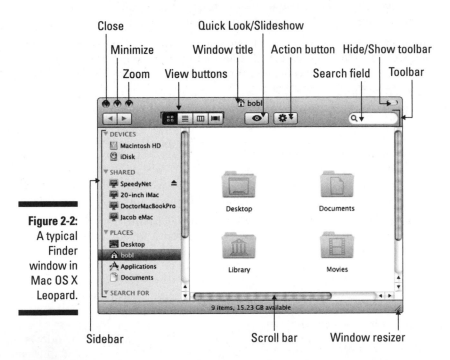

Figure 2-2:
A typical
Finder
window in
Mac OS X
Leopard.

Sidebar   Scroll bar   Window resizer

If your windows don't look exactly like the one shown in Figure 2-2, don't be concerned. You can make your windows look and feel any way you like. As I explain later in this section, moving and resizing windows are easy tasks. Chapter 3 explains how to customize how certain window features look and feel. Chapter 5 focuses on ways you can change a window's view specifically when you're using the Finder.

Meanwhile, here's what you see (clockwise from top left):

- **Close, Minimize, and Zoom (gumdrop) buttons:** Shut 'em, shrink and place 'em in the Dock, and make 'em grow.

- **View buttons:** Choose among four exciting views of your window: icon, list, column, and cover flow. Find out more about views in Chapter 5.

- **Quick Look/Slideshow button:** Gives you a quick peek at the contents of the selected item. If more than one item is selected, it gives you a quick peek of one item and next and previous buttons so you can view the others slide show style.

- **Action button:** This button is really a pop-up menu of commands you can apply to currently selected items in the Finder window.

- **Window title:** Shows the name of the window.

- **Search field:** Type a string of characters here, and Mac OS X Leopard digs into your system to find items that match.

- **Hide/Show Toolbar button:** Causes your computer to melt into a puddle of molten silicon slag. Just kidding! This button actually does what its name implies — hides or shows the toolbar (and Sidebar) of a window.

- **Toolbar:** Buttons for frequently used commands and actions live here.

- **Window resizer:** Click and drag here to resize the window.

- **Scroll bars:** Use the scroll bars for moving around a window pane.

- **Sidebar:** Frequently used items live here.

- **Forward and Back buttons:** These buttons take you to the next or previous folder displayed in this particular window.

  If you're familiar with Web browsers, the Forward and Back buttons in the Finder work exactly the same way. The first time you open a window, neither button is active. But as you navigate from folder to folder, these buttons remember your breadcrumb trail so you can quickly traverse backward or forward, window by window. You can even navigate this way from the keyboard by using the shortcuts ⌘+[for Back and ⌘+] for Forward.

The Forward and Back buttons remember only the other folders you've visited that appear in *that* open window. If you've set a Finder Preference so that a folder always opens in a new window — or if you forced a folder to open in a new window, which I describe in a bit — the Forward and Back buttons won't work. You have to use the modern, OS X–style window option, which uses a single window, or the buttons are useless.

This frosts me. If you hide the toolbar, the Sidebar is also hidden, whether you like it or not. Conversely, if you want to see the toolbar, you have no choice but to also see the Sidebar. So if you want to hide the toolbar and see the Sidebar, or vice versa, you're out of luck. If I had my druthers, I'd hide the toolbar (which I rarely use) and keep the Sidebar (which I use constantly). For some unfathomable reason, Apple doesn't allow that.

Top o' the window to ya!

Take a gander at the top of a window — any window. You see three buttons in the upper-left corner and the name of the window in the top center. The three buttons (called *gumdrop buttons* by some folks because they look like, well, gumdrops) are officially known as Close, Minimize, and Zoom, and their colors (red, yellow, and green, respectively) pop off the screen. Here's what they do:

- ✔ **Close (red):** Click this button to close the window.

- ✔ **Minimize (yellow):** Click this button to minimize the window. Clicking Minimize appears to close the window, but instead of making it disappear, Minimize adds an icon for the window in the Dock. To view the window again, click the Dock icon for the window that you minimized. If the window happens to be a QuickTime movie, the movie continues to play, albeit at postage-stamp size, in its icon in the Dock. (I discuss the Dock in Chapter 4.)

- ✔ **Zoom (green):** Click this button to make the window larger or smaller, depending on its current size. If you're looking at a standard-size window, clicking Zoom *usually* makes it bigger. (I say *usually* because if the window is larger than its contents, clicking this button shrinks the window to the smallest size that can completely enclose the contents without scrolling.) Click the Zoom button again to return the window to its previous size.

Some people still call the Zoom button by its Mac OS 9 name, Grow.

A scroll new world

Yet another way to see more of what's in a window or pane is to scroll through it. Scroll bars appear at the bottom and right sides of any window or pane that contains more stuff — icons, text, pixels, or whatever — than you can see in the window. Figure 2-3, for example, shows two instances of the same window: Dragging the scroll bar on the right side of the front window reveals the items above Font Book and iCal and below Photo Booth and Preview, which you can see in the expanded window in the background. Dragging the scroll bar on the bottom of the window reveals items to the left and right, such as Exposé, iChat, Image Capture, and iTunes.

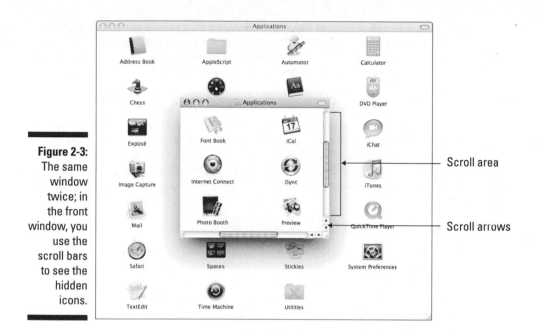

Figure 2-3:
The same
window
twice; in
the front
window, you
use the
scroll bars
to see the
hidden
icons.

Scroll area

Scroll arrows

Simply click and drag a scroll bar to move it up or down or side to side. And yes, the scroll bars also look a bit gumdrop-like. As best as I can tell, Steve Jobs (Apple's charismatic CEO) has a thing for gumdrops.

You can scroll in the following four ways:

✔ **Click a scroll bar and drag.** The content of the window scrolls proportionally to how far you drag the scroll bar.

✔ **Click in the scroll bar area but not on the scroll bar itself.** The window scrolls either one page up (if you click above the scroll bar) or down (if you click below the scroll bar). You can change a setting in your General System Preferences pane to cause the window to scroll proportionally to where you click.

For what it's worth, the Page Up and Page Down keys on your keyboard function the same way as clicking the grayish scroll bar area (the vertical scroll bar only) in the Finder and many applications. But these keys don't work in every program; don't become too dependent on them. Also, if you've purchased a mouse, trackball, or other pointing device with a scroll wheel, you can scroll vertically in the active (front) window with the scroll wheel or press and hold the Shift key to scroll horizontally.

✔ **Click a scroll arrow at the top or bottom of a scroll area.** By default, both arrows appear at the bottom of the scroll bar, as shown in Figure 2-3. You can set your General System Preferences so that you see one arrow at each end of the scroll area, as I explain in Chapter 3.

✔ **Use the keyboard.** In the Finder, first click an icon in the window and then use the arrow keys to move up, down, left, or right. Using an arrow key selects the next icon in the direction it indicates — and automatically scrolls the window, if necessary. In other programs, you might or might not be able to use the keyboard to scroll. The best advice I can give you is to try it — either it'll work or it won't.

(Hyper) Active windows

To work within a window, the window must be *active*. The active window is always the frontmost window, and inactive windows always appear behind the active window. Only one window can be active at a time. To make a window active, click it anywhere — in the middle, on the title bar, or on a scroll bar. It doesn't matter where you click, with one proviso: You can't click the red, yellow, or green gumdrop buttons or the clear Hide/Show button of an inactive window to activate it.

Look at Figure 2-4 for an example of an active window in front of an inactive window (the Applications window and the Utilities window, respectively).

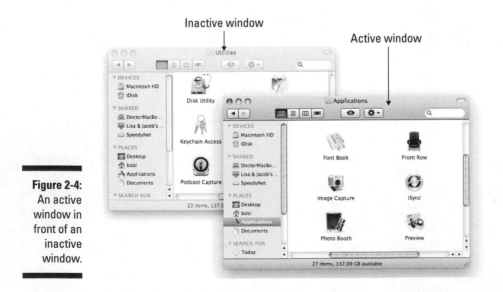

Inactive window

Active window

Figure 2-4:
An active window in front of an inactive window.

The following is a list of the major visual cues that distinguish active from inactive windows:

- ✔ **The active window's title bar:** The Close, Minimize, and Zoom buttons are red, yellow, and green. The inactive windows' buttons are not.

  This is a nice visual cue — colored items are active, and gray ones are inactive. Better still, if you move your mouse over an inactive window's gumdrop buttons, they light up in their usual colors so you can close, minimize, or zoom an inactive window without first making it active. Neat!

- ✔ **Other buttons and scroll bars in an active window:** They're bright. In an inactive window, these features are grayed out and more subdued.

- ✔ **Bigger and darker drop shadows in an active window:** They grab your attention more than those of inactive windows.

Dialog Dealie-Boppers

Dialogs are special windows that pop up over the active window. You generally see them when you select a menu item that ends in an ellipsis (. . .).

Dialogs can contain a number of standard Macintosh features (I call them *dealie-boppers*), such as radio buttons, pop-up menus, tabs, text-entry fields, and check boxes. You see these features again and again in dialogs. Take a moment to look at each of these dealie-boppers in Figure 2-5.

- ✔ **Radio buttons:** *Radio buttons* are so named because, like the buttons on your car radio (if you have a very old car), only one at a time can be active. (When they're active, they appear to be pushed in, just like the old radio buttons.) Radio buttons always appear in a group of two or more; when you select one, all the others are automatically deselected.

  Here's a nifty and undocumented shortcut: You can usually select check boxes and radio buttons by clicking their names (instead of the buttons or boxes).

- ✔ **Tabs:** When a dialog contains more information than can fit in a single window, the info is divided among tabs. In Figure 2-5, the New Document tab is selected on the left, and the Open and Save tab is selected on the right.

- ✔ **Pop-up menus:** These menus are appropriately named because that's what they do — they pop up when you click them. In Figure 2-5, the Encoding menu has been clicked and is popped up; the four other pop-up menus — Opening Files, Saving Files, Document Type, and Styling — are unclicked and unpopped.

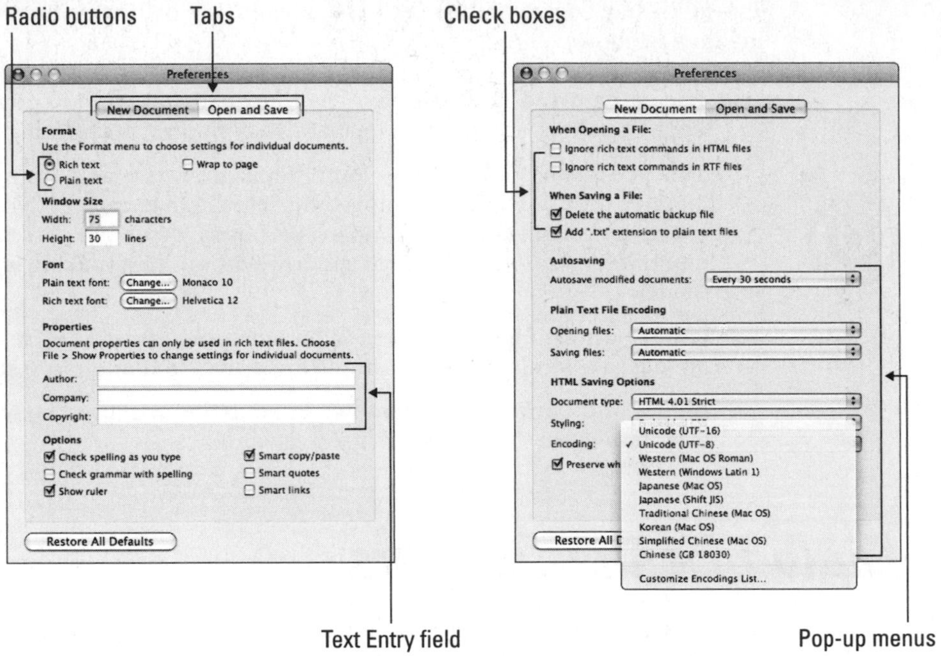

Radio buttons   Tabs   Check boxes

Figure 2-5:
This window offers most dealie-boppers you're ever likely to encounter.

Text Entry field   Pop-up menus

You can always recognize a pop-up menu because it appears in a slightly rounded rectangle and has a double-ended arrow symbol (or a pair of triangles, if you like) on the right.

Have you figured out yet what radio buttons, tabs, and pop-up menus have in common? *Hint:* All three enable you to make a single selection from a group of options. (Well, okay, that was more of an answer than a hint.)

✔ **Text-entry fields:** In text-entry fields, you type text (including numbers) from the keyboard. In Figure 2-5, the Window Width, Window Height, Author, Company, and Copyright options are text-entry fields.

✔ **Check boxes:** The last dealie-bopper that you see frequently is the check box. In a group of check boxes, you can select as many options as you like. Check boxes are selected when they contain a check mark, and they are deselected when they're empty, as shown in Figure 2-5.

Some applications have what they call *tri-state* check boxes (and no, I'm not talking geography here). These special check boxes are empty when nothing in the group is enabled, sport an *x* when everything in the group is enabled, and sport a minus sign (–) when *some* items in the group are enabled and some are not. This type of check box is often used for the Custom Install screen of Mac OS X installers.

Working with Windows

In the following sections, I give you a closer look at windows themselves: how you move them, size them, and use them. And although Mac OS X windows are similar to windows you've used in other versions of Mac OS, they have some new wrinkles.

If you're relatively new to the Mac, you might want to read this section while sitting at your computer, trying the techniques as you read them. You might find it easier to remember something you read if you actually do it. If you've been using your Mac for a while, you've probably figured out how windows work by now.

Opening and closing windows

To start peering into windows on your Mac, you first need to know how to open and close them. When you're working in the Finder, you can choose the following commands from the File menu. In many other programs, you can probably find some similar commands on the File menu of that program.

You'll use many of these commands frequently, so it would behoove you to memorize the keyboard shortcuts. If you're not sure how keyboard shortcuts work, check out "Using keyboard shortcut commands," later in this chapter.

- ✓ **New Finder Window (⌘+N):** Opens a new Finder window. In other programs, ⌘+N might open a new document, project, or whatever that program helps you create.
- ✓ **Open (⌘+O):** Opens the selected item, be it an icon, a window, or a folder.
- ✓ **Close Window (⌘+W):** Closes the active window. If no windows are open or if no window is selected, the Close Window command is grayed out and can't be chosen. Or if you prefer, you can close a window by clicking the red Close button in the upper-left corner.

   If you also hold down the Option key with the File menu open, the Close Window command changes to Close All. This very useful command enables you to close all open Finder windows. But it shows up only when you press the Option key; otherwise, it remains hidden.

Resizing windows

If you want to see more (or less) of what's in a window, use the resizer in the extreme lower-right corner of a window. (Refer to Figure 2-2 to see the resizer; it's in the lower-right corner and has little diagonal grippy lines on it.) Just drag the resizer downward and/or to the right to make a window larger. Or drag it upward and/or to the left to make a window smaller. In other words, after you grab the resizer, you can make a window whatever size you like.

Resizing window panes

Display windows, like those in the Finder, frequently consist of multiple panes. If you look at Figure 2-2, the line divides the blue Sidebar to the left of it and the actual contents of the window to the right. When your mouse hovers over the resizing area of this bar, the cursor changes to a vertical bar (or it could be horizontal if the panes are one above the other) with little arrows pointing out of both sides. When you see this cursor, you can click and drag anywhere in the strip that divides the Sidebar from the rest of the window. Doing so resizes the two panes relative to each other; one will get larger and one smaller.

Moving windows

To move a window, click anywhere in a window's title bar (or anywhere in the metallic part of a display window, except on a button, menu, search field, scroll bar, or resizer) and drag the window to wherever you want it. The window moves wherever you move the mouse, stopping dead in its tracks when you release the mouse button.

Shuffling windows

I've already spent plenty of pages giving you the scoop on how to work with windows. But wait; there's more . . . the commands on the Window menu provide tools that you can use to manage your windows. (Refer to Figure 2-1.) Here is a brief look at each of the items on the Window menu (and if you're unfamiliar with menus and keyboard shortcuts, I explain how they work later in this chapter):

- ✔ **Minimize Window (⌘+M):** Use this command to minimize the active Finder window to the Dock and unclutter your Desktop. It's the same as clicking the yellow gumdrop button.

- ✔ **Zoom:** This command does the same thing as the green gumdrop button. If you've forgotten what the green gumdrop does already, just turn back a few pages to the "Anatomy of a Window" section and read it again.

- **Cycle Through Windows (⌘+`):** Each time you choose this command or use the keyboard shortcut for it, a different window becomes active. So if you have three windows — call 'em window 1, window 2, and window 3 — and you're using window 1, this command deactivates window 1 and activates window 2. If you choose it again, the command deactivates window 2 and activates window 3. Choose it one more time, and it deactivates window 3 and reactivates window 1.

  This command actually has been available in several earlier versions of Mac OS X, but only as a keyboard shortcut. Leopard marks the first time it appears in a Finder menu.

- **Bring All to Front:** In Mac OS X Leopard, windows from different applications interleave. For example, you can have a Finder window, a Microsoft Word window, an Adobe Photoshop window, another Microsoft Word window, and another Finder window in front-to-back order. Choosing Bring All to Front while the Finder is the active application enables you to have both of the Finder windows in this example move in front of those belonging to Word and Photoshop.

  If you want to bring the all windows belonging to the Finder (or any other program, for that matter) to the front at the same time, you can also click the appropriate Dock icon (the Finder, in this case).

  If you hold down the Option key when you pull down the Window menu, Minimize Window changes to Minimize All, and the Bring All to Front command changes to the useful Arrange in Front command, which arranges all your Desktop windows neatly — starting near the upper-left corner of the Desktop, as shown in Figure 2-6.

- **Other items:** The remaining items on the Window menu are the names of all currently open Finder windows. Click a window's name to bring it to the front.

In addition to the commands on the Window menu, Mac OS X has a program called Exposé that lets you display all open windows (or all the windows open in the application you're currently using) by rearranging the windows on-screen and graying out everything else. It can also hide all windows so you can see your desktop (what a concept).

By default, you use the function keys to choose the way Exposé displays your windows:

- To see all open windows, press F9.

- To see all open windows belonging to the current application, press F10.

- To hide all open windows and display the Desktop, press F11.

- To summon forth the Dashboard (which displays your widgets, as I explain in Chapter 3), press F12.

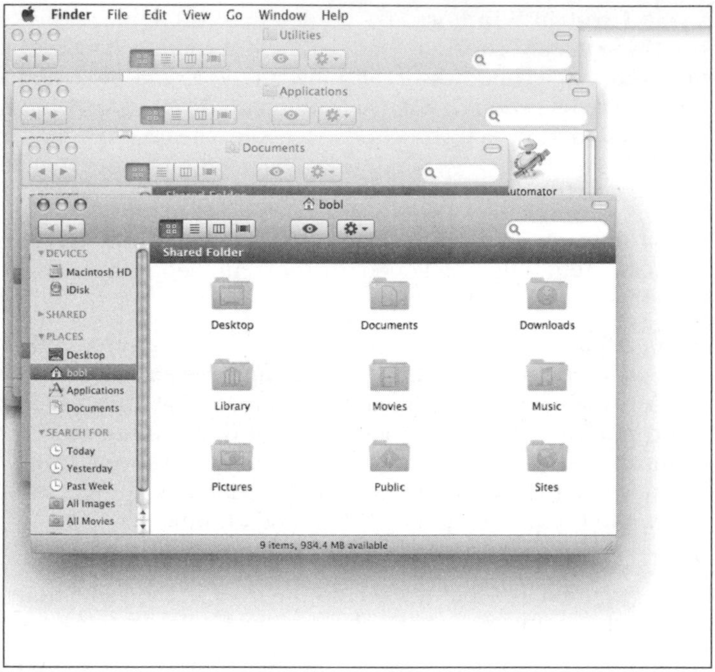

Figure 2-6:
The Arrange in Front command stacks up your windows neatly in the corner.

A picture is worth a thousand words, so take a gander at Figure 2-7, where I have several applications running with multiple windows open in each of them.

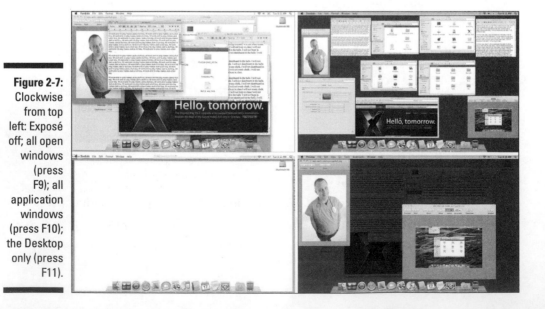

Figure 2-7:
Clockwise from top left: Exposé off; all open windows (press F9); all application windows (press F10); the Desktop only (press F11).

When using Exposé, if you point to a window but don't click, the window's title appears. If you click any window — even one that's grayed out — at any time, Exposé deactivates, and that window becomes active.

By the way, Exposé is enabled by default. You can disable it or change its keyboard shortcuts in the Exposé & Spaces System Preferences pane. Find out more about using and customizing Exposé (and its sister application Spaces) in Chapter 3.

Menu Basics

Mac menus are often referred to as *pull-down menus*. To check out the Mac OS X menus, click the Finder button in the Dock to activate the Finder and then look at the top of your screen. From left to right, you see the Apple menu, the Finder menu, and six other menus. To use an OS X menu, click its name to make the menu appear and then pull (drag) down to select a menu item. Piece of cake!

Ever since Mac OS 8, menus stay down after you click their names until you either select an item or click outside the menu's boundaries.

The ever-changing menu bar

Before you start working with OS X menus, you really, really should know this about menus in general: *They can change unexpectedly.* Why? Well, the menus you see on the menu bar at the top of the screen always reflect the program that's active at the time. When you switch from the Finder to a particular program — or from one program to another — the menus change immediately to match whatever you switched to.

For example, when the Finder is active, the menu bar looks like Figure 2-6, shown earlier. But if you launch the TextEdit application (discussed in Chapter 13), the menu bar changes to what you see in Figure 2-8.

An easy way to tell which program is active is to look at the application menu — it's the leftmost menu with a name, just to the right of the Apple menu. When you're in the Finder, of course, the application menu reads *Finder.* But if you switch to another program (by clicking its icon in the Dock or by clicking any window associated with the program) or launch a new program, that menu changes to the name of the active program.

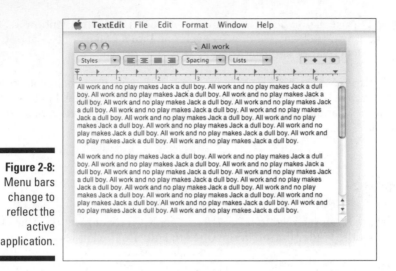

When you have an application open, the commands on the menu change, too — but just a little bit. What makes this cool is that you have access to some standard application menu items whether you're running Mail or Safari. You can find much more about commands for applications in Part III, which explains how applications that come with Mac OS Leopard can help you get things you want to do done.

Contextual menus: They're sooo sensitive

Contextual menus are, as the name implies, context sensitive; they list commands that apply only to the item that is currently selected. Contextual menus might be available in windows, on icons, and in most places on the Desktop.

To use them, you either hold down the Control key and click — which you can call a *Control+click* to sound cool to your Mac friends — or, if your mouse has two or more buttons, *right-click*.

Actions appear in contextual menus only if they make sense for the item that you Control+click or right-click. That's why people call 'em *contextual!* They stick to the immediate context. Figure 2-9 shows the contextual menu that appears when you Control+click (or right-click) a document icon on the left and the contextual menu for the Desktop on the right.

Contextual menu
for a document

Contextual menu
for the Desktop

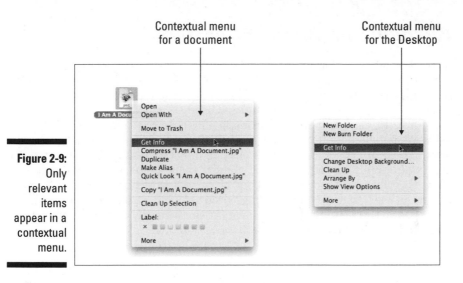

Figure 2-9:
Only
relevant
items
appear in a
contextual
menu.

Contextual menus are also available in many applications. Open your favorite app and try Control+clicking to find out whether those menus are there. In most cases, using a contextual menu is a quick way to avoid going to the menu bar to choose a command. In some programs — such as AppleWorks 6, iMovie, iTunes, and many more — contextual menus are the only way to access certain commands.

To make the Finder-related contextual menus available to users who didn't have the foresight to purchase this book, Apple added the Actions button to the toolbar. So these days, people who don't know about Control+clicking or right-clicking (or have only one free hand) can access their contextual menus by clicking the Actions button and displaying its contextual menu. You, on the other hand, gentle reader, know how to get at these commands without having to run your mouse all the way up to the Action button in the toolbar.

I'm a big fan of multibutton mice, and contextual menus are a huge reason for this preference. Thankfully, Apple now includes multibutton mice with all its desktop computers (except the Mac Mini, which doesn't include a mouse, keyboard, or monitor). If you have an older Mac with a single-button mouse, you might want to replace the mouse with one that offers you at least two buttons. With a multibutton mouse, you need only one hand to access these beautiful little contextual menus.

Get in the habit of Control+clicking (or right-clicking if your mouse has more than one button) items on your screen. Before you know it, using contextual menus will become second nature to you.

Recognizing disabled options

Menu items that appear in black on a menu are currently available. Menu items that aren't currently available are grayed out, meaning that they're disabled for the time being. You can't select a disabled menu item.

In Figure 2-10, the File menu on the left is pulled down while nothing is selected in the Finder; this is why many of the menu items are disabled (in gray). These items are disabled because an item (such as a window or icon) must be selected for you to use one of these menu items. For example, the Show Original command is grayed out because it works only if the selected item is an alias. In the picture on the right, I selected a document before I pulled down the menu; notice that many of the formerly disabled commands are enabled when an icon is selected.

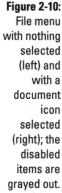

Figure 2-10:
File menu
with nothing
selected
(left) and
with a
document
icon
selected
(right); the
disabled
items are
grayed out.

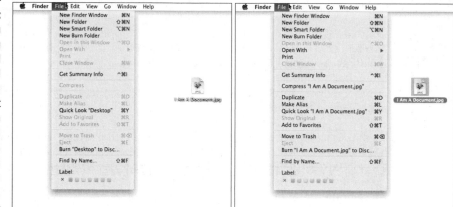

Navigating submenus

Some menu items have more menus attached to them, and these are called *submenus* — menus that are subordinate to a menu item. If a menu has a black triangle to the right of its name, it has a submenu.

To use a submenu, click a menu name once (to drop the menu down) and then slide your cursor down to any item with a black triangle. When the item is highlighted, move your mouse to the right just slightly. The submenu should pop out of the original menu's item, as shown in Figure 2-11.

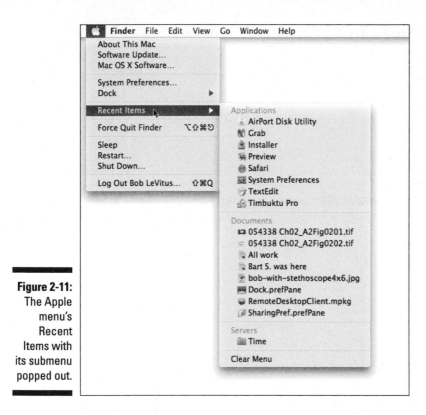

Figure 2-11:
The Apple
menu's
Recent
Items with
its submenu
popped out.

Underneath the Apple menu tree

On the far left side of the menu bar sits a little , which, if you click it, actually displays a menu. No matter what application is active, the menu is available up in the top-left corner of your menu bar.

From top to bottom, the menu gives you a number of options, including the following:

✔ **About This Mac:** Choose this item to see what version of Mac OS X you're running, what kind of Mac and processor you're using, and how much memory your Mac has. The window that appears also sports a Get Info button that will launch Apple System Profiler; there, you can find out more than you'll probably ever want or need to know about your Mac's hardware and software.

If you click the version number in this window, it changes to the *build number* (Apple's internal tracking number for versions). If you click the build number in this window, it changes to the serial number of your Mac. Finally, if you click the serial number of your Mac in this window, it changes to the version number again. This interesting effect is shown in Figure 2-12. Any or all of this information might come in handy for troubleshooting, repair, upgrades, or who knows what else. At least now you know how to find it.

Figure 2-12:
Click the version, build, or serial number to cycle through these three variations in the About This Mac window.

About This Mac	About This Mac	About This Mac
Mac OS X	**Mac OS X**	**Mac OS X**
Version 10.5	Build 9A499	Serial Number W864300UX2J
Software Update...	Software Update...	Software Update...
Processor 2.33 GHz Intel Core 2 Duo	**Processor** 2.33 GHz Intel Core 2 Duo	**Processor** 2.33 GHz Intel Core 2 Duo
Memory 3 GB 667 MHz DDR2 SDRAM	**Memory** 3 GB 667 MHz DDR2 SDRAM	**Memory** 3 GB 667 MHz DDR2 SDRAM
Startup Disk Macintosh HD	**Startup Disk** Macintosh HD	**Startup Disk** Macintosh HD
More Info...	More Info...	More Info...
TM & © 1983–2007 Apple Inc. All Rights Reserved.	TM & © 1983–2007 Apple Inc. All Rights Reserved.	TM & © 1983–2007 Apple Inc. All Rights Reserved.

✔ **Software Update:** If you're connected to the Internet, choose this item to have your Mac check with the mothership (Apple) to see whether any updates are available for OS X or its included applications (or even for Apple-branded peripheral devices, such as the iPod or iPhone).

✔ **System Preferences:** Choose this item to open the System Preferences window (which I discuss further in Chapter 3 and elsewhere).

✔ **Dock (submenu):** This lets you mess with, well, the Dock! Scour Chapter 4 for more info on the Dock.

✔ **Recent Items:** This lets you quickly access applications, documents, and servers you've used recently as shown in Figure 2-11.

✔ **Shut down options:** The commands here can tell your Mac to Force Quit (⌘+Option+power button) when a program freezes or otherwise becomes recalcitrant, sleep, restart, shut down, or log out. See Chapter 1 for details about turning off your Mac.

Using keyboard shortcut commands

Most menu items, or at least the most common ones, have *keyboard shortcuts* to help you quickly navigate your Mac without having to haggle so much with the mouse. Using these key combinations activates menu items without using the mouse; to use them, you press the Command (⌘) key and then press another key (or keys) without releasing the ⌘ key. Memorize the shortcuts that you use often.

Some people refer to the Command key as the *Apple key*. That's because on many keyboards, that key has both the pretzel-like Command-key symbol (⌘) *and* an Apple logo (🍎) on it. To avoid confusion, I always refer to ⌘ as the Command key.

Here are five things to know that will give you a handle on keyboard shortcuts:

✔ **Keyboard shortcuts are shown in menus.** For example, Figure 2-10 shows that the keyboard shortcut for the Find command appears on the menu after the word *Find*: ⌘+F. Any menu item with one of these pretzel-symbol+letter combinations after its name can be executed with that keyboard shortcut. Just hold down the ⌘ key and press the letter shown in the menu — *N* for New Finder Window, *F* for Find, and so on — and the appropriate command executes.

✔ **Capital letters don't mean that you have to press Shift as part of the shortcut.** Although the letters next to the ⌘ symbol in the Finder menus are indeed capitals, they just identify the letter on the keyboard. For example, if you see ⌘+P, just hold down the ⌘ key and then press *P*. Some programs have keyboard combinations that require the use of ⌘ *and* the Shift key, but those programs tell you so by calling the key combination something like ⇧+⌘+S or ⇧+⌘+O. A very few (usually older) programs indicate when you need to use the Shift key by using the word *Shift* rather than the ⇧ symbol.

✔ **Recognize the funky-looking Option key symbol.** You'll see one other symbol sometimes used in keyboard shortcuts: It represents the Option key (sometimes abbreviated in keyboard shortcuts as *Opt* and, on some keyboards, also labeled *Alt*). Check it out next to the Hide Others command, shown in Figure 2-13.

What this freakish symbol means in the Finder menu item (Hide Others in Figure 2-13) is that if you hold down both the ⌘ and Option keys as you press the H key, all applications other than the Finder will be hidden.

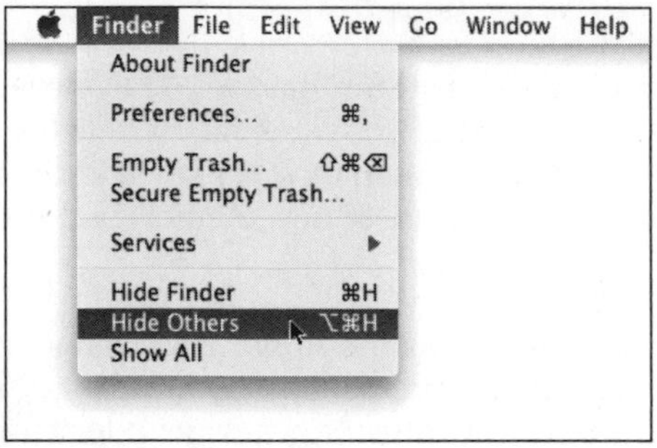

Figure 2-13:
Some
keyboard
shortcuts,
such as
Hide Others,
use the
Option
key in
combination
with the
Command
key.

| Finder | File | Edit | View | Go | Window | Help |

About Finder

Preferences...   ⌘,

Empty Trash...   ⇧⌘⌫
Secure Empty Trash...

Services   ▶

Hide Finder   ⌘H
Hide Others   ⌥⌘H
Show All

TIP

✔ **Okay, there was more than one more symbol.** Occasionally, you'll see a *caret* (^) used as the abbreviation for the Control key. For example, ^⌘I on a menu means that you need to press Control+⌘+I.

✔ **If it makes sense, it's probably a shortcut.** Most keyboard shortcuts have a mnemonic relationship with their names. For example, here are some of the most basic keyboard shortcuts:

Command	*Mnemonic Keyboard Shortcut*
New Finder Window	⌘+N
New Folder	⌘+Shift+N
Open	⌘+O
Get Info	⌘+I
Select All	⌘+A
Copy	⌘+C
Duplicate	⌘+D

More menus 4 U

If you like the menus you've seen so far, have I got a treat for you: Mac OS X Leopard includes 25 additional special-purpose menus, known as Menu Extras, that you can install if you like. Some — including Sound, Displays, Battery, and others — can be enabled from the appropriate System Preferences pane. But the easiest way is to open the Menu Extras folder (`/System/ Library/CoreServices/Menu Extras`) and double-click each Menu Extra you want to install.

The following figure shows a handful of Menu Extras installed in the menu bar.

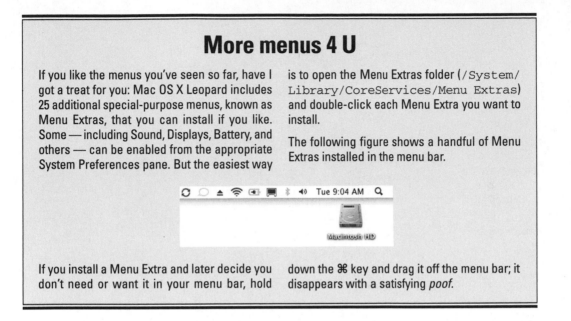

If you install a Menu Extra and later decide you don't need or want it in your menu bar, hold down the ⌘ key and drag it off the menu bar; it disappears with a satisfying *poof.*

Chapter 3

Have It Your Way

*E*veryone works a bit differently, and everyone likes to use the Macs in a certain way. In this chapter, you find out how to tweak various options so everything is just the way you like it. The first things most people like to do are set their background and screen saver and populate the Dashboard with handy widgets. You can begin with that stuff, but keep in mind that you can do much more.

You can change the colors in windows, the standard font, and more if you like. Your Mac lets you choose how on-screen elements behave and how your hardware — such as the keyboard, mouse, and any wireless Bluetooth gadgets — interacts with your Mac.

Introducing System Preferences

You should start by becoming familiar with System Preferences, which appear on the Apple (🍎) menu and in the Dock.

The following steps explain how to move around the System Preferences window, no matter what you're trying to tweak:

1. **Open the System Preferences window, shown in Figure 3-1.**

    You can do this three different ways:

    • Choose 🍎➪System Preferences.

    • Open the System Preferences icon in your Applications folder.

    • Click the System Preferences icon on your Dock.

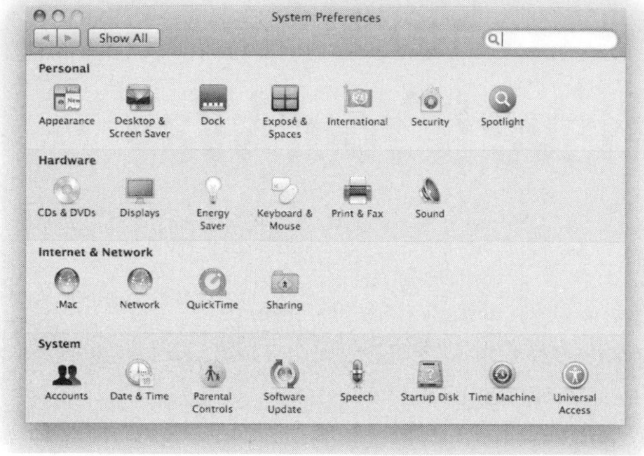

Figure 3-1:
The System
Preferences
window:
Change
your world.

2. **Click any of the icons here.**

   The bottom part of the window changes to reflect the options for the icon that you click. When this happens, I call the bottom part of the window a *pane*. So, for example, when you click the Appearance icon in the System Preferences window, the bottom part of the window becomes the Appearance System Preferences pane.

3. **When you finish working with a System Preferences pane, click the Show All button to return to the window with icons for all available System Preferences panes, or use the keyboard shortcut ⌘+L.**

   Or, if you want to work with a different System Preferences pane, you can choose it from the View menu, as shown in Figure 3-2. Also notice that you can navigate to the next or previous pane you've viewed with the Back and Forward buttons below the red and yellow gumdrops (shortcuts ⌘+[and ⌘+] respectively). Back and Forward commands also appear on the View menu.

You can get rid of the categories altogether and display the icons in alphabetical order. As a bonus, it makes the System Preferences window roughly 25 percent smaller on-screen. To do so, choose View⇨Organize Alphabetically. The categories disappear, the window shrinks, and the icons are alphabetized, as shown in Figure 3-2. To switch from alphabetical view back to category view, choose View⇨Organize by Categories.

System Preferences is actually an application that you can find in the Applications folder. The menu item and Dock icon are merely shortcuts that open the System Preferences application. The actual files for preferences panes are stored in the Preference Panes folder, inside the Library folder in the System folder. If you choose to install third-party preference panes, they should go either in the Preference Panes folder in the Library folder at the top level of your startup disk (if you want them to be available to all users) or in the Preference Panes folder in the Library inside your Home folder (if you want to keep them to yourself).

Figure 3-2:
The View menu and the System Preferences window organized alphabetically.

Putting a Picture on the Desktop

In Figure 3-3, you can see my Desktop with a beautiful black-and-white background picture of lightning striking a distant city. (If you want a reminder of what the default Desktop background looks like, refer to Figure 3-2.)

Here's how you can change your Desktop picture if you care to:

1. **From the Desktop, choose ⌘⇨System Preferences or Control+click or right-click the Desktop itself and choose Change Desktop Background from the contextual menu.**

   The System Preferences window appears.

2. **Click the Desktop & Screen Saver icon.**

   The Desktop & Screen Saver preferences pane appears, as shown in Figure 3-4.

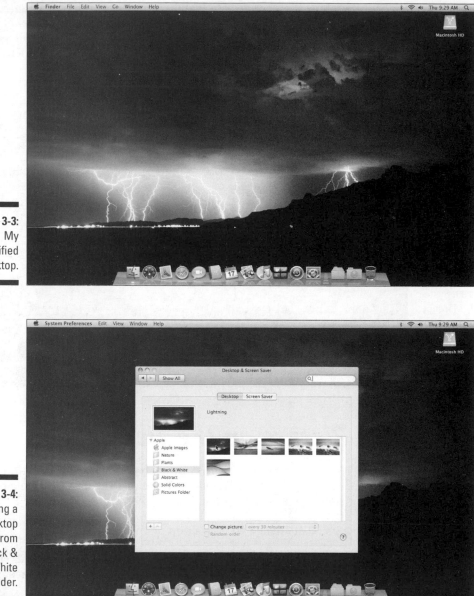

Figure 3-3:
My
beautified
Desktop.

Figure 3-4:
Selecting a
Desktop
picture from
the Black &
White
folder.

Note: This step isn't necessary if you used the contextual menu technique in Step 1.

3. **Click a folder in the column on the left and then click a picture in the area on the right.**

   I'm clicking a picture called Lightning in Figure 3-4. As you can see, it's one of the items in the Black & White folder. If you want to show one of your own pictures on the Desktop, it's probably in the Pictures folder.

You have at least three other ways to change your Desktop picture:

- Drag a picture file from the Finder onto the *picture well* (the little rectangular picture to the left of the picture's name).

- Select the Pictures Folder in the list of folders on the left side of the Desktop & Screen Saver System Preferences pane and then select a folder by using the standard Open File dialog. That folder then appears in the list; you can use any picture files it contains for your Desktop picture.

  If you don't know how to choose a folder that way, see Chapter 5.

- Click one of the iPhoto Albums items in the column on the left side of the Desktop & Screen Saver System Preferences pane.

One last thing before moving on: Although I love having a beautiful Desktop picture, from this point forward, I use a plain white Desktop (obtained by clicking Solid Colors in the list and then clicking the white color swatch). The plain Desktop will make it easier for you to see fine details.

Setting Up a Screen Saver

Mac OS X comes with several screen-saver modules. To set up your screen saver, follow these steps:

1. **Open System Preferences, select the Desktop & Screen Saver option, and click the Screen Saver tab to see the options shown in Figure 3-5.**

2. **In the Screen Savers column on the left side of the pane, select a screen saver option that interests you.**

3. **(Optional) To see what the selected module looks like in action, click the Test button. Press any key to end the test.**

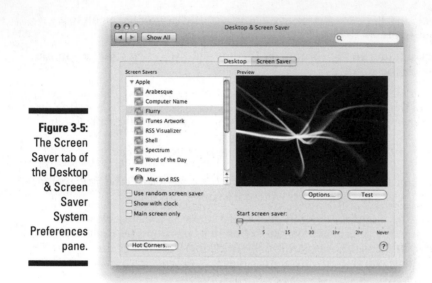

4. **After you've chosen a screen saver, drag the Start Screen Saver slider to the number of minutes you want the Mac to wait before activating the screen saver.**

   If you can't decide, you can select the Use Random Screen Saver check box to have your Mac choose a new screen saver at random each time the screen saver kicks in.

5. **Select the Show with Clock check box to display a digital clock along with the screen saver.**

6. **(Optional) Click the Hot Corners button to choose which corner of your screen activates the screen saver and which disables it.**

   Now when you move your cursor to a selected corner, you activate or disable the screen saver until you move the cursor elsewhere.

   Note that hot corners are optional and are turned off by default.

7. **When you're done, close the Desktop & Screen Saver pane.**

You can require a password to wake your Mac from sleep or a screen saver. To do so, follow these steps:

1. **Choose System Preferences Security.**

2. **Click the General tab at the top of the preference pane.**

3. **Select the *Require Password to Wake This Computer from Sleep or Screen Saver* check box.**

   From now on, you need to supply the user account password to wake up this computer.

If you like Screen Savers/Effects, you can find plenty more available at your favorite downloadable software repository. (My favorite is `www.version tracker.com`.) Many are free, but some cost a few bucks. Some of those, such as Marine Aquarium in Figure 3-6 (from `www.serenescreen.com`), are even worth paying for. I paid my $19.95, and it was worth every penny. It's so lifelike that I sometimes believe those are real fish in my monitor. Plus, unlike other fish I've owned, these never float belly up (or explode from overfeeding). I love this saver/effect; it's the only one I use anymore.

Figure 3-6:
Search the
Web for
other cool
screen
savers.

Putting Widgets on the Dashboard

Dashboard offers a way-cool set of *widgets,* Apple's name for the mini-applications that live inside the Dashboard layer. You see, Dashboard takes over your screen when you invoke it (as shown in Figure 3-7) by clicking Dashboard's Dock icon or pressing its keyboard shortcut, F12. In Figure 3-7, Dashboard is shown with just a few of its default widgets: Calculator, Weather, World Clock, and Calendar.

Widgets are small, single-function applications that work only within Dashboard. Some widgets talk to applications on your hard drive, such as Address Book, iTunes, and iCal. Other widgets — such as Flight Tracker, Stocks, and Weather — gather information for you via the Internet.

Figure 3-7:
Dashboard
lives in its
own gray
overlay
layer,
floating
above any
Finder or
application
windows
open at the
time.

The following tips can help you work with widgets:

- ✔ **Each time you invoke Dashboard, widgets that were open the last time you used it will be on your screen.**

- ✔ **To close an open widget,** click the encircled X in its upper-left corner. If you don't see an X, press the Option key and move the cursor over the widget, and you will.

- ✔ **To access widgets other than the four on your screen by default,** click the Open button (the large encircled plus sign shown earlier in the lower-left corner of Figure 3-7) to open the Widget Bar, shown at the bottom of Figure 3-8.

Figure 3-8:
The Widget
Bar (bottom
of screen)
and the
Translation
widget
(middle of
screen).

Widget Bar sounds like a trendy watering hole downtown, but I assure you that's the official, Apple-sanctioned name. Really.

✔ **To open a widget window,** click the widget. In Figure 3-8, the Translation widget is open in the middle of the screen, all set to do my bidding. Or you can click and drag a widget from the Widget Bar to a preferred location on your screen.

✔ **To see more widgets,** click the tiny arrows on the left and right sides of the Widget Bar.

✔ **To move a widget around on your screen,** click almost anywhere on the widget and then drag it to the appropriate location.

✔ **To manage your widgets,** click the Manage Widgets button above the Widget Bar on the left side. The Widget Manager appears in the middle of the screen. For example, in Figure 3-9 I've disabled the Ski Report and Tile Game widgets, which I never use.

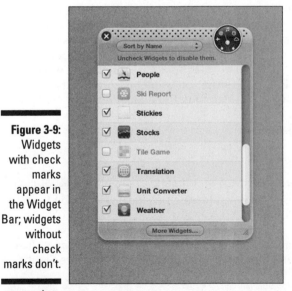

Figure 3-9:
Widgets
with check
marks
appear in
the Widget
Bar; widgets
without
check
marks don't.

You can manage widgets only if the Widget Bar is open.

At the bottom of the Widget Manager window is a button titled More Widgets. Clicking it launches your Web browser and shows you additional widgets you can download from the Apple Web site.

✔ **To uninstall a third-party widget that you no longer want,** merely open the Widget Manager and click the red minus sign next to its name. Your Mac politely asks whether you want to move this widget to the trash. You do.

Think of your Dashboard widgets as being handy yet potent miniprograms available at any time with a keystroke or click. Widgets are just so danged cool that I want to give you a quick look at a couple I consider particularly useful. Read on for details.

Translation

The Translation widget could be a lifesaver. You've been able to do this trick on the Web for a while, but now you can do it right on your desktop. This widget translates words from one language to another. It offers more than a dozen language choices — including French, German, Spanish, Russian, Dutch, Chinese, and more — and can translate in either direction.

I love the Translation widget so much that, sometimes, it hurts.

It's fun at parties, too. Try this: Type a paragraph or two of your purplest prose into Translation. Now translate back and forth to any language a few times. Howl when prose written as "It was a dark and stormy night when our heroine met her untimely demise" turns into something like "It was one night dark and stormy where our heroin met an ugly transfer." It doesn't get much better than this, folks. I used to leave my MacBook Pro at home if I wasn't absolutely going to need it. But the Translation widget is so wicked cool and useful that lately I've been taking my MacBook Pro almost everywhere I go.

Flight Tracker

Flight Tracker, shown in Figure 3-10, can find flights on most airlines and report the flight's status in real time — a terrific timesaver when you have to meet a flight.

When you have to meet someone's flight, this widget can be a lifesaver. Just open Dashboard every few minutes, and you know exactly what the flight's status is at that moment.

This is a really good tip — You can open more than one instance of a widget. So if you're trying to track two flights or want to know the weather in more than one city, just click the appropriate widget in the Widget Bar, and another instance of it appears.

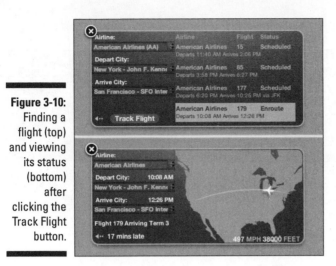

Figure 3-10:
Finding a
flight (top)
and viewing
its status
(bottom)
after
clicking the
Track Flight
button.

Business and People

The Business and People widgets (shown in Figure 3-11) are like having white-page and yellow-page directories at your fingertips. You can quickly find local (or not local) phone numbers for businesses or people.

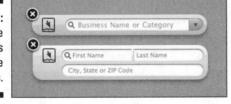

Figure 3-11:
The
Business
and People
widgets.

Some widgets, including the Business widget, have drop-down menus or More Info buttons in their lower-right corner. Click the little *i* (visible in the middle picture in Figure 3-12) and the widget appears to flip around, exposing its backside and additional options (right picture in Figure 3-12).

Figure 3-12:
The
Business
widget's
drop-down
menu (left),
results
(middle),
and More
Info (right).

Giving Buttons, Menus, and Windows a Makeover

Computers don't care about appearances, but if you want your Mac to look a bit more festive (or, for that matter, businesslike), you have options in the Appearance pane (see Figure 3-13) at your disposal. To open this pane, choose ➪System Preferences➪Appearance.

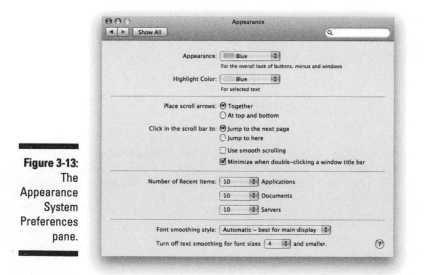

Figure 3-13:
The
Appearance
System
Preferences
pane.

First up are the general appearance options:

✔ **Appearance pop-up menu:** Use this menu to choose different appearances and change the overall look of buttons, such as the three gumdrop buttons in the upper-left corner of most windows, as well as the gumdrop buttons that appear in scroll bars.

Apple, however, in its infinite wisdom, provides only two choices: Blue and Graphite.

✔ **Highlight Color pop-up menu:** From here, you can choose the color that text becomes surrounded by when you select it in a document or in an icon's name in a Finder window. This time, Apple isn't so restrictive: You have eight highlight colors to choose among, plus Other, which brings up a color picker from which you can choose almost any color.

The next area in the Appearance System Preferences pane enables you to set scroll bar and title bar behavior:

✔ **The Place Scroll Arrows radio buttons** let you choose whether you have the default of both arrows together at the bottom and to the right of the scroll bars (left in Figure 3-14) or the old-school single arrow at either end of the scroll bar (right in Figure 3-14).

Figure 3-14:
Scroll arrows
together
(left) or at top
and bottom
(right).

✔ **The Click in the Scroll Bar To radio buttons** give you the option of moving your view of a window up or down by a page (the default) or to the position in the document roughly proportionate to where you clicked in the scroll bar.

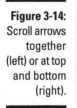

Select the Jump to Here radio button if you often work with long (multi-page) documents. It's quite handy for navigating long documents. And don't forget — the Page Down key does the same thing as selecting the Jump to the Next Page choice, so you lose nothing by selecting Jump to Here.

✔ Selecting the **Use Smooth Scrolling check box** makes documents more legible while you scroll. Give it a try; if you think it's making things feel sluggish, turn it off.

✔ **The Minimize When Double-Clicking a Window Title Bar check box** does just what it says when selected — it shrinks a window to the Dock when you double-click its title bar. For what it's worth, the yellow gumdrop button does exactly the same thing.

The next area in the Appearance pane controls the Number of Recent Items that are remembered and displayed in your ⌘⇨Recent Items submenu. The default is 10, but I like having access to more than 10 applications and documents in my Recent Items submenu, so I crank mine up to the max — 50 of each. Here's what each pop-up menu means:

✔ **Applications:** When you choose to display any number of applications, you can open any application you've used recently from your Recent Items submenu.

✔ **Documents:** This setting tells Leopard to show specific documents you've opened recently in Recent Items.

✔ **Servers:** Determines the number of recently accessed remote computers Leopard displays in the Recent Items submenu.

The last area offers a few options for how your fonts look. The Font Smoothing Style pop-up menu offers five settings for anti-aliasing (smoothing) fonts on screen. The categories are

✔ **Automatic – Best for Main Display:** Usually your best choice.

✔ **Standard – Best for CRT:** Your standard, clunky tube-type monitor. If your monitor isn't a flat-panel LCD, this is probably your best bet.

✔ **Light:** Just a hint of the essence of smoothing for your text.

✔ **Medium – Best for Flat-Panel:** For those sleek, flat-panel monitors and notebooks, too.

✔ **Strong:** Mondo-smoothing. I happen to like it on my flat-panel display, but you might not.

Ignore Apple's editorial comments and try all five. Then choose the one that looks best to your eyes.

The Turn Off Text Smoothing for Font Sizes *x* and Smaller pop-up menu (where *x* is the pop-up menu setting) does just what it says. Fonts that size and smaller are no longer *anti-aliased* (smoothed) when displayed.

If you find that type in small font sizes is hard for you to read, try increasing or decreasing this setting.

Spaced Out! Defining Screen Spaces

Actually, the Spaces feature is anything but spacey. Both Spaces and Exposé help you manage Finder windows and Application windows by organizing them on-screen according to preferences you set in the Exposé & Spaces preferences pane. To access this pane, simply choose ⌘⇨System Preferences⇨ Exposé & Spaces.

Exposé has been around since Panther; Spaces is brand new in Leopard. This new feature lets you organize applications into groups and then switch from group to group with a single keystroke. When you use Spaces, only two kinds of windows are shown: windows from applications associated with the active Space and windows from applications launched while that Space is active.

You set the preferences for Spaces on the Spaces tab of the Exposé & Spaces System Preferences pane, shown in Figure 3-15. The following steps walk you through the setup and customization of Spaces:

1. **Click the Spaces tab, shown in Figure 3-15, to begin setting up your Spaces.**

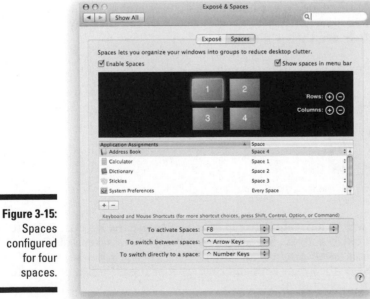

Figure 3-15: Spaces configured for four spaces.

2. **Set up the number of spaces you want by clicking the circled + (plus) buttons next to the Rows and Columns labels.**

Clicking the + button adds a row or column. In Figure 3-15 for example, I have two rows and two columns, to create a total of four spaces on my screen.

3. **In the Application Assignments area, assign applications to the Spaces you've set up by first selecting an Application name and then selecting the Space you want to assign it to from the pop-up menu on the right.**

   In Figure 3-16, Space 1 is configured for the Calculator only. Space 2 is configured for Dictionary only. Space 3 is configured to show only Stickies. And Space 4 shows only Address Book. Finally, if the System Preferences application is running, it appears in all four spaces.

4. **Use the pop-up menus at the bottom of the screen to select how you want to activate and switch between your Spaces.**

   The ^ symbol stands for the Control key.

5. **When you're done, simply close the preference pane and begin working with your Spaces by using the keyboard shortcut you designated in Step 4.**

   The settings are sticky until you return to this pane to change them.

   With my settings in place, when I switch from one space to another using either of the "switch" keyboard shortcuts, the windows in the current space are hidden, and the windows in the space I've switched to appear. At the same time, a handy pop-up indicator appears on-screen; as shown in Figure 3-16, the indicator tells me I switched from Space 4 (arrow) to Space 1 (all white).

Figure 3-16:
This pop-up indicator tells me how I switched Spaces.

Another way to navigate between spaces is to use the keyboard shortcut you selected to activate Spaces (F8 by default). Your screen displays all your spaces, as shown in Figure 3-17. Select the one you want with either the mouse or the arrow keys and then click or press Return or Enter to activate the selected space.

6. **(Optional) Choose options in the four Active Screen Corners pop-up menus (on the Exposé tab of the Exposé & Spaces System Preferences pane) to configure the corners of your screen to activate and deactivate Exposé and Spaces features.**

Figure 3-17:
The Activate
Spaces
shortcut
displays
representa-
tions of all
four of my
spaces on
the screen.

For example, if you set the upper-left corner to Spaces, as shown in Figure 3-18, all you have to do is move the cursor to the upper-left corner, and then all your spaces appear on-screen, as shown in Figure 3-17. Other features you can activate with corners include all four Exposé modes (discussed in Chapter 2) and Start or Disable Screen Saver (discussed earlier in this chapter).

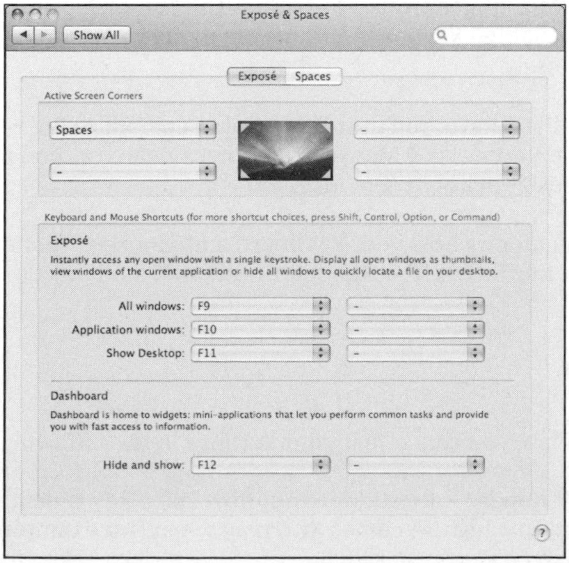

Figure 3-18:
The Exposé
& Spaces
preferences
pane's
Exposé tab.

7. **(Optional) Use the pop-up menus in the Keyboard and Mouse Shortcuts area of the Spaces tab to change or disable the keys or mouse actions for Spaces.**

   You can disable the keyboard commands completely by choosing the dash — as shown in all menus but the upper-left-corner menu in Figure 3-18.

You can also set other custom keyboard shortcuts on your Mac, but those work in a slightly different way. See "Creating Custom Keyboard Shortcuts" later in this chapter for details.

Spaces is particularly useful if you have a smaller display. It's an acquired taste, so even if you have a small screen, you might hate it.

My advice: Try it for a while, and if you decide you hate it, turn it off and be done with it.

Adjusting the Keyboard, Mouse, and Other Hardware

No one uses the keyboard and mouse in the same way. Some folks don't use a mouse at all. (You might not even use the keyboard much if you use voice-recognition software or other devices, as I explain in Chapter 16.) If you're using Mac OS X on a notebook, you might have a *trackpad,* that little surface where you move your finger around to control the cursor. Or perhaps you have a Bluetooth-enabled keyboard and mouse so that you can hook them up to your Mac wirelessly.

Regardless of what you have, you probably want to customize the way it works. To do so, open the Keyboard & Mouse preferences pane by choosing ⌘➪ System Preferences➪Keyboard & Mouse.

This pane lets you modify how your keyboard and mouse respond. It offers three tabs (plus a fourth tab, Trackpad, for notebook models).

Keyboard

On the Keyboard tab, you can adjust your settings in the following ways:

  ✔ Drag **the Key Repeat Rate slider** to set how fast a key repeats when you hold it down. This feature comes into play when (for example) you hold down the dash (-) key to make a line or the asterisk (*) key to make a divider.

✔ Drag **the Delay Until Repeat slider** to set how long you have to hold down a key before it starts repeating.

You can type in the box that says Type Here to Test Settings to test your settings before exiting this tab.

If you have a notebook Mac (such as a PowerBook, iBook, MacBook, or MacBook Pro), you also see one or more of these additional features:

✔ **Use All F1, F2 Keys As Standard Function Keys:** If this check box is selected, the F keys at the top of your keyboard control the active software application. To use the special hardware features printed on each F key (display brightness, screen mirroring, sound volume, mute, and so on) you need to press the Fn key before pressing the F key. If the check box is left deselected, you need to press the Fn key if you want to use the F keys with a software application. Got it? Good.

✔ **Illuminate Keyboard in Low Light Conditions:** This check box turns your laptop's ambient keyboard lighting on and off.

✔ **Turn Off When Computer Is Not Used For:** This slide control lets you determine how long the ambient keyboard lighting remains on when your computer isn't in use.

Of course, if your notebook computer doesn't *have* ambient keyboard lighting, as many don't, you don't see the last two items.

Ambient keyboard lighting is a cool feature, but remember that it reduces battery life. My recommendation is to use it only when you really need it.

Trackpad

You see this tab only if you have a notebook Mac with a trackpad (the mouse that isn't a mouse). This tab lets you set the tracking speed, as well as the clicking and gesturing behavior of your trackpad.

✔ Move **the Tracking Speed slider** to change the relationship between finger movement on the trackpad and cursor movement on-screen. A faster tracking speed setting (moving the slider to the right) sends your cursor flying across the screen with a mere flick of the finger; slower mouse speed settings (moving the slider to the left) make the cursor crawl across in seemingly slow motion, even when your finger is flying. Set this setting as fast as you can stand it — I like the fastest speed. Try it: You might like it.

✔ **The Double-Click Speed setting** determines how close together two clicks must be for the Mac to interpret them as a double-click and not as two separate clicks. Move the slider arrow to the leftmost setting (Slow) for the slowest. With this setting, you can double-click at a leisurely pace. The rightmost position (Fast) is the fastest setting, which I prefer. The middle area of the slider represents a double-click speed somewhere in the middle.

✓ **The Trackpad Gestures check boxes** do what their names imply.

- Select the *Use Two Fingers to Scroll check box,* and when you use two fingers right next to each other on the trackpad, you cause the window to scroll (rather than moving the cursor, as would happen with a single finger).

- The *Zoom While Holding check box* lets you zoom in and out by holding down a specific key (the default is the Control key) and dragging two fingers on the trackpad. When you zoom in or out, items on-screen get bigger or smaller. Click the arrow to the left of the Options button to open the menu and select a different modifier key.

- If you select the *Clicking check box,* you can tap your finger on the trackpad once to make your Mac recognize that gesture as a click.

- Select the *Dragging check box* to tap and drag on the trackpad without having to click the trackpad button.

- Select the *Drag Lock (tap again to release) check box* to keep an item selected after dragging until you tap the trackpad again.

✓ **The Trackpad Options check boxes** let you tell your laptop to ignore the trackpad while you're typing or when a mouse is present.

Mouse

The Mouse tab is where you set your mouse speed and double-click delays.

✓ Move **the Tracking Speed slider** to change the relationship between hand movement of the mouse and cursor movement on-screen. This slider works just like the slider for trackpads, as I explain in the preceding section.

✓ **The Double-Click Speed setting** determines how close together two clicks must be for the Mac to interpret them as a double-click and not as two separate clicks. Move the slider arrow to the leftmost setting, Very Slow, for the slowest. The rightmost position, Fast, is the fastest setting, which I prefer.

✓ If your mouse has a scroll ball or scroll wheel, you also see a **Scrolling Speed slider,** which lets you adjust how fast the contents of a window scroll when you use the scroll wheel or ball.

✓ If your mouse has more than one button, you see a pair of **Primary Mouse Button radio buttons.** These let you select which button — left or right — will be your primary (regular) click. Conversely, the other mouse button (the one you didn't select) becomes your secondary (Control or right) click.

This is the setting many lefties like to change. Set the primary button as the right button, and you can click with the index finger on your left hand.

✔ Last but not least, the **Zoom Using Scroll Wheel While Holding** check box lets you zoom in and out by turning the scroll wheel or ball while holding down a particular key. The default is the Control key, so if you scroll while holding down the Control key, items on-screen get bigger or smaller. Click the arrow to the left of the Options button, shown in Figure 3-19, to open the menu and select a different modifier key.

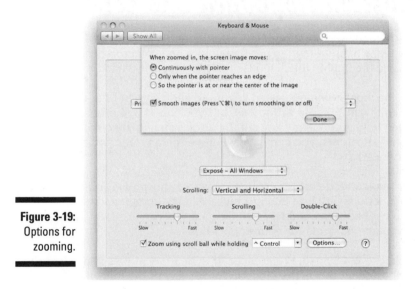

Figure 3-19: Options for zooming.

The Options button opens a sheet with options for how the screen image moves when you're zoomed in, as well as a check box for smoothing images.

Smoothing images might slow down your Mac, so if things feel sluggish when you zoom in, try clearing this check box.

Changes in the Mouse System Preferences pane take place immediately, so you should definitely play around a little and see what settings feel best for you. You can test the effect of your changes to the Double-Click Speed setting in the Double-Click Here to Test text box just below the slider before you close this preferences pane.

Bluetooth

Bluetooth is a technology that lets you make wireless connections between your Mac and devices such as Bluetooth mice and phones. You can see a

Bluetooth tab in the Keyboard & Mouse System Preferences pane if your Mac has Bluetooth. Some Macs do; some don't.

If your Mac does, the Bluetooth tab shows you the battery level of your Bluetooth mouse or keyboard. It also offers a check box to add a Bluetooth status menu to your menu bar and a check box to let Bluetooth devices wake your computer from sleep.

Creating Custom Keyboard Shortcuts

If you really hate to use your mouse or if your mouse is broken, keyboard shortcuts can be really handy. I tend to use them more on my laptop because I really don't like using the built-in touch-mouse thing (technically called a *trackpad*).

I introduce the most commonly used keyboard shortcuts in Chapter 2. You probably don't want to mess with those, but you can assign other commands you use often to just about any key combination you like. By creating your own keyboard shortcuts, you can have whatever commands you need literally at your fingertips.

Not only can you add, delete, or change keyboard shortcuts for many operating system functions (such as taking a picture of the screen and using the keyboard to choose menu and Dock items), but you can also add, delete, or change keyboard shortcuts for your applications.

To begin, choose ⌘➪System Preferences➪Keyboard & Mouse and select the Keyboard Shortcuts tab. On the tab, you can do any of the following:

- ✔ **To change a shortcut,** double-click it and then hold down the new shortcut keys.
- ✔ **To add a new shortcut,** click the + button. Choose the appropriate application from the Application pop-up menu, type the exact name of the menu command you want to add into the Menu Title field, and then type the shortcut you want to assign to that command in the Keyboard Shortcut field. It really is that simple.
- ✔ **To delete a shortcut,** select it and then click the – button.

The Keyboard Shortcuts tab also offers options for changing the Tab order. The Full Keyboard Access radio buttons control what happens when you press the Tab key in a window or dialog box.

- ✔ If you select **the Text Boxes and Lists Only radio button,** the Tab key moves the cursor from one text box to the next or from one list item to the next item (usually alphabetically).

✔ If you select **the All Controls radio button**, you can avoid using the mouse for the most part, if that's your preference.

When All Controls is selected, the Tab key moves the focus from one item to the next in a window or dialog box. So in an Open file dialog, each time you pressed the Tab key the focus would move, for example, from the Sidebar to the file list to the Cancel button to the icon view button and so on. Each item is highlighted when it's selected, and you can activate the highlighted item from the keyboard by pressing the spacebar.

You can toggle this setting by pressing F7 or Fn-F7 (depending on whether or not the **Use All F1, F2 Keys as Standard Function Keys** check box is selected on the Keyboard tab.

Styling Your Sound

Out of the box, Mac OS X Leopard comes with a preset collection of beeps and controls, but through the Sound preferences pane, you can change the way your Mac plays and records sound by changing settings on each of the three tabs: Sound Effects, Output, and Input.

Three items appear at the bottom of the Sound pane no matter which of the three tabs is active:

✔ To make your Mac's volume louder or softer, use the Output Volume slider. You can also change or mute the volume with the designated volume and mute keys found on most Apple keyboards.

✔ Select the Mute check box to turn off all sound.

✔ Click the Show Volume in Menu Bar check box to add a volume control menu to your menu bar.

A shortcut to the Sound System Preferences pane is to press Option while pressing any of the volume keys (usually the volume keys on a standard Apple extended keyboard, but the F4 and F5 keys on laptops and other keyboards).

Changing sound effects

On the Sound Effects tab, choose an alert (beep) sound by clicking its name; set its volume by using the Alert Volume slider control.

You can also specify the output device through which sound effects play (if you have more than one device) by selecting it from the Play Alerts and Sound Effects Through pop-up menu.

The Play User Interface Sound Effects check box turns on sound effects for actions, such as dragging a file to the Trash.

The Play Feedback When Volume is Changed check box tells your Mac to beep once for each press of the increase or decrease volume key.

Selecting output options

If you have more than one sound-output device (in addition to the built-in speakers), you can select it here. The Balance slider makes one stereo speaker — left or right — louder than the other.

Selecting input options

If you have more than one sound-input device (in addition to the built-in microphone on many Macs or an iSight camera, which contains its own mic), you can select it here. The Input Volume slider controls the Input Level (how loud input from that device will be), which is displayed as a row of blue dots. If the dots light up all the way to the right side, your input volume is too loud. Ideally, the input level should light up around ¾ of the little blue dots and no more.

Chapter 4

What's Up, Dock?

In This Chapter

- Getting to know the Dock
- Discovering the default Dock icons
- Talkin' Trash
- Delving into Dock customization
- Adjusting Dock preferences

Take a minute to look at the row of icons at the bottom of your display. That row, good friend, is the *Dock* (shown in Figure 4-1), and those individual pictures are known as *icons* (which I discuss in greater detail momentarily).

Figure 4-1: The Dock and all its default icons.

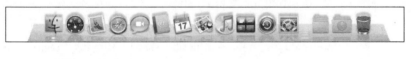

TIP: Dock icons are odd ducks — they're activated with a single-click. Most other icons are *selected* (highlighted) when you single-click and are *opened* when you double-click. So Dock icons are kind of like links on a Web page — you need only a single click to open them.

A Quick Introduction to Using The Dock

Single-click a Dock icon to open the item it represents:

- If the item is **an application,** the application opens and becomes active.
- If the item is **a document,** that document opens in its appropriate application, which becomes the active application.

> ✔ If the item is **a folder icon,** you see a stacked menu of its subfolders, and the Finder becomes the active application. Click Show in Finder to open the folder in a Finder window.

If the item is open already when you click its Dock icon, it becomes active.

The default icons of the Dock

By default, the Dock contains a number of commonly used Mac OS X applications, and you can also store your own applications, files, or folders there. (I show you how to do that in the "Adding Dock icons" section later in this chapter.)

But first, look at the items you find in a standard Mac OS X Leopard Dock. If they aren't familiar to you, they certainly will be as you get to know Mac OS X.

I admit that I can't do justice to all the programs that come with Mac OS X Leopard that aren't, strictly speaking, part of the operating system. Alas, some of the programs in the default Dock are ones you won't be seeing much more of. But I'd hate to leave you wondering what all those icons in the Dock are, so Table 4-1 gives you a brief description of each default Dock icon (moving from left to right on-screen). If additional coverage of an item appears elsewhere in the book, the table tells you where.

To quickly discover the name of a Dock icon, just move your cursor over any item in the Dock, and the item's name appears above it (as shown in the middle of Figure 4-4 later in this chapter). And as I describe in the section "Resizing the Dock" later in this chapter, you can resize the Dock to make the icons smaller (which does make them more difficult to see). Hovering the cursor to discover the name of a teeny icon makes this feature even more useful.

Table 4-1		Icons in the Dock	
Icon	*Name*	*What It Is*	*Go Here for More Info*
	Finder	The always-running application that manages the Desktop, files, folders, disks, and more.	Chapters 4, 5, and 6
	Dashboard	A layer containing small special-use applications called widgets.	Chapter 3

Icon	Name	What It Is	Go Here for More Info
	Mail	An e-mail program.	Chapter 10
	Safari	A Web browser.	Chapter 9
	iChat	An instant-messaging program.	Chapter 9
	Address Book	An address book application.	Chapter 10
	iCal	Apple's calendar program.	Chapter 8
	Preview	Apple's PDF and graphic-viewing program.	Chapter 12
	iTunes	An audio player and iPod manager (part of the iLife package).	Chapter 11
	Spaces	Helps you manage windows by organizing them into groups.	Chapter 3

(continued)

Table 4-1 (continued)

Icon	Name	What It Is	Go Here for More Info
	Time Machine	Automated data backup system.	Chapter 17
	System Preferences	The System Preferences application lets you configure the way many aspects of your Mac work.	Chapters 3, 14, and 15
	Downloads folder (empty)	An empty folder that *will* contain files you download using Safari.	Chapter 9
	Documents folder (empty)	An empty folder that *will* contain files you put into it.	Chapter 6
	Trash	The Trash icon isn't a file or application. Instead, you drag files and folders onto this icon to get rid of them or drag removable discs onto it to eject them.	Chapter 4 (this chapter!)

If you bought a new Mac with Leopard preinstalled, you might or might not see icons for the iLife applications — iMovie, iDVD, iPhoto, iWeb, and GarageBand — in your Dock. It was unclear at press time whether *every* new Mac shipped with Leopard on it was going to include the iLife suite.

Trash talkin'

The *Trash* is a special container where you put the icons that you no longer want on your hard drive or removable media storage device (such as a Zip or floppy disk). Got four copies of TextEdit on your hard drive? Drag three of them to the Trash. Tired of tripping over old letters that you don't want to keep? Drag them to the Trash, too. To put something in the Trash, just drag its icon on top of the Trash icon and watch it disappear.

As with other icons, you know that you've connected with the Trash while dragging when the icon is highlighted. And as with other Dock icons, the Trash icon's name appears when you move the cursor over the icon.

If you accidentally drag something to the Trash, you can magically put it back where it came from, but only if you act quickly. Immediately after dragging the item(s) to the Trash, choose Edit➪Undo or use the shortcut ⌘+Z. Don't hesitate — the Undo command is ephemeral and works only until you perform another action in the Finder. In other words, as soon as you do anything else in the Finder, you can no longer undo what you moved to the Trash.

You know how the garbage in the can on the street curb sits there until the sanitation engineers come by and pick it up each Thursday? The Mac OS X Trash works the same way, but without the smell. Items sit in the Trash waiting for you to empty it. The Trash basket shows you that it has files waiting for you there . . . as in real life, your unemptied Trash is full of crumpled papers.

- ✔ **To open the Trash and see what's in there,** just click its icon in the Dock. A Finder window called Trash opens, displaying any files it contains.

- ✔ **To keep an item that's already in the Trash,** drag it back out, either onto the Desktop or back into the folder where it belongs.

- ✔ **To empty the Trash,** when you put something in the Trash, it sits there until you choose the Finder➪Empty Trash command or use the keyboard shortcut ⌘+Shift+Delete.

    If the Trash window is open, you see an Empty button just below its toolbar on the right. Clicking the button, of course, also empties the Trash.

    You can also empty the Trash from the Dock by pressing the mouse button and holding it down on the Trash icon for a second or two. The Empty Trash menu pops up like magic. Move your cursor over it to select it and then release the mouse button.

Think twice before you invoke the Empty Trash command. After you empty the Trash, the files that it contained are (usually) gone forever. My advice: Before you get too bold, read Chapter 17 and back up your hard drive several times. After you get proficient at backups, chances improve greatly that even though the files are technically gone forever from your hard drive, you can get them back if you like (at least in theory).

Opening application menus in the Dock

Every application icon in the Dock — such as TextEdit, iTunes, and others — hides a menu of handy commands. (Folder icons in the Dock have a different but no less handy menu, which I discuss in a moment.)

To make this menu appear, as shown in Figure 4-2, press (click but don't let go) a Dock icon. Control+clicking a Dock icon gives you the same result as pressing and holding. The cool part is that the menu pops up immediately when you Control+click.

In addition to useful program-specific commands, Dock menus for applications that have multiple windows offer a list of windows on their menus (iTunes, The Compleat Beatles, Texas Rock, and so on), as shown in Figure 4-2.

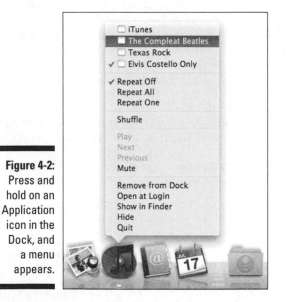

Figure 4-2:
Press and hold on an Application icon in the Dock, and a menu appears.

Reading Dock icon body language

As you use the Dock or when you're just doing regular stuff on your Mac, the Dock icons like to communicate with you. They can't talk, so they have a few moves and symbols that indicate things you might want to know. Table 4-2 clarifies what's up with your Dock icons.

Table 4-2	What Dock Icons Are Telling You
Icon Movement or Symbol	*What It Means*
The icon moves up and out of its place on the Dock for a moment, as shown in Figure 4-3.	You single-clicked a Dock icon, and it's letting you know that you've activated it.
The icon does a little bouncy dance when that program is open but isn't active (that is, its menu bar isn't showing, and it isn't the frontmost program).	The program desires your attention; give its icon a click to find out what it wants.
An glowing white dot appears below its Dock icon, as shown on the right in Figure 4-3.	This application in the Dock is open.
An icon that isn't ordinarily in the Dock magically appears.	You see a temporary Dock icon for every program that's currently open on the Dock until you quit that application. The icon appears because you've opened something. When you quit, its icon magically disappears.

Figure 4-3:
A raised
Dock icon
(middle)
with before
(left) and
after (right)
shots.

Opening files from the Dock

One useful function of the Dock is that you can easily use it to open icons. The following tips explain several handy ways to open what you need from the Dock:

✔ **You can drag a document icon onto an application's Dock icon.** If the application knows how to handle that type of document, its Dock icon is highlighted, and the document opens in that application. If the application can't handle that particular type of document, the Dock icon isn't highlighted, and you can't drop the document on it.

I'm getting ahead of myself here, but if the application can't handle a document, try opening the document this way: Select the icon and choose File➪Open With, or Control+click the document icon and use the Open With menu to choose the application you want to open the document with.

If you hold down the Option key, the Open With command changes to Always Open With, which enables you to change the default application for this document permanently.

✔ **You can find the original icon of any item you see in the Dock by choosing Show in Finder from its Dock menu.** This trick opens the window containing the item's actual icon and thoughtfully selects that icon for you.

Customizing the Dock

The Dock is a convenient way to get at oft-used icons. By default, the Dock comes stocked with icons that Apple thinks you'll need most frequently (refer to Table 4-1), but you can customize it to contain any icons that you choose, as you discover in the following sections. You also find out how to resize the Dock to fit your new set of icons and how to tell Dock icons what your preferences are.

Adding Dock icons

You can customize your Dock with favorite applications, a document you update daily, or maybe a folder containing your favorite recipes — use the Dock for anything you need quick access to.

Adding an application, file, or folder to the Dock is as easy as 1-2-3:

1. **Open a Finder window that contains an application, a file, a folder, a URL, or a disk icon that you use frequently.**

2. **Click the item you want to add to the Dock.**

   As shown in Figure 4-4, I chose the TextEdit application. (It's highlighted.) I use TextEdit constantly to type and edit quick text notes to myself and others, so having its icon in the Dock is very convenient for me.

3. **Drag the icon out of the Finder window and onto the Dock.**

   An icon for this item now appears in the Dock.

Folder, disk, and URL icons must be on the right side of the divider line in the Dock; Application icons must be on the left side of it. Why does the Dock force these rules upon you? I suppose someone at Apple thinks this is what's best for you — who knows? But that's the rule: apps on the left; folders, disks, and URLs on the right.

Figure 4-4:
Adding an
icon to the
Dock is
as easy as
1-2-3: Just
drag the
icon onto
the Dock.

You can add several items to the Dock at the same time by selecting them all and dragging the group to the Dock. However, you can delete only one icon at a time from the Dock.

Adding a URL to the Dock works slightly differently. Here's how to quickly add a URL to the Dock:

1. **Open Safari and go to the page with a URL that you want to save on the Dock.**

2. **Click the small icon that you find to the left of the URL in the address bar and drag it to the right side of the dividing line in the Dock.**

3. **Release the mouse button when the icon is right where you want it.**

   The icons in the Dock slide over and make room for your URL, as shown in Figure 4-5. From now on, when you click the URL icon that you moved to your Dock, Safari opens to that page.

If you open an icon that normally doesn't appear in the Dock and you want to keep its temporary icon in the Dock permanently, you have two ways to tell it to stick around after you quit the program:

✔ Control+click (or click and hold) and then choose Keep in Dock from the menu that pops up.

✔ Drag the icon (for an application that's currently open) off and then back to the Dock (or to a different position in the Dock) without letting go of the mouse button.

Figure 4-5:
Drag the icon from the address bar (top) to the right side of the Dock (middle). The URL appears as a Dock icon (bottom).

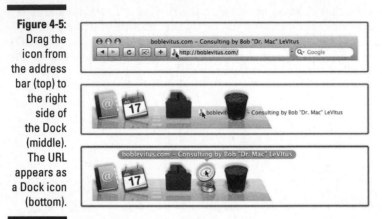

Removing an icon from the Dock

Removing an item from the Dock is as easy as 1-2 (there is no 3): Just drag its icon out of the Dock, and it disappears with a cool *poof* animation, as shown in Figure 4-6.

Figure 4-6:
To remove an icon, drag it off the Dock, and *poof* — it's gone.

Choosing Remove from Dock from the item's Dock menu does the same thing. Last but not least, you can't remove the icon of a program that's running from the Dock until you quit that program.

By moving an icon out of the Dock, you aren't moving, deleting, or copying the item itself — you're just removing its icon from the Dock. The item is unchanged. Think of it like a library catalog card: Just because you remove the card from the card catalog doesn't mean that the book is gone from the library.

Resizing the Dock

If the default size of the Dock bugs you, you can make the Dock smaller and save yourself a lot of screen real estate. This space comes in especially handy when you add your own stuff to the Dock.

To shrink or enlarge the Dock (and its icons) without opening the Dock Preferences window, follow these steps:

1. **Make the sizer appear (as shown in the left margin) by moving your cursor over the dotted line that you find on the right side of the Dock.**

2. **Drag the sizer down to make the Dock smaller, holding down the mouse button until you find the size you like.**

   The more you drag this control down, the smaller the Dock gets.

3. **To enlarge the Dock again, just drag the sizer back up.**

   Bam! Big Dock! You can enlarge the Dock until it fills your screen from side to side.

What should you put in YOUR Dock?

Put things in the Dock that you need quick access to and that you use often, or add items that aren't quickly available from menus or the sidebar. If you like using the Dock better than the Finder window sidebar, for example, add your Documents, Movies, Pictures, Music, or even your Home folder or hard drive to the Dock.

I suggest adding these items to your Dock:

✔ **A word-processing application:** Most people use word-processing software more than any other application.

✔ **A project folder:** You know, the folder that contains all the documents for your thesis, or the biggest project you have at work, or your massive recipe collection . . . whatever. If you add that folder to the Dock, you can access it much quicker than if you have to open several folders to find it.

   If you click a folder icon, a handy stacked menu of its contents appears, as shown in Figure 4-7. Better still, the same goes for disk icons. Figure 4-7 shows my Downloads folder as a stacked menu. Give this trick a try — it's great.

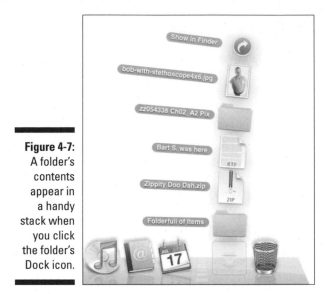

Figure 4-7:
A folder's contents appear in a handy stack when you click the folder's Dock icon.

✔ **A special utility or application:** The Preview application is an essential part of my work because I receive a lot of different image files every day. You might also want to add programs (such as AOL), your favorite graphics application (such as Photoshop Elements), or the game you play every afternoon when you think the boss isn't watching.

✔ **Your favorite URLs:** Save links to sites that you visit every day — ones that you use in your job, your favorite Mac news sites, or your personalized page from an Internet service provider (ISP). Sure, you can make one of these pages your browser's start page or bookmark it, but the Dock lets you add one or more additional URLs. (See "Adding Dock icons" earlier in this chapter for details.)

You can add several URL icons to the Dock, but bear in mind that the Dock and its icons shrink to accommodate added icons, thus making them harder to see. Perhaps the best idea — if you want easy access to several URLs — is to create a folder full of URLs and put that folder on the Dock. Then you can just press and hold your cursor on the folder (or Control+click the folder) to pop up a menu with all your URLs.

Even though you can make the Dock smaller, you're still limited to one row of icons. The smaller you make the Dock, the larger the crowd of icons you can amass. You have to determine for yourself what's best for you: having lots of icons available in the Dock (even though they might be difficult to see because they're so tiny) or having less clutter but fewer icons in your Dock.

After you figure out which programs you use and don't use, it's a good idea to relieve overcrowding by removing the ones you never (or rarely) use.

Setting your Dock preferences

You can change a few things about the Dock to make it look and behave just the way you want it to. To do so, just choose Dock⇨Dock Preferences from the menu (or the *Apple menu,* meaning the menu below that symbol in the upper-left corner of the Finder menu bar). The System Preferences application opens, showing an active Dock pane (see Figure 4-8).

You can also open the Dock Preferences by right-clicking or Control+clicking the Dock resizer and choosing Dock Preferences from the contextual menu.

Now you can adjust your Dock with the following preferences:

- ✔ **Size:** Note the slider bar here. Move this slider to the right (larger) or left (smaller) to adjust the size of the Dock in your Finder. As you move the slider, watch the Dock change size. (Now *there's* a fun way to spend a Saturday afternoon!)

     As you add items to the Dock, each icon — and the Dock itself — shrinks to accommodate the new ones.

- ✔ **Magnification:** This slider controls how big icons grow when you pass the arrow cursor over them. Or you can deselect this check box to turn off magnification entirely.

- ✔ **Position on Screen:** Choose from these three radio buttons to attach the Dock to the left side, the right side, or the bottom of your screen (the default). Personally, I prefer it on the bottom, but you should probably try all three before you decide.

- ✔ **Minimize Using:** From this handy pop-up menu (PC users would call it a drop-*down* list, but what the heck; there's no gravity in a computer screen anyway), select the animation that you see when you click a window's Minimize button (the yellow gumdrop). The Genie Effect is the default, but the Scale Effect seems a bit faster to me.

- ✔ **Animate Opening Applications:** Mac OS X animates (bounces) Dock icons when you click them to open an item. If you don't like the animation, deselect this check box, and the bouncing ceases evermore.

- ✔ **Automatically Hide and Show the Dock:** Don't like the Dock? Maybe you want to free up the screen real estate on your monitor? Then select the Automatically Hide and Show the Dock check box; after that, the Dock displays itself only when you move the cursor to the bottom of the screen where the Dock would ordinarily appear. It's like magic! (Okay, it's like Windows that way, but I hate to admit it.)

If the Dock isn't visible, deselect the Automatically Hide and Show the Dock check box to bring it back. The option remains turned off unless you change it or choose Dock⇨Turn Hiding Off from the menu (or press ⌘+Option+D).

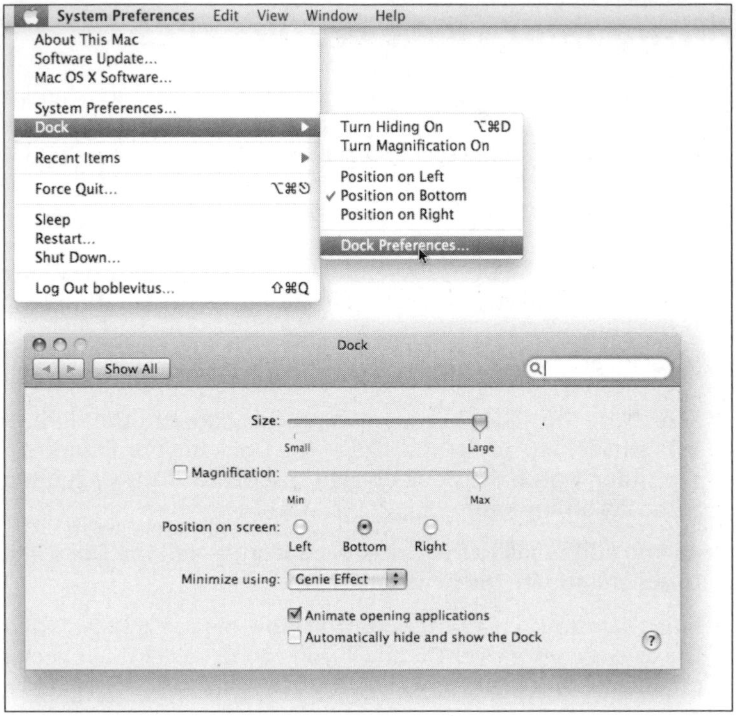

Figure 4-8: The Dock menu and Dock Preferences window.

Chapter 5

The Finder and Its Icons

*O*n your Mac, the Finder is your starting point — the centerpiece of your Mac experience, if you will — and it's always available. In Finder windows (or the Finder's Desktop), you can double-click your way to your favorite application, your documents, or your folders. And so in this chapter, I show you how to get the most from the Mac OS X Finder.

The Finder has, among other things, a special type of window. It's a very talented window, but it's a window just the same. (For the lowdown on windows in general, see Chapter 2.)

Introducing the Finder and Your Desktop

A Finder window is a handy friend. And the Finder is indeed a window (or multiple windows) in OS X. Use the Finder to navigate through files, folders, and applications on your hard drive — or to connect to other Macs and Internet servers — right from your Desktop.

Figure 5-1 shows a typical Finder window with all the standard features highlighted. You find out the details about how each feature works in the sections that follow.

Back and Forward buttons   Quick Look/Slideshow

Folder name   Hide/Show the Toolbar, Sidebar, and Status bar

View buttons   Search field

Action menu   Toolbar

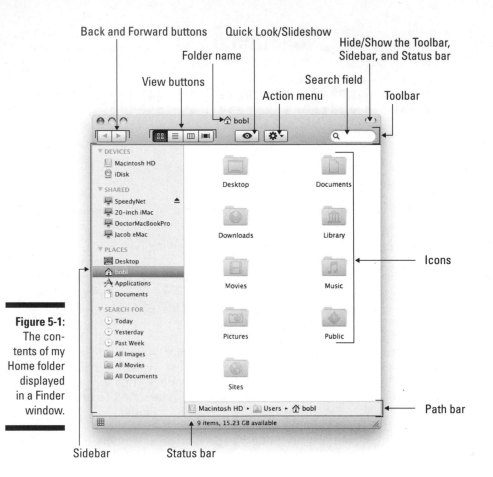

Icons

Figure 5-1:
The con-
tents of my
Home folder
displayed
in a Finder
window.

Path bar

Sidebar   Status bar

The Desktop is the backdrop for the Finder. It's always available and is where you can usually find your hard drive icon(s).

Your hard drive (and other disk) icons appear in the upper-right corner of the Desktop by default. In "Setting Finder preferences" later in this chapter, you find out how to make them *not* appear there if you so desire, but unless you have a good reason to do so, my advice is to leave them showing so that you can always find them on the Desktop if you need them. If you don't see a disk icon on your Desktop, skip ahead in this chapter to the section "Setting Finder preferences," which is where you choose whether to see disks on your Desktop.

At the bottom of the Finder window are two optional bars. The status bar tells you how many items are in each window and, if any are selected, how many you've selected out of the total, and how much space is available on the hard drive containing this window. And just above the status bar is the Path bar, which shows the path from the top level of your hard drive to the selected folder (bobl in Figure 5-1). You can show or hide the status bar by choosing View⇨Hide/Show Status Bar, and show or hide the Path bar by choosing View⇨ Hide/Show Path Bar.

If you're not familiar with the Desktop, here are a few tips that will come in handy as you become familiar with the icons that hang out there:

✐ **Icons on the Desktop behave the same as icons in a window.** You move them and copy them just like you would icons in a window. The only difference is that icons on the Desktop aren't in a window. Because they're on the Desktop, they're more convenient to use.

✐ **The first icon you should get to know is the icon for your hard drive (see Figure 5-2).** You can usually find it on the upper-right side of the desktop. Look for the name Macintosh HD or something like that, unless you've already renamed it. (I renamed my hard drive LeopardHD in Figure 5-2; see the section on renaming icons in Chapter 6 if you'd like to rename your own hard drive.) You can see how selected and deselected hard drive icons look in Figure 5-2, too.

✐ **Other disc or hard drive icons appear on the Desktop by default.** When you insert a CD or DVD or connect an external hard drive, the disc or drive icon appears on the Desktop just below your startup hard drive icon (space permitting).You can find details about working with discs and drives in Chapter 7.

✐ **You can move an item to the Desktop so that you can find it right away.** Simply click its icon in any window and then, without releasing the mouse button, drag it out of the window and onto the Desktop. Then release the mouse button.

Icon with name selected

Unselected icon   Selected icon

Figure 5-2:
Selected and deselected hard drive icons.

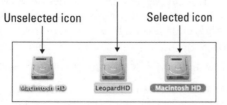

The true home of your Desktop icons

If you're curious about the inner workings of your Mac, you might find it interesting to check out the Desktop folder in your Home directory. Just click the Home icon in any Finder window's Sidebar (or use the shortcut ⌘+Shift+H to open a window displaying Home), and you see a folder named *Desktop,* which contains the same icons you place on the Desktop (but not the hard drive icons). The reason for this folder is that each user has an individual Desktop. You find out much more about Home, users, and all that jazz in the upcoming chapters.

Getting to Know the Finder Menu

One of the first features you notice in the Finder is its menu, which is packed with useful goodies. Here are a few of the main items you can find on the Finder menu:

- **About Finder:** Choose this command to find out which version of the Finder is running on your Mac.

  Okay, so this menu item isn't particularly useful — or at least not for very long. But when a different application is running, the About Finder item becomes `About application_name` and usually gives information about the program's version number, the developers (the company and the people), and any other tidbits that those developers decide to throw in. Sometimes these tidbits are useful, sometimes they're interesting, and sometimes they're both.

- **Preferences:** Use the choices here to control how the Desktop looks and acts. Find out the details in "Setting Finder preferences" later in this chapter.

- **Services:** One of the really cool features of Mac OS X applications is the accessibility of Services. You can send a file to someone via e-mail, spell-check a document or selection (even if the program you're using didn't come with a spell-checker), start a Google search instantly, and much more, as shown in Figure 5-3.

  Unfortunately, quite a few applications still don't support Services.

- **Hide Finder (⌘+H):** Use this command when you have Finder windows open and they're distracting you. Choosing it makes the Finder inactive (another currently program becomes active) and hides any open Finder windows. To make the Finder visible again, either choose Show All from the Finder menu (or whatever it's called in the active application — the command should still be there) or click the Finder button, shown in the margin here, in the Dock.

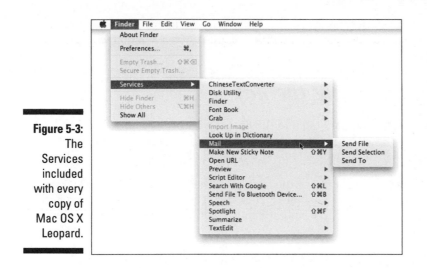

Figure 5-3:
The
Services
included
with every
copy of
Mac OS X
Leopard.

The advantage to hiding the Finder — rather than closing or minimizing all your windows to get a clean screen — is that you don't have to open them all again when you're ready to get the windows back. Instead, just choose Show All or click the Finder button in the Dock.

✔ **Hide Others (Option+⌘+H):** This command hides all windows associated with all running programs except the active program. It appears in most application's Application menus and is good for hiding distractions so you can focus on one thing — the unhidden application.

Another easy way to hide all open applications and windows while activating the Finder is to hold down the ⌘ and Option keys and click the Finder button in the Dock. This technique works with whatever application is active, not just the Finder. So if you're surfing the Web and decide you want to see only Safari's windows on your screen, ⌘+Option+click the Safari button in the Dock, and it will happen instantly.

✔ **Show All:** Use this command as the antidote to both of the Hide commands. Choose this, and nothing is hidden anymore.

You can achieve much of the same effect as all this hide-and-show jazz by using Exposé, described in Chapter 2, and/or Spaces, discussed in Chapter 3.

Navigating the Finder: Up, Down, and Backward

In addition to the Sidebar (mentioned in Chapter 2) and some good, old-fashioned double-clicking, the Mac OS X Finder window offers navigation aids. Several of these are on the toolbar — namely, the Back and Forward buttons, as well as the extra-helpful view buttons. You can find other handy features on the Go menu. The following sections explain how each one works.

Belly up to the toolbar

Right below the title bar, you find the Finder window's toolbar (refer to Figure 5-1). On it are tools and buttons that let you navigate quickly and act on selected icons. To activate a toolbar button, click it once.

You say you don't want to see the toolbar at the top of the window? Okay! Just choose View➪Hide Toolbar or click the little gray jelly bean thing in the upper-right corner of every Finder window, and it's gone. (If only life were always so easy!)

Alas, hiding the toolbar also hides the useful Sidebar and status bar. If only you could choose to hide them independently. . . . I find this fact annoying because I use the Sidebar a lot but don't use the toolbar nearly as often.

When the toolbar is hidden, opening a folder opens a *new* Finder window rather than reusing the current one (which is what happens when the toolbar is showing unless you've changed this preference in Finder preferences or are using Column view).

If you've customized your toolbar by choosing View➪Customize Toolbar, it won't look exactly like this. But here's the lowdown on the toolbar's default buttons, from left to right:

- ✓ **Forward and Back buttons:** Clicking the Forward and Back buttons displays the folders that you've viewed in this window in sequential order. If you've used a Web browser, it's a lot like that.

  Here's an example of how the Back button works. Say you're in your Home folder; you click the Favorites button, and a split-second later you realize that you actually need something in the Home folder. Just a quick click of the Back button and — *poof!* — you're back Home. As for the Forward button, well, it moves you in the opposite direction through folders that you've visited in this window. Play around with them both — you'll find them invaluable.

  The keyboard shortcuts ⌘+[for Back and ⌘+] for Forward are more useful (in my opinion) than using the buttons.

- ✓ **View buttons:** The four view buttons change the way that the window displays its contents. Stay tuned for an entire section on views coming up in just a few pages.

  You have four ways to view a window: Column view, Icon view, List view, and Leopard's new Cover Flow view. Some people like columns, some like icons, and others love lists or flows. To each her own. Play with the four Finder views to see which one works best for you. For what it's worth, I usually prefer Column view with a dash of List view thrown in when I need a folder's contents sorted by creation date or size. And the new Cover Flow view is great for folders with documents because you can see the contents of many document types right in the window, as I explain shortly.

The following sections give you a peek at each view and explain how it works.

✔ **Action:** Click this button to see a pop-up menu of all the context-sensitive actions you can perform on selected icons, as shown in Figure 5-4.

Figure 5-4: Find a common action on the Action menu.

✔ **Search:** The toolbar's Search box is a nifty way to search for files or folders. Just type a word or even just a few letters, and after a few seconds, the window fills with a list of files that match.

A more precise way to find files or folders is the File⇨Find command (shortcut: ⌘+F), which opens a special Finder window. When you use this technique:

• You have a choice of where to search. This Mac is selected in Figure 5-5.

- You can choose additional search criteria, such as the kind of file (PDF in Figure 5-5) and last date the file was opened (within last 60 days in Figure 5-5), as well as other attributes, including modification date, creation date, keywords, label, file contents, and file size.

- To add another criterion, simply click the + button on the right side of the window.

- To save a search for reuse in the future, click the Save button on the right side of the window.

You can find out about searching for files in more detail in Chapter 6.

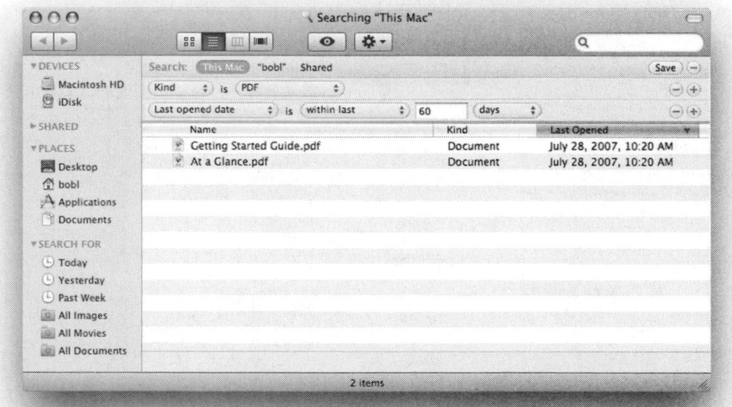

Figure 5-5:
When the toolbar's Search text box isn't good enough, use the Find command instead.

Moving through folders fast in Column view

Column view is a darn handy way to quickly look through a lot of folders at once, and it's especially useful when those folders are filled with graphics files. The Column view is my favorite way to display windows in the Finder.

To display a window in Column view, shown in Figure 5-6, click the Column view button on the toolbar (as shown in the margin), choose View⇨As Columns from the Finder's menu bar, or use the keyboard shortcut ⌘+3.

Here's how I clicked around in Column view to see the list of folders and files you see in Figure 5-6:

1. When I click the Macintosh HD icon in the Sidebar, its contents appear in the column to the right.

2. When I click the Applications folder in this column, its contents appear in the second column.

3. When I click the Utilities folder in the second column, its contents appear in the third column.

4. When I click the Java folder in the third column, its contents appear in the fourth column.

5. Finally, when I click Java Web Start in the fourth column, a big icon plus some information about this file appears (it's an application, 1.1MB in size, created on 7/28/07, and so on). That's the Preview column.

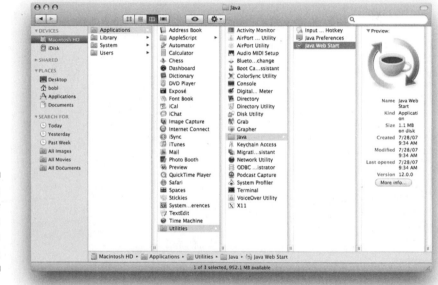

Figure 5-6:
A Finder window in Column view.

When you're poking around your Mac in Column view, the following tips are good to know:

✔ **You can have as many columns in a Column view window as your screen can handle.** Just use the window sizer (also known as the resize control) in the lower-right corner to enlarge your window horizontally so new columns have room to open. Or click the green Zoom (also known as Maximize) gumdrop button to expand the window to its maximum width instantly.

✔ **You can use the little grabber handles at the bottom of a column to resize the column widths.** When you drag this handle left or right, the column to its left resizes; if you hold down the Option key when you drag, *all* the columns resize at the same time. Furthermore, if you double-click one of these little handles, the column to its left expands to the width of the widest item it contains. And if you Option+double-click any handle, all the columns expand to the width of the widest item at the same time.

✔ **The preview column displays information about the highlighted item to its left, but only if that item isn't a folder or disk.** (If it is a folder or disk, its contents would be in this column.) For most items, the picture is an enlarged view of the file's icon, as shown earlier in Figure 5-6. But if that item is a graphic file (even a PDF) saved in a format that QuickTime can interpret (most graphic file formats), a preview picture appears instead, as shown in Figure 5-7. If you don't like having the preview displayed, you can choose View⇨Show View Options and turn off Show Preview Column.

Figure 5-7:
The preview of a graphic file is a picture instead of an icon.

Perusing in Icon view

Icon view is a free-form view that allows you to move your icons around within a window to your heart's content. Check out the Finder window shown in Figure 5-1, earlier in this chapter, to see what Icon view looks like.

To display a window in Icon view, click the Icon view button in the toolbar (shown in the margin), choose View⇨As Icons from the Finder's menu bar, or use the keyboard shortcut ⌘+1.

Icon view: The ol' stick-in-the-mud view

In all fairness, I must say that many perfectly happy Macintosh users love Icon view and refuse to even consider anything else. Fine. But as the number of files on your hard drive increases (as it does for every Mac user), screen real estate becomes more and more valuable. In my humble opinion, the only real advantages that Icon view has over Column or List view are the ability to arrange the icons anywhere you like within the window and to put a background picture or color behind your icons. Big deal.

I offer this solution as a compromise: If you still want to see your files and folders in Icon view, make them smaller so that more of them fit in the same space on-screen. This is what I do with any icons I have on my Desktop (because the Desktop allows only Icon view).

To change the size of a window's icons, choose View⇨Show View Options (or press ⌘+J). In the View Options window that appears, drag the Icon Size slider that you find there to the left. This makes the icons in the active window smaller. Conversely, you could make 'em all bigger by dragging the Icon Size slider to the right. Bigger icons make me crazy, but if you like them that way, your Mac can accommodate you. You can also alter the space between icons by dragging the Grid Spacing slider left or right.

When you're satisfied with your choices in the View Options window, if you want to apply those settings to *every* window when it's in Icon view, click the Use as Defaults button at the bottom of the View Options window. This affects all windows displayed in Icon view. (Read more on the View Options window coming up in a page or two. . . .)

Note: If you like Icon view, consider purchasing a larger monitor — I hear that monitors now come in a 30-inch size.

The Finder's View menu also offers a few commands that might help you glance through your icons more easily:

✔ **Choosing View⇨Clean Up:** Choose this command to align icons to an invisible grid; you use it to keep your windows and Desktop neat and tidy. (If you like this invisible grid, don't forget that you can turn it on or off for the Desktop and individual windows by using View Options.) Clean Up is available only in Icon view or when no windows are active. If no windows are active, the command instead cleans up your Desktop. (To deactivate all open windows, just click anywhere on the Desktop.)

If you're like me, you've taken great pains to place icons carefully in specific places on your Desktop. Cleaning up your Desktop destroys all your beautiful work and moves all your perfectly arranged icons. And alas, cleaning up your Desktop is not something you can undo.

✔ **Choosing View➪Arrange By:** This command rearranges the icons in the active window in your choice of six ways:

- Name (shortcut ⌘+Control+1)

- Date Modified (shortcut ⌘+Control+2)

- Date Created (shortcut ⌘+Control+3)

- Size, Kind, or Label (shortcuts ⌘+Control+4, 5, and 6, respectively)

Like Clean Up, Arrange By is available only for windows viewed as icons.

Listless? Try touring folders in List view

Now I come to my second-favorite view, List view (shown in Figure 5-8). The main reason why I like it so much is the little triangles to the left of each folder, known as *disclosure triangles,* which let you see the contents of a folder without actually opening it. This view also allows you to select items from multiple folders at once.

To display a window in List view, click the List view button on the toolbar (shown in the margin), choose View➪As List from the Finder's menu bar, or use the keyboard shortcut ⌘+2.

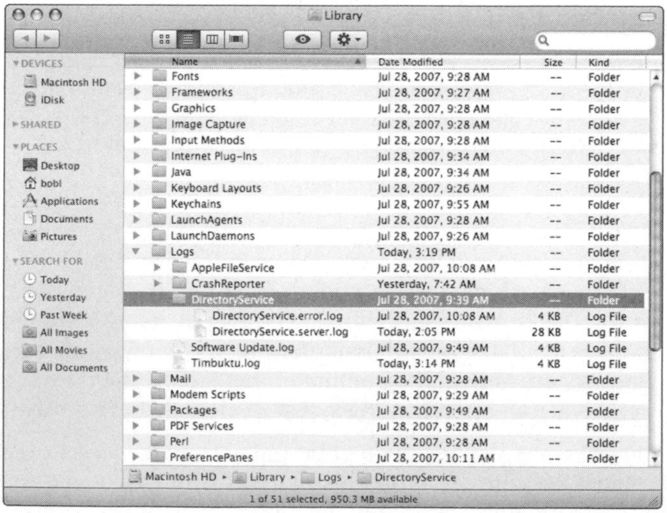

Figure 5-8:
A window
in List view.

The alternating stripes are a new Leopard feature that makes it easier to look at long lists like this one.

When you're in List view, the following tips can help you breeze through your folders to find what you're looking for:

✔ **To disclose a folder's contents, merely click the triangle to its left.** In Figure 5-8, the Logs and DirectoryService folders are disclosed.

✔ **Click the column header to sort items in List view.** Notice the little triangle at the right edge of the selected column (the Name column in Figure 5-8). If this little arrow points up, the items in the corresponding column sort in descending order; if you click the header (Name) once, the arrow points down, and the items are listed in the opposite (ascending) order. This behavior is true for all columns in List view windows.

✔ **You can change the order in which columns appear in a window.** To do so, press and hold a column's name and then drag it to the left or right until it's where you want it. Release the mouse button, and the column moves.

The exception (isn't there always an exception?) is that the Name column always appears first in List view windows; you can move all other columns about at will. And, in fact, you can even hide and show columns other than Name if you like, as you see in "On using view options" later in this chapter.

You gotta go with the flow

Leopard has a new view: the Cover Flow view. If you're familiar with the Cover Flow feature in iTunes or if you own an iPhone (which does a Cover Flow thing when you turn it sideways in its iPod music player mode), you're already familiar with Cover Flow.

To display a window in Cover Flow view, click the Cover Flow view button on the toolbar (shown in the margin), choose View⇨As Cover Flow from the Finder's menu bar, or use the keyboard shortcut ⌘+4. Figure 5-9 shows the Cover Flow view.

The Cover Flow view has two cool features. First, the item that's selected in the list (Dr bob-with-stethomouse.jpg in Figure 5-9) appears in a preview in the upper part of the window. Second, you can flip through the previews by clicking the images to the left or right of the current preview image (me wearing a stethomouse in the figure) or by sliding the black scroll bar below the preview to the left or right.

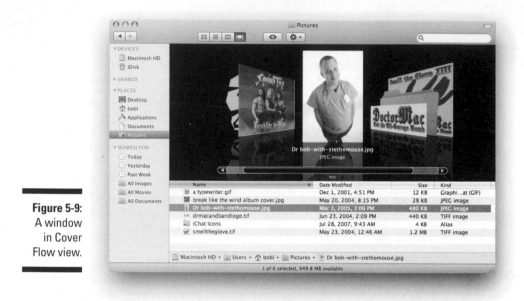

Figure 5-9:
A window
in Cover
Flow view.

Like a road map: The current folder drop-down menu

In the center of the window's title bar is the name of the folder that you're viewing in this window — the highlighted folder. You know that already. What you might not know is that it offers a hidden road map to this folder from the top level. The following steps explain how it works:

1. **⌘+click and hold the folder's name (Desktop) in the title bar, as shown in Figure 5-10.**

   A drop-down menu appears with the current folder (Desktop in Figure 5-10) at the top.

2. **Select any folder in the menu, and it becomes the highlighted folder in the current window; release the mouse button, and that folder's contents are displayed.**

   Put another way, in Figure 5-10, the contents of the Desktop folder are displayed (actually, they would be displayed if there were any, but there aren't) in the window. If I released the mouse button, the contents of the highlighted folder (bobl) would appear.

3. **After jumping to a new folder, you can click the Back button.**

   Hey, you're right back where you were before you touched that pop-up menu.

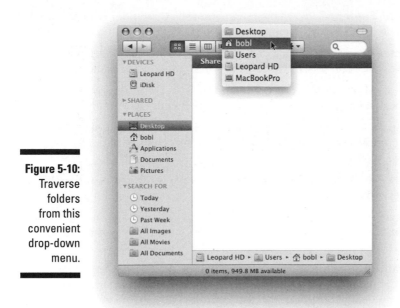

Figure 5-10: Traverse folders from this convenient drop-down menu.

If you like this feature a lot, use the Customize Toolbar command (on the View menu) to add a Path button to your toolbar. It displays the menu of folders previously described without your having to hold down the ⌘ key. (If you decide later to remove this item from the toolbar, simply hold down the ⌘ key and drag it out of the toolbar. When you release the mouse button, the item disappears with a satisfying *poof.*) And don't forget that you can display the Path bar near the bottom of the window (it's showing in Figure 5-10) by choosing View➪Show Path Bar.

Going places with the Go menu

The Go menu is chock-full of shortcuts. The items on this menu take you to places on your Mac — many of the same places that you can go with the Finder window toolbar — and a few other places.

The following list gives you a brief look at the items on the Go menu:

- **Back (⌘+[ ):** Use this menu option to return to the last Finder window that you had open. It's equivalent to the Back button on the Finder toolbar, in case you have the toolbar hidden.

- **Forward (⌘+]) :** This command is the opposite of using the Back command, moving you forward through every folder you open. Remember that if you haven't gone back, you can't go forward.

✔ **Enclosing Folder (⌘+↑) :** This command tells the Finder window to display the folder where the currently selected item is located.

✔ **Computer (⌘+Shift+C):** This command tells the Finder window to display the Computer level, showing Network and all your disks.

✔ **Home (⌘+Shift+H):** Use this command to have the Finder window display your Home folder (which is named with your short name).

✔ **Desktop (⌘+Shift+D):** Use this command to display the Desktop folder, which contains the same icons as the Desktop you see behind open windows.

✔ **Network (⌘+Shift+K):** This command displays whatever is accessible on your network in the Finder window.

✔ **iDisk:** Use this submenu to mount your iDisk (⌘+Shift+I), another user's iDisk, or another user's iDisk Public Folder. (You find out more about iDisk in Chapter 9.)

✔ **Applications (⌘+Shift+A):** This command displays your Applications folder, the usual storehouse for all the programs that came with your Mac (and the most likely spot where the programs you install will be placed).

✔ **Utilities (⌘+Shift+U):** This command gets you to the Utilities folder inside the Applications folder in one fell swoop. The Utilities folder is the repository of such useful items as Disk Utility (which lets you erase, format, verify, and repair disks) and Disk Copy (which you use to create and mount disk-image files). You find out more about these useful tools in Chapter 18.

✔ **Recent Folders:** Use this submenu to quickly go back to a folder that you recently visited. Every time you open a folder, Mac OS X creates an alias to it and stores it in the Recent Folders folder. You can open any of these aliases from the Recent Folders command on the Go menu.

✔ **Go to Folder (⌘+Shift+G):** This command summons the Go to Folder dialog, shown in Figure 5-11. Look at your Desktop. Maybe it's cluttered with lots of windows, or maybe it's completely empty. Either way, suppose you're several clicks away from a folder that you want to open. If you know the path from your hard drive to that folder, you can type the path to the folder that you want in the Go to the Folder text box (separating folder names with a forward slash [/]) and then click Go to move (relatively) quickly to the folder that you need.

The first character you type must also be a forward slash, as shown in Figure 5-11, unless you're going to a subfolder of the current window.

This particular window is clairvoyant; it tries to guess which folder you mean by the first letter or two that you type. For example, in Figure 5-11, I typed the letter **A** and paused, and the window guessed that I wanted *Applications*. Then I pressed the right-arrow key to accept the guess and typed **U**, and the window guessed the rest (tilities) and filled it in for me.

✔ **Connect to Server (⌘+K):** If your Mac is connected to a network or to the Internet, use this command to reach those remote resources.

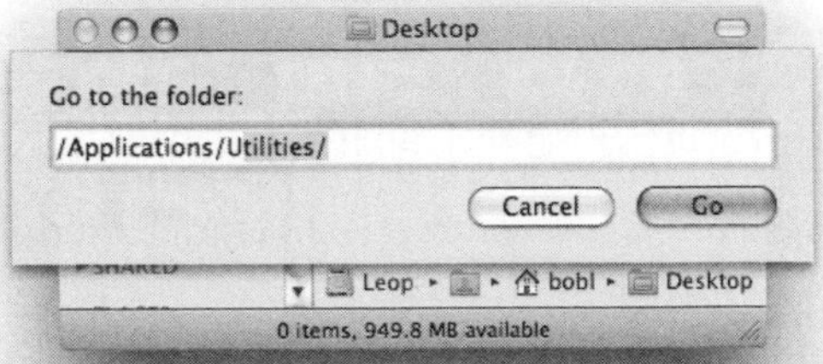

Figure 5-11:
Go to a
folder by
entering
its path.

Go to the folder:

/Applications/Utilities/

Cancel   Go

Leop ▸ ▤ ▸ ⌂ bobl ▸ ▤ Desktop

0 items, 949.8 MB available

Customizing the Finder Window

The Finder is outrageously handy. It not only gives you convenient access to
multiple windows, but also offers ways to tweak what you see till you get
what works best for you. So whereas earlier sections in this chapter explain
what the Finder is and how it works, the following sections ask, "How would
you like it to be?"

Your main task when customizing the Finder is setting the preferences. View
Options also offers settings for Icon, List, Column, and Cover Flow views. But
that's not all. Remember the Action menu? Well, it might be too egghead for
you, but you can customize that menu, too, so that your favorite actions are
at your fingertips.

Adding folders to the Sidebar

Adding whatever folder you like to the Sidebar is easy. All you need to do is
select the item you want to add and choose File⇨Add to Sidebar from the
menu bar (or press ⌘+T). You can now reach the item by clicking it in any
Finder window's Sidebar.

Setting Finder preferences

You can find Finder and Desktop preferences by choosing Finder⇨Preferences.
In the Finder Preferences window that appears, you find four panes: General,
Labels, Sidebar, and Advanced, all of which are shown in Figure 5-12.

In the **General pane,** you find the following options:

  ✔ **Show These Items on the Desktop check boxes:** Select or deselect these
     check boxes to choose whether icons for hard drives, CDs, DVDs, and

other types of disks and servers appear on the Desktop. Mac OS X selects all three options by default (which mimics earlier versions of Mac OS). But if you don't want disk icons cluttering your beautiful Desktop, you have the option of deselecting (clearing) these check boxes. If they're deselected, you can still work with CDs, DVDs, and other types of disks. You just have to open a Finder window and click the one you want in the Sidebar.

✔ **New Finder Windows Open pop-up menu:** Here, you can choose whether opening a new Finder window displays your Home folder, the Computer window, or some other folder. (Home is the default.)

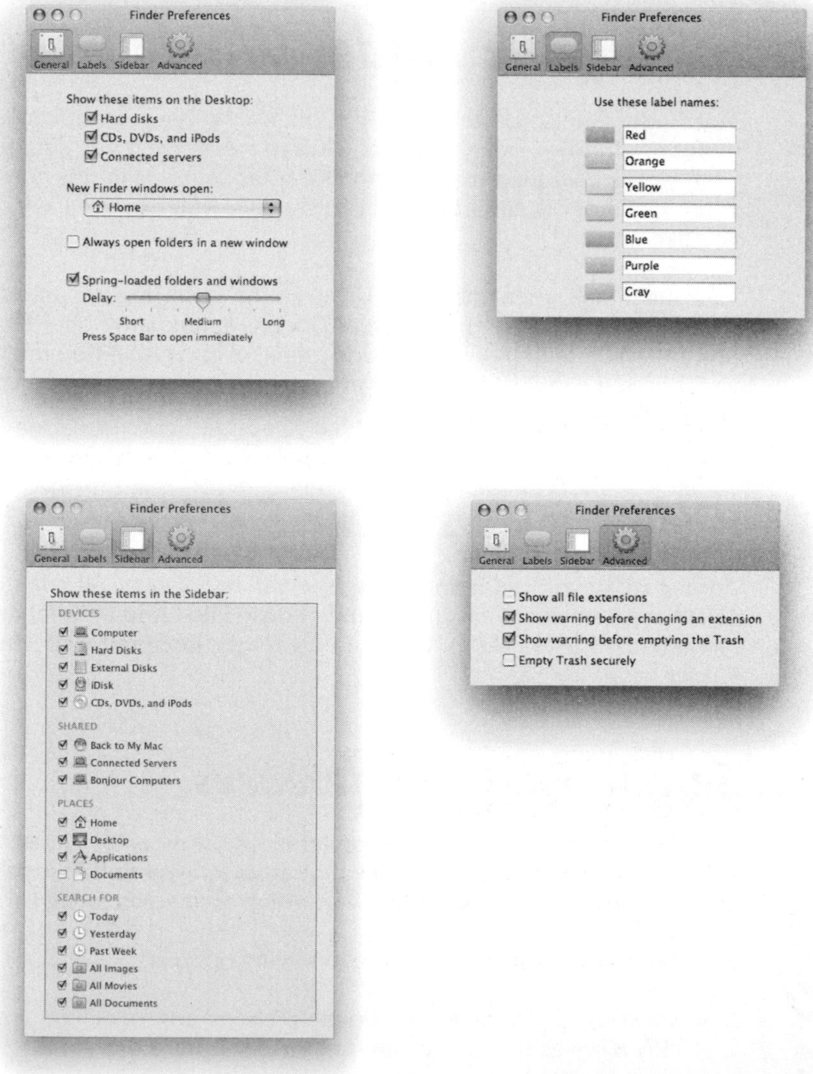

Figure 5-12:
Set Finder preferences here.

✔ **Always Open Folders in a New Window check box:** Selecting this box makes OS X work the same way as Mac OS 9.

Try it the OS X way — with windows opening "in place" to prevent window clutter. Press ⌘ before double-clicking to force a folder to open in a new window. I've learned to love this new way, although I hated it at first. Now, between this feature and Column view, I rarely need more than two or three windows on-screen, and I get by most of the time with a single window in Column view.

The **Labels pane** lets you rename the colored labels that appear in the File menu. The default names are the same as their color, but you can change them to anything you like by entering new labels in the text boxes shown in Figure 5-12.

To assign a label to any icon, select the icon, choose File⇨Label, and click one of the colored dots. The selected icon takes on that color. Why would you want to do that? Well, partly because colorized icons are festive, but mostly because you can then use the label as one of the criteria for searches, as described earlier in the chapter.

Here's an example: If you apply the red label to every file and folder associated with, say Project X — all of the folders, DOC files, PDF files, JPEG files, and so on — you can later search for items with the red label and see all these items at once, regardless of what folder they're stored in or what application created them.

Another use for labels is to use them to designate folders you want a third-party backup utility, such as EMC/Dantz Development's Retrospect, to copy automatically. (Backups are covered in detail in Chapter 17.)

That said, many users find labels useless and go years without ever applying a single label to a file or folder.

The **Sidebar pane** lets you choose which items are displayed in the Sidebar. Select the check box to display the item; deselect the check box to not display it.

The **Advanced pane** is just big enough to offer the following check boxes:

✔ **The Show All File Extensions check box** tells the Finder to display the little three-, four-, or more-character filename suffixes (such as .doc in summary.doc) that make your Mac's file lists look more like those of a Windows user. The Finder hides those from you by default, but if you want to be able to see them in the Finder and when you open or save files, you need to turn on this option.

✔ **The Show Warning before Emptying the Trash check box** (on by default) allows you to turn off the nagging dialog telling you how many items are in the Trash and asking whether you really want to delete them.

✔ **The Show Warning before Changing an Extension check box** allows you to turn off the other nagging dialog that appears if you attempt to change the three-, four-, or more-character file extension.

✔ **The Empty Trash Securely check box** makes Secure Empty Trash the default. The Secure Empty Trash feature overwrites deleted files with meaningless data so the files can't be recovered.

On using view options

The View Options window lets you soup up the way any window looks and behaves. You can do this either globally (so that all windows use the same view when opened) or on a window-by-window basis.

To find these options, follow these steps:

1. **Decide whether you want to modify Icon, List, Column, or Cover Flow view by displaying the window in that view.**

   The choice of window view determines what options you see in the View Options window. The following sections describe those options.

2. **Choose View➪Show View Options (or use the keyboard shortcut ⌘+J).**

   The View Options window appears. The choices you set in this window affect only the active Finder window unless you click the Use As Defaults button, which I get to in a moment.

Icon view options

The following list describes the View Options that you see after you choose Icon view (see Figure 5-13):

✔ **Always Open in Icon View:** Does just what the name implies — it causes this window (bobl in Figure 5-13) to always open in Icon view even if you switched it to a different view the last time you used it.

✔ **Icon Size:** Use the Icon Size slider to make icons larger or smaller. To save valuable screen space, I recommend keeping your icons small. The largest icon size is nothing short of huge.

✔ **Grid Spacing:** Use the Grid Spacing slider to change the distance between icons.

Watch the active Finder window as you move the sliders so you can monitor the icons' size and spacing as they shrink or grow depending on how far you move the slider.

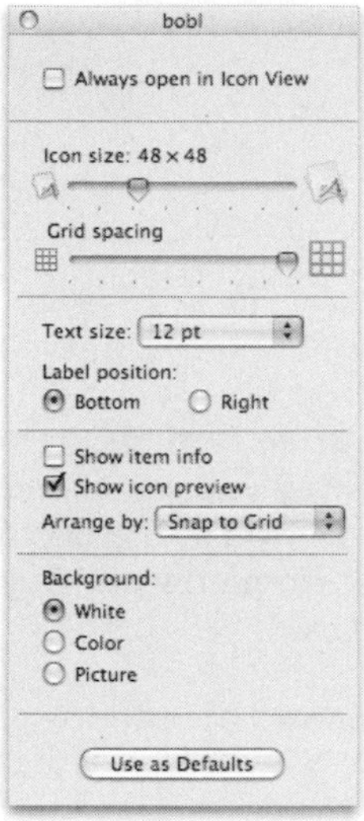

Figure 5-13:
The options
for Icon
view.

▶ **Text Size:** What it says . . . the size of the icon's name. Just choose the point size that you want from the pop-up menu.

▶ **Label Position:** Select either the Bottom or the Right radio button to set where the icon's name appears — below it or to its right.

▶ **Icon Arrangement:** Okay, *Icon Arrangement* doesn't label this group of check boxes, but icon arrangement is what these options do. With these check boxes, you specify whether those icons should be penned up or free-range:

 • *Show Item Info:* Adds a line of text below the icon's name with info about the file (or folder).

 • *Show Icon Preview:* Makes the icon look like the picture the document contains, assuming that the document contains a picture (that is, if it's a TIFF, JPEG, PDF, or other graphic file type), as shown in Figure 5-14.

 • *Arrange By:* Lets you specify the sort order for your icons from the pop-up menu. Your choices are None, Snap to Grid, Name, Date Modified, Date Created, Size, Kind, and Label.

▶ **Background:** From this list of radio buttons, you can pick a color or picture for your windows or opt for none at all (white, the default). Figure 5-15 shows what a folder looks like with a picture in its background. I'm not sure that windows should have pictures in their backgrounds, but if you like them, this is how it's done.

Whatever you choose — insert a picture, choose a color, or plain white — appears in the currently active window unless you click the Use As Defaults button, which makes it appear in every window.

Figure 5-14:
An icon with its preview off (left) and on (right).

RedMicIcon.tiff   RedMicIcon.tiff

If you want *all* your Icon view windows to use these settings, here's what to do: First, set all the preceding options just the way you want them for Icon view windows. Then, click the Use As Defaults button at the bottom of the View Options window. That's it — you're done! From now on, all your windows in Icon view will have those characteristics.

When you're done, close the View Options window.

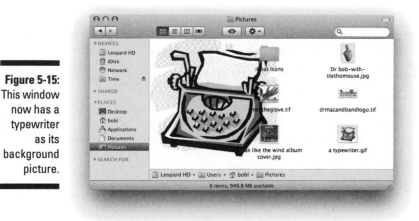

Figure 5-15:
This window now has a typewriter as its background picture.

List view (and Cover Flow) options

Suppose that you prefer List view (instead of Icon view) and want to change the options for viewing your items this way. (The Cover Flow view options are similar to the List view options, because Cover Flow includes a List view at the bottom.) To change these view options, follow these steps:

1. **With the View Options window still open, open a Finder window in List view.**

2. **From the cluster of check boxes beneath the Show Columns heading, shown in Figure 5-16, select the ones you want to appear in this List view window.**

Figure 5-16:
Choose which fields to display in List view.

Most of the options here tell Mac OS X which fields to display or hide. The choices depend on what information you want displayed, such as

- *Date Modified:* Notes the last time someone saved a change to the file or an item in a folder.

- *Date Created:* Shows when a file or folder was created.

- *Size:* Indicates the item's size in kilobytes, megabytes, or gigabytes.

- *Kind:* Indicates the item's type — folder, PDF file, and so on.

- *Version:* Indicates a file's version number (if available).

- *Comments:* Displays comments typed in the Spotlight Comments field in the icon's Get Info window.

The Spotlight Comments field in the Get Info window can help you find files or folder more easily. For example, add a project name or the word *urgent,* or any description that will help you find the file later. (You discover more about the Get Info window later in this Chapter and more about Spotlight searches in Chapter 6.)

- *Label:* Displays the Label assigned to that icon (if a label has been assigned, as discussed earlier in the chapter).

You can always change your selections later if you find that you aren't using a particular field.

The first three — modification date, creation date, and size — can be useful if you want to sort the items by something other than name.

3. **Select the Use Relative Dates check box if you want Mac OS X to intelligently substitute relative word equivalents — such as *yesterday* or *today* — for numerical dates.**

4. **Select the Calculate All Sizes check box if you want to instruct Mac OS X to (yup) calculate all sizes. Select this view to see how much stuff is in each folder when you look at it in List view.**

   The items (including folders) in the active window are sorted in descending order, from biggest to smallest, when you sort by size.

   If you don't select the Calculate All Sizes check box, items other than folders are sorted by size, with all folders — regardless of their size — appearing at the bottom of the list (or top, if the sort order is ascending).

5. **Near the top of the View Options window, you find the Icon Size radio buttons; select one of these two radio buttons to choose small or large icons in your List views.**

   For my money, I think the smallest ones make windows appear noticeably faster — and they definitely allow more items to be shown. (Your mileage may vary.)

   If you want to make all your List view windows use these settings, it's no problem. First, set everything above just the way you want it for all your List view windows. Then click the Use As Defaults button at the bottom of the View Options window. That's it!

6. **Select the Show Icon Preview check box to make icons look like the picture the document contains, assuming that the document contains a picture (that is, if it's a TIFF, JPEG, PDF, or other graphic file type).**

7. **Select the Always Open in List View check box to cause this window to always open in List view even if you switched it to a different view the last time you used it.**

8. **Close the View Options window.**

Column view options

Last but not least, to alter your options for windows in Column view, follow these steps:

1. **With the View Options window open, open a Finder window in Column view.**

2. **Set the options you want to use in this Column view window.**

   Only four options are available for windows in Column view:

   - *Text Size:* Choose the size you want from the pop-up menu.

   - *Show Icons:* Deselect this check box, and you see only text in the columns instead of both text and icons.

   - *Show Preview Column:* Determines whether you see a preview in the rightmost column when a file is selected (as shown in Figure 5-6, earlier in this chapter).

- *Arrange By:* This pop-up menu lets you choose the order in which items in the columns are displayed. Your options are Name, Date Modified, Date Created, Size, Kind, and Label.

  I find arranging columns by any of the options but Name totally disconcerting.

If you want *all* your Column view windows to use these settings, it's no problem. First, set all the options just the way you want them for all of your Column view windows. Then click the Use As Defaults button at the bottom of the View Options window. That's it!

3. **Select the Always Open in Column View check box to cause this window to always open in Column View even if you switched it to a different view the last time you used it.**

4. **Close the View Options window.**

Customizing the Finder with Folder Actions

Apple has this really cool technology called AppleScript. It's been around since System 7 was released and hasn't ever really gotten the respect it deserves. AppleScript lets you program repetitive tasks so you don't have to go through all the steps every time you want to perform the task. (You find a bit more info on AppleScript in Chapter 16.)

Having an AppleScript run when items are added to a closed folder sounds like a great tool for drop-box-style folders to me — how about you? For example, you could have Mail launch and send a notification to your project leader or project team whenever a new file was added to the folder. Here's what you need to do:

1. **Create or obtain AppleScripts to perform the tasks you want done.**

   Programming AppleScript is beyond the purview of this book. In fact, a book telling you all about programming AppleScript is the size of this entire book — it's *AppleScript For Dummies,* 2nd Edition, by Tom Trinko (Wiley). Closer to hand, you can find ready-to-go scripts for Folder Actions on your hard drive at

   ```
   Library/Scripts/Folder Action Scripts
   ```

   and even more at the Apple Web site in the AppleScript pages (www. apple.com/macosx/features/applescript).

2. **Enable Folder Actions by right-clicking or Control+clicking the folder icon and choosing More⇨Enable Folder Actions from the contextual menu.**

3. **Configure a Folder Action by right-clicking or Control+clicking the folder icon and choosing More⇨Attach a Folder Action from the contextual menu.**

   This opens a Choose a File dialog (really an Open dialog, which I tell you about in Chapter 6). The dialog conveniently defaults to the Folder Action Scripts folder mentioned previously.

4. **Select your Folder Action script, click Choose, and you're set to go.**

   If you want to know more about writing Folder Action scripts, check out www.apple.com/applescript/folderactions.

Knowing Thy Finder Icons

Now is the time to take a closer look at some of the different icons you'll encounter in the Finder. In the broadest sense, icons represent things you work with on your Mac, such as programs, documents, and folders.

Don't confuse Dock icons with Finder icons — they're two different animals. *Dock and Sidebar icons* are simply pointers to items on your hard drive. Icons in Finder windows, on the other hand, represent real things on your hard drive — your folders, applications, and documents. The big difference, though, is that you can select regular Finder icons with a single click and open them with a double click; Dock and Sidebar icons can't be selected, and you click just once to open them.

Finder icons come in several shapes and sizes. After you've been around the Macintosh for a while, you develop a sixth sense about what an icon contains, and you know just by looking at it. The three main types of icons are applications, documents, and folders. Well, there are actually four types — aliases are an icon type in their own right. But don't worry — I show you all four icon types right now:

- **Application icons** are *programs* — the software that you use to accomplish tasks on your Mac. Mail, Safari, and iCal are applications. So are Microsoft Word and Adobe Photoshop.

  Application icons come in a variety of shapes. For example, application (that is, program) icons are often square-ish. Sometimes they're diamond-shaped, rectangular, or just oddly shaped. In Figure 5-17, you can see application icons of various shapes.

- **Document icons** are files that are created by applications. A letter to your mom, which you create in TextEdit, is a document, and so are my latest column written in Microsoft Word and my Quicken data files. Document icons are almost always reminiscent of a piece of paper, as shown in Figure 5-18.

Figure 5-17:
Application
icons come
in many
different
shapes.

✔ **Folder icons** are the Mac's organizational containers. You can put icons — and the applications or documents they stand for — in folders. You can also put folders inside other folders. Folders look like, well, manila folders (what a concept) and can contain just about any other icon. You use folders to organize your files and applications on your hard drive. You can have as many folders as you want, so don't be afraid to create new ones. The thought behind the whole folders thing is pretty obvious — if your hard drive is a filing cabinet, folders are its drawers and folders (duh!). Figure 5-19 shows some typical folder icons.

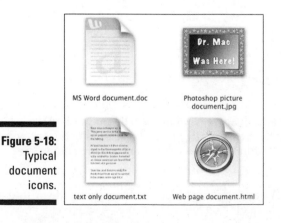

Figure 5-18:
Typical
document
icons.

Figure 5-19:
Some run-
of-the-mill
folder icons.

✔ **Aliases** are wonderful — no, *fabulous* — organizational tools. I like aliases so much, in fact, that I think they deserve their very own section. Read on for more info on this ultra-useful tool.

If you're looking for details about how to organize your icons in folders, move them around or delete them, and much more, check out Chapter 6, which explains everything you need to know about file organization and management.

Aliases: Greatest Thing Since Sliced Bread

An *alias* is a tiny file that automatically opens the file, folder, disk, or network volume that it represents. Although an alias is technically an icon, it's different from other icons — it actually does nothing but open another icon automatically when you double-click it.

Put another way, aliases are organizational tools that let you have an icon appear in more than one place without having to create multiple copies of the file that icon represents.

An alias is very different from a duplicated file. For example, the iTunes application uses around 90 megabytes (MB) of hard drive space. A *duplicate* of iTunes gives me two files, each requiring around 90MB of space on my hard drive. An *alias* of iTunes, on the other hand, uses a mere 68 kilobytes (K).

So you put aliases of programs and files you use often in convenient places such as the Desktop.

In effect, Microsoft stole the alias feature from Apple. (If you've used Windows, you may know aliases as *shortcuts*.) But what else is new? And for what it's worth, aliases usually don't break when you move or rename the original file; shortcuts do.

Why else do I think that aliases are so great? Well, they open any file or folder on any hard drive from anywhere else on any hard drive — which is a very good trick. But there are many other reasons I think aliases rock:

✔ **Convenience:** Aliases enable you to make items appear to be in more than one place, which on many occasions is exactly what you want to do. For example, keep an alias of your word processor on your Desktop and another in your Documents folder for quick access. Aliases enable you to open your word processor quickly and easily without navigating into the depths of your Applications folder each time you need it.

While you're at it, you might want to put an icon for your word processor in both the Dock and the Sidebar to make it even easier to open your word processor without a lot of clicking.

✔ **Flexibility and organization:** You can create aliases and store them anywhere on your hard drive to represent the same document in several different folders. This is a great help when you need to file a document that can logically be stored in any of several files. If you write a memo to Fred Smith about the Smythe Marketing Campaign to be executed in the fourth quarter, which folder does the document go in? Smith? Smythe? Marketing? Memos? 4th Quarter? Correct answer: With aliases, it can go in all of the above, if you like. Then you can find the memo wherever you look instead of guessing which folder it was filed in.

With aliases, it doesn't matter. You can put the actual file in any folder and then create aliases of the file, placing them in any other applicable folder.

✔ **Integrity:** Some programs must remain in the same folder as their supporting files and folders. Many programs, for example, won't function properly unless they're in the same folder as their dictionaries, thesauruses, data files (for games), templates, and so on. Thus, you can't put the actual icon for such programs on the Desktop without impairing their functionality. An alias lets you access a program like that from anywhere on your hard drive.

Creating aliases

When you create an alias, its icon looks the same as the icon that it represents, but the suffix *alias* is tacked onto its name, and a tiny arrow called a *badge* appears in the lower-left corner of its icon. Figure 5-20 shows both an alias and its *parent* icon (that is, the icon that opens if you double-click the alias).

To create an alias for an icon, do one of the following:

✔ **Click the parent icon and choose File⇨Make Alias.**

✔ **Click the parent icon and press ⌘+L.**

✔ **Click any file or folder, press and hold down ⌘+Option, and then drag the file or folder while continuing to hold down ⌘+Option.**

Presto! An alias appears where you release the mouse button.

Figure 5-20:
An alias
icon (right)
and its
parent.

> I am the parent icon   I am the parent icon's alias

 ✔ **Click an icon while holding down the Control key and then choose the Make Alias command from the contextual menu that appears.**

   The alias appears in the same folder as its parent. (You can explore contextual menus — which are very cool — in Chapter 2.)

When I first create a file, I save it in its proper folder inside the Documents folder in my Home folder. If it's a document that I plan to work on for more than a day or two (such as a magazine article or book chapter), I make an alias of the document (or folder) and plop it on the Desktop. After I finish the article or chapter and submit it to an editor, I trash the alias, leaving the original file stashed away in its proper folder.

Deleting aliases

This is a short section because deleting an alias is such an easy chore. To delete an alias, simply drag it onto the Trash icon in the Dock. That's it! You can also Control+click it and choose Move to Trash from the contextual menu that appears, or select the icon and use the keyboard shortcut ⌘+Delete.

Deleting an alias does *not* delete the parent item. (If you want to delete the parent item, you have to go hunt it down and kill it yourself.)

Hunting down an alias's parent

Suppose that you create an alias of a file, and later you want to delete both the alias and its parent file, but you can't find the parent file. What do you do? Well, you can use the Finder's Find function to find it (try saying that three times real fast), but here are three faster ways to find the parent icon of an alias:

 ✔ Select the alias icon and choose File➪Show Original.

 ✔ Select the alias icon and use the keyboard shortcut ⌘+R.

 ✔ Control+click the alias icon and choose Show Original from the contextual menu.

Digging for Icon Data in the Info Window

Every icon has an Info window that gives you — big surprise! — information about that icon and enables you to choose which other users (if any) you want to have the privilege of using this icon. (I discuss sharing files and privileges in detail in Chapter 15.) The Info window is also where you lock an icon so that it can't be renamed or dragged to the Trash.

To see an icon's Info window, click the icon and choose File➪Get Info (or press ⌘+I). The Info window for that icon appears. Figure 5-21 shows the Info window for the QuickTime Player icon.

Figure 5-21:
A typical
Info window
for an
application
(QuickTime
Player, in
this case).

> **QuickTime Player Info**
>
> **QuickTime Player**   8.3 MB
> Modified: Jul 28, 2007 9:28 AM
>
> ▶ **Spotlight Comments:**
>
> ▼ General:
>   Kind: Application (Universal)
>   Size: 8.3 MB on disk (7,300,633 bytes)
>   Where: /Applications
>   Created: Saturday, July 28, 2007 9:28 AM
>   Modified: Saturday, July 28, 2007 9:28 AM
>   Version: 7.2.1, Copyright © 1989–2007
>   Apple Inc. All Rights Reserved
>   Label: [×] ▪ ▪ ▪ ▪ ▪ ▪ ▪
>
>   ☐ Open using Rosetta
>   ☐ Locked
>
> ▶ More Info:
> ▶ Name & Extension:
> ▶ Preview:
> ▶ Languages:
> ▶ Plug-ins:
> ▶ Sharing & Permissions:

Documents, folders, and disks each have slightly different Info windows. In this section, I give you highlights on the type of information and options that you can find.

The gray triangles reveal what information for an icon is available in this particular Info window. The sections that you see for most icons include the following:

✓ **Spotlight Comments:** Provides a field in which you can type your own comments about this icon for Spotlight to use in its searches. (I talk about this a little earlier in this chapter and discuss Spotlight searches in Chapter 6.)

✓ **General:** For information of the general kind, such as

- *Kind:* What kind of file this is — an application, document, disk, folder, and so on.

- *Size:* How much hard drive space this file uses.

- *Where:* The path to the folder that contains this file.

- *Created:* The date and time that this file was created.

- *Modified:* The date and time that this file was last modified (that is, saved).

- *Version:* Copyright information and the file's version number.

- *Label:* Choose or change the color label for this item.

- *Open Using Rosetta* (check box): Some applications — known as *Universal* applications — are designed to work on both Intel-based Macintosh computers and PowerPC-based Macs. Some of these Universal applications might use extensions or plug-ins that won't work in an Intel-based Mac unless you select this check box.

  If you have an Intel-based Mac and a program doesn't seem to work with it, try selecting this check box.

✔ **More Info:** When the icon was last opened.

✔ **Name & Extension:** Tells the full name, including the (possibly hidden) extension.

✔ **Preview:** When you select a document icon, the menu offers a Preview option that you use to see a glimpse of what's in that document. You can also see this preview when you select a document icon in Column view — it magically appears in the rightmost column. If you select a QuickTime movie or sound, you can even play it right there in the preview pane without launching a separate application. Neat.

✔ **Languages:** Manages the language that the application uses for menus and dialogs.

  This option appears only if you're using an Info window to look at certain application programs (usually the sort that contain multiple `.lproj` folders within their Contents/Resources folders).

✔ **Plug-Ins:** Shows plug-in components for applications that have plug-in architecture, such as QuickTime Player.

  This option appears only if you're using an Info window to look at certain application programs (usually the sort that contain multiple `.lproj` folders within their Contents/Resources folders).

✔ **Sharing & Permissions:** Governs which users have access to this icon and how much access they are allowed. (See Chapter 15 for more about access privileges.)

And that's about it for icons, which are among the most fundamental parts of what makes your Mac a Mac (and not a toaster or an Xbox).

Part II

Leopard Taming (Or "Organization for Smart People")

The 5th Wave   By Rich Tennant

"The funny thing is he's spent 9 hours organizing his computer desktop."

In this part . . .

Peruse the chapters in this part to discover how to organize just about everything in your Leopard. Don't get all worked up — this stuff is easy. In fact, I think of this part as "The Lazy Person's Guide to Getting and Staying Organized."

I start by showing you more about the all-important Finder, including the two most important skills of all: saving and opening files. Then you discover the joys of dealing with disks (and discs) — a good thing to know indeed! Next is a short discourse on managing and synchronizing your calendars and other important information without tearing your hair out.

It might sound imposing, but I assure you this part is (mostly) painless.

Chapter 6

Organizing and Managing Files and Folders

*T*his could be the most important chapter in this book. If you don't under-stand how to open and save files using the Open dialog and Save sheets or how to use the file and folder system, you'll have a heck of a time getting the hang of your Mac. Ask any longtime Mac user — the old lament is pretty common: "Well, I saved the file, but now I don't know where it went." It happens all the time with new users; if they don't master these essential techniques, they often become confused about where files are located on their hard drives.

This chapter is the cure-all for your file and folder woes. Hang with me and pay attention; everything soon becomes crystal clear.

You work with Open dialogs and Save sheets within applications. You see them only *after* you launch a program and use that program's File menu to open or save a file. (For more on launching applications, read the parts of Chapter 5 that discuss icons; for more on creating and opening documents, see the documentation for the program that you're using.)

Understanding the Mac OS X Folder Structure

Start by looking at the folder structure of a typical Mac OS X installation. Open a Finder window and click the icon for your hard drive (which is typically called

Macintosh HD) in the Sidebar. You should now see at least four folders — Applications, Library, System, and Users.

Within the User folder, each person who uses this Mac has his or her own set of folders that contain documents, preferences, and other information that belong to that person.

If you're the sole person who accesses your Mac, you probably have only one user. Regardless, the folder structure that Mac OS X uses is the same, whether you have one user or dozens.

Within the Users folder, you find your personal Home folder and a Shared folder, where you can put files you want to share with other users.

All these files are stored in a nested folder structure that's a bit tricky to understand at first. This structure makes more sense after you spend a little time with it and figure out some basic concepts.

If you display the Path bar at the bottom of your windows by choosing View➪Show Path Bar, it'll start to make sense that much sooner.

If you take a look at Figure 6-1, you can see how these main folders are related to one another. In the sections that follow, you take a look at each of these folders in more depth and find out more about what's nested inside each one.

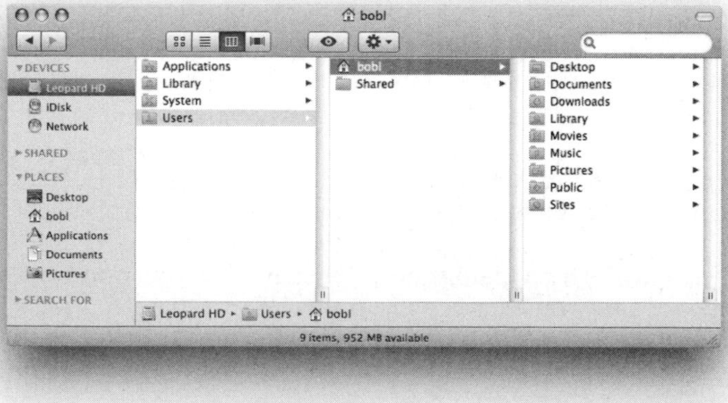

Figure 6-1:
A bird's-eye view of key folders on your Mac and their structure.

Understanding nested folders

Folders within other folders are often called *nested folders*. To get a feel for the way nested folders work in Mac OS X, check out Figure 6-2. You can see the following from the figure:

✔ Folder 1 is one level deep.

✔ Folder 2 is inside Folder 1, which is one level deeper than Folder 1, or two levels deep.

✔ Folder 3 is inside Folder 2 and is three levels deep.

✔ The files inside Folder 3 are four levels deep.

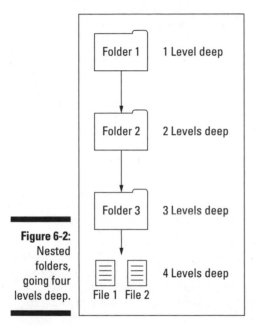

Figure 6-2:
Nested
folders,
going four
levels deep.

If the previous list makes sense to you, you're golden. What's important here is that you're able to visualize the path to Folder 3. That is, to get to files inside Folder 3, you open Folder 1 and then open Folder 2 to be able to open Folder 3. Understanding this concept is important to understanding the relationships between files and folders. Keep reviewing this section, and eventually the concept will click — you'll slap yourself in the head and say, "Now I get it!"

From the top: The Computer folder

I start with the Computer folder, which is the top level of the folder hierarchy. The Computer folder shows all the storage devices (hard drives, CD- or DVD-ROM, Zip disk, and so forth) that are currently connected to your Mac. The following steps show how you can start at the Computer folder and drill down through the folder structure:

1. **To find the Computer folder, choose Go⇨Computer or use the keyboard shortcut ⌘+Shift+C.**

In Figure 6-3, the Computer folder is called MacBookPro, and it contains a hard drive icon (LeopardHD) and a Network icon, with which you can access servers or other computers on your local network. (Don't quite know what that means? Read Chapter 15 for the whole scoop on sharing files with other Macs and sharing your Mac with other users.)

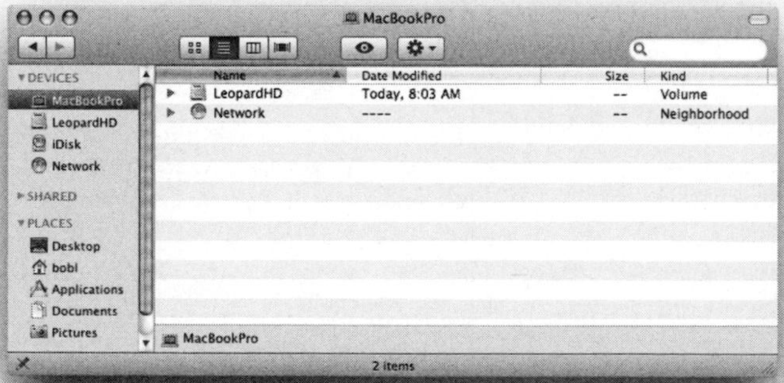

Figure 6-3:
The contents
of the
Computer
folder.

If you don't see a Computer icon in your Sidebar, choose Finder⇨ Preferences, click the Sidebar icon at the top, and then select the Computer check box. You can change the computer name (MacBookPro in Figure 6-3) in the Sharing System Preferences pane, which you can access by launching the System Preferences application (from the Applications folder, the Dock, or the Apple menu) and then clicking the Sharing icon.

You might have more or fewer icons in your Computer folder than what you see in Figure 6-3 (depending on how many disks you have mounted).

2. **Double-click the icon that holds your Mac OS X stuff. (Technically, this is called your boot drive.)**

   In Figure 6-3, that hard drive is called LeopardHD. Of course, I have no idea what yours is called; if you haven't changed it, it's probably called Macintosh HD.

3. **Check out the folders you find there.**

   You should see at least four folders (unless you've added some — if you installed the Xcode programming tools, for example, you have more). In the next few sections, I walk you through what you can find in each one.

Peeking in the Applications folder

The Applications folder, located at the root level of your boot drive (the one with OS X installed on it), is accessible with a click of the Applications icon in the Sidebar, from the Go menu, or by using the keyboard shortcut ⌘+Shift+A. In this folder, you find applications and utilities that Apple includes with Mac OS X. All users of a given Mac have access to the items in the Applications folder.

Finding fonts (and more) in the public Library folder

The Library folder at the root level of your Mac OS X hard drive is like a public library — it stores items that everyone with access to this Mac can use. You can find two different Library folders on your hard drive — the one at the root level of your OS X disk and another in your Home folder.

Okay, I wasn't entirely truthful, but only for your own good: There's actually a third Library folder inside the System folder, which I discuss in a page or two. But for now, heed this warning: **Leave the \System\Library folder alone** — don't move, remove, or rename it or do anything within it. It's the nerve center of your Mac. In other words, you should never have to touch this third Library folder.

You find a bunch of folders inside the Library folder at root level (the public Library folder). Most of them contain files that you never need to open, move, or delete.

By and large, the public Library subfolder that gets the most use is the Fonts folder, which houses many of the fonts installed on the Mac. For the most part, fonts can be made available in one of two ways:

- **To everyone who uses the Mac:** If that's the case, they're stored here in the Fonts folder.
- **To a single user:** In this case, you place the fonts in the user's Library folder (the one in the user's Home folder).

I discuss fonts more in Chapter 13. Meanwhile, some other public Library subfolders that you might use or add to are the iMovie, iTunes, iPhoto, and iDVD folders (where you put plug-ins for those programs); the Scripts folder (which houses AppleScripts accessible to all users); and the Desktop Pictures folder (where you can place pictures to be used as Desktop backgrounds).

Leave the "public" Library folder pretty much alone unless you're using the Fonts folder or know what you're adding to one of the other folders. Don't remove, rename, or move any files or folders. Mac OS X uses these items and is very picky about where they're kept and how they're named.

Note: Under most circumstances, you won't actually add or remove items from folders in this Library yourself. Software installers usually do the heavy lifting for you by placing all their little pieces into appropriate Library folders. You shouldn't need to touch this Library often, if ever. That said, knowing what these folders are — and who can access their contents — might come in handy down the road a piece.

If your Mac is set up for multiple users, only users with administrator (admin) privileges can put stuff into the public (root level) Library folder. (For more information on admin privileges, check out Chapter 15.)

Let it be: The System folder

The System folder contains the files that Mac OS X needs to start up and keep working.

Leave this folder alone — don't move, remove, or rename it or anything within it. It's part of the nerve center of your Mac.

The usability of the Users folder

When you open the Users folder, you see a folder for each person who uses the Mac, as well as the Shared folder.

The Shared folder that you see in the Users folder allows everyone who uses the Mac to use the files stored there. If you want other people who use your Mac to have access to a file or folder, the Shared folder is the proper place to stash it. You can see my Shared folder right below my Home folder (bobl) earlier in Figure 6-1.

I realize that a lot of people don't share their Macs with others. And if you're one of these folks, you might wonder why I keep mentioning sharing and multiple users and the like. Well, Mac OS X is based on the UNIX operating system — a multiuser operating system found on high-end servers and workstations that are often shared by several people. Mac OS X has both the benefit of this arrangement and a bit of the confusion caused when a single user (could it be you?) fires up a computer that could be set up for several people. That's why Mac OS X folders are organized the way they are — with different hierarchies for each user and for the computer as a whole.

There's no place like Home

From the Users folder, you can drill down into the Home folder to see what's inside. When the user logs onto this Mac, his Home folder appears whenever he clicks the Home icon in the Sidebar, chooses Go⇨Home, or uses the keyboard shortcut ⌘+Shift+H.

Your Home folder is the most important folder to you as a user — or at least the one where you stash most of your files. I strongly recommend that you store all the files you create in a subfolder within your Home folder, preferably in a subfolder in your Home/Documents folder. The advantage of doing so is that your Home/Documents folder is easy to find, and many programs use it as the default folder for opening or saving a file.

When you open your Home folder, you see a Finder window with a little house icon and your short username in the title bar. Seeing your short username in the title bar tells you that you're in *your* Home folder. Every user has a Home folder named after his or her short username (as specified in the Accounts System Preferences pane). In Figure 6-4, you can see that my Home folder is named bobl — the short name I used when I first set up my Mac.

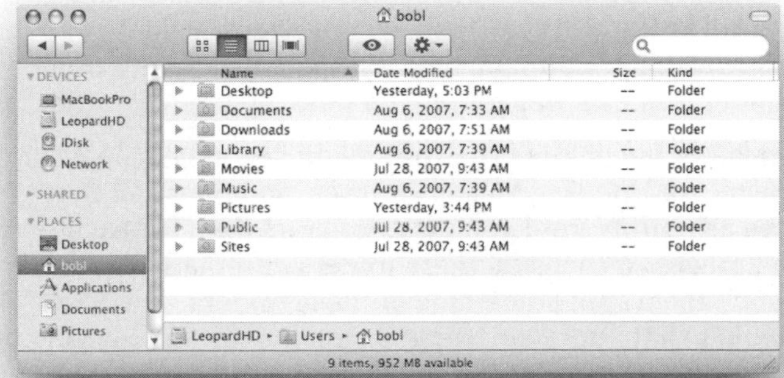

Figure 6-4:
My Home
folder.

If your Mac has more than one user, you can see the other users' Home folders in your Users folder, but Mac OS X prevents you from opening files from or saving files to them.

Your Home folder, by default, has several folders inside it created by Mac OS X. The following four are the most important:

✔ **Desktop:** If you put items (files, folders, applications, or aliases) on the Desktop, they're actually stored in the Desktop folder.

✔ **Documents:** This is the place to put all the documents (letters, spreadsheets, recipes, and novels) that you create.

✔ **Library:** Preferences (files containing the settings you create in System Preferences and other places) are stored in the Library folder, along with fonts that are available only to you (as described previously in this chapter) and other stuff to be used by you and only you.

✔ **Public:** If others on your local area network use file sharing to connect with your Mac, they can't see or use files or folders in your Home folder. But they can share files you've stored in your Home folder's Public folder. (Read more about file sharing and Public folders in Chapter 15.)

You can create more folders if you like. In fact, every folder that you *ever* create (at least every one you create on this particular hard drive or volume) *should* be within your Home folder. I explain more about creating folders and subfolders and organizing your stuff inside them later in this chapter.

The following are a few more tidbits to keep in mind as you dig around your Home folder:

✔ If you decide you don't want an item on the Desktop anymore, delete it by dragging its icon from the Desktop folder to the Trash or by dragging its icon from the Desktop itself to the Trash. Both techniques yield the same effect: The file is in the Trash, where it remains until you empty the Trash. Or if you don't want it on the Desktop anymore but don't want to get rid of it either, you can drag it from the Desktop into any other folder you like.

✔ The other five folders that you might see in your Home folder are Downloads, Movies, Music, Pictures, and Sites. All these folders except Sites are empty until you (or a program like iTunes, iPhoto, or iMovie that creates files inside these folders automatically the first time you launch them) put something in these folders. The Sites folder contains a few files that your Mac needs if you enable Web Sharing in the Sharing System Preferences pane, as I describe in Chapter 15.

Your personal Library card

The Library subfolder of your Home folder is the repository of everything that Mac OS X needs to customize *your* Mac to *your* tastes. If you want to add something to a Library folder, it's usually best to add it to your `Home/ Library` folder. You won't spend much time (if any) adding things to the Library folder or moving them around within it, but it's a good idea for you to know what's in there. In the "Finding fonts (and more) in the public Library folder" section earlier in this chapter, I discuss the Library folder that's used to specify preferences for the Mac as a whole. But *this* Library folder is all about you and your stuff.

I'm getting a little ahead of myself, but I'm afraid if I don't mention this now it might confuse you: Previous versions of Mac OS X placed downloaded files on your Desktop by default; Mac OS X 10.5 Leopard places downloaded files in the (new in Leopard) Downloads folder in your Home folder by default. (I'll tell you more about downloading and Web browsing with Safari, but not until Chapter 9.)

Be cautious with the Library folder because OS X is very persnickety about how its folders and files are organized. As I discuss earlier in the chapter, you can add and remove items safely from most Library folders, but *leave the folders themselves alone.* If you remove or rename the wrong folder, you could render OS X inoperable. It's like the old joke about the guy who said to the doctor, "It hurts when I do that," and the doctor replies, "Then don't do that."

To find the Library folder, click the Home icon in the Sidebar of any Finder window or use the shortcut ⌘+Shift+H and then open the Library folder. You should see several folders; the exact number depends on the software that you install on your Mac. For example, if you have an e-mail account, you should see folders called Addresses and Mail. (If you don't have an e-mail account set up, of course, those folders might not be there.)

Some of the most important standard folders in the Library folder include the following:

- **Documentation:** Some applications store their Help files here. Others store theirs in the main (root-level) public Library folder.

- **Fonts:** This folder is empty until you install your own fonts here. The fonts that come with Mac OS X aren't stored here, but in the Library folder at root level for everyone who uses this Mac. I discuss this earlier in this chapter. If you want to install fonts so that only you have access to them, put them in the Fonts folder in *your* Library folder.

To install a font, drag its icon to the Fonts folder inside your `Home/Library` folder. It's available only when you're logged in; other users can't use a font stored here. To install a font that's available to anyone who uses this Mac, drag it into the Fonts folder in the public Library folder — the one at root level that you see when you open your hard drive's icon.

- **Preferences:** The files here hold the information about whichever things you customize in Mac OS X. Whenever you change a system or application preference, that info is saved to a file in the Preferences folder.

Don't mess with the Preferences folder! You should never need to open or use this folder unless something bad happens — for example, you suspect that a particular preferences file has become *corrupted* (that is, damaged). My advice is to just forget about this folder and let it do its job. In fact, let me take it a step further and say, "Don't mess with any of the folders inside your `Home/Library` folder unless you have a darn good reason." If you don't know why you're doing something to a folder (other than the Fonts folder) in your `Home/Library`, *don't do it.*

Saving Your Document Before It's Too Late

If you have a feel for the Mac OS X folder structure, you can get down to the important stuff — namely, how to save documents and where to save them. You can create as many documents as you want, using one program or dozens of 'em, but all is lost if you don't save the files to a storage device such as your hard drive or other disk.

When you *save* a file, you're committing a copy to a disk — whether it's a disk mounted on your Desktop, one available over a network, or a removable disk such as a Zip or floppy.

In these sections, I show you how to save your masterpieces. Prevent unnecessary pain in your life by developing good saving habits. I recommend you save your work

- ✔ Every few minutes
- ✔ Before you switch to another program
- ✔ Before you print a document
- ✔ Before you stand up

Hiding your stuff under the right rock

In previous versions of Mac OS, the rules about where to store things were a lot looser. Storing everything within your Documents folder wasn't at all important. But Mac OS X arranges its system files, applications, and other stuff a bit differently from the way the older versions did.

I strongly advise you to store all your document files and the folders that contain them in the Documents folder within your Home folder or your Home folder's Movies folder, Music folder, or Pictures folder, if that's where the application (such as iMovie, iTunes, or iPhoto) recommends. Files that you place outside the Documents folder are likely to get lost while you navigate through a maze of aliases and folders that belong to (and make sense to) particular programs or parts of the system software — and not to you

as a user. An exception to this rule is to place files you need to share with other users in the Shared folder, inside the Users folder in which your Home folder resides.

If other people use your Mac and they changed privilege settings to give you access to their directories (see Chapter 15), you could even save a file in another user's folder by accident, in which case you'd probably *never* find it again.

So trust me when I say that the Documents folder in your Home folder is the right place to start, not only because it's easy to remember, but also because it's only a menu command (Go⇨Home) or keyboard shortcut (⌘+Shift+H) away, wherever you're working on your Mac.

If you don't heed this advice and the program that you're using crashes while switching programs, printing, or sitting idle (which, not coincidentally, are the three most likely times for a crash), you lose everything that you did since your last save. The fact that a program crash doesn't bring down the entire system (as it did under Mac OS 9) is small consolation when you've lost everything you've typed, drawn, copied, pasted, or whatever since the last time you saved.

The keyboard shortcut for Save in almost every Mac program is ⌘+S. Memorize it. See it in your dreams. Train your finger muscles to do it unconsciously. Use it (the keyboard shortcut) or lose it (your unsaved work).

Stepping through a basic Save

When you choose to save a file for the first time (by choosing File⇨Save or pressing ⌘+S), a Save sheet appears in front of the window that you're saving, as shown in Figure 6-5. I call this a basic Save sheet (as opposed to an expanded Save sheet, which I get to in a moment). The following steps walk you through all the options so that you can save your file the way you want the first time you save:

1. **In the Save As field, type a name for your file.**

   When a Save sheet appears for the first time, the Save As field is active and displays the name of the document. The document name (usually `Untitled`) is selected; when you begin typing, the name disappears and is replaced by the name you type.

2. **Check whether the Where pop-up menu lists the location where you want to save your file. If so, select it from the list and proceed to Step 5. If not, click the disclosure triangle (see Figure 6-5).**

   You can choose any folder or volume listed in a Finder window's Sidebar by clicking a basic Save sheet's Where pop-up menu and taking your pick. Or if you click the disclosure triangle, the sheet expands so that you can navigate folders just as you would in the Finder: by opening them to see their contents.

   In a basic Save sheet, the Where pop-up menu acts like a shortcut menu to all the items in a Finder window's Sidebar. The Where pop-up menu lists one or more places where you may save your files (Documents, Home) as well as other folders where you have opened or saved files recently. If you switch to expanded view by clicking the disclosure triangle (you see the expanded view in Figure 6-6), the Where pop-up menu traces the folder path (as all Save sheets did in Mac OS versions of yore).

Disclosure triangle

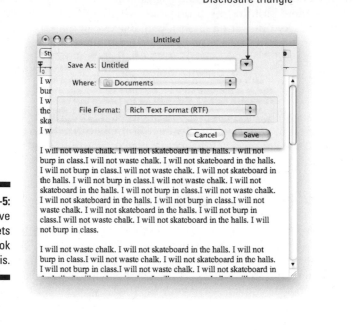

Figure 6-5:
Basic Save
sheets
usually look
like this.

Figure 6-6:
Expanded
Save sheets
usually look
like this (List
view on left,
Icon view
in center,
Column view
on right).

3. **To begin navigating the expanded Save sheet to find the folder where you want to save your file, choose among views by clicking the Icon (new in Leopard), List, or Column view button. (The buttons look like their counterparts in Finder windows.)**

   Click and hold the Icon view button to adjust the icon size and label position.

   In Icon view, you double-click a folder to open it. List view offers no disclosure triangles (as you see in List view Finder windows), so you double-click folders to open them and see their contents. In Column view, you click an item on the left to see its contents on the right, just as you do in a Column view Finder window.

In an expanded Save sheet, the pop-up menu shows a path from the currently selected folder; it's similar to the menu you see when you ⌘+click a Finder window's title but with Recent Places grafted onto its bottom.

You can also use the Forward and Back buttons or the Sidebar, both available only in an expanded Save dialog, to conveniently navigate your disk. Many of these navigation aids work just like the ones in the Finder; flip to Chapter 5 for more details.

You can enlarge the Save sheet to see more the same way you enlarge a Finder window — drag the lower-right corner of the sheet down or to the right.

If you can't find the folder in which you want to save your document, type the folder's name in the Search box. Three buttons appear just below the Where pop-up menu. Click the Computer button (MacBookPro in the previous figures) to search everywhere, the Home button (bobl in the previous figures) to search only in your Home folder, or the active folder button (labeled with the name of the active folder) to search only within the active folder. You don't even have to press Enter or Return; the Save sheet updates itself to show you only items that match the characters as you've typed them.

4. **Select the folder where you want to save your file in the Where pop-up menu. If you want to create a new subfolder of the selected folder to save your file in, click the New Folder button, give the new folder a name, and then save your file in it.**

In Figure 6-7, I've selected the Novels folder. You can tell it's selected by the highlight on the folder name and because it appears in the expanded Save sheet's Where pop-up menu. Remember that the selected folder is where your file will be saved.

The keyboard shortcut for New Folder is ⌘+Shift+N. I've never seen this shortcut documented in Mac Help (or anywhere else, for that matter), so it may well be a *Mac OS X Leopard For Dummies* exclusive.

5. **In the File Format pop-up menu, make sure the format selected is the one you want.**

6. **If you want to turn off the display of file extensions (such as** `.rtf`**,** `.pdf`**, or** `.txt`**) in Save sheets, select the Hide Extension check box.**

7. **Double-check the Where pop-up menu one last time to make sure the correct folder is selected. Then click the Save button to save the file to the active folder.**

If you click Save, the file now appears in the folder you selected. If you change your mind about saving this file, clicking Cancel dismisses the Save sheet without saving anything anywhere. In other words, the Cancel button returns things to the way they were before you displayed the Save sheet.

Figure 6-7:
Saving a
file in the
Novels
folder.

TIP

After you've saved a file for the first time, choosing File⇨Save or pressing ⌘+S doesn't bring up a Save sheet anymore. It just saves the file again without any further intervention on your part. Get into the habit of pressing ⌘+S often. It can't hurt and just might save your bacon someday.

REMEMBER

In Figures 6-5 and 6-6, you see, respectively, the Save sheet for the TextEdit program, basic and expanded. In programs other than TextEdit, the Save sheet might contain additional options, fewer options, or different options, and therefore might look slightly different. For example, the File Format menu is a feature specific to TextEdit and might not appear in other applications' Save sheets. Don't worry. The Save sheet always *works* the same way, no matter what options it offers.

Looks like Save, acts like Save — why's it called Save As?

The Save As command — which you can find on the File menu of almost every program ever made (at least those that create documents) — lets you resave a file that has already been saved by giving it a different name.

Why would you want to do that? Here's a good (albeit kind of rude) example:

Suppose you have two cousins, Kate and Nancy. You write Kate a long, chatty letter and save this document with the name `Letter to Kate`. At some point afterward, you decide you want to send almost the same letter to Nancy, too, but you want to change a few things. So you change the part about your date last night (Nancy isn't as liberated as Kate) and replace all references to Kate's husband, Kevin, with Nancy's husband, Norman. (Aren't computers grand?)

So you make all these changes to `Letter to Kate`, but you haven't saved this document yet. And although the document on your screen is actually a letter to Nancy, its filename is still `Letter to Kate`. Think of what would happen if you were to save it now without using the Save As feature: `Letter to Kate` reflects the changes that you just made (the stuff in the letter meant for Kate is blown away, replaced by the stuff that you write to Nancy). Thus, the file name `Letter to Kate` is inaccurate. Even worse, you would no longer have a copy of the letter you sent to Kate!

Tabbing around the Save sheet

In the expanded view, if you press the Tab key while the Save As field is active, it becomes inactive, and the Search box becomes active. Press Tab again, and the Sidebar becomes active. Press the Tab key one more time, and the file list box (more accurately known as the *detail pane* — the part with Icon, List, or Column view in it) becomes active. That's because the file list box, the Search box, the Sidebar, and the Save As field are mutually exclusive. Only one can be active at any time.

You can always tell which item is active by the thin blue or gray border around it.

When you want to switch to a different folder to save a file, click the folder in the Sidebar or click anywhere in the file list box to make the file list active.

The following tricks help you get a hold on this whole active/inactive silliness:

✔ Look for the thin blue border that shows you which part of the Save sheet is active.

✔ If you type while the file list box is active, the list box selects the folder that most closely matches the letter(s) that you type. It's a little strange because you won't see what

you type: You'll be typing blind, so to speak. Go ahead and give it a try.

✔ When the file list is active, the letters that you type don't appear in the Save As field. If you want to type a filename, you have to activate the Save As field again (by clicking in it or using the Tab key) before you can type in it.

✔ If you type while the Sidebar is active, nothing happens. You can, however, use the up- and down-arrow keys to move around in the Sidebar.

✔ Regardless of which box or field is active at the time, when you press the Tab key, the next in sequence becomes active.

✔ Pressing Shift reverses the order of the sequence. If you press Shift+Tab, the active item moves from the Save As field to the file list box to the Sidebar to the Search box and back to the Save As field again.

If you don't feel like pressing the Tab key, you can achieve the same effect by clicking the file list box, the Sidebar, or the Save As field to make it active.

The solution? Just use Save As to rename this file `Letter to Nancy` by choosing File➪Save As. A Save sheet appears, in which you can type a different filename in the Save As field. You can also navigate to another folder, if you like, and save the newly named version of the file there.

Now you have two distinct files: `Letter to Kate` and `Letter to Nancy`. Both contain the stuff they should, but both started life from the same file. *That's* what Save As is for.

Here's another reason you might use Save As: If you had a TIFF graphic file open in Preview and wanted to convert it to a JPEG file, you'd do so by using Save As.

An even better idea is to choose Save As just before you begin modifying the document and give it the new name. That way, when you're done with your changes, you don't have to remember to choose Save As — you can just perform your habitual Save. It also protects you from accidentally saving part of the letter to Nancy without changing its name first (which you're likely to do if you're following my advice about saving often). So when you decide you're going to reuse a document, Save As *before* you begin working on it, just to be safe.

Open Sez Me

You can open any icon — whether it's a file or a folder — in at least six ways. (Okay, there are at least *seven* ways, but one of them belongs to aliases, which I discuss in Chapter 5.) Anyway, here are the ways:

✐ **Click the icon once to select it and then choose File➪Open.**

✐ **Click the icon twice in rapid succession.**

If the icon doesn't open, you double-clicked too slowly. You can test your mouse's sensitivity to double-click speed as well as adjust it in the Keyboard & Mouse System Preferences pane, which you can access by launching the System Preferences application (from the Applications folder, the Dock, or the Apple menu) and then clicking the Keyboard & Mouse icon.

✐ **Select the icon and then press either ⌘+O or ⌘+↓.**

✐ **Right-click or Control+click it and then choose Open from the contextual menu.**

✐ **If the icon is a document, drag it onto an application icon (or the Dock icon of an application) that can open that type of document.**

✐ **If the icon is a document, right-click or Control+click it and then choose an application from the Open With submenu of the contextual menu.**

Of course, you can also open any document icon from within an application. Here's how it works:

1. **Just launch your favorite program and choose File⇨Open (or use the keyboard shortcut ⌘+O, which works in 98 percent of all programs ever made).**

   An Open dialog appears, like the one shown in Figure 6-8.

   When you use a program's Open dialog, only files that the program knows how to open appear enabled (in black rather than light gray) in the file list. In other words, the program filters out the files it can't open, so you barely see them in the Open dialog. This method of selectively displaying certain items in Open dialogs is a feature of most applications. Therefore, when you're using TextEdit, its Open dialog dims all your spreadsheet files (that's because TextEdit can open only text, Rich Text, Microsoft Word, and some picture files). Pretty neat, eh?

2. **In the dialog, simply navigate to the file you want to open (using the same techniques you use in a Save sheet).**

3. **With the file you want to open selected, click the Open button.**

   If I were to click the Open button in Figure 6-8, the file Scary Novel would open in TextEdit, the program I'm using.

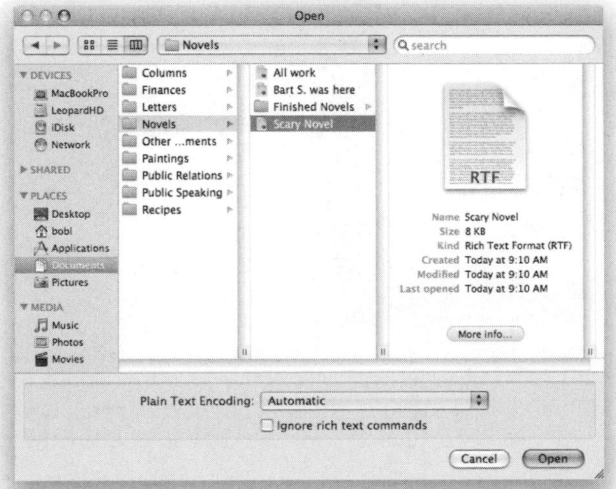

Figure 6-8:
The Open dialog in all its glory.

Some programs — such as AppleWorks, Microsoft Word, and Adobe Photoshop — have a Show or Format menu in their Open dialogs. This menu lets you specify the type(s) of files you want to see in the Open dialog. You can usually open a file that appears dimmed by choosing All Documents from the Show or Format menu (in those applications with Open dialogs that offer such a menu).

Mac OS X also offers a few tricks that help you find files you want to open and that enable you to decide what application opens a file. Check out the following sections for more tips, tricks, and troubleshooting help.

With a Quick Look

The Quick Look command is new in Leopard and displays the contents of the currently selected file in a floating window without launching an application, as shown in Figure 6-9. This feature can be handy if you want to peek at the contents of a file before you open it, to make sure you have the right one. Simply select the file and then choose File⇨Quick Look, press ⌘+Y, or, easiest of all, merely press the spacebar.

Figure 6-9:
The Quick Look window with a graphic file (a picture of me named *I am a graphic file*) selected.

Notice the double-arrow button at the bottom of the Quick Look window. It expands the contents of the Quick Look window to occupy the entire screen.

If you hold down Option before choosing Quick Look from the File menu, the command changes from Quick Look to Slideshow, and its shortcut changes from ⌘+Y to ⌘+Option+Y. When you choose Slideshow, the contents of the Quick Look window expand to occupy the entire screen immediately, without your having to click the aforementioned button.

In Slideshow (full-screen) mode, press Esc to return to the Quick Look window.

If you select multiple items before you invoke Quick Look, a set of slideshow controls appears at the bottom of the Quick Look window (or screen if you're viewing it as a slideshow) to let you move forward or backward one item at a time, or view all of the selected items at the same time (called an *index sheet*).

When you're finished with Quick Look window, click the X button in the top-left corner or use the shortcut ⌘+Y to close it.

With drag-and-drop

Macintosh *drag-and-drop* is usually all about dragging text and graphics from one place to another. But there's another angle to drag-and-drop — one that has to do with files and icons.

You can open a document by dragging its icon onto that of the proper application. For example, you can open a document created with Microsoft Word by dragging the document icon onto the Microsoft Word application's icon. The Word icon highlights, and the document launches. Of course, it's usually easier to just double-click a document's icon to open it; the proper application opens automatically when you do — or at least it does most of the time. Which reminds me. . . .

When your Mac can't open a file

If you try to open a file but Mac OS X can't find a program to open the file, Mac OS X prompts you with an alert window, as shown in Figure 6-10. You can either click Cancel (and abort the attempt to open the file) or pick another application to open by clicking the Choose Application button.

Figure 6-10:
Oops! Mac
OS X helps
you find the
correct
application.

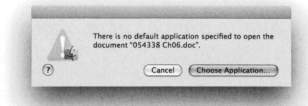

There is no default application specified to open the document "054338 Ch06.doc".

Cancel   Choose Application...

If you click the Choose Application button, a dialog appears (conveniently opened to your Applications folder and shown in Figure 6-11). Applications that Mac OS X doesn't think can be used to open the file are dimmed. For a wider choice of applications, choose All Applications (instead of Recommended Applications) from the Enable pop-up menu.

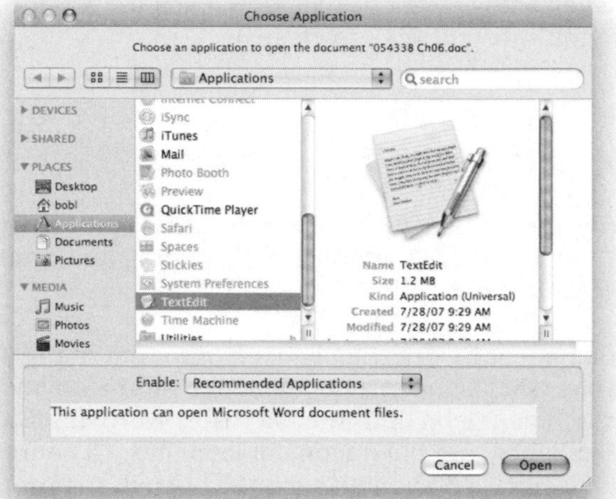

Figure 6-11: Choosing an application to open this document file.

Here's a better way: If you click Cancel, you can use drag-and-drop to open a file using a program other than the one that would *ordinarily* launch when you open the document.

You can't open every file with every program. For example, if you try to open an MP3 (music) file with Microsoft Excel (a spreadsheet), it just won't work — you get an error message or a screen full of gibberish. Sometimes you just have to keep trying until you find the right program; other times, you don't have a program capable of opening the file.

With the application of your choice

I don't know about you, but people send me files all the time that were created by applications I don't use . . . or at least that I don't use for that document type. Mac OS X lets you specify the application in which you want to open a document in the future when you double-click it. More than that, you can specify that you want all documents of that type to open with the specified application. "Where is this magic bullet hidden?" you ask. Right there in the file's Show Info window.

Assigning a file type to an application

Suppose that you want all .tiff graphic files that default to opening in Preview to open in GraphicConverter (one of my favorite pieces of OS X–savvy shareware) instead. Here's what to do:

1. **Just click one of these files in the Finder.**

2. **Choose File⇨Get Info (⌘+I).**

3. **In the Info window, click the gray triangle to disclose the Open With pane, as shown in Figure 6-12.**

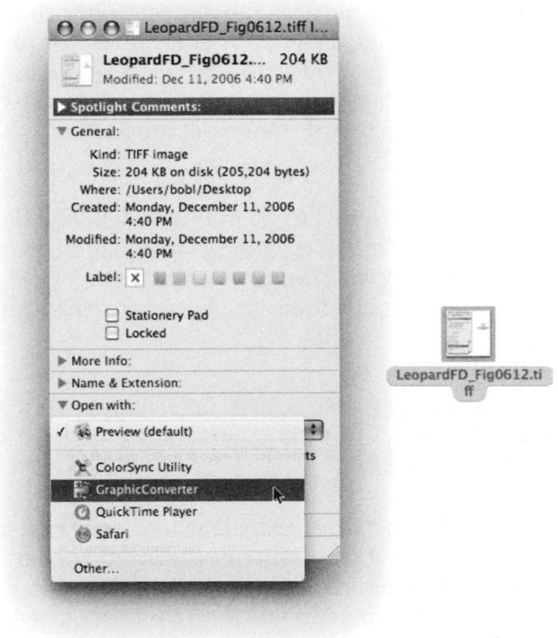

Figure 6-12:
Select an application to open this document.

4. **From the pop-up menu, choose from the applications that Mac OS X believes will open this document type.**

   In Figure 6-12, I'm choosing GraphicConverter. Now GraphicConverter opens when I double-click this particular document.

5. **(Optional) If you click the Change All button at the bottom of the Open With pane (you can't see it in Figure 6-12 because it's hidden by the pop-up menu), you make GraphicConverter the default application for all .tiff documents that would otherwise be opened in Preview.**

Opening a file with an application other than the default

One last technique works great when you want to open a document with a program other than its default. Just drag the file onto the application's icon or alias icon or Dock icon, and presto — the file opens in the application.

For example, if I were to double-click an MP3 file, the file would open in iTunes. But I frequently want to listen to MP3 files using QuickTime Player (so they're not added to my iTunes music library). Dragging the MP3 file onto QuickTime Player's icon in the Applications folder or its Dock icon (if it's in the Dock) solves this conundrum quickly and easily.

If the icon doesn't highlight and you release the mouse button anyway, the document ends up in the same folder as the application with the icon that didn't highlight. If that happens, just choose Edit⇨Undo (or press ⌘+Z), and the mislaid document magically returns to where it was before you dropped it. Just remember — don't do anything else after you drop the file, or Undo might not work. If Undo doesn't work, you must move the file back to its original location manually.

Only applications that *might* be able to open the file will highlight when you drag the document on them. That doesn't mean the document will be usable — just that the application can *open* it. Suffice to say that Mac OS X is smart enough to figure out which applications on your hard drive can open what documents — and to offer you a choice.

Organizing Your Stuff in Folders

I won't pretend to be able to organize your Mac for you. Organizing your files is as personal as your taste in music; you develop your own style with the Mac. But now that you know how to open and save documents when you're using applications, these sections provide food for thought — some ideas about how I organize things — and some suggestions that can make organization easier for you regardless of how you choose to do it yourself.

So these sections look at the difference between a file and a folder, how to set up nested folders, and how some special folder features work. After you know these things, you will almost certainly be a savvier — and better organized — Mac OS X user.

Files versus folders

When I speak of a *file,* I'm talking about what's connected to any icon except a folder or disk icon. A file can be a document, an application, an alias of a file or an application, a dictionary, a font, or any other icon that *isn't* a folder or disk. The main distinction is that you can't put something *into* most file icons.

The exceptions are icons that represent Mac OS X packages. A *package* is an icon that acts like a file but isn't. Examples of icons that are really packages include many software installers and applications as well as "documents" saved by some programs (such as Keynote or GarageBand). When you open an icon that represents a package the usual way (double-click, File⇨Open, ⌘+O, and so on), the program or document opens. If you want to see the contents of an icon that represents a package, you have to Control+click the icon first and then choose Show Package Contents from the contextual menu. If you see that item, the icon is a package, and you can see the files and folders it contains by choosing Show Package Contents; if you don't see a Show Package Contents item on the contextual menu, the icon represents a file, not a package.

When I talk about *folders,* I'm talking about things that work like manila folders in the real world. Their icons look like folders, like the one in the margin to the left; they can contain files or other folders, called *subfolders.* You can put any icon — any file or folder — into a folder.

Here's an exception: If you put a disk icon into a folder, you get an alias to the disk unless you hold down the Option key. Remember that you can't put a disk icon into a folder on itself. In other words, you can copy a disk icon only to a different disk. Put another way, you can never copy a disk icon into a folder that resides on that disk. For more about aliases, flip to Chapter 5; for details on working with disks, see Chapter 7.

File icons can look like practically anything. If the icon doesn't look like a folder or one of the numerous disk icons, you can be pretty sure it's a file.

Organizing your stuff with subfolders

As I mention earlier in this chapter, you can put folders inside other folders to organize your icons. A folder that's inside another folder is called a *subfolder.*

You can create subfolders according to whatever system makes sense to you — but why reinvent the wheel? Here are some organizational topic ideas and naming examples for subfolders:

- **By type of document:** Word-Processing Documents, Spreadsheet Documents, Graphics Documents
- **By date:** Documents May–June, Documents Spring '03
- **By content:** Memos, Outgoing Letters, Expense Reports
- **By project:** Project X, Project Y, Project Z

When you notice your folders swelling and starting to get messy (that is, filling up with tons of files), subdivide them again by using a combination of these methods that makes sense to you. Suppose that you start by subdividing your

Documents folder into multiple subfolders. Later, when those folders begin to get full, you can subdivide them even further, as shown in Figure 6-13.

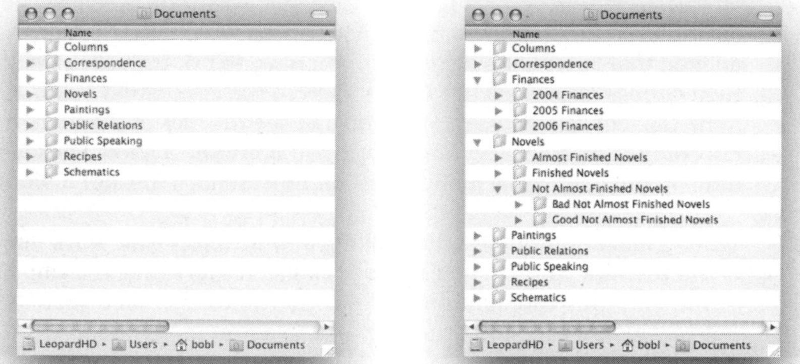

Figure 6-13:
Before (left) and after (right) organizing the Novels and Finance folders with subfolders.

Creating subfolders . . . or not

How full is too full? When should you begin creating subfolders? That's impossible to say, but having too many items in a folder can be a nightmare, as can having too many subfolders with just one or two files in them. My guideline is this: If you find more than 15 or 20 files in a single folder, begin thinking about ways to subdivide it.

On the other hand, some of my bigger subfolders contain things that I don't often access. For example, my Bob's Correspondence 1992 folder contains more than 200 files. But because I want to keep this folder on my hard drive in case I do need to find something there — even though I don't use it very often — its overcrowded condition doesn't bother me. (Your mileage may vary.)

Here are some tips to help you decide whether to use subfolders or just leave well enough alone:

✔ **Don't create subfolders until you need them.** In other words, don't create a bunch of empty folders because you think you might need them someday. Wait to create new folders until you need them; that way, you avoid opening an empty folder when you're looking for something else — a complete waste of time.

✔ **Let your work style decide the file structure.** When you first start working with your Mac, you might want to save everything in your Documents folder for a week or two (or a month or two, depending on how many new documents you save each day). When a decent-sized group of documents has accumulated in the Documents folder, consider taking a look at them and creating logical subfolders for them.

My point (yes, I do have one!): Allow your folder structure to be organic, growing as you need it to grow. Let it happen. Don't let any one folder get so full that it's a hassle to deal with. Create new subfolders when things start to get crowded. I explain how to create folders in the next section.

If you want to monkey around with some subfolders yourself, a good place to start is the Documents folder — it's inside your Home folder (that is, the Documents folder is a *subfolder* of your Home folder).

If you use a particular folder a great deal, put it in your Dock or make an alias of it and move the alias from the Documents folder to your Home folder or to your Desktop (for more info on aliases, see Chapter 5) to make the folder easier to access. Or drag the folder (or its alias) to the Sidebar, where it's always available, even in Open dialogs and Save sheets. For example, if you write a lot of letters, you could keep an alias to your Correspondence folder in your Home folder, in the Dock, or on your Desktop for quick access. (By the way, there's no reason you can't have a folder appear in all three places if you like. That's what aliases are all about, right?)

If you create your own subfolders in the Documents folder, you can click it in the Dock to reveal them, as shown in Figure 6-14. I show you how to customize the Dock in Chapter 4.

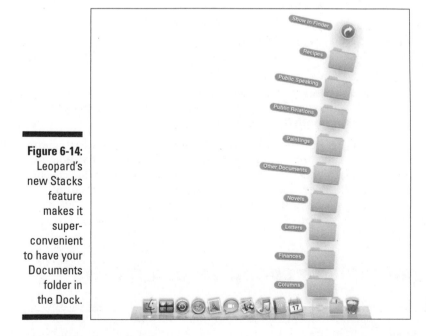

Figure 6-14: Leopard's new Stacks feature makes it super-convenient to have your Documents folder in the Dock.

Creating new folders

So you think Apple has already given you enough folders? Can't imagine why you'd need more? Think of creating new folders the same way you'd think of labeling a new folder at work for a specific project. New folders help you keep your files organized, enabling you to reorganize them just the way you want. Creating folders is really quite simple.

To create a new folder, just follow these steps:

1. **Decide which window you want the new folder to appear in and then make sure that window is active.**

   If you want to create a new folder right on the Desktop, make sure *no* window is active.

   You can make a window active by clicking it, and you can make the Desktop active if you have windows on-screen by clicking the Desktop itself.

2. **Choose File⇨New Folder (or press ⌘+Shift+N).**

   A new, untitled folder appears in the active window with its name box already highlighted, ready for you to type a new name for it.

3. **Type a name for your folder.**

   If you accidentally click anywhere before you type a name for the folder, the name box is no longer highlighted. To highlight it again, select the icon (single-click it) and then press Return (or Enter) once. Now you can type its new name.

Give your folders relevant names. Folders with nebulous titles like sfdghb or Stuff — or, worst of all, Untitled — won't make it any easier to find something six months from now.

For folders and files you might share with users of non-Macintosh computers, here's the rule for maximum compatibility: no punctuation and no Option-key characters in the folder name. Periods, slashes, backslashes, and colons in particular can be reserved for use by other operating systems. When I say Option key characters, I'm talking about ones like ™ (Option+2), ® (Option+R), ¢ (Option+4), and even © (Option+G).

Navigating with spring-loaded folders

A *spring-loaded folder* pops open when you drag something onto it without releasing the mouse button. Spring-loaded folders work with all folder or disk icons in all views and in the Sidebar. Because you just got the short course on folders and subfolders and various ways to organize your stuff, you're ready for your introduction to one of my favorite ways to get around my disks, folders, and subfolders.

Here's how they work:

1. **Select any icon except a disk icon.**

   The folder highlights to indicate that it's selected.

2. **Drag the selected icon onto any folder or disk icon — but don't release the mouse button.**

   I call this *hovering* because you're doing just that — hovering the cursor over a folder or disk icon without releasing the button.

   In a second or two, the highlighted folder or disk flashes twice and then springs open, right under the cursor.

   You can press the spacebar to make the folder spring open immediately.

3. **After the folder springs open, some more handy operations are possible:**

   - You can continue to traverse your folder structure this way. Subfolders continue to pop open until you release the mouse button.

   - If you release the mouse button, the icon you've been dragging is dropped into the active folder at the time. That window remains open — but all the windows you traversed clean up after themselves by closing automatically and leaving your window clean and uncluttered.

   - If you want to cancel a spring-loaded folder, drag the cursor away from the folder icon or outside the boundaries of the sprung window — the folder pops shut.

After you get used to spring-loaded folders, you'll wonder how you ever got along without them. They work in all four window views, and they work with icons in the Sidebar or Dock. Give 'em a try, and you'll be hooked.

You can toggle spring-loaded folders on or off in the Finder's Preferences window. There's also a setting for how long the Finder waits before it springs the folders open. See Chapter 5 for more on Finder preferences.

Smart Folders

Now, as Steve Jobs is fond of saying near the end of his annual keynote addresses, "There is one more thing." Those things are called Smart Folders.

Smart Folders let you save search criteria and then work in the background to reflect those criteria in real time. In other words, Smart Folders are updated continuously, so they always find all the files on your computer that match the search criteria. So, for example, you can create a Smart Folder that contains all the Rich Text files on your computer that you've opened in the past two weeks, as shown in Figure 6-15. Or create a Smart Folder that displays graphics files, but only ones bigger (or smaller) than a specified file size. Then all those files appear in one convenient Smart Folder.

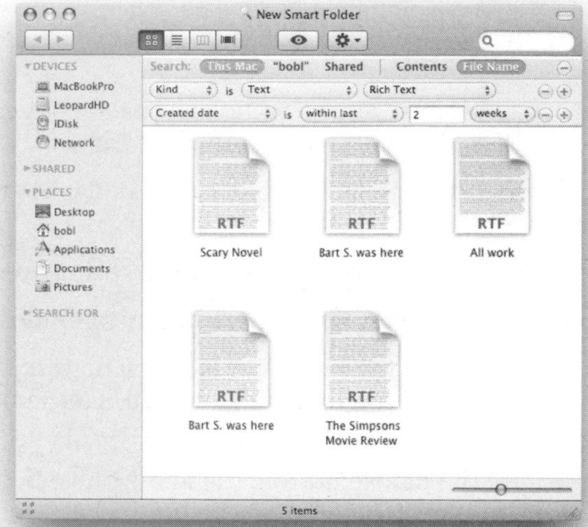

Figure 6-15:
A Smart Folder that gathers only Rich Text files created in the past two weeks.

The possibilities are endless. And because Smart Folders use alias-like technology to display items, the actual files reside in only one location — the folder where you originally put them. In other words, Smart Folders don't gather files in a separate place; rather, they gather aliases of files, leaving the originals right where you stashed them. Neat!

Also, because Spotlight (discussed in the final section of this chapter) is built deep into the bowels of the Mac OS X file system and kernel, Smart Folders are always current, even if you've added or deleted files on your hard drive since you created the Smart Folder.

Smart Folders are so useful that Apple provides five different ways to create one. The following steps show you how:

1. **Start your Smart Folder using any of the following methods:**

   • Choose File⇨New Smart Folder from the Finder menu bar.

   • Use the keyboard shortcut ⌘+Option+N.

   • Choose File⇨Find.

   • Use the keyboard shortcut ⌘+F.

   • Type at least one character into the Search box in a Finder window.

2. **Refine the criteria for your search by clicking the + button to add a criterion or the – button to delete one.**

3. **When you're satisfied and ready to turn your criteria into a Smart Folder, click the Save button below the Search box.**

   A sheet drops down.

4. **Choose where you want to save your folder.**

   While the Save sheet is displayed, you can add the Smart Folder to the Sidebar if you like by clicking the Add to Sidebar check box.

5. **When you're finished editing criteria, click the Save button to save the folder with its criteria.**

After you create your Smart Folder, you can move it anywhere on any hard drive and then use it like any other folder. If you want to change the criteria for a Smart Folder, open it and click the Action menu button and choose Show Search Criteria, as shown in Figure 6-16. Then click the Save button to resave your folder. You might be asked whether you want to replace the previous Smart Folder of the same name; you (usually) do.

Smart Folders can save you a lot of time and effort, so if you haven't played with them much (or at all) yet, be sure to give 'em a try.

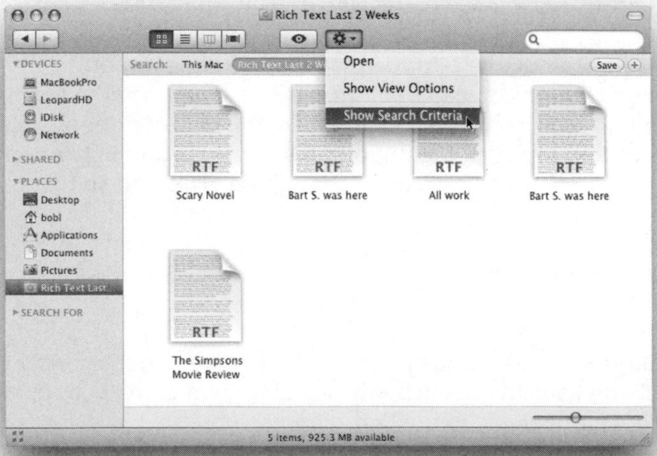

Figure 6-16:
Open a
Smart Folder
you've
created and
click the
Action menu
button to
change its
search
criteria.

Shuffling Around Files and Folders

Sometimes, keeping files and folders organized means moving them from one place to another. Other times, you want to copy them, rename them, or compress them to send to a friend. These sections explain all those things and more.

All the techniques I discuss in the following sections work at least as well for windows that use List or Column view as they do for windows using Icon view. In other words, I use Icon view in the figures in this section only because it's the best view for pictures to show you what's going on. For what it's worth, I find moving and copying files much easier in windows that use List or Column view.

Comprehending the Clipboard

Before you start moving your files around, let me introduce you to the Clipboard. The *Clipboard* is a holding area for the last thing that you cut or copied. That copied item can be text, a picture, a portion of a picture, an object in a drawing program, a column of numbers in a spreadsheet, any icon except a disk, or just about anything else that can be selected. In other words, the Clipboard is the Mac's temporary storage area.

Most of the time, the Clipboard works quietly in the background, but you can ask the Clipboard to reveal itself by choosing Edit⇨Show Clipboard from the Finder menu bar. This command summons the Clipboard window, which lists the type of item (such as text, picture, or sound) on the Clipboard and a message letting you know whether the item on the Clipboard can be displayed.

As a storage area, the Clipboard's contents are temporary. *Very* temporary. When you cut or copy an item, that item remains on the Clipboard only until you cut or copy something else. When you do cut or copy something else, the new item replaces the Clipboard's contents and in turn remains on the Clipboard until you cut or copy something else. And so it goes.

Of course, whatever is on the Clipboard heads straight for oblivion if you crash, lose power, log out, or shut down your Mac, so don't count on it too heavily or for too long.

The Clipboard commands on the Edit menu are enabled only when they can actually be used. If the currently selected item can be cut or copied, the Cut and Copy commands in the Edit menu are enabled. If the selected item can't be cut or copied, the commands are unavailable and are dimmed (gray). If the Clipboard is empty or the current document can't accept what's on the Clipboard, the Paste command is dimmed. Finally, when nothing is selected, the Cut, Copy, and Clear commands are dimmed.

Icons cannot be cut; they can only be copied or pasted. So when an icon is selected, the Cut command is always gray.

Copying files and folders

One way to copy icons from one place to another is to use the Clipboard.

When a file or folder icon is selected, choose Edit⇨Copy (or use its shortcut, ⌘+C) to copy the selected icon to the Clipboard. Note that this doesn't delete the selected item, but just makes a copy of it on the Clipboard. To then paste the copied icon in another location, choose Edit⇨Paste (or use its shortcut, ⌘+V).

Other methods of copying icons from one place to another include

- **Drag an icon from one folder icon onto another folder icon while holding down the Option key.** Release the mouse button when the second folder is highlighted. This technique works regardless of whether the second folder's window is open. If you don't hold down the Option key, you move the icon to a new location rather than copy it, as I explain a little later in this section.

- When you copy something by dragging and dropping it with the Option key held down, the cursor changes to include a little plus sign (+) next to the arrow, as shown in the margin. Neat!

- **Drag an icon into an open window for another folder while holding down the Option key.** Drag the icon for the file or folder that you want to copy into the open window for a second folder (or removable media, such as a floppy disk).

- **Choose File⇨Duplicate (⌘+D) or Control+click the file or folder that you want to duplicate and then choose Duplicate from the contextual menu that appears.** This makes a copy of the selected icon, adds the word *copy* to its name, and then places the copy in the same window as the original icon. You can use the Duplicate command on any icon except a disk icon.

You can't duplicate an entire disk onto itself. But you can copy an entire disk (call it Disk 1) to any other disk (call it Disk 2) as long as Disk 2 has enough space available. Just hold down Option and drag Disk 1 onto Disk 2's icon. The contents of Disk 1 are copied to Disk 2 and appear on Disk 2 in a folder named Disk 1.

You can cut an icon's name, but you can't cut the icon itself; you may only copy an icon.

To achieve the effect of cutting an icon, select the icon, copy it to the Clipboard, paste it in its new location, and then move the original icon to the Trash.

If you're wondering why anyone would ever want to copy a file, trust me: Someday you will. Suppose that you have a file called Long Letter to Mom in a folder called Old Correspondence. You figure that Mom has forgotten that letter by now, and you want to send it again. But before you do, you want to change the date and delete the reference to Clarence, her pit bull, who passed away last year. So now you need to put a copy of `Long Letter to Mom` in your `Current Correspondence` folder. This technique yields the same result as making a copy of a file by using Save As, which I describe earlier in this chapter.

When you copy a file, it's wise to change the name of the copied file. Having more than one file on your hard drive with exactly the same name isn't a good idea, even if the files are in different folders. Trust me, having 10 files called `Expense Report` or 15 files named `Doctor Mac Consulting Invoice` can be confusing, no matter how well organized your folder structure is. Add distinguishing words or dates to file and folder names so they're named something more explicit, such as `Expense Report 10-03` or `Doctor Mac Consulting Invoice 4-4-05`.

You can have lots of files with the same name *on the same disk* (although, as I mention earlier, it's probably not a good idea). But your Mac won't let you have more than one file with the same name *in the same folder*.

Pasting from the Clipboard

As I mention previously, to place the icon that's on the Clipboard someplace new, click where you want the item to go and then choose Edit➪Paste or use the keyboard shortcut ⌘+V to paste what you've copied or cut.

Pasting doesn't purge the contents of the Clipboard. In fact, an item stays on the Clipboard until you cut, copy, restart, shut down, log out, or crash. This means that you can paste the same item over and over and over again, which can come in pretty handy at times.

Almost all programs have an Edit menu and use the Macintosh Clipboard, which means you can usually cut or copy something from a document in one program and paste it into a document in another program.

Usually.

Moving files and folders

You can move files and folders around within a window to your heart's content as long as that window is set to Icon view. Just click and drag any icon to its new location in the window.

Some people spend hours arranging icons in a window so that they're just so. But because using Icon view wastes so much screen space, I avoid using icons in a window.

You can't move icons around in a window that is displayed as a List, Columns, or Cover Flow, which makes total sense when you think about it. (Well, you can move them to put them in a different folder in List, Column, or Cover Flow view, but that's not moving them around, really.)

As you might expect from Apple by now, you have choices for how you move one file or folder into another folder. You can use these techniques to move any icon — folder, document, alias, or program icon — into folders or onto other disks.

 ✔ **Drag an icon onto a folder icon:** Drag the icon for one folder (or file) onto the icon for another folder (or disk) and then release when the second icon is highlighted (see Figure 6-17). The first folder is now inside the second folder. Put another way, the first folder is now a subfolder of the second folder.

   This technique works regardless of whether the second folder's window is open.

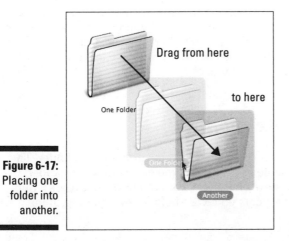

Figure 6-17:
Placing one folder into another.

 ✔ **Drag an icon into an open folder's window:** Drag the icon for one folder (or file) into the open window for a second folder (or disk), as shown in Figure 6-18.

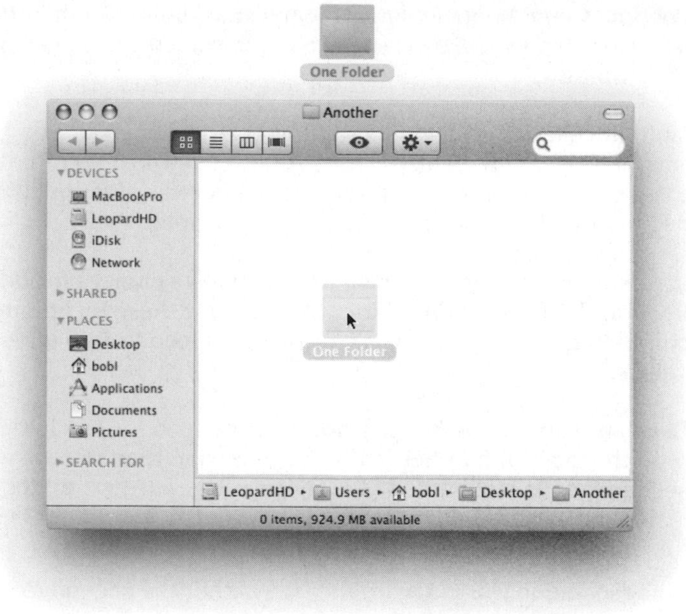

Figure 6-18:
You can also
move a file
or folder by
dragging it
into the
open
window of
another
folder.

If you want to move an item from one *disk* to another disk, you can't use the preceding tricks. Your item is copied, not moved. If you want to *move* a file or folder from one disk to another, you have to hold down the ⌘ key when you drag an icon from one disk to another. The little Copying Files window even changes to read *Moving* Files. Nice touch, eh?

Selecting multiple icons

Sometimes you want to move or copy several items into a single folder. The process is pretty much the same as it is when you copy one file or folder (that is, you just drag the icon to where you want it and drop it there). But you first need to select all the items you want before you can drag them, *en masse,* to their destination.

If you want to move all the files in a particular folder, simply choose Edit⇨Select All or press ⌘+A. This command selects all icons in the active window, regardless of whether you can see them onscreen. Or if no window is active, using Select All selects every icon on the Desktop.

But what if you want to select only some of the files in the active window or on the Desktop? Here's the most convenient method:

1. **To select more than one icon in a folder, do one of the following:**

   • Click once within the folder window (don't click any one icon) and drag your mouse while continuing to hold down the mouse button. You see an outline of a box around the icons while you drag, and all icons within or touching the box become highlighted (see Figure 6-19).

Figure 6-19: Select more than one icon with your mouse.

   • Click one icon and then hold down the Shift key while you click others. As long as you hold down the Shift key, each new icon that you click is added to the selection. To deselect an icon, click it a second time while still holding down the Shift key.

   • Click one icon and then hold down the Command (⌘) key while you click others. The difference between using the Shift and ⌘ keys is that using the ⌘ key doesn't select everything between it and the first item selected when your window is in List or Column view. In Icon view, it really doesn't make much difference.

   To deselect an icon, click it while holding down the ⌘ key.

2. **After you select the icons, click one of them (clicking anywhere else deselects the icons) and drag them to the location where you want to move them (or Option+drag to copy them).**

   Be careful with multiple selections, especially when you drag icons to the Trash. You can easily — and accidentally — select more than one icon, so watch out that you don't accidentally put the wrong icon in the Trash by not paying close attention. I explain how the Trash icon works in more detail later in this chapter.

Playing the icon name game: Renaming icons

Icon, icon, bo-bicon, banana-fanna fo-ficon. Betcha can change the name of any old icon! Well, that's not entirely true. . . .

If an icon is locked, busy (an application that's currently open), or you don't have the owner's permission to rename that icon (see Chapter 15 for details about permissions), you can't rename it. Similarly, you should never rename certain reserved icons (such as the Library, System, and Desktop folders).

To rename an icon, you can either click the icon's name directly (don't click the icon itself, because that selects the icon) or click the icon and then press Return (or Enter) once.

Either way, the icon's name is selected and surrounded with a box, and you can now type a new name (as shown in Figure 6-20). In addition to selecting the name, the cursor changes from a pointer to a text-editing I-beam. An *I-beam cursor* (shown in the left margin) is the Mac's way of telling you that you can type now. At this point, if you click the I-beam cursor anywhere in the name box, you can edit the icon's original name. If you don't click the I-beam cursor in the name box but just begin typing, the icon's original name is replaced by what you type.

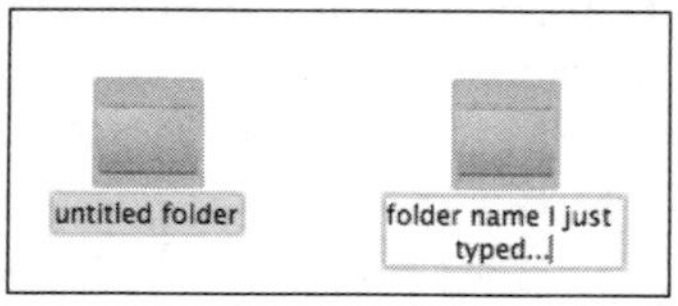

Figure 6-20:
Change an
icon's name
by typing
over the
old one
when it's
highlighted.

If you've never changed an icon's name, give it a try. And don't forget: If you click the icon itself, the icon is selected, and you won't be able to change its name. If you do accidentally select the icon, just press Return (or Enter) once to edit the name of the icon.

Compressing files

If you're going to send files as an e-mail enclosure, creating a compressed archive of the files first and sending the archive instead of the originals saves you time sending the files and saves the recipient time downloading them. To create this compressed archive, simply select the file or files and then choose File⇨Compress. This creates a compressed .zip file out of your selection. The compressed file is smaller than the original, sometimes by quite a bit.

Getting rid of icons

To get rid of an icon — any icon — merely drag it to the Trash on your Dock.

Trashing an alias gets rid of only the alias, not the parent file. But trashing a document, folder, or application icon puts it in the Trash, where it will be deleted permanently the next time you empty the Trash. The Finder menu offers a couple of commands that help you manage the Trash:

✔ **Finder⇨Empty Trash:** Deletes all items in the Trash from your hard drive — period.

 I'll probably say this more than once: *Use this command with a modicum of caution.* After a file is dragged into the Trash and the Trash is emptied, the file is gone, gone, gone. (Okay, maybe ProSoft Engineering's Data Rescue II or other third-party utility can bring it back, but I wouldn't bet the farm on it.)

✔ **Finder⇨Secure Empty Trash:** Choosing this option makes the chance of recovery by even the most ardent hacker or expensive disk-recovery tool difficult to virtually impossible. Now the portion of the disk that held the files you're deleting will be overwritten 1, 7, or 35 times (your choice in the submenu) with randomly generated gibberish.

If you put something in the Trash by accident, you can almost always return it whence it came: Just invoke the magical Undo command. Choose Edit⇨Undo or use the keyboard shortcut ⌘+Z. The accidentally trashed file returns to its original location. Usually.

Unfortunately, Undo doesn't work every time — and it remembers only the very last action that you performed when it *does* work — so don't rely on it too much.

Finding Your Stuff, Fast

Even if you follow every single bit of advice provided in this chapter, a time will come when you won't be able to find a file or folder, although you know for certain it's right there on your hard drive. Somewhere. Fortunately, Leopard includes a fabulous technology called Spotlight that can help you find almost anything on any mounted disk in seconds. Spotlight can

- ✔ Search for files
- ✔ Search for folders
- ✔ Search for text inside documents
- ✔ Search for files and folders by their metadata (for example, creation date, modification date, kind, size, and so on)

Spotlight finds what you're looking for and then organizes its results logically, all in the blink of an eye (on most Macs).

Spotlight is both a technology and a feature. The technology is pervasive throughout Leopard and is the underlying power behind the search boxes in many Apple applications and utilities such as Mail, Address Book, System Preferences, and Finder. You can also use it right from the Spotlight menu — the little magnifying glass on the right side of the menu bar. Also, you can reuse Spotlight searches in the future by turning them into Smart Folders (which I explain earlier in this chapter).

Finding files and folders has never been faster or easier than it is in Leopard. So in these sections, I look at the two separate but related ways Spotlight helps you find files, folders, and even text inside document files — the Search box in Finder windows and the Spotlight menu.

In addition to the Spotlight tools discussed here, the Find command kicks some butt. Find out the details of how it works in Chapter 5.

The Search box in Finder Windows

If you used previous versions of Mac OS X, you might think you know how the Search box on the toolbar of Finder windows works. But you don't. Even though it looks almost the same as before, it's a Search box on major-league steroids. With its power provided by Spotlight, this definitely isn't your father's Search box.

So what's new and different? Glad you asked. The following steps walk you through all the features:

1. **As soon as you type a single character in the Search box, as shown in Figure 6-21, notice that the window changes completely.**

Figure 6-21: As soon as you type the first character in the Search box, the results begin to appear.

2. **(Optional) You can use the Search For items in the Sidebar to limit your search.**

   The default items are Today, Yesterday, Past Week, All Images, All Movies, and All Documents. Click one before you begin typing in the Search box to use it.

   If you want to change the criteria for one or more of these items, it's the same as changing criteria for a Smart Folder — click the item in the Sidebar and then click the Action menu button and choose Show Search Criteria. When you're done changing the search criteria, click the Save button to resave your folder.

3. **If the folder or volume you want to search isn't This Mac or your Home folder, open the folder you want to search and type your query into the Search box in that folder's window.**

4. **Click either the Contents or File Name button to search for the contents of a document or the name of a file or folder.**

5. **When you find the file or folder, you can open any item in the list by double-clicking it.**

   Last but not least, if you want to know where a file or folder resides on your hard drive, look at the very bottom row of the window, where you can see the path to that file.

So there you have it — fast searches made easy in the Finder. But there are many ways to access the power of Spotlight, and the Search box in the toolbar of Finder windows is merely one of them.

Using the Spotlight menu

Another way to search for files and folders is to use the Spotlight menu itself — the aqua magnifying-glass icon on the far right in your menu bar. Click the icon to open Spotlight's Search box and then type a character, word, or series of words in the Search box to find an item, as shown in Figure 6-22.

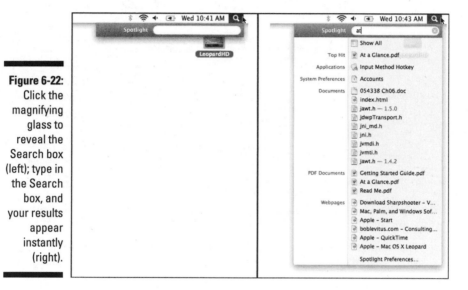

Figure 6-22: Click the magnifying glass to reveal the Search box (left); type in the Search box, and your results appear instantly (right).

Another way to open the Spotlight Search box is with its keyboard shortcut, which is ⌘+spacebar by default.

You can change this shortcut to whatever you like in the Spotlight System Preferences pane.

Spotlight is more than just a menu, though. You can also use the Spotlight window to create and perform more sophisticated searches.

You can access this window two ways:

✔ Click the Show All item in the Spotlight menu or use its keyboard short-cut (⌘+Option+spacebar by default).

   You can change this shortcut to whatever you like in the Spotlight System Preferences pane.

✔ In the Spotlight window, use the Search For items in the Sidebar — Today, Yesterday, Past Week, All Images, All Movies, and All Documents — to fine-tune your search.

TIP

✔ Use the criteria at the top of the window to narrow your search.

This is exactly the same process you used to create Smart Folders! The only difference is that you won't click the Save button at the end to create a Smart Folder from your search.

Regardless of which method you choose to invoke it — the Search box in a Finder window, the Spotlight Search box in the menu bar, or the Spotlight window — Spotlight saves you time and effort.

Finding files by color

If you're the type of person who thinks in color, color labels (preference for these labels are discussed in Chapter 5) offer another neat trick that helps you find files quickly. For the labels to work, you need to think ahead and choose File⇨Color Label to apply a colored label to the selected icon. Then, when you want to find all the files that are tagged with a particular

color, you can press ⌘+F and choose the Color Labels option. Then simply select the color you're looking for.

Tip: When you're applying colors, the Color Label item also appears on an icon's contextual (Control+click) menu; it's often easier to use it instead of the File menu.

Chapter 7

Dealing with Disks

*I*n this chapter, I show you disk basics: how to format them, how to format them so that your Windows-using brethren (and sisteren) can use them, how to eject them, how to copy or move files between disks, and much more. Onward!

This chapter offers lots of info that applies to every Mac user — including folder management and moving or copying files to and from disks other than your internal hard drive. I also show you how to work with optical media such as CD-R, CD-RW, DVD-R, DVD+R, DVD-RW, DVD+RW, and DVD+R DL (dual layer) — all of which many Mac users deal with regularly. If you have a recently minted Mac, for example, you probably have an internal SuperDrive (CD and DVD player/burner). Or you might have added an external USB flash drive or optical disc player/recorder.

The bottom line is that external disk or disc drives allow you to easily copy files for friends, regardless of whether they use a Mac or a PC, and to move your files between home and work.

Comprehending Disks

You should think of the disk icons that appear on the Desktop (and/or in the sidebar of Finder windows) as though they were folders. That's because your Mac sees disks as nothing *but* giant folders. When you double-click them, their contents appear in a Finder window, just like a folder. You can drag stuff in and out of a disk's window, and you can manipulate the disk's window in all the usual ways, just like a folder.

Although for all intents and purposes, disks are folders, disks do behave in unique ways sometimes. The following sections explain what you need to know.

Is that a disk or a disc?

So how do you spell this critter, anyway? Sometimes you see it spelled d-i-s-k; other times you see it spelled d-i-s-c. If you're wondering what's up with that, here's the skinny. In the good old days, the only kind of computer disk was a disk with a k: floppy disk, hard drive, Bernoulli disk, and so on. Then one day, the compact disc (you know, a CD) was invented. And the people who invented it chose to spell it with a c instead of a k, probably because it's round like a discus (think track and field). From that time on, both spellings have been used more or less interchangeably.

Now some people will tell you that magnetic media (floppy, hard, Zip, Jaz, and so on) are called *disks* (spelled with a k). And that optical media — that is, discs that are read with a laser, such as CD-ROMs, CD-RWs, audio CDs, and DVDs — are called *discs* (spelled with a c). Maybe that's true, but the two terms have been used pretty much interchangeably for so long that you can't depend on the last letter to tell you whether a disk is magnetic or optical.

The bottom line is that I'm going to compromise. When I'm speaking generally about something that could be either a disk or a disc, I stick with the term *disk*. But if I'm speaking strictly about optical media (CDs and DVDs), I use the term *disc*.

I hope that's clear. If not, my editors *made* me do it.

Some disks need to be formatted first

Brand-new disks sometimes need to be *formatted* — prepared to receive Macintosh files — before you can use them.

When you pop in an unformatted disk, your Mac usually pops up a dialog that asks what you want to do with the disk. One option is usually to *format* (or *initialize*) the disk — that is, to get it ready to record data. If you choose to format the disk, the Disk Utility program launches itself so you can format the disk from the Erase tab.

If you ever need to format or initialize a blank disk and don't see the dialog, all you have to do is open Disk Utility manually (it's in your `Applications/Utilities` folder) and use its Erase tab to format the disk.

Moving and copying disk icons

Moving a file icon from one on-screen disk to another works the same as moving an icon from one folder to another, with one notable exception: When you move a file from one disk to another, you automatically make a copy of it, leaving the original untouched and unmoved. If you want to move a file or folder completely from one disk to another, you have to delete that leftover original by dragging it to the Trash or by holding down the ⌘ key when you drag it from one disk to the other.

You can't remove a file from a read-only disc (such as a CD-R or DVD-R) or from a folder to which you don't have write permission. But you should be able to move or delete files and folders from all other kinds of disks that you might encounter.

Copying the entire contents of any disk or volume (CD, DVD, or external hard drive, among others) to a new destination works a little differently. To do this, click the disk's icon and then, while holding down the Option key, drag the disk icon onto any folder or disk icon or any open Finder window. When the copy is completed, a folder bearing the same name as the copied disk appears in the destination folder or disk. The new folder contains each and every file that was on the disk of the same name.

Copying files in this way is handy when you want to grab all the files from a CD or DVD and put them on your hard drive.

If you don't hold down the Option key when you drag a disk icon to another destination, it creates an *alias* of the disk (that is, a link back to the original) instead of a copy of its contents. As you might expect, the alias will be almost worthless after you eject the disk — if you open it, it will ask you to insert the original disk.

If you like using the Duplicate command, note that you can't use the Duplicate keyboard shortcut (⌘+D) on a disk, although you can use it on a folder.

For the full details of moving, copying, and pasting, flip to Chapter 6.

Surprise: Your PC Disks Work, Too!

One of the most excellent features of Mac OS X (if you have friends unfortunate enough not to own Macs and you want to share files with them) is that it reads and writes CDs and DVDs that can be read by PCs.

Although your Mac can read disks formatted by a PC, the *files* on them might or might not work for you. If the files are documents, such as Microsoft Word .doc or Microsoft Excel .xls files, one of your Mac programs can probably open them. If the files are Windows programs (these often sport the .exe extension, which stands for *executable*), your Mac can't do anything with 'em without additional software designed to run Windows programs.

That additional software depends upon the processor in your Mac. If you have a PowerPC processor, you need *Virtual PC* from Microsoft (www.microsoft.com). If you have an Intel processor, you need a program like Parallels Desktop from Parallels (www.parallels.com). Both programs emulate a Pentium-based PC so you can run genuine Microsoft Windows operating systems (Windows XP Professional or XP Home, Windows 2000, Windows Me, and Windows 98) on your Mac.

So with a copy of Virtual PC (around $200; includes a copy of Windows) or Parallels Desktop (around $80; does not include a copy of Windows), your Mac *can* run those .exe files (and most Windows programs, as well).

Unfortunately, because emulating a Pentium processor and PC video card demands a lot from your Mac, the performance you get from Virtual PC is slower than even a cheap PC, even on the fastest G5-based Macs. So although it's a useful program for running most Windows applications (including Web browsers, which run decently under Virtual PC), fast-moving games (such as Doom, Quake, and Unreal Tournament) are unplayable. Bummer. The Windows-bundled Solitaire game, on the other hand, works pretty well under Virtual PC.

Parallels Desktop achieves much more usable speeds with most Windows applications. Depending upon which Intel-based Mac you have, it might even be speedy enough to play first-person shooters such as Doom, Quake, and Unreal Tournament. For most other stuff (including the Windows-bundled Solitaire), Parallels Desktop on an Intel-based Mac is one heck of a lot faster than Virtual PC on a PowerPC-based Mac — and a heck of a lot faster than many Dells, Lenovos, and HPs, too.

Burning CDs and DVDs

With Mac OS X (10.1 or later), you can play, create, and publish audio and video on optical media. Depending upon which type of optical drive your Mac is equipped with, you can burn some or all of the following types of discs: CD-R, CD-RW, DVD-R, DVD+R, DVD-RW, DVD+RW, and DVD+R DL (dual layer).

How can I tell what kind of discs my Mac can burn?

Great question. If you don't know what types of discs your Mac can burn, here's an easy way to find out:

1. **In your Applications folder, open the Utilities folder and then open the System Profiler application.**

2. **In the Contents pane on the left, click Hardware and then Disc Burning, as shown in the following figure.**

The right side of the window now reveals lots of information about the disc-burning capabilities of this Macintosh.

3. **Check the CD-Write and DVD-Write information near the bottom for the types of discs in your Mac.**

This info will note whether you can burn CD-R, CD-RW, DVD-R, DVD+R, DVD-RW, DVD+RW, and DVD+R DL (dual layer) optical discs.

In the sections that follow, I show you two ways to burn files onto a CD or DVD. For the first way, you insert a disc and then select the files you want to burn. The second method, creating a Burn folder, enables you to save the list of files you've burned.

Burning on the fly

One way to burn files to a CD or DVD is to simply insert a disc and select files on the fly. Just follow these steps:

1. **Insert a blank disc.**

   You see an alert (as shown in Figure 7-1) that asks you what you want to do with the disc.

Figure 7-1:
Insert a
blank CD in
your optical
media drive
and get
ready to feel
the burn.

You inserted a blank CD. Choose an action from the pop-up menu or click Ignore.

Action: Open Finder

☐ Make this action the default

(?)   (Eject)   (Ignore)   (OK)

In this case, the blank disc was a CD-R, but the same thing happens if you insert a recordable DVD.

2. **Now select Open Finder from the Action pop-up menu.**

   Open Finder is the default choice unless you've changed that default in the CDs & DVDs System Preferences pane or as explained in this tip.

   The other choices are Open iTunes and Open Disk Utility. If you select the first, iTunes automatically opens when you insert a blank CD; if you select the second, Disk Utility automatically opens. If you want to make either of these actions the default so it occurs the next time you insert a blank disc (and every time thereafter), select the Make This Action the Default check box. For the purposes of these steps, I go with Open Finder for now.

3. **Click OK.**

   Your blank CD *mounts* (appears as an icon) on the Desktop just like any other removable disc, but its distinctive icon tells you that it's a recordable CD (or DVD), as shown in Figure 7-2.

4. **Drag files or folders onto the disc icon on your Desktop until the disc contains all the files you want on it.**

Figure 7-2:
Recordable
optical
discs get a
distinctive,
labeled icon.

5. **(Optional) If you like, you can change the disc's name from Untitled CD (or DVD) the same way you change the name of any file or folder.**

MP3 players play files in the order in which they're written, which is alphabetically. So if you want them to play in a particular order, be sure to name them with sequential numbers at the beginning. Fortunately, iTunes makes that easy with the Create File Names with Track Number option in your Importing preferences.

6. **When you're ready to finish (burn) your CD (or DVD), open its disc icon and click the Burn button in the upper-right corner of the disc's window, or click the Burn icon (which looks like the warning symbol for radioactivity) to the right of the disc in the Sidebar, both shown in Figure 7-3.**

Burn button

Figure 7-3:
Click the
Burn button
in the
window or
the burn
icon next to
the disc's
icon in the
sidebar to
burn your
disc.

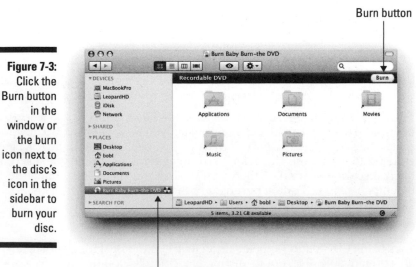

Burn icon in the Sidebar

Alternatively, you could

- Control+click or right-click the disc's icon and choose Burn Disc
  (yes, Apple spells it with a *c*) from the contextual menu (right in
  Figure 7-4).

- Select the icon and choose Burn *Disc Name* from the File menu (left
  in Figure 7-4). If you choose Eject, from either the contextual menu
  or the File menu, you're asked whether you want to burn the disc first.

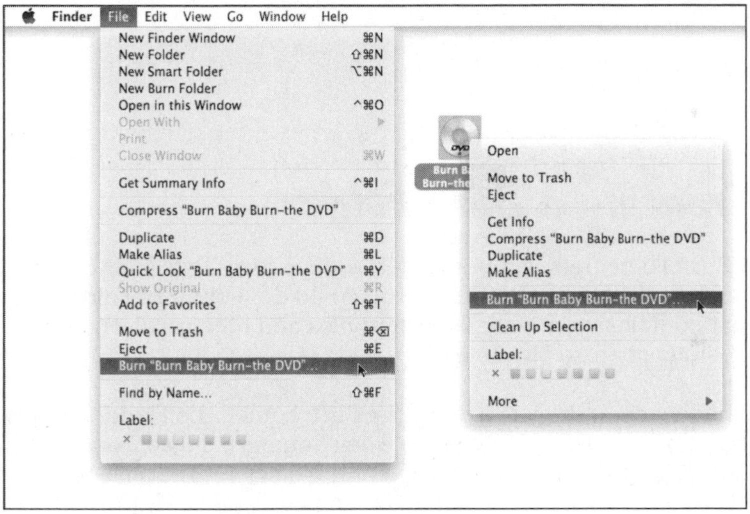

Figure 7-4:
Two more
ways to
burn a disc.

- If you drag the disc icon to the Trash/Eject Disk icon in your Dock,
  the Trash/Eject Disk icon turns into the Burn Disc icon (which still
  looks like the warning symbol for radioactivity). Drop the disc icon
  on the radioactivity icon in the Dock, and the burning begins.

7. **After you've chosen to burn a disc, you see the dialog shown in Figure
   7-5. Select a speed from the Burn Speed pop-up menu; then click the
   Burn button, and you're done.**

   I usually use a slower (2x) but more reliable burn speed unless I'm in a
   huge hurry. I've had many discs fail at the higher speeds. (You can call
   those discs "drink coasters.")

   Select the Save Burn Folder To check box if you think you might want to
   burn another copy of this disc someday.

One last thing: Burning a music CD is a different process that's performed
using iTunes. Don't worry — you find out all about that process in Chapter 11.

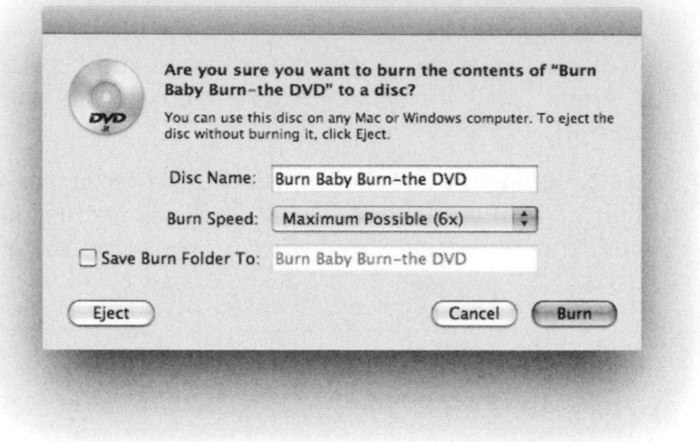

Figure 7-5:
The last
step before
the burning
begins.

> Are you sure you want to burn the contents of "Burn Baby Burn-the DVD" to a disc?
>
> You can use this disc on any Mac or Windows computer. To eject the disc without burning it, click Eject.
>
> Disc Name: Burn Baby Burn-the DVD
>
> Burn Speed: Maximum Possible (6x)
>
> ☐ Save Burn Folder To: Burn Baby Burn-the DVD
>
> Eject   Cancel   Burn

Creating a Burn Folder

A Burn Folder lets you burn selected files to a CD or DVD many times. Perhaps the most useful thing you could do with Burn Folder is create one that contains your most important files and then regularly burn the current versions of those files to a CD or DVD as a backup.

Whenever you drag an item to the Burn Folder, the Finder creates an alias of that item in the Burn Folder. So when you burn a disc using a Burn Folder, the parent (original) files are burned to the disc, not the aliases.

Here's how to create and use a Burn Folder:

1. **Choose File⇨New Burn Folder.**

   A folder titled Burn Folder appears on the desktop.

2. **Name the Burn Folder.**

3. **Drag some icons into the Burn Folder.**

4. **When you're ready to burn the folder's contents to a disc, double-click it and click Burn.**

5. **Insert a disc and follow the on-screen instructions.**

If the Finder can't find the parent file for an alias, it asks whether you want to cancel the burn or to continue without that item. If you cancel, the disc remains empty.

If a Burn Folder is in the Sidebar of a Finder window, you can quickly burn its contents to a disc by clicking the burn icon to its right, as shown in Figure 7-6.

Figure 7-6:
One of the
ways you
can burn
items in a
Burn Folder
to disc.

Another way to burn the contents of a burn folder is to right-click or
Control+click it and then choose Burn Disc from the contextual menu.

Getting Disks out of Your Mac

The preceding sections tell you almost everything there is to know about
disks except one important thing: how to eject a disk. Piece of cake, actually.
Here are several ways, all simple to remember:

- Click the disk's icon to select it and then choose File⇨Eject (or use the
  keyboard shortcut ⌘+E).

- Drag the disk's icon to the Trash. When you drag a disk's icon, the Trash
  icon in the Dock changes into an Eject icon, like the one shown in the
  left margin.

  The preceding method of ejecting a disk is something that used to drive
  me (and many others) crazy before Mac OS X. In the olden days, the
  Trash icon didn't change into an Eject icon. And this confused many new
  users, who then asked me the same question (over and over and over):
  "But doesn't dragging something to the Trash erase it from your disk?"

- Click the little Eject icon to the right of the disc's name in the Sidebar.

- Press the Eject key on your keyboard if it has one. (If it has one, it probably has the Eject icon on it.)

TIP

If your keyboard doesn't have an Eject key, press the F12 key and continue to hold it down for a second or two. On many keyboards that don't have an Eject key, this is the keyboard shortcut to eject a disc.

✔ Right-click or Control+click the disk icon and then choose Eject from the contextual menu.

There's one more way if you like little menus on the right side of your menu bar. To install your own Eject menu on the menu bar, navigate to `System/Library/CoreServices/MenuExtras` and then open (double-click) the Eject.menu icon. Your Eject menu appears on the right side of your menu bar.

Chapter 8

Organizing Your Life

*W*hen you buy Mac OS X Leopard, the folks at Apple generously include applications that can help simplify and organize your everyday affairs, namely iCal, Stickies, and iSync (and .Mac).

In fact, Mac OS X comes with a whole folder full of applications — software you can use to do everything from surfing the Internet to capturing an image of your Mac's screen to playing QuickTime movies to checking the time. Technically, most of these applications aren't even part of Mac OS X. Rather, the vast majority of them are what are known as *bundled* apps — programs that come with the operating system but are unrelated to its function. Readers (bless them) tend to complain when I skip over bundled applications, so I mention almost all of them in this book.

But in this chapter, you get a look at only the applications that help you organize your everyday life — your appointments, to-do items, notes to yourself, and all the various gadgets you may attach to and detach from your Mac.

The applications discussed in this chapter are stored in (where else?) the Applications folder, which you can get to in three ways:

✔ Click the Applications folder in the Sidebar in any Finder window.

✔ Choose Go⇨Applications.

✔ Use the keyboard shortcut ⌘+Shift+A.

Other bundled apps you might be especially interested in include Safari (Chapter 9), Address Book and Mail (Chapter 10), iTunes (Chapter 11), a whole handful of multimedia applications that enable you to play video and more on your Mac (Chapter 12), and Text Edit (Chapter 13). For even more information on the Mac OS X bundled applications, check out *Macs For Dummies,* 9th Edition, by *USA Today* columnist Edward C. Baig.

Keeping Track with iCal

iCal is a wonderful program that combines a comprehensive daily/weekly/ monthly appointment calendar and a to-do list. It offers multiple color-coded calendars, several types of reminder alarms, repeating event scheduling, and more. You can publish your calendar(s) on the Web for others to view (which requires a .Mac account or other WebDav server), and you can subscribe to calendars published by other iCal users.

It's a handy-dandy memory-enhancing tool, and if you make a habit of recording appointments and things to do in iCal, you'll almost never forget them.

I love iCal and keep it open at all times on my Macs. In the sections that follow, I share a handful of the features I find most useful.

Navigating iCal views

iCal lets you display the main iCal window just the way you like it.

- ✔ **You can view your calendar by the day, week, or month.** Figure 8-1 shows a weekly view. To select a view, click the Day, Week, or Month button at the top of the window.

- ✔ **To move back or forward,** click the arrow buttons on either side of the Day, Week, and Month buttons. You see the previous or next week in weekly view, you move back or forward by day in Day view, and so on.

- ✔ **To show or hide the Event Info, Mini Calendar(s), Notifications, Search Results, To Dos, and All-Day Events,** click the Show/Hide button for that feature. (Refer to Figure 8-1.)

- ✔ **To go to today's date,** click the Go to Today button.

- ✔ **To jump to any date, week, or month** (depending on the view you've selected), simply click it in the mini calendar in the lower left.

You can find all these items, most of which have handy keyboard shortcuts, in the iCal View menu, as shown in Figure 8-2. This menu offers almost total control over what you see and how you navigate

Calendars

Go to Today button

Previous day/week/month

Current time

Next day/week/month

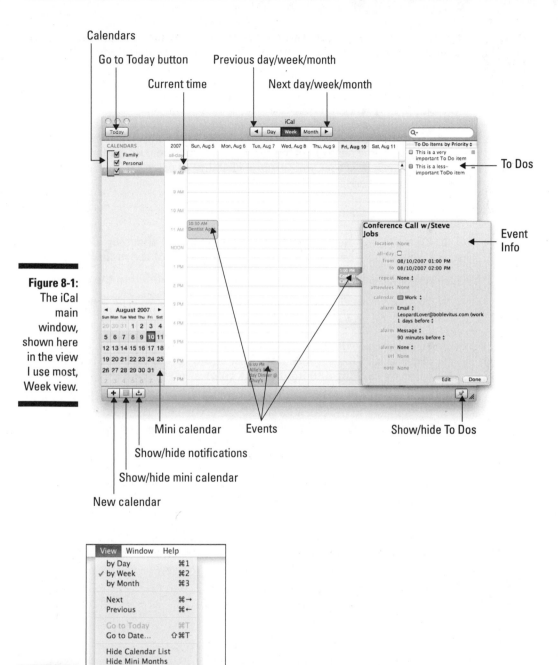

To Dos

Event Info

Mini calendar

Events

Show/hide To Dos

Show/hide notifications

Show/hide mini calendar

New calendar

If you want to master iCal, it would behoove you to spend some time experimenting with these view and navigation commands and options.

Creating calendars

If you refer to Figure 8-1, you see check boxes for Family, Personal, and Work in the upper left. These check boxes represent different calendars set up in iCal. The check boxes let you turn the visibility of calendars on (checked) and off (unchecked).

To create a new calendar in iCal:

1. **Choose File⇨New Calendar, use the keyboard shortcut ⌘+Option+N, or click the + button in the bottom-left corner of the main iCal window.**

   A new calendar named Untitled is created and added to the calendar list.

2. **To give your calendar a name, select Untitled and type a new name.**

   You can also add a description of this calendar if you want.

3. **To color-code the entries for this calendar, first select the calendar (by clicking it). Then choose File⇨Get Info or press ⌘+I and then select a color by clicking and holding the color swatch, as shown in Figure 8-3.**

   Now any item you create while this calendar is selected in the list on the left appears in the calendar in the color you selected. And when a calendar is selected in the list on the left, events that belong to the calendar are displayed in a brighter shade of the color.

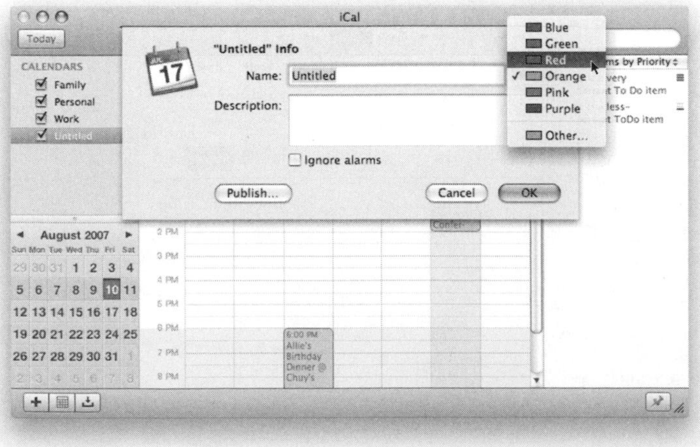

Figure 8-3:
Change the
color of a
calendar
by clicking
the color
swatch in
the drawer.

TIP

In my humble opinion, Other is the really handy choice, because it lets you select colors other than the six boring default colors.

Grouping calendars

You can also organize calendars into groups that contain more than one calendar. To create a new calendar group in iCal:

1. **Choose File⇨New Calendar Group, use the keyboard shortcut ⌘+Shift+N, or press Shift and then click the + button in the bottom-left corner of the main iCal window.**

   A new calendar group named Group is created and added to the calendar list.

2. **Give the new group a name by selecting Group and typing a new name.**

3. **To add calendars to the group, simply drag them below the group name in the list, as shown in Figure 8-4.**

   You can now show or hide all calendars in the group by selecting or deselecting a single check box. And of course, you can still show or hide individual calendars by selecting or deselecting their check boxes.

Figure 8-4:
Add
calendars to
a calendar
group by
dragging
them under
the group
name, like
this.

Here's how you might deploy this feature. You could create individual calendars for each member of your family and then put all the individual family calendars into a group called Family. Then you could make all the family-member calendars visible or invisible with a single click of the group calendar's check box.

If you have a .Mac account (as discussed in Chapter 9), you can publish your calendars and invite others to subscribe to them by choosing Calendar⇨Publish. The others receive an e-mail inviting them to subscribe to your calendar. This is what my family does. Each of us maintains and publishes his or her own calendar and subscribes to everyone else's. That way, we can all see at a glance who is doing what and when they're doing it. This is by far the slickest solution we've found.

In any event

The heart of iCal is the event. To create a new one, follow these steps:

1. **Choose File⇨New Event, press ⌘+N, or double-click anywhere on the calendar.**

   A newly created event in my Work calendar is shown in Figure 8-5.

Figure 8-5: You modify an event by changing the value of the items displayed in its pop-up event info.

2. **If the event doesn't appear in the proper place, just click it and drag it wherever you like.**

3. **To change the values of the event's items — event name, location, time and duration, repeat, attendees, calendar, alarm, URL, and notes — click the Show Info button in the lower-right corner.**

- *To show or hide the event info,* click the Show/Hide Info button (the *i* button shown in the margin), which you can find in the lower-right corner of the iCal window.

- *To change the date, time, or duration of the event,* click the appropriate item to select it and type a new value for that item.

- *To make an event repeat daily, weekly, monthly, or on a custom schedule you create,* click and hold the double-headed arrow next to the word *Repeat,* as shown in Figure 8-6.

Figure 8-6:
Making this
event repeat
every week
on the same
day.

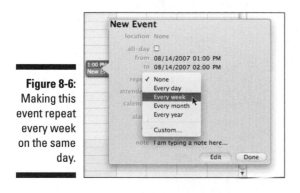

- *To invite others to attend an event,* select people you want to invite to a scheduled event. To add attendees, you can either open Address Book or the iCal Address Panel (Window⇨Address Panel or ⌘+Option+A) and drag the contacts onto the event in iCal. Alternatively, you can type the first few letters of the name in the Attendees field, and names that match magically appear. For example, in Figure 8-7, I typed the letters *st,* and iCal offered me a choice of my two contacts with names that start with *st* — namely Steve LeVitus and Stanley Steamer. Sweet! (If you're unfamiliar with Address Book, flip to Chapter 10 for details.)

- *To set an alarm,* just click the word *None* with the double-headed arrow just to the right of the word *alarm.* A menu appears. Choose the type of alarm you want from the menu and then change its values to suit your needs. I find the Message with Sound and Email alarms so useful that I use both for almost every event I create.

  You can have as many alarms as you like for each event. When you add an alarm to an event, a new alarm item appears below it. Just click the word *None* with the double-headed arrow just to the right of the word *alarm* to create a second (or third or fifteenth) alarm. To remove an alarm, click the word *alarm* and choose *None* from the pop-up menu.

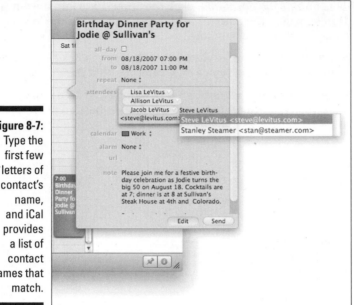

Figure 8-7:
Type the
first few
letters of
a contact's
name,
and iCal
provides
a list of
contact
names that
match.

All the features mentioned so far are wonderful, but my very favorite iCal feature has to be alarms. I rarely miss an important event anymore — iCal reminds me of them with time to spare.

To do or not to do

iCal has one more trick up its sleeve to help you stay organized — the To Do item. Unlike an event, a To Do item isn't necessarily associated with a particular day or time and can be assigned a priority level: Very Important, Important, Not Important, or None.

To create a new To Do item, choose File➪New To Do, press ⌘+K, or double-click anywhere on the To Do list.

To show or hide the To Do list, click the push-pin button (shown in the margin), which you can find in the lower-right corner of the iCal window.

Stickies

Stickies are electronic sticky notes for your Mac. They're convenient places to jot quick notes or phone numbers. Some Stickies are shown in Figure 8-8.

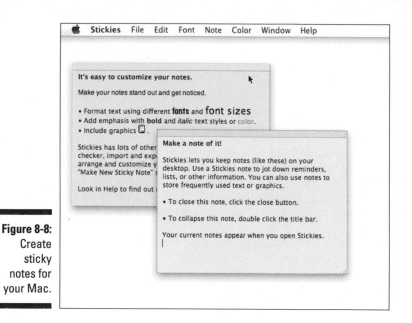

Figure 8-8:
Create
sticky
notes for
your Mac.

Stickies are supremely flexible.

- ✔ Move them around on-screen (just drag 'em by their title bars).
- ✔ Change their text to any font and color you desire by using the Note menu.
- ✔ Make your Stickies any color you like by using the Color menu.
- ✔ Collapse a Sticky by double-clicking its title bar.
- ✔ Print a Sticky and import or export text files from the Stickies application menu.

If you hover the cursor over a Sticky without clicking, the creation and modification dates and times pop up in a little tool-tip-style window, as shown in Figure 8-8.

Anything that you type on a Sticky is automatically saved as long as you keep that note open. But when you close a note (by clicking its Close box, choosing File⇨Close, or using the keyboard shortcut ⌘+W), you lose its contents forever. Fortunately, Stickies give you a warning and a second chance to save the note in a separate file on your hard drive. You can also export Stickies (choose File⇨Export Text) and save them as plain text, Rich Text Format (RTF) files, or as RTF with attachments (RTFD) files. The last two formats support fonts and other formatting that plain-text format does not.

Other Stickies goodies include a spell checker and spoken notes, both found on the Edit menu.

iSync

iSync is Leopard's synchronizing software that lets you synchronize your Address Book entries and iCal calendars with more than 20 cell-phone models (Bluetooth is required on both the Mac and the phone to take advantage of this feature), your iPod, and/or your PDA (Palm, Visor, and others). It also lets you synchronize your Address Book entries, iCal calendars, and Safari bookmarks among multiple Macs in different locations via a .Mac account.

You can find a list of devices supported by iSync here: `www.apple.com/macosx/features/isync/devices.html`.

Here's a quick overview of how to synchronize data on your Mac with various devices:

- **Bluetooth cell phone:** Open System Preferences, and click the Bluetooth icon. In the Devices tab, click the little plus sign to add your phone. The Bluetooth Setup Assistant will launch automatically and walk you through the process.

- **iPod or iPhone:** Configure synchronization by selecting your iPod or iPhone in the iTunes Devices list (on the left) and then clicking the appropriate tabs.

- **Other Macs (requires .Mac subscription):** Open System Preferences (from the Applications folder, Dock, or menu) and click the .Mac icon. Click the Sync tab, and check the boxes for items you want to synchronize with other Macs — Automator library, bookmarks, calendars, Dashboard widgets, Dock items, Stickies, and so on. Now do the same thing on every Mac you want to synchronize these items with.

- **Palm, Visor, Blackberry, or other PDA:** Refer to the documentation that came with your device.

Part III
Do Unto Leopard: Getting Things Done

The 5th Wave   By Rich Tennant

"Wow, I didn't know OS X could redirect an email message like _that_."

In this part . . .

Moving right along, Part III comprises how to do stuff with your Mac. In this section, it's off to the Internet first — how to get it working and what to do with it after that. Next you discover two of Apple's most imaginatively named programs: The excellent e-mail application called Mail and the wonderful address book called Address Book. That's followed by a pair of chapters devoted to working with media — music, movies, DVDs, and digital photos. Finally, you discover the basics of processing words and using fonts.

This is an excellent section, chock-full of useful information (if I do say so myself), and it's one you definitely don't want to miss.

Chapter 9

Internet-Working

- -

In This Chapter

▶ Getting an overview of the Internet

▶ Presurfing with the Network System Preferences pane

▶ Finding out about the .Mac (*dot-Mac*) services

▶ Surfing the Web with Safari

▶ Searching with Google

▶ Chatting with iChat AV

- -

*T*hese days, networking online is easier than finding a log to fall off: You simply use the Internet to connect your Mac to a wealth of information residing on computers around the world. Luckily for you, Mac OS X has the best and most comprehensive Internet tools ever shipped with a Mac operating system.

Mac OS X offers built-in Internet connectivity right out of the box. For example, Mac OS X Leopard comes with

✔ Apple's **Safari Web browser,** which you use to navigate the Web, download remote files via FTP, and more

✔ **iChat AV,** Apple's live online chatting client that works with other iChat users, people using AOL Instant Messaging (AIM) clients, people using Jabber (an open-source chatting protocol), and Bonjour (which discovers other users on your local area network)

✔ The **Mail** application (for e-mail)

In this chapter, I cover the top two things most people use the Internet for: the *World Wide Web* (that's the *www* you see so often in Internet addresses) and *live chatting* with iChat AV. You can find all about Mail and Address Book in Chapter 10.

But before I can talk about browsers, e-mail software, and chatting, I have to help you configure your Internet connection. When you're finished, you can play with your browsers, mail, and chat applications to your heart's content.

Setting Up for Surfing

Before you can surf the Internet, you need to get a few small tasks out of the way. In this section, I walk you through them all. If you're a typical home user, you need three things to surf the Internet:

- ✔ **A modem or other connection to the Internet,** such as a Digital Subscriber Line (DSL), a cable modem, an Integrated Services Digital Network (ISDN), or a satellite Internet service.

  If you use technology other than a regular (analog) modem, DSL, or cable modem to connect your computer to the Internet, your network administrator (the person you run to at work when something goes wrong with your computer) or ISP might have to help you set up your Mac because setting up those other configurations is (sigh) beyond the scope of this book.

- ✔ **An account with an ISP** (an Internet service provider such as EarthLink, Comcast, or RoadRunner) or AOL.

- ✔ **Mac OS X Leopard default installation.** You might need to tweak a few settings, as I explain in the upcoming section "Plugging in your Internet connection settings."

After you set up each of these components, you can launch and use Safari, Mail, iChat AV, or any other Internet application.

Setting up your modem

If you have a cable modem, DSL, or other high-speed Internet connection or are thinking about getting any of these, you can use them with your Mac. In most cases, you merely connect your Mac to the Internet via a cable plugged into the Ethernet port of your Mac and into an external box, which is connected to either a cable or phone outlet, depending on what kind of access you have to the Internet.

Your cable or DSL installer person should set up everything for you. If he doesn't, you have to call that service provider for help — troubleshooting a high-speed connection is pretty abstruse (which puts it beyond the purview of this book).

Your Internet service provider and you

After you make sure that you have a working modem, you have to select a company to provide you access to the Internet. These companies are called *Internet service providers* (ISPs). The prices and services that ISPs offer vary, often from minute to minute. Keep the following in mind when choosing an ISP:

Old school: About analog modems

A *modem* is a small, inexpensive device that turns data (that is, computer files) into sounds and then squirts those sounds across phone lines. At the other end, another modem receives these sounds and turns them back into data (that is, your files). Before the days of ubiquitous broadband Internet access (such as cable modem and DSL), all Macs included an internal modem. Alas, all Macs sold today require you to purchase an external USB modem if you intend to use a *dial-up* Internet connection. *Tip:* Apple sells one called the Apple USB Modem for around $50.

To use an analog modem, you merely plug a plain old telephone line into it.

✔ **On Macs with internal modems,** that simply means plugging one end of the phone cable into the phone-plug-shaped port on the side or back of your Mac and the other end into a live phone outlet (or the phone jack on a surge suppressor that has a phone line running to your phone outlet).

✔ **If you have an external modem,** plug the phone cable into the modem and plug the modem into a USB port. Finally, plug the

modem into an AC power source if it requires AC power. (Some modems don't because they obtain power from your Mac's USB port.)

The modem port on Macs with internal modems looks a lot like the Ethernet port, but it's smaller. You could plug a phone cable into the Ethernet port, but it wouldn't fit right, and it wouldn't connect you to the Internet. The modem port is the smaller of the two — look for the phone icon next to it. Conversely, the Ethernet port is the larger of the two. Look for an icon that looks something like this: <•>. Check out the differences: Both ports and their icons appear in the following figure (the Ethernet port is on the left).

Just in case you visit a store populated by computer geeks, a phone connector is called an RJ-11, and an Ethernet connector is called an RJ-45.

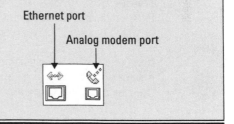

Ethernet port

Analog modem port

✔ **If you're using a cable modem, your ISP is probably your cable company.** In most cases, the same applies to DSL — except that your provider is either your local phone company or an ISP that you've chosen to get your service connected through your phone company. In that case, your ISP usually contacts the phone company and arranges installation and setup for you.

In other words, the choice of ISP is pretty much made for you when you decide on cable or DSL service.

✔ **The going rate for unlimited broadband access to the Internet starts at around $25 per month.** If your service provider asks for considerably more than that, find out why. Higher-throughput packages for cable modem, DSL, or other high-speed connections might run you twice that much. My highest-speed DSL, for example, is $60 a month from AT&T.

Because most Mac users like things to be easy, Mac OS X includes a cool feature in its Setup Assistant to help you find and configure an account with an ISP. When you installed OS X (assuming that you did and that it didn't come preinstalled on your Mac), the Installer program might have asked you a bunch of questions about your Internet connection and then set everything up for you. This process is detailed in this book's appendix. If you didn't have an Internet connection (an ISP) at that time, you need to configure the Network System Preferences pane yourself. Although I cover the Network System Preferences pane in depth in the next section, how to configure it so that your Mac works with your ISP is something you have to work out with that ISP. If you have questions or problems not answered by this book, your ISP should be able to assist you. And if your ISP can't help, it's probably time to try a different ISP.

Plugging in your Internet connection settings

If you didn't set up your Internet connection when you installed OS X, you need to open System Preferences (from the Applications folder, the Dock, or the menu) and click the Network icon. The Network pane offers options for connecting your Mac to the Internet or to a network. The easiest way to use it is to click the Assist Me button at the bottom and let your Mac do the heavy lifting. That said, here are some tips and tricks to get you started.

If you're part of a large office network, check with your system administrator before you change anything in this pane. If you ignore this advice, you run the risk of losing your network connection completely.

Setting up your Internet connection manually in the Network System Preferences pane is beyond the purview of this book. That said, here's a very brief overview of the things you need to do should you feel inclined to configure your network connection manually.

Depending on the type of connection you have, you need to configure some or all of the items in the following list.

Once again, I highly recommend clicking the Assist Me button at the bottom of the Network System Preferences pane and letting your Mac set up your connection for you. If it asks you a question you can't answer, ask your ISP or network administrator for the answer. I can't possibly tell you how in this book, because there are just too many possible configurations, and each depends on your particular ISP and service.

That said, here's a brief rundown on the most common things you might need to know to set up a network connection:

- *TCP/IP:* TCP/IP is the language of the Internet. You might be asked to specify things such as your IP address, domain name servers, and search domains.

- *PPP or PPPoE:* These acronyms stand for *Point-to-Point Protocol* and *Point-to-Point Protocol over Ethernet.* Which one you see depends on what service you're using to connect. All analog modems use PPP; some cable and DSL modems use PPPoE.

- *AppleTalk:* AppleTalk is a homegrown network protocol invented by Apple. Some (but not all) networked printers require it to be turned on for them to function.

- *Proxies:* If you're on a large network or your Mac is behind a firewall, you might need to specify one or more proxy servers. If so, your network administrator or ISP can help you configure it. If you're a home user, you'll probably never need to touch this tab. Finally, some ISPs require you to specify proxy servers; if you need to do this, ask your ISP what to do.

If you use your Mac in more than one place, you can set up a separate configuration for each location and then choose it from this menu. A location, in this context, consists of all settings in all items in the Network System Preferences pane. After you have this entire pane configured the way that you like, pull down the Location menu and choose Edit Locations. Click the little gear button at the bottom of the Locations column and choose Create New Location. Type a descriptive name for the new location (AirPort at Starbucks, Ethernet at Joe's Office, and so on), select the check box for the service or services this location uses, and then click Done. From now on, you can change all your network settings at the same time by choosing the appropriate location from the Location pop-up menu.

If, on the other hand, your Mac has a single network or Internet connection (as most home users have), just leave the Location menu set to Automatic and be done with it.

Using the Network Setup Assistant (click the Assist Me button at the bottom of the Network System Preferences pane) to create a network connection usually makes it unnecessary for you to have to deal with most of these items. Still, I thought you should at least know the basics.

Starting up a .Mac account

.Mac (pronounced *dot-Mac*) is a set of optional, Internet-based services that integrate nicely with Mac OS X and cost around $100 a year. Although .Mac isn't specifically a Mac OS X feature, it is an Internet-based service that I happen to think is worth paying for (and I do pay for it). So I'd be remiss if I didn't at least tell you a little bit about it.

At the time of this writing, .Mac offers e-mail, Web page hosting, an image gallery feature, 10GB of storage (called iDisk, for e-mail, backups, Web pages, and so on), and much more. Check www.mac.com for the most current details and look for a 60-day free trial so you can test drive it before you pay a nickel.

 The .Mac pane lets you configure your .Mac subscription and iDisk (if you have them). It offers four tabs:

- ✔ **Account:** If you have a .Mac account, you can type your name and password here so that you don't have to type them every time you use your iDisk or Mail. (See the nearby sidebar, "A quick overview of .Mac," for details.)

    Click the Sign Up button, and your Web browser opens and takes you to the Apple .Mac Sign Up page.

- ✔ **Sync:** The Sync tab is where you can specify which synchronization services you want to employ. You can use iSync to manage Safari bookmarks; iCal calendars; Address Book information; keychains; and Mail rules, mail accounts, signatures, and smart mailboxes.

- ✔ **iDisk:** This tab shows how much of your iDisk (your remote disk maintained on Apple's servers for .Mac members) is used, how much is available, and how you have allocated space between disk storage and mail storage. It also allows you to keep a local copy of your iDisk on your hard drive, synchronize it automatically or manually, and make your Public Folder Read/Write or Read-Only with or without a password.

- ✔ **Advanced:** Use this pane to register several Macs for synchronization through your .Mac account.

Browsing the Web with Safari

With your Internet connection set up, you're ready to browse the Web. In the following sections, I concentrate on browsing the Web with Safari because it's the Web browser installed with OS X Leopard. (If you don't like Safari, I recommend taking a look at either OmniWeb or Firefox, which are both filled with features you can't find in Safari.)

To begin, just open your Web browser. No problem. As usual, there's more than one way. You can launch Safari by using the following methods:

✔ Clicking the Safari icon in the Dock (look for the big blue compass that looks like a stopwatch, as shown in the margin)

✔ Double-clicking the Safari icon in your Applications folder

✔ Single-clicking a URL link in an e-mail or other document

✔ Double-clicking a URL link document in the Finder

When you first launch Safari, it automatically connects you to the Internet and displays the default Apple start page (see Figure 9-1). In the sections that follow, I cover the highlights of using Safari, starting at the top of the screen.

Figure 9-1: The Apple start page.

Navigating with the toolbar buttons

The buttons along the top of the window do pretty much what their names imply. From left to right, these buttons are

- ✔ **Back/Forward:** When you open a page and then move to a second page (or third or fourth), the Back button takes you to a previously visited page. Remember that you need to go back before the Forward button will work.

- ✔ **Reload/Stop:** Click Reload to make sure you're getting the most up-to-date version of a page. Stop tells a sluggish page to quit trying to appear so that you can move on.

- ✔ **Open This Page in Dashboard:** Creates a widget out of the page or the portion of the page you select. The page/widget remains available in Dashboard until you close it. (Press Option and click the X that appears above the upper-left corner.)

- ✔ **Add Bookmark:** When you find a page you know you'll want to return to, clicking this button tells Safari to remember it for you. I explain bookmarks in more detail a little later in this chapter.

Play with the buttons a bit, and you'll see what I mean.

Other available buttons include Home, AutoFill, Text Size, Print, and Bug (report a bug to Apple); you can add or delete them by choosing View⇨Customize Address Bar.

Below the Address field are some bookmark buttons that take you directly to pages that might interest you, such as Amazon.com, eBay, and Yahoo!

The News item in this row of buttons is a pop-up (actually, pop-down) menu, as shown in Figure 9-2. Clicking any of these buttons or choosing an item from the News pop-down menu transports you to that page.

Figure 9-2:
The News button is actually a menu.

To the right of the top row of buttons is the Address field. This is where you type Web addresses, or *URLs* (Uniform Resource Locators), that you want to visit. Just type one and press Return to surf to that site.

Web addresses almost always begin with `http://www`. But Safari has a cool trick: If you just type a name, you usually get to the appropriate Web site that way — without typing `http`, `//`, or `www`. For example, if you type **apple** in the Address field and then press Return, you go to `www.apple.com`. Or if you type **boblevitus**, you're taken to `www.boblevitus.com`. Try it — it's pretty slick.

Bookmarking your favorite pages

When you find a Web page you want to return to, you bookmark it. Here's how it works:

1. **Click the Add Bookmark (+) button in the Safari toolbar, choose Bookmarks⇨Add Bookmark, or use the shortcut ⌘+D.**

   A sheet appears. In it, you can rename the bookmark or use the name provided by Safari.

2. **(Optional) To put this bookmark into an existing folder, choose the folder from the pop-up menu below the bookmark's name.**

   You can choose where to store the bookmark — the bookmark bar, the bookmark menu, or a folder in either place — from the pop-up menu beneath the bookmark name. These folders let you group your bookmarks so that you can return to them more easily.

3. **Click the Add button to save the bookmark.**

4. **When you want to return to a bookmarked page, choose Bookmarks⇨Show All Bookmarks, type the keyboard shortcut ⌘+Option+B, or click the Show All Bookmarks button (shown in margin).**

   The Bookmarks window appears, as shown in Figure 9-3.

   You can view the contents of any Collection (that is, a folder full of bookmarks) by clicking its name in the Collections pane. Figure 9-3 shows, in particular, the contents of the Bookmarks Bar folder with the contents of the News subfolder expanded.

If you enable Auto-Click for a collection of bookmarks, when you click the collection's button, you don't get a pop-down menu. Instead, all the pages in that collection open at once, each in its own separate tab. You can still use the pop-down menu, but you have to click and hold the button rather than just click.

To organize your Bookmarks window or place bookmarks on the toolbar or Bookmarks menu, move bookmarks by dragging them. You can place bookmarks and folders of bookmarks on the Safari Bookmarks bar or Bookmarks menu by dragging them to the appropriate folder. If you drag a folder of bookmarks to the Bookmarks Bar folder (or directly onto the Bookmarks bar itself), the result is a drop-down menu, as shown earlier in Figure 9-2.

Figure 9-3:
The
Bookmarks
window in
all its glory.

5. **Open bookmarked pages in the Bookmarks window by double-clicking them.**

   To delete a bookmark, select it in the Bookmarks window and then press Delete or Backspace.

Bookmarks are favorites, and favorites are bookmarks. Both words describe exactly the same exact thing — shortcuts to Web sites. In this chapter, I use *bookmarks* because that's what Safari calls them. Some other browsers call them *favorites*.

Your copy of Safari comes preloaded with bookmarks that take you to other nifty Mac sites to check out. You can find links to Apple sites, hardware and software vendors, Mac publications, and more. Take a look at the folders full of great Web pages that your pals at Apple have put together — Mac, Kids, Sports, Entertainment, and so on. Be sure to explore all the included bookmarks when you have some time; most, if not all, are worth knowing more about.

Simplifying surfing with RSS feeds

One of the biggest buzzes in Web browsing these days (other than *blogs,* a form of Web-published personal journal) is *RSS,* which stands for *Really Simple Syndication* (according to most people who know about it). You see synopses of what's available at the site providing the *RSS feed* — which gives you an adjustable-length overview with a link to the full story. Here's how they work:

1. When a Web page has an RSS feed (that's what the special RSS links are called) associated, you see a little RSS icon at the right end of the address bar, just like the one shown earlier in Figure 9-1.

2. Click it to see all the RSS synopses for the site, as shown in Figure 9-4.

3. Click it again, and the RSS synopses disappear and are replaced by the page contents, as shown earlier in Figure 9-1.

Figure 9-4: The RSS synopses for the Apple start page, shown earlier in Figure 9-1.

If you like this RSS thing (and why wouldn't you?), keep in mind that Safari includes plenty of interesting feeds to choose among. Click the little book icon (below the Back arrow near the top-right corner of the window) and then click the All RSS Feeds collection on the left. A lengthy list of available RSS feeds appears on the right; double-click one or more items in the Bookmark list on the right to see its feed.

Searching with Google

Looking for something on the Internet? Check out Google, a fantastic search engine integrated with Safari to help you hunt down just about anything on the Internet quickly and easily.

In this section, you discover how to use Google to search the Internet and find almost anything, as well as how to get help with Google when all else fails.

To search the Internet with Google, follow these steps:

1. **Merely type a word or phrase in the Google field to the right of the address bar near the top of the Safari window.**

2. **Press Return or Enter to start the search.**

   Google almost immediately offers a list of results, as shown in Figure 9-5.

Figure 9-5:
A Google search for a King Ranch Chicken recipe.

3. **Click one of the result links — they appear in blue and are underlined — and you'll be taken instantly to that particular page.**

4. **If it's not just what you're looking for, click the Back button and try another result link.**

5. **If Google offers too many results that aren't just right, click the Advanced Search link near the top of the results page and refine your search.**

   You can refine your search by using a multitude of options, as shown in Figure 9-6.

6. **Click the Google Search button.**

   A refined results page quickly appears. As before, click a result link to visit that page. If it's not just what you're looking for, click the Back button and try a different result link.

Figure 9-6:
A Google advanced search for a King Ranch Chicken recipe.

One last feature you might like to know about is the drop-down menu that remembers your recent Google searches. Click the triangle next to the magnifying glass in the Google field to see your previous search terms, as shown in Figure 9-7.

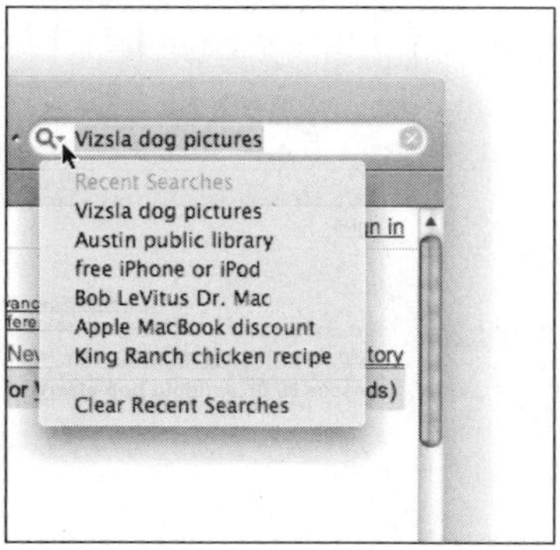

Figure 9-7: Choosing a previous search term from the drop-down menu.

That's pretty much all you need to know to have a great time surfing the Web with Google.

Checking out Help Center

Actually, Safari has a lot more features, and I could write an entire chapter about using Safari, but one of the rules we *For Dummies* authors must follow is that our books can't run 1,000 pages long. So I'm going to give you the next-best thing: Open the Help Center (by choosing Help⇨Safari Help). A special Safari Help window appears; you can search for any Safari-related topic or solution to any Safari-related problem right here.

Communicating via iChat AV

Instant messaging and chat rooms provide for interactive communication among users all over the world. If you're into instant messaging, iChat AV gives you immediate access to all the other users of AIM, Jabber, and .Mac. All you need are their screen names, and you're set to go. You can even join any AOL chat room just by choosing File⇨Go to Chat.

Chit-chatting with iChat

Your text chats can be one to one, or they can be group bull sessions. iChat AV is integrated with the Address Book, so you don't have to enter your buddies' information twice. It also communicates directly with the Mail application. Here's all the essential info you need to get started:

- **To start a chat,** open iChat, select a buddy in your buddy list, and choose Buddies⇨Invite to Chat.

  Each participant's picture (or icon) appears next to anything she says, which is displayed in a cartoon-like thought bubble, as shown in Figure 9-8. If you find the thought bubbles a little too childish, you can turn them off from the View menu.

Figure 9-8:
A chat with myself. (I have two Macs on the same network.)

- **To invite a third or fourth person to your chat,** select the buddy in your buddy list and choose Buddies⇨Invite to Chat.

- **To attach a picture to a person in your Address Book** (as I have for myself with a photo on one Mac and a cartoon image on the other), copy a picture of that person to the Clipboard in your favorite graphics application (Preview, for example). Now open Address Book and display the card for the person you want to add a picture to. Click the empty picture box at the top of the card and paste the picture on the Clipboard. You should now see that picture on the Address Book card and also when you iChat with the person. Neat!

- **To transfer files,** just drag the document's icon to the message box, as demonstrated in Figure 9-9, and press Return or Enter. The file zips across the ether. This is a very convenient way to share photos or documents without resorting to file sharing or e-mail.

- **To send an e-mail from iChat,** just select a buddy in iChat AV's buddy list and then choose Buddies⇨Send Email (or use the keyboard shortcut ⌘+Option+E). Mail launches (if it's not already open) and addresses a new message to the selected buddy, ready for you to begin typing.

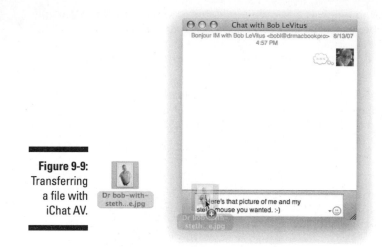

Figure 9-9:
Transferring
a file with
iChat AV.

Dr bob-with–
steth...e.jpg

Gimme an A! Gimme a V!

The greatest iChat feature is audio/video chatting, which is what the *AV* in its name stands for. iChat's audio and video features are easy to set up and use.

The latest enhancement to iChat's AV capabilities is that you can now conference a video chat with up to three other people at the same time and audio chat with up to nine other folks at the same time.

To conduct a video or audio chat:

1. **Connect a FireWire camera and/or a supported microphone to your Mac.**

   Although many FireWire camcorders work fairly well for video chatting, Apple's iSight camera/microphone combination is designed just for this purpose (and works even better in most cases). It's built into all Mac notebooks and iMacs these days, so likely you won't have to buy a thing to video (and audio) chat.

   When you have appropriate hardware connected to your Mac, your buddies' names in the buddy lists display little green telephone or camera icons if they have the right hardware on their end.

2. **To start an audio- or videoconference, click the appropriate green icon(s).**

   Your buddies receive an invitation to begin an audio or video chat.

3. **If they accept the invitation, a Video Chat window appears, as shown in Figure 9-10.**

TIP

If you have an iSight camera or FireWire camcorder handy or if your Mac has a built-in iSight camera, why not give it a try? My chat handle is `boblevitus @mac.com`; feel free to invite me to video chat if you see me online.

Figure 9-10:
I'm iChatting with my buddy Dave Hamilton.

Sending files and messages with Bonjour and iChat

Mac OS X's built-in Bonjour (Apple used to call it Rendezvous) support makes chatting even better. With Bonjour, Mac OS X can automatically recognize others on a local network who are available to chat. So you can send a quick message or files from one computer to another quickly and easily. For example, with Bonjour enabled, I've sent and received messages from/to my AirPort-equipped PowerBook from/to my desktop computer without any network configuration and without having to add anyone to my buddy list manually. Just choose Window⇨Bonjour and select the person with whom you want to chat from the Bonjour window. From there, you can send a message or file.

For Bonjour to connect to another computer, both users need to have Bonjour enabled and must either be connected to the same network or have AirPort for wireless networking built in. Beyond that, the connection is configuration free; you don't have to do anything to be part of a Bonjour network, because your Mac configures itself and joins up automatically.

iChat with Bonjour is also a great, quick way you can send a file from one Mac to another without the bother of setting up file sharing or even adding someone to your buddy list. Just choose Buddies⇨Send File (or use the shortcut ⌘+Option+F) and use iChat instead.

Remote Screen Sharing — remarkable and superbly satisfying

I'd like to call your attention to one last iChat feature. It's called Remote Screen Sharing, and it's brand new and possibly the most useful iChat feature ever. It lets you control another Mac anywhere in the world, or another Mac user can control your Mac from any location.

So now when Mom calls you and says, "I'm trying to get my mail, but the thing that I click disappeared," you don't have to try to decipher her description and explain how to replace the Mail icon in the Dock. Instead, you calmly say to her, "Mom, just open up iChat and let me show you how to fix that." Here's how it works:

1. She launches iChat on her Mac. You launch iChat on yours.

2. She clicks your name in her Buddy list and chooses Buddies⇨Share My Screen (or you click her name in your Buddy list and choose Buddies⇨Share Remote Screen).

3. A window pops up on mom's screen, where she grants you permission to control her screen; once permission is granted, you can see her screen on *your* Mac and control her Mac with your mouse and keyboard.

   More specifically, after she grants you permission, you see a proxy image of her screen that says `Switch to Mom's Computer`, as shown in Figure 9-11. (It actually says `Switch to Bob LeVitus's Computer` in the figure because my mom wasn't available when I shot the figure. So just think of me as Mom for the rest of this exercise, okay?)

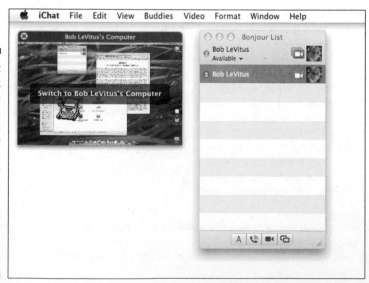

Figure 9-11: If I click anywhere in the Bob LeVitus's Computer window on the left, my screen is replaced by Bob LeVitus's Computer's screen.

4. When I click anywhere in the little Bob LeVitus's (Or Mom's, or Whomever's) Computer window shown on the left in Figure 9-11, my screen changes, and instead of my stuff, I see the remote screen, as shown in Figure 9-12.

5. To go back to my Mac screen, I just click the My Computer window at top left in Figure 9-12, and the remote computer screen disappears and mine comes back.

This is the best way to help another Mac user accomplish anything. In fact, my consulting business has been using similar software to help Mac users for years. It's fantastic to be able to talk to folks on the phone while you're controlling their Mac. You can fix things in a fraction of the time it would take to explain how to do it over the phone alone.

Before you get too excited, there are a few provisos:

✔ You and the other user must both be running Mac OS X 10.5 Leopard.

✔ You and the other user must both have an iChat account (on .Mac, AIM, Jabber, or Google Talk).

✔ You and the other user both need high-speed Internet access.

You can combine this feature with the iChat file-sharing feature described earlier to collaborate with others on documents or projects.

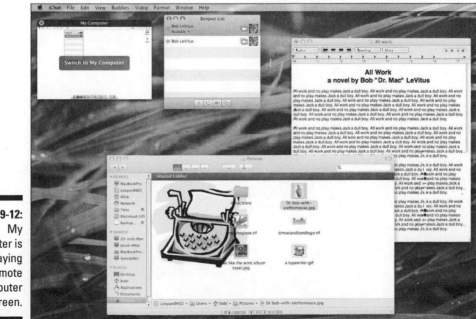

Figure 9-12: My computer is displaying the remote computer screen.

When you share your screen, the person you share it with has the same degree of access to your files that you have. It follows that you should share your screen only with people you deeply trust. Furthermore, if you have files on your Mac that you would prefer the other person didn't see, I suggest you hide them deep in a subfolder somewhere or delete them before you begin your screen-sharing session.

Chapter 10

E-Mail Made Easy

1n this chapter, you look at a pair of programs that work together and make managing your contacts and e-mail a breeze. You find out how both of these eponymous programs — Address Book and Mail — work, and how to use them individually and as a team.

Keeping Contacts Handy with Address Book

The Address Book is where you store contact information for your family, friends, and anyone else you want to keep track of. It works seamlessly with the Mail application, enabling you to quickly look up e-mail addresses when you're ready to send a message.

In fact, Address Book works with several applications, both on and beyond your Mac, including the following:

✔ Use it with iChat (covered in Chapter 9) to quickly chat with your online friends.

✔ Use it with iCal by choosing Window⇨Address Panel or pressing ⌘+Option+A. You can then drag any person in your Address Book from the Address Panel to any date and time on the calendar, and a special Meeting event is created automatically by iCal. The event even has a Send Invitation button — if you click it, it launches Mail and sends the person an invitation to this meeting. Very cool stuff.

✔ The Address Book application can also work with any other application whose programmers choose to make the connection or with any device that is compatible with Address Book. For example, my Sony Ericsson wireless phone can obtain my contact information (wirelessly!) from Address Book through the magic of Bluetooth, as described in Chapter 8.

You can find a list of such devices here: www.apple.com/macosx/features/isync/devices.html.

In the following sections, you find out the best ways to fill Address Book with contacts and keep those contacts organized.

Adding contacts

Follow these steps to create a new entry in the Address Book:

1. **Launch the Address Book application by double-clicking its icon in the Applications folder or clicking its Dock icon.**

   The Address Book appears. The first time that you open Address Book, you see two cards: Apple Computer and the one with the personal identification information you supplied when you created your account.

2. **To create a new entry, click the + button at the bottom of the Address Book's Name column.**

   An untitled address card appears. The First name text field is initially selected. (You can tell because it's highlighted, as shown in Figure 10-1.)

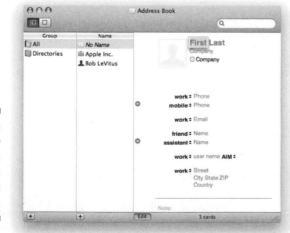

Figure 10-1: A new address card in Address Book.

The little up and down arrows you see in Figure 10-1 between the labels and their contents fields are pop-up menus that offer alternative labels for the field. For example, if you were to click the arrows next to the word *Work,* you could choose Home, Mobile, Main, Home Fax, Work Fax, Pager, Other, or Custom to replace the label Work.

3. **Type the person's first name in the First text field.**

   Here, I type **Doctor**.

4. **Press Tab.**

   Your cursor should now be in the Last text field.

   You can always move from one field to the next by pressing Tab — in fact, this shortcut works in almost all Mac programs that have fields like these. (You can move to the previous field by pressing Shift+Tab.)

5. **Type the last name for the person you're adding to your Address Book.**

   Here, I type **Mac**.

   Continue this process, filling in the rest of the fields shown in Figure 10-2.

6. **When you're done entering information, click the Edit button to exit the editing mode.**

   The contact I created with this step appears in Figure 10-2.

   The little contact card is called a *vCard* (virtual business card).

   To add more info about any Address Book entry, select the name in the Name column (<Doctor Mac> in Figure 10-2. You can tell when a name is selected because it is highlighted, as Doctor Mac is in Figure 10-2. Then click the Edit button at the bottom of the Address Book window, and make your changes.

Repeat this process for everyone you know and want to keep in touch with.

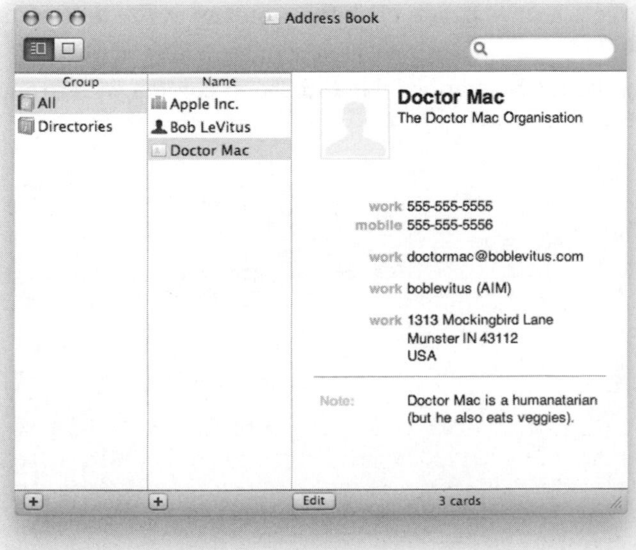

Figure 10-2:
The address card displayed in the Address Book window.

		Address Book	
Group	Name		
All	Apple Inc.	**Doctor Mac**	
Directories	Bob LeVitus	The Doctor Mac Organisation	
	Doctor Mac		

work 555-555-5555
mobile 555-555-5556

work doctormac@boblevitus.com

work boblevitus (AIM)

work 1313 Mockingbird Lane
Munster IN 43112
USA

Note: Doctor Mac is a humanatarian
(but he also eats veggies).

3 cards

Importing contacts from other programs

If you already have contacts you created in another program, you might be able to import them into Address Book. Address Book can import contacts in vCard, LDIF, or Text file format.

The first thing you need to do is export the data from the other program in one of these formats. Then, choose File⇨Import⇨vCard (or LDIF or Text file, as the case may be), choose the exported data file in the Open File dialog, and then click the Open button.

Creating a basic group

Now let me explain how to organize your contacts into groups. Why would you want to organize your contacts into groups? The main reason, at least for me, is that I can send e-mail to everyone in a group that I've defined with a single click. So when it's time to send out a press release, I can simply send it to my Press group, shooting the e-mail off to all 50 people I have in that group. And when I want to send an e-mail to all the parents of kids on my son's indoor football team, I merely address it to my Flag Football Parents group, and all 12 families in that group receive it.

Here's how to create a group and add contacts to it:

1. **Launch the Address Book application by double-clicking its icon in the Applications folder or clicking its Dock icon.**

2. **To create a new group, click the + button at the bottom of the Group column.**

   An untitled Group appears in the Group column with Group Name highlighted, as shown in Figure 10-3.

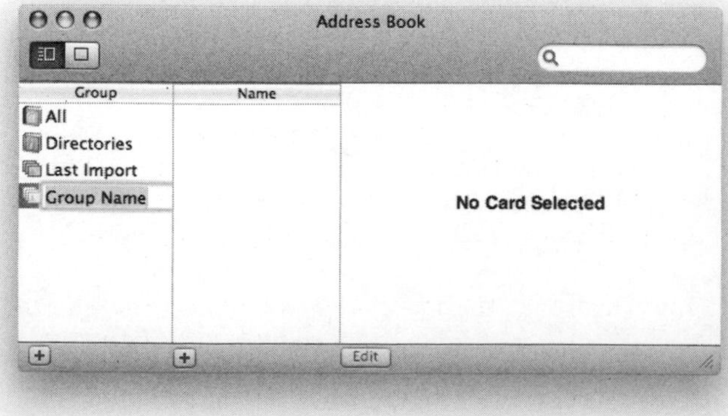

Figure 10-3: A newly created group ready to be named.

3. **Type a descriptive name for this group and then press Enter or Return.**

   I named mine PR, which stands for Public Relations.

4. **Click the All group in the Group column to show all your contacts in the Name column.**

5. **Click the contacts you want in the group in the Name column, holding down the ⌘ key as you click if you want to select more than one contact.**

6. **Drag the selected contact names onto the group, as shown in Figure 10-4.**

   Address Book considerately displays the number of contacts you're dragging, which happens to be two in this instance.

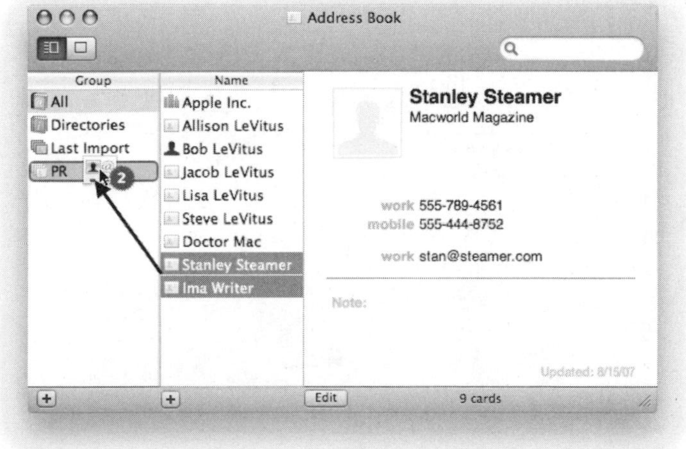

Figure 10-4:
Adding two contacts to the PR group.

And that's all there is to creating your own groups.

Setting up a Smart Group (based on contact criteria)

A second type of group — called a Smart Group — might be even more useful to you. A Smart Group gathers contacts in your Address Book based on criteria you specify. So, for example, you could create a group that automatically selects Apple staff members, as I demonstrate in a moment.

The big advantage of a Smart Group over a regular group is that when I add a new contact who works at Apple, that contact automatically becomes a member of the Smart Group with no further action on my part.

To create a Smart Group, follow these steps:

1. **Choose File⇨ New Smart Group, use its keyboard shortcut (⌘+Option+N), or press the Option key and then click the + button at the bottom of the Group column.**

   A Smart Group sheet appears in front of the Address Book window, as shown in Figure 10-5.

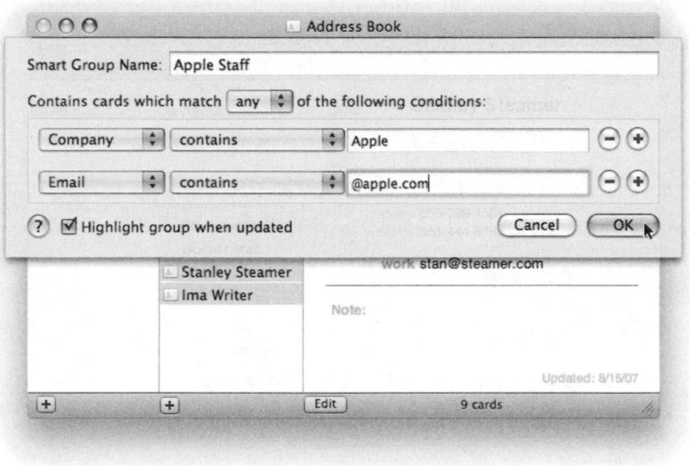

Figure 10-5:
Creating a new Smart Group.

2. **Give the Smart Group a name.**

3. **Select the appropriate items from the menus — Any, Company, Contains, Email, and so on.**

   In Figure 10-5, I've created a Smart Group that includes any contact with Apple in the Company field or `@apple.com` in any e-mail field.

4. **When you're happy with the criteria specified, click OK.**

To delete a contact, group, or Smart Group from your Address Book, click to select it and then press Delete or Backspace.

Sending e-mail to a contact or group

This section looks at how you can create and send an e-mail message to a contact or group in your Address Book.

You don't even have to open Address Book to send an e-mail to a contact or group contained in your Address Book. In the next section, you see how Mail finds contacts or groups for you without launching Address Book. But if you already have Address Book open, this technique for sending e-mail to a contact or group is probably most convenient.

To create a blank e-mail message to a contact, click and hold the label next to the e-mail address and choose Send Email from the pop-up menu that appears, as shown in Figure 10-6.

Figure 10-6:
Sending
e-mail to
someone
in your
Address
Book is as
easy as
clicking
here.

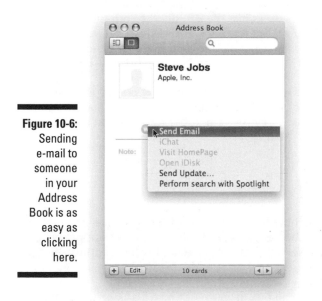

The Mail program becomes active, and a blank e-mail message addressed to the selected contact appears on your screen. Just type your e-mail as you normally would.

In Figure 10-6, I've hidden the Group and Name columns by clicking the little square button just below the yellow and green gumdrop buttons. To make the columns reappear, click the button just to the left — the little square with lines on its left side (to represent the Group and Name columns). The buttons in the margin on the left are the ones I'm talking about.

Sending and Receiving E-Mail with Mail

Mail is a program for sending, receiving, and organizing your e-mail.

Mail is fast and easy to use, too. Click the Mail icon in the Dock or double-click the Mail icon in the Applications folder to launch Mail. The Mail icon looks like a canceled postage stamp, as shown in the margin.

You can use other applications to read Internet mail. Mozilla (Thunderbird) and AOL, for example, have their own mail readers, as does Microsoft Office (Entourage). And lots of power users like the BBEdit-like editing features in MailSmith (BareBones Software). But for Macs, the easiest and best mail reader around (meaning the best one on your hard drive by default) is almost certainly Mail. And of course, you can't beat the price — it's free!

The following sections, in some cases, offer you starting points. Even so, you should find everything perfectly straightforward. If you run into a question that the following sections don't answer, remember that you can always call upon the assistance of Help⇨Mail Help.

Setting Up Mail

If this is your first time launching Mail, you need to set up your e-mail account before you can proceed. A set of New Account screens appears automatically. Just fill in the blanks on each screen and click the Continue button until you're finished.

If you don't know what to type in one or more of these blank fields, contact your ISP (Internet service provider) or mail provider for assistance.

After you've set up one or more e-mail accounts, you see a Welcome message asking whether you'd like to see what's new in Mail. If you click Yes, Help Viewer launches and shows you the What's New in Mail page, while Mail's main window, which looks like Figure 10-7, appears in the background. Or if you click No, Mail's main window appears as the active window immediately.

Mail's main window is actually called a *viewer window* or *message viewer window.* You can have more than one of them on your screen, if you like — just choose File⇨New Viewer Window or press ⌘+Option+N.

Composing a new message

Here's how to create a new e-mail message:

1. Choose File ⇨ New Message, click the New button on the toolbar, or press ⌘+N.

A new window appears; this is where you compose your e-mail message, as shown in Figure 10-8.

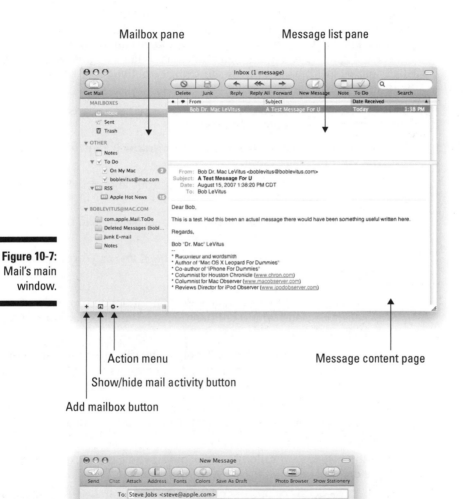

Mailbox pane

Message list pane

Action menu

Show/hide mail activity button

Add mailbox button

Message content page

Figure 10-7: Mail's main window.

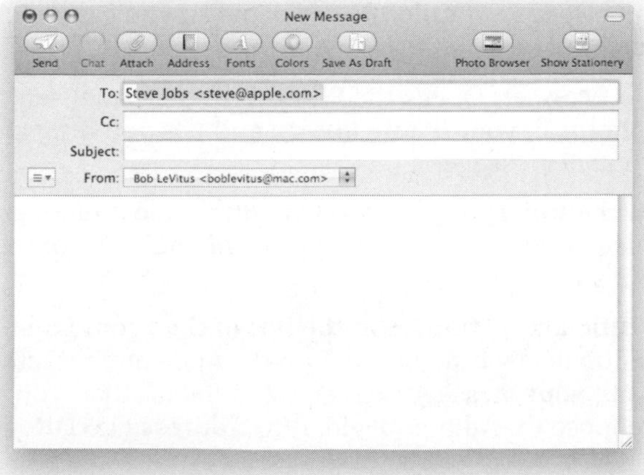

Figure 10-8: Composing an e-mail message.

2. **Place your cursor in the To field and type someone's e-mail address.**

   Use my address (Leopard4Dummies@boblevitus.com) if you don't know anyone else to send mail to.

   If the recipient is already in your Address Book (as Steve Jobs is in mine), Mail will automatically complete the addressee's name after you've typed a few characters. So, for example, in Figure 10-8 I typed *st,* and Mail filled in the rest, *eve Jobs <Steve@apple.com>,* which is high-lighted in Figure 10-8. If more than one contact name begins with *st,* a list of all contacts with names that begin with *st* would appear below the To field. Neat, huh?

3. **Press the Tab key twice to move your cursor to the Subject text field and then type a subject for this message.**

4. **Click in the main message portion of the window (refer to Figure 10-8) and type your message there.**

   Just for the record, here's what the other buttons shown in Figure 10-8 are all about:

   • **Attach:** Opens a standard Open File sheet so you can pick a file or files to enclose with this message.

     To enclose multiple files, hold down the ⌘ key as you click each file you want to enclose.

     If the recipient of this message uses Windows, you probably want to select the Send Windows-Friendly Attachments check box at the bottom of the Open File sheet.

   • **Address:** Opens the Address Panel, a miniature representation of your Address Book. You can then drag contacts or groups from the Address Panel to the To or CC field of the message.

   • **Fonts:** Opens the Fonts panel, where you can change the font type-face, size, color, underline, strikethrough, shadow, document color, and more.

   • **Colors:** Opens the Color Picker panel so you can quickly change the color of selected text in your message.

   • **Photo Browser:** Opens the Photo Browser panel, which displays the photos in your iPhoto library and lets you drag and drop them into a mail message.

   • **Show Stationery:** Opens a sheet with a selection of stationery you can use for your e-mail message. (You find out more about this fea-ture in a few pages.)

   • **The little arrow thingie to the left of the From pop-up menu:** This little doohickey is actually a pop-down menu that lets you add fields to your message header. What fields? Glad you asked. . . . You can choose CC Address Field, BCC Address Field, Reply-To Address

Field, or Priority Field. Or if you choose Customize, you see all the available fields with check boxes next to them so you can turn them on or off at will.

Note that changes you make using this menu become the default. In other words, if you add a BCC field to this message, all subsequent messages also have a BCC field.

5. **When you're finished writing your message, click the Send button to send the e-mail immediately or choose File⇨Save to save it in the Drafts mailbox so you can work on it later.**

If you save your message to the Drafts mailbox (so you can write more later, perhaps), you can send it when you're ready by opening the Drafts mailbox, double-clicking the message, and then clicking the Send button.

A quick overview of the toolbar

Before you go any further, look at the nine handy buttons on the viewer window's toolbar by default:

- ✔ **Delete:** Deletes selected message or messages ("A test message for U" in Figure 10-7, shown earlier).

  To select more than one message in the list, hold down the ⌘ key when you click the second and subsequent messages.

- ✔ **Junk:** Marks the selected message or messages as junk mail. Mail has built-in junk-mail filtering that can be enabled or disabled in Mail Preferences. (Choose Mail⇨Preferences and then click the Junk Mail icon on the toolbar.) If you receive a piece of *spam* (junk mail), select it and click this button to help train Mail's junk-mail filter.

  If a message has been marked as junk mail, the button changes to read Not Junk.

  For more info on junk-mail filtering, click the question-mark button in the Junk Mail pane of the Mail Preferences window.

- ✔ **Reply:** Creates a reply to the sender only.

- ✔ **Reply All:** Creates a reply to the sender and everyone on the CC list.

- ✔ **Forward:** Creates a copy of this message you can send to someone other than the sender or other recipients.

- ✔ **New:** Creates a new, blank e-mail message.

- ✔ **Get Mail:** Checks for new e-mail.

✔ **Note:** Creates a new, blank note. You can write yourself a note (or copy and paste information into a note) and save it for future reference. By default, it's placed in the Notes mailbox when you save it, but you can drag it into any mailbox you like.

✔ **To Do:** Creates a new To Do item, puts a copy in Mail's To Do mailbox, and adds it to your To Do list in iCal. (See Chapter 8 for details about To Do items in iCal.)

Finally, on the toolbar is a Search field that finds a word or phrase in any item stored in Mail, as shown in Figure 10-9. Click the buttons at the top of the list pane to limit your search to specific mailboxes or to search only specific parts (From, To, Subject, and so on) of messages.

Searching in Mail should be familiar to you — it works the same way as searching in the Finder. So, for example, if you want to save a search as a Smart Mailbox (Mail's version of a Smart Folder in the Finder), you click the Save button.

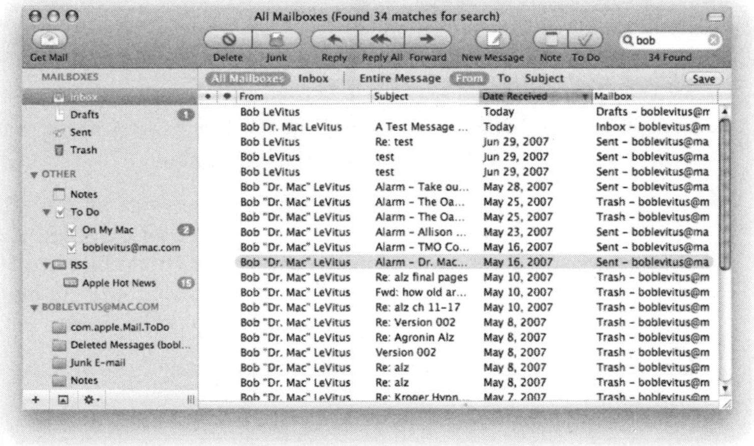

Figure 10-9:
Searching
for items
from
"bob" in all
mailboxes
reveals
34 items.

Working with stationery

Stationery for e-mail messages is new in Leopard, and although I personally find it dorky, you might think it's the greatest thing since kittens, so here are some tips for working with it. To use it, click the Show Stationery button in a New Message window.

I'm a Luddite when it comes to e-mail. When I started using e-mail a long, long time ago, it was considered bad form to add anything but text to an e-mail message. It was generally agreed that e-mail messages should include only what was necessary to convey the information and nothing more. That's why all these froufrou flowers and borders irritate me and why I find them a waste of bandwidth. So please do me a favor: If you decide to send me an e-mail message, please don't use goofy stationery.

Here are some tips to help you have more fun with stationery:

- ✔ **Adding favorites:** If you find you're using a particular stationery a lot, you can add it to the Favorites category to make it easier to use. To do so, merely click the appropriate category in the list on the left (Simple, Photos, Greetings, or Invitations); then click the stationery you want to make a favorite and drag it onto the word *Favorites* in the list on the left. When *Favorites* highlights, drop the stationery, and presto — that piece of stationery will appear in the Favorites category evermore.

- ✔ **Greeking out:** You can change the Greek text that appears in all the stationery by selecting it, deleting it, and typing whatever text you want to appear. You have to do it only once — the text you type in any stationery appears in all other stationaries.

- ✔ **Replacing pictures:** You can replace any picture in any stationery with a picture of your own. Just drag a picture — from the Photo Browser (Window➪Photo Browser) or the Finder — onto any picture in any piece of stationery. I've replaced the boilerplate text and all three of the dorky pictures in the Air Mail stationery, as you can see in Figure 10-10.

- ✔ **Removing stationery:** If you decide you don't want to use stationery with a message after you've applied it, click the Simple category and choose the Original stationery, which changes the message back to a clean, blank page.

Figure 10-10:
Drag and drop your own pictures anywhere you see a picture in a stationery.

Checking your mail

How do you check and open your mail? Easy. Just click the Get Mail button at the top of the main Mail window (refer to Figure 10-9).

✔ **To read a new message,** select it. Its contents appear in the Message Content pane.

✔ **To delete a selected message,** click the Delete button on the toolbar.

✔ **To retrieve a message you accidentally deleted,** click Trash on the left and drag the message into the Inbox or other mailbox.

✔ **To configure Mail to send and check for your mail every *X* minutes,** choose Mail⇨Preferences and then click the General icon at the top of the window. Pull down the Check for New Mail pop-up menu and make a selection — every 1, 5, 15, 30, or 60 minutes — or choose Manually if you don't want Mail to check for mail automatically at all. (The default setting is to check for mail every five minutes.)

✔ **To add a sender to Address Book,** when someone who isn't already in your Address Book sends you an e-mail message, simply choose Message⇨Add Sender to Address Book (shortcut: ⌘+Y).

Adding a sender to your Address Book has an additional benefit: It guards messages from that person against being mistaken for junk mail. In other words, your Address Book is a *white list* for the spam filter; if specific senders appear in your Address Book, their messages will never be mistakenly marked as junk mail.

Dealing with spam

Speaking of junk mail, although e-mail is a wonderful thing, some people out there try to spoil it. They're called *spammers,* and they're lowlifes who share their lists among themselves — and before you know it, your e-mail box is flooded with get-rich-quick schemes, advertisements for pornographic Web sites and chat rooms, and all the more traditional buy-me junk mail.

Fortunately, Mail comes with a Junk Mail filter that analyzes incoming message subjects, senders, and contents to determine which ones are likely to contain bulk or junk mail. When you open Mail for the first time, it's running in its training mode, which is how Mail learns to differentiate between what it considers junk mail and what you consider junk mail; all it needs is your input. Mail identifies messages it thinks are junk, but if you disagree with its decisions, here's what you do:

✔ Click the Not Junk button in the brown bar for any message that *isn't* junk mail.

✔ Conversely, if a piece of junk mail slips past Mail's filters and ends up in the Inbox, select the message and then click the Junk button in the Mail window's toolbar.

After a few days (or weeks, depending upon your mail volume), Mail should be getting it right almost all the time. When you reach that point, choose Automatic mode on the Junk Mail tab of Mail's preferences pane. Mail starts moving junk mail automatically out of your Inbox and into a Junk mailbox, where you can scan the items quickly and trash them when you're ready.

If (for some reason that escapes me) you prefer to receive and manually process your junk mail, you can turn off junk-mail processing by disabling it on the Junk Mail tab of Mail's preferences pane.

Changing your preferences

Actually, Mail's preferences are more than you might expect from the name. This is the control center for Mail, where you can

✔ Create and delete e-mail accounts.

✔ Determine which fonts and colors are used for your messages.

✔ Decide whether to download and save attachments (such as pictures).

✔ Decide whether to send formatted mail or plain text.

✔ Decide whether to turn on the spell checker.

The default is to check spelling as you type, which many people (myself included) find annoying.

✔ Decide whether to have an automatic signature appended to your messages.

✔ Establish rules to process mail that you receive.

Mail rules rule

If you really want to tap the power of Mail, you need to set *rules*. With some cool rules, you can automatically tag messages with a color; file them in a specific mailbox; reply to/forward/redirect the messages automatically (handy when you're going to be away for a while); automatically reply to messages; and *kill-file* messages (just delete them without even bothering to look at them — what better fate for mail from people you hate?).

There's no way I can do rules justice in the few pages I have left for this chapter, but here's a quick look at how to create one:

1. **Choose Mail ⇨ Preferences.**

2. **Click the Rules icon on the toolbar of the Preferences window.**

3. **Click the Add Rule button.**

   The first condition should say From in its first pop-up menu and Contains in its second pop-up menu. Look at your options in these menus but return them to their original state — From and Contains — when you're done looking.

4. **In the field to the right of the Contains pop-up menu, type** LeVitus.

   Below the condition you just created, you should see an action under the words *Perform the Following Actions*. It should say Move Message in its first pop-up menu and No Mailbox Selected in its second pop-up menu.

5. **Look at the options on these menus, but this time, change the first one from Move Message to Play Sound and the second one from No Mailbox Selected to Blow.**

6. **Type a description of the rule, such as** Message from LeVitus, **in the Description field.**

   Your rule should look identical to Figure 10-11 now.

7. **Click OK.**

   Mail asks whether you want to apply your rule(s) to the selected mailboxes.

8. **Choose Apply if you want Mail to run this rule on the selected mailboxes or choose Don't Apply if you don't.**

   And that's how you build a rule. From this point forward, every time you get a message from me, you hear the Blow sound.

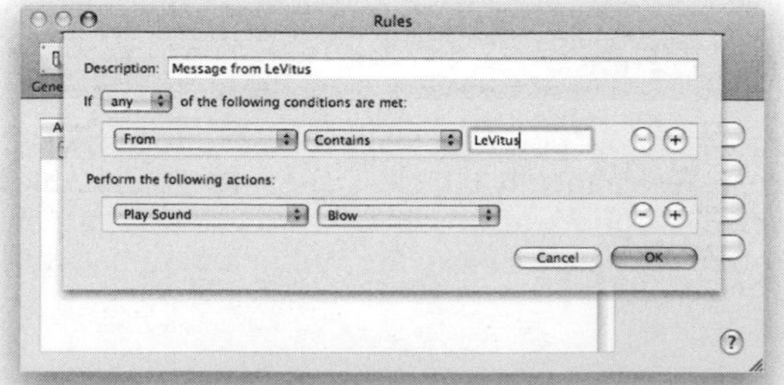

Figure 10-11:
When
you get a
message
from me,
Mail plays
the Blow
sound.

Notice the little + (plus) and – (minus) buttons to the right of each condition and action. Use the + button to add more conditions or actions and the – button to delete a condition or action. If you have multiple conditions, you can choose Any or All from the pop-up menu above them, which executes this rule when either any of the conditions or all of the conditions are met. Either way, all the actions you create are always executed when this rule is triggered.

Mailboxes smart and plain

The following sections take a closer look at both types of mailboxes — plain and smart.

Plain old mailboxes

Plain mailboxes are just like folders in the Finder — you create them and name them, and they're empty until you put something in them. They even look like folders in Mail's mailbox pane. You use mailboxes to organize any messages you want to save.

Here are several ways to create a plain mailbox:

- Choose Mailbox⇨New Mailbox.
- Click the little + sign at the bottom of the mailbox pane on the left side of the viewer window.
- Click the Action menu at the bottom of the mailbox pane (the one that looks like a gear) and choose New Mailbox.
- Right-click or Control+click in the mailbox pane and choose New Mailbox from the contextual menu.

Whichever way you choose, the next thing that happens is that a sheet drops down with a Location pop-up menu and a field for you to type the name you want to give this mailbox. Choose On My Mac from the Location menu and name the mailbox anything you like. Click OK, and the mailbox is created in the mailbox pane.

You can create mailboxes inside other mailboxes to further subdivide your messages. To do so, click a mailbox to select it before you create a new mailbox using any of the techniques in the preceding list.

In Figure 10-12, I've divided my Books mailbox into three submailboxes: Dr. Mac: The OS X Files, iPhone For Dummies, and Mac OS X Leopard For Dummies.

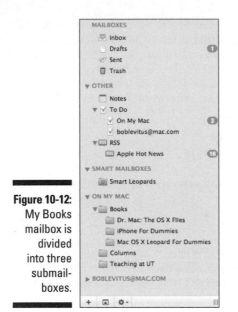

Figure 10-12:
My Books mailbox is divided into three submail-boxes.

You can also drag and drop a mailbox from the top level of the list (such as Columns or Teaching in Figure 10-12) onto another mailbox (such as Books or any of its three submailboxes) to make them submailboxes. If you drag a mailbox into a submailbox, it becomes a sub-submailbox. And so on.

To delete a mailbox, click it to select it and then

- ✔ Choose Mailbox➪Delete.
- ✔ Click the Action menu at the bottom of the mailbox pane (the one that looks like a gear) and choose Delete.

Intelligent smart mailboxes

A smart mailbox is Mail's version of the Finder's smart folder. In a nutshell, smart mailboxes are mailboxes that display the results of a search. The mes-sages you see in a smart mailbox are *virtual,* meaning that they aren't really in the smart mailbox itself. The smart mailbox displays a list of messages stored in other mailboxes that match whatever criteria you've defined for that smart folder. And like smart folders in the Finder, smart mailboxes update automati-cally when new messages that meet the criteria are received.

Here are several ways to create a smart mailbox:

- ✔ Choose Mailbox➪New Smart Mailbox.
- ✔ Hold down Option and click the little + sign at the bottom of the mailbox pane on the left side of the viewer window.

✔ Click the Action menu at the bottom of the mailbox pane (the one that looks like a gear) and choose New Mailbox.

✔ Right-click or Control+click in the mailbox pane and choose New Mailbox from the contextual menu.

Whichever way you choose, the next thing that happens is that a sheet drops down with a field for the smart mailbox's name, plus some pop-up menus, buttons, and check boxes, as shown in Figure 10-13.

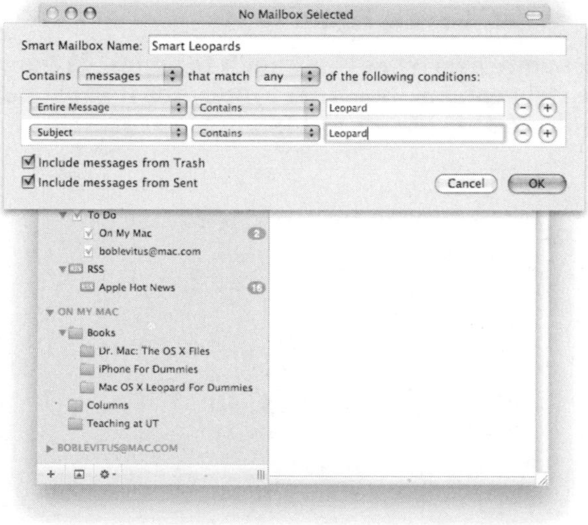

Figure 10-13: This smart mailbox gathers messages with the word *Leopard* in their body or subject.

Name your smart mailbox; determine its criteria by using the pop-up menus, plus and minus buttons, and check boxes; and then click OK. The smart folder appears in the mailbox pane with a little gear on it to denote that it's smart. You can see the Smart Leopards smart mailbox in Figure 10-12. Notice that it has a gear, and plain mailboxes don't.

Sign here, please

If you're like me, you'd rather not type your whole "signature" every time you send an e-mail message. And you don't have to with Mail. If you create canned signatures, you can use them in outgoing messages without typing a single character.

Here's how it works:

1. **Choose Mail⇨Preferences or use the shortcut ⌘+, (that's ⌘+comma).**

2. **Click the Signatures icon in the Preferences window's toolbar.**

3. **Click the name of the mail account you want to create this signature for in the left column (boblevitus@mac.com in Figure 10-14).**

4. **Click the little + sign at the bottom of the middle column to create a new, blank signature.**

5. **Type a descriptive name for this signature to replace the default name Signature #1 (BL Long in Figure 10-14).**

6. **Type the signature exactly as you want it to appear in outgoing messages in the right column. (Regards, Bob "Dr. Mac" LeVitus -- * Raconteur etc. in Figure 10-14).**

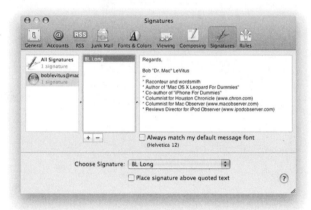

Figure 10-14:
My newly
created
BL Long
signature.

That's about it for signatures. If you have more than one signature, you can choose the one you want to use as the default for each account by selecting the account in the column on the left and then choosing the appropriate signature from the Choose Signature pop-up menu.

If you have more than one signature, another cool thing happens: A Signature menu appears in new messages, as shown in Figure 10-15, so you can choose a signature other than the one you chose from the pop-up menu as the default, if you like (BL Short in Figure 10-15).

Figure 10-15:
Choosing
my BL Short
signature
from the
Signature
menu.

(Slide) show me the photos

One last cool feature, and you're finished with Mail. That cool new feature
is the Slideshow button, which appears in the header of any message you
receive that contains more than one picture. If you click the Slideshow
button, your screen turns black with a photo in the middle of it and a set of
control buttons — Back, Play, Next, Index Sheet, Fit to Screen, Add to iPhoto,
and Close — beneath the photo, as shown in Figure 10-16.

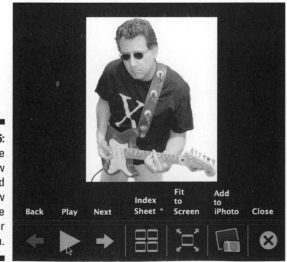

Figure 10-16:
Click the
Slideshow
button, and
a slide show
like this one
fills your
screen.

Here's the lowdown on those buttons:

- ✔ **Play/Pause:** Click this button to start or pause the slide show. It displays each of the enclosed pictures for around five seconds with a smooth dissolve transition between them.

- ✔ **Back/Next:** Click these buttons to see the previous or next picture.

- ✔ **Index Sheet:** Displays all the enclosed pictures at the same time, shrinking them to a smaller size if necessary to fit them all on the screen. Click a picture once to see its name; click a picture twice to display it full screen.

- ✔ **Fit to Screen:** Adjusts the picture so it fills the screen.

- ✔ **Add to iPhoto:** Click this button to cause your Mac to melt down into a steaming heap of molten slag. Just kidding. As you probably guessed, this button adds the current picture to your iPhoto library.

- ✔ **Close:** Exits the slide show.

So there you have it — most of what you need to know to get the most out of Leopard's Address Book and Mail programs. I cover a lot of material in not a lot of space, so if there's something you want to find out about Address Book or Mail that I don't cover in this chapter, don't forget about the wonderful assistance you can find in Help⇨Mail Help.

Chapter 11

The Musical Mac

A long time ago, before the iPod and the iTunes Store were born, iTunes was a program you used to store and manage your MP3 music files. Over the ensuing years, it has grown into much more. Today, iTunes not only manages your music collection, but manages your video collection as well. And if you use devices such as an iPod, Apple TV, or iPhone, you manage *them* using iTunes, too.

In fact, today iTunes does so much more than manage your tunes that I'm surprised Apple hasn't renamed it iMedia, iAV, or something like that.

So the anachronistically named iTunes is the program you use to manage audio and video files on your hard drive as well as your iPod, Apple TV, or iPhone devices.

Although entire books have been dedicated to iTunes alone, I share the most important stuff — the handful of things you really need to know — in this chapter.

Introducing iTunes

iTunes has to be the Swiss Army knife of multimedia software. After all, what other program lets you play audio CDs; create (burn) your own audio or MP3 CDs; listen to MP3, AIFF, AAC, WAV, and Audible.com files; view album cover art; enjoy pretty visual displays; view and manage TV shows, movies, and other video files; manage iPods (or other MP3 players), Apple TVs, and/or iPhones; listen to Internet radio stations; and more? On top of all that, it's your interface to the Apple iTunes Store, the world's leading (legitimate) source of downloadable music and video content. (Whew!)

I start with an overview of iTunes interface elements, as shown in Figure 11-1.

In a nutshell, whatever you select in the Source List on the left is reflected in the main list on the right. In Figure 11-1, the Music library is selected. At the bottom of the window, you can see that there are 4,194 items in my Music library, which would take 13.2 days to listen to from start to finish and uses 19.3GB of space on my hard drive.

Rather than try to explain what every item shown in Figure 11-1 does, I encourage you to click anything and everything you see in the main iTunes window. Experiment with the views, show and hide the browser and album art, click different items in the Source List, and see what happens.

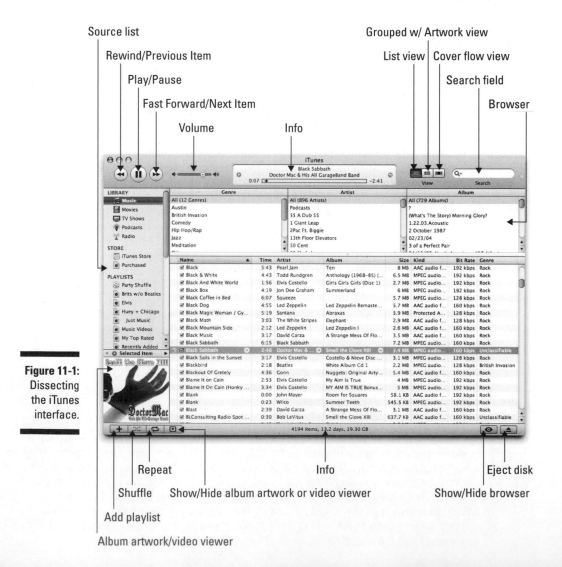

Figure 11-1:
Dissecting
the iTunes
interface.

I'd like you to take note of a few other items:

- ✔ iTunes offers a ten-band graphic equalizer that can make your music (or video) sound significantly better. Just choose View➪Show Equalizer to invoke it on-screen. You can see the equalizer in the lower part of Figure 11-2.

- ✔ Another cool feature is that iTunes main window shrinks to a much more manageable size when you click its green gumdrop button, as shown in the upper part of Figure 11-2. Click the green gumdrop again to expand it back to its normal size.

- ✔ Don't miss the iTunes Visualizer, which offers a groovy light show that dances in time to the music, as shown in Figure 11-3. You turn it on by choosing View➪Turn on Visualizer or using the keyboard shortcut ⌘+T.

Figure 11-2: The iTunes equalizer and minimized main window.

Figure 11-3: The iTunes psychedelic light show is known as the Visualizer.

When you get sick of the Visualizer (as you surely will), just choose View➪Turn off Visualizer or use the keyboard shortcut ⌘+T to make it disappear.

If you like the Visualizer, you can find tons of free and inexpensive third-party Visualizer plug-ins at sites like VersionTracker (www.versiontracker.com).

Working with Media

iTunes is first and foremost a media manager and player, so the next thing I examine is how to get your favorite media *into* iTunes. Of course, there are a number of ways, depending upon the type of media and where the files reside. For example, you can add song or video files you've downloaded from Web sites or received as enclosures in e-mail messages. Or you can add songs by ripping audio CDs. You can buy music, movies, TV shows, audiobooks, and iPod games at the iTunes Store. You can subscribe to free podcasts at the iTunes Store as well. And you can listen all sorts of music on the Internet radio stations included with iTunes.

Note that the iTunes Store and Internet radio require that you be connected to the Internet before you can use them. And although both work over a dial-up Internet connection (more or less), both features work much better when used over a broadband connection.

In the following sections, you discover the various ways to add media — songs, movies, videos, and podcasts — to your iTunes library, followed by a quick course in listening to iTunes Internet radio stations.

Adding songs

You can add songs from pretty much any source, and the way you add a song to iTunes depends on where that song comes from. Here are the most common ways people add their songs:

✔ **To add a song file such as an MP3 or AAC document from your hard drive,** either drag the document into the iTunes window, as shown in Figure 11-4, or choose File⇨Import (shortcut: ⌘+Shift+O) and choose the file in the Open File dialog. In either case, the file is added to your iTunes Music library.

✔ **If you want to add songs from a store-bought or homemade audio CD,** launch iTunes and insert the CD. A dialog should appear, asking whether you would like to import the CD into your iTunes library. Click the Yes button, and the songs on that CD are added to your iTunes Music library.

Figure 11-4: Drag-and-drop songs to the iTunes window to add them to your Music library.

If you don't see a dialog when you insert an audio CD, you can import the songs on that CD anyway. Just select the CD in the Source List on the left, and click the Import button near the bottom-right corner of the iTunes window.

If your computer is connected to the Internet, iTunes magically looks up the song title, artist name, album name, song length, and genre for every song on the CD. Note that this works only for store-bought CDs containing somewhat popular music and that iTunes might not be able to find information about a very obscure CD by an even more obscure band, even if it is store bought. And in most cases, it can't look up information for homemade (home-burned) audio CDs.

✔ **The final way you can get your songs into iTunes is to buy them from the iTunes Store.** To do it, first click the iTunes Store option in the Source List on the left. From the iTunes Store's home screen, you can either click a link or type a song title, album title, artist name, or keyword or phrase in the Search field and then press Return or Enter to start the search.

When you've found an item that interests you, you can double-click any song to listen to a 30-second preview of it or click the Buy Song or Buy Album button to purchase the song or album, as shown in Figure 11-5.

The first time you make a purchase from the iTunes Store, you have to create an Apple account, if you don't already have one. To do so, just click the Sign In button and then click the Create New Account button in the Sign In dialog. After your account is established, future purchases require just one or two clicks.

Click here to shop   Buy Album button   Search field

Sign In button

Figure 11-5:
At the
iTunes
Store,
buying a
song is as
easy as
clicking the
Buy Song
button.

Buy song button

Adding movies and videos

To add a video file such as an MOV or MPEG document from your hard drive, either drag the document to the iTunes window, as shown in Figure 11-4, earlier in this chapter, or choose File⇨Import (shortcut: ⌘+Shift+O) and choose the file in the Open File dialog. In either case, the file is added to your iTunes Movie library.

You can also buy movies, TV shows, and other video content from the iTunes Store. Shopping for video is almost the same as shopping for music. Here are the steps:

1. **Click the iTunes Store in the Source List on the left.**

2. **Either click a link or type a movie title, music-video name, actor or director name, or other keyword or phrase in the Search field. Press Return or Enter to start the search.**

3. **When you find a video item that interests you, double-click it to see a 30-second preview or click the Buy Episode or Buy Video button to purchase the episode or video.**

Adding podcasts

Podcasts are like radio shows, but you can subscribe and listen to them, using iTunes or your iPod, at any time you like. Thousands of podcasts are available, and many (or most) are free.

To find podcasts, follow these steps:

1. **Click the iTunes Store in the Source List on the left.**

2. **Click the Podcasts link on the store's home screen.**

3. **Click a link on the Podcasts screen or type a keyword or phrase in the Search field.**

4. **When you find a podcast that appeals to you, double-click it to listen to a preview, click the Get Episode button to download the current episode of that podcast, or click the Subscribe button to receive all future episodes of that podcast automatically.**

   Figure 11-6 shows all of these things for Car Talk's Call of the Week podcast from National Public Radio.

   For more information on most podcasts, click the little *i* button on the right side of the description field to see the details, as shown in Figure 11-7.

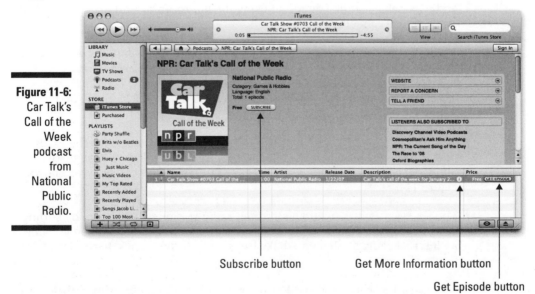

Figure 11-6: Car Talk's Call of the Week podcast from National Public Radio.

Subscribe button   Get More Information button

Get Episode button

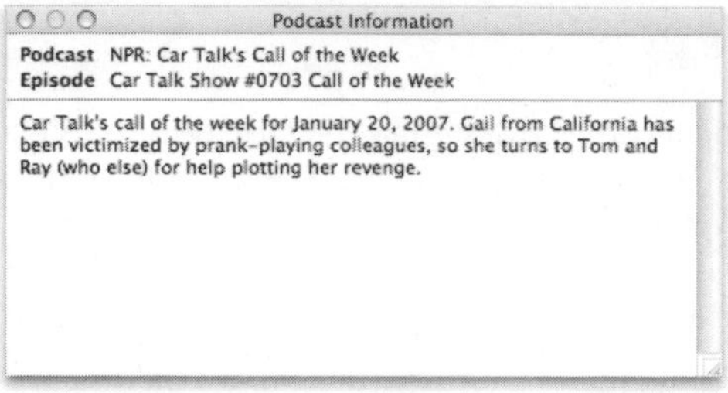

Figure 11-7:
More
information
about Car
Talk's Call of
the Week
podcast.

○ ○ ○   Podcast Information
Podcast NPR: Car Talk's Call of the Week
Episode Car Talk Show #0703 Call of the Week

Car Talk's call of the week for January 20, 2007. Gail from California has
been victimized by prank-playing colleagues, so she turns to Tom and
Ray (who else) for help plotting her revenge.

If you're interested in things Macintosh (and you probably are if you're reading this book), check out the MacNotables podcast, which features an all-star cast of Mac book authors, feature writers, columnists, and editors (sometimes even including yours truly), who get together to discuss what's new and interesting in Macintosh computing at least once a week. Hosted by the ever-inquisitive Chuck Joiner, it's worth a try, if I do say so myself. Search for MacNotables at the iTunes Store or visit www.macnotables.com to check it out.

Listening to Internet radio

Streaming audio is delivered over the Internet in real time. Think of streaming audio as being just like radio but using the Internet rather than the airwaves as its delivery mechanism.

There are two ways to listen to streaming Internet radio stations with iTunes: the easy way and the less easy way. The easy way is to listen to one of the hundreds of Internet radio stations included with iTunes. They're even organized into convenient categories such as Alt/Modern Rock, Blues, Country, Jazz, Public, Top 40/Pop, Urban, and many more.

To listen to one of iTunes' included Internet radio stations, click the Radio item in the Source List on the left and then click a disclosure triangle to the left of each category name to reveal the stations in that category, as shown in Figure 11-8.

The less easy way is to find an Internet radio station on your own by surfing or searching the Web using Safari (or another Web browser). When you find an Internet radio station you'd like to listen to using iTunes, here's how to get it into iTunes:

1. **Copy its address (its URL) by highlighting it and choosing Edit ⇨ Copy (shortcut: ⌘+C).**

2. **Switch to (or launch) iTunes.**

3. **Choose Advanced ⇨ Open Stream (shortcut: ⌘+U).**

4. **Choose Edit⇨Paste (shortcut: ⌘+V).**

5. **Click OK.**

The station appears in your iTunes library.

Figure 11-8: Listening to Rock & Roll.fm, one of 28 streams in the Classic Rock category.

Strangely, there's no way to make an Internet radio station you've added yourself appear in iTunes' Radio category. Apparently, only Apple is allowed to decide what is and is not "radio." Harrumph.

All About Playlists

Playlists are a big deal in iTunes. Playlists let you manage unmanageable amounts of media, like the 4,000+ songs I have in my iTunes library. Playlists let you create subsets of a large collection, so it's easier to enjoy exactly the kind of music you want in iTunes or on your iPod.

Two types of playlists exist:

✔ **Regular playlists** contain the songs (or videos, podcasts, or radio stations) that you specify by dragging them to the playlist.

✔ **Smart playlists,** on the other hand, select songs from your library based on criteria you specify. Furthermore, smart playlists are updated automatically if you add new items to your library that meet the criteria.

Creating a regular playlist

To create a regular playlist, follow these steps:

1. **Either click the + button in the lower-left corner of the iTunes window or choose File⇨New Playlist (shortcut: ⌘+N).**

   A new playlist named "untitled playlist" appears in the Source List.

2. **(Optional) To rename the playlist something meaningful, click its name to highlight it and then type the new name.**

3. **To add a song to a playlist, click the song in your library and then drag it to the playlist's name. When the playlist's name highlights, release the mouse button.**

   The song is added to that playlist. Note that adding a song to a playlist doesn't remove it from the library. So if you delete a song from a playlist, the song isn't deleted from your library. And if you delete a playlist from the Source List, the songs it contains aren't deleted from your library. In other words, think of songs in playlists as being aliases of songs in your library.

4. **When you're done, all you have to do is select the playlist in your Source List and click Play to listen to the songs it contains.**

If you don't want to drag songs to your playlist one by one, there's an easier way. To create a regular playlist that includes songs you've selected from your library, ⌘+click the songs you want to include in the playlist and choose File⇨New Playlist from Selection (shortcut: ⌘+Shift+N), as shown in Figure 11-9.

Figure 11-9:
How to
create a
playlist
from songs
you've
selected in
your Music
library.

Working with smart playlists

To create a smart playlist that builds a list based on criteria and updates itself automatically, follow these steps:

1. **Either Option+click the + button in the lower-left corner of the iTunes window or choose File➪New Smart Playlist (shortcut: ⌘+Option+N).**

   The Smart Playlist window appears, as shown in Figure 11-10.

2. **Use the pop-up menus to select the criteria that will build your smart playlist. Click the + button to add more criteria.**

3. **Click OK when you're done.**

   The playlist appears alongside your other playlists in the Source List.

   To modify the criteria of a smart playlist after it's been created, hold down the Option key and double-click the smart playlist to reopen the Smart Playlist window and change the smart playlist's criteria.

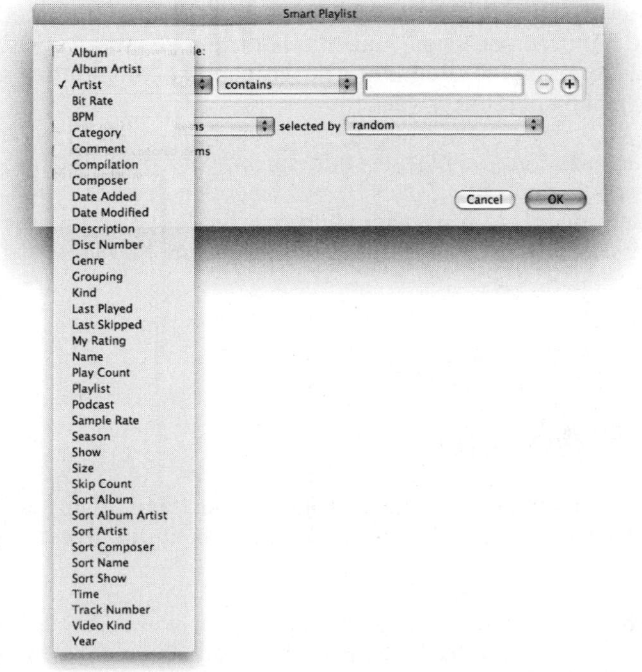

Figure 11-10:
The Smart Playlist window lets you specify the criteria for your smart playlist.

Burning a playlist to CD

Another use for playlists is for burning audio CDs you can listen to on almost any audio CD player. The only trick is to make sure the total playing time of the songs in the playlist is less than the capacity of the blank CD you're using, which is usually 74–80 minutes. When you have all the songs you want on your CD on the playlist, choose File➪ Burn Playlist to Disc or click the Burn Disk button in the lower-right corner of the main iTunes window. In a few minutes, you have an audio CD that contains all the songs on the playlist and will play them in the order they appeared on the playlist.

Note that although the default type of disc iTunes burns is an audio CD, it can also burn two other types — MP3 CDs or Data CDs (and DVDs).

MP3 CD is a special format that can be played in many new CD audio players. The cool thing about an MP3 CD is that rather than holding a mere 74–80 minutes of music, it can hold more than 100 songs! The uncool thing about MP3 CDs is that many older audio CD players won't play them.

Finally, a data CD or DVD is nothing more than a disc formatted to be read and mounted by any computer, Mac or Windows. So if you wanted to give your friend hundreds of songs, you could fit them all on a single CD or DVD that would mount on his computer's desktop, and he could then import it into his own copy of iTunes. Neat.

To determine which format iTunes burns from your playlist, choose iTunes➪ Preferences (shortcut: ⌘+,). Click the Advanced icon on the toolbar and then click the Burning tab. You see radio buttons that let you choose Audio CD, MP3 CD, or Data CD or DVD. Click the one you want, and you're golden.

Protecting (Backing Up) Your iTunes Media

After spending a bunch of time and money ripping and buying songs to populate your iTunes library, you might want to protect your investment by backing up your music.

Actually, you should back up all your data files, as you discover in Chapter 17. But if you decide against backing up all your data, consider this: Apple won't replace music you've bought at the iTunes Store if you lose it.

Fortunately, iTunes makes it easy to back up your Music library with its built-in back-up-your-music command. To back up *your* music:

1. **In iTunes, choose File ⇨ Back Up to Disc.**

   The iTunes Backup dialog appears, as shown in Figure 11-11.

   You have two options for backing up your iTunes library: You can back up the entire iTunes library or back up only items you've purchased at the iTunes Store. Regardless of which you choose, you have the option of backing up only items that have been added or modified since your last iTunes Backup.

2. **Make your choices and then click the Back Up button to start.**

3. **Insert a blank CD or DVD, and the process begins.**

   If your backup requires more than one disc, iTunes ejects the current disc, and you have to insert another.

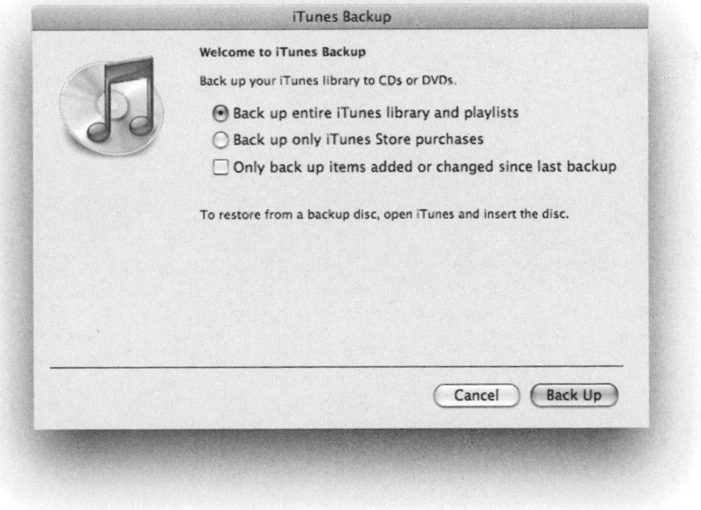

Figure 11-11:
The iTunes
Backup
dialog offers
you these
choices.

iTunes Backup

Welcome to iTunes Backup

Back up your iTunes library to CDs or DVDs.

⊙ Back up entire iTunes library and playlists
○ Back up only iTunes Store purchases
☐ Only back up items added or changed since last backup

To restore from a backup disc, open iTunes and insert the disc.

(Cancel) (Back Up)

It's a good idea to label these discs — iTunes Backup Disc 1, iTunes Backup Disc 2, and so on. That way, if you ever have to *use* your backup discs, you can insert the correct one when iTunes asks.

The cool part about using the iTunes built-in backup feature is that it performs incremental backups, which reduces the number of discs you need. In other words, it backs up only the items added or changed since the last backup.

By the way, discs you create using the iTunes backup feature can be used only to restore your playlists and can't be played in an audio CD or video DVD player.

To restore your music from an iTunes backup, merely launch iTunes and insert the disc (or the first disc, if the backup required more than one disc); then choose File⇨Back Up to Disc and click Restore.

Chapter 12

The Multimedia Mac

Media is more than just music (the topic of Chapter 11), and your Mac is ready, willing, and able to handle almost any type of media you can throw at it. Which is why, in addition to the aforementioned iTunes, Mac OS X Leopard includes applications for viewing and working with media such as DVD movie discs; QuickTime movie files; and graphics in a variety of file formats such as PDF, TIFF, and JPEG.

In this chapter, you look at three bundled applications you can use to work with such media — namely, DVD Player, QuickTime Player, and Preview — followed by a brief tutorial about importing your own media (photos and videos) into your Mac.

Watching Movies with DVD Player

The DVD Player application includes snazzy little on-screen controllers, as shown in Figure 12-1. They enable you to watch your movies on your Mac, pretty much like you'd watch them on your TV with your DVD player, as follows:

1. **Insert a DVD into a Mac with DVD Player.**

   This step automatically launches the DVD Player application; if it doesn't, you can double-click the DVD Player icon in the Applications folder to start it.

Figure 12-1:
DVD
Player's
on-screen
controller
gadgets.

If you don't see the little controller gadgets, you can choose Window➪Show Controller (shortcut: ⌘+Option+C) to display the gray remote control–looking gadget shown at the top of Figure 12-1, or you can move your cursor to the very bottom of the screen to see the transparent overlay controls shown at the bottom of Figure 12-1.

The transparent overlay works only in Full Screen mode.

2. Use the controls to play, stop, or pause your DVD and more.

The controls themselves should be self-explanatory to anyone who has ever used a set-top DVD player. If they're not familiar to you, hover the cursor over any control to reveal a tool tip. This works for buttons on either type of controller.

3. Use the Controller drawer if you like to give DVD Player less commonly used, but still useful, commands.

To open (top right, Figure 12-1) or close (top left, Figure 12-1) the little Controller drawer, choose Controls➪Open/Close Control Drawer, use the keyboard shortcut ⌘+], or click the little pull tab (where you see the arrow cursors in Figure 12-1) and drag.

The controller might disappear after a few seconds. To make it reappear, jiggle the mouse or choose Window➪Show Controller (shortcut ⌘+Option+C).

If you're in Full Screen mode, the menu bar won't appear unless you move the cursor to the top of the screen. And the transparent controller won't appear unless you move the cursor to the bottom of the screen.

4. Sit back and enjoy the inserted DVD movie on your Mac screen.

There really isn't much more to it than that, but here are a couple of other useful tips and hints for using DVD Player:

- ✔ The View menu lets you choose viewing sizes for your movie, including Full Screen, which usually looks best.

- ✔ The Go menu lets you navigate to the DVD menu, beginning of the disc, previous or next chapter, or forward or back five seconds, with convenient keyboard shortcuts for each of these commands.

Troubleshooting DVD Player settings

DVD Player is a pretty-easy-to-use application. However, you might find it's not working as expected for a couple of reasons:

✔ You've changed the default setting — Open DVD Player When You Insert a Video DVD — in the CDs & DVDs System Preferences pane, which you find in the System Preferences application.

✔ Certain external DVD players won't be recognized by DVD Player. If that's the case, you need to use either the viewing software that came with the drive or a program such as *VLC* (VideoLAN Client).

✔ Your Mac might not have a DVD player, although this situation is probably true only if you have a somewhat older Mac. If you choose ⌥About This Mac in the Finder, the About this Mac window has a More Info button. Click it to launch an application called System Profiler. Or you can launch System Profiler (which you find in the Utilities folder) the old-fashioned way — by double-clicking its icon. Either way, it can tell you whether you have a DVD drive in your Mac. Just click the Disc Burning item in the contents column on the left; the details appear on the right.

✔ Many user-configurable options are available in the Preferences window: DVD Player⇨Preferences (keyboard shortcut: ⌘+,).

✔ For more information about almost any DVD Player feature, choose Help⇨DVD Player Help.

This application is present only on Macs that have an Apple-recognized DVD player or a SuperDrive DVD player/burner. Also, if you've changed your preferences, DVD Player might not start automatically. See the nearby sidebar for details.

Playing Movies and Music in QuickTime Player

QuickTime is Apple's technology for digital media creation, delivery, and playback. It's used in a myriad of ways by programs such as Apple's iMovie and Final Cut, by Web sites such as YouTube (www.youtube.com), and in training videos delivered on CD or DVD.

QuickTime Player is the Mac OS X application that lets you view QuickTime movies as well as streaming audio and video, QuickTime VR (Virtual Reality), and many types of audio files as well. The quickest way to launch it is by clicking its icon in the Dock. It also opens automatically when you open any QuickTime movie document file.

To play a QuickTime movie, merely double-click its icon, and QuickTime Player launches itself.

Using QuickTime Player couldn't be easier. All its important controls are available right in the player window, as shown in Figure 12-2.

Figure 12-2:
QuickTime
Player is
easy to use.

Here are a few more QuickTime Player features you might find useful:

✔ **The Movie Inspector window** (Window⇨Show/Hide Movie Inspector or ⌘+I) provides a lot of useful information about the current movie, such as its location on your hard drive, file format, frames per second, file size, and duration.

✔ **The A/V Controls window** (Window⇨Show/Hide A/V Controls or ⌘+K) lets you adjust the volume, stereo balance, bass, treble, brightness, color, contrast, playback speed, and several other characteristics of the current movie.

✔ **The Content Guide window** (Window⇨ Show/Hide Content Guide or ⌘+Option+K) displays a window full of links to a variety of video and audio files. Click one, and it appears in QuickTime Player, iTunes, or Safari, depending on what type of file it is.

Viewing and Converting Images and PDFs in Preview

You use Preview to open, view, and print PDFs as well as most graphics files (TIFF, JPEG, PICT, and so on). *PDF files* are formatted documents that include text and images. User manuals, books, and the like are often distributed as PDF files. You can't edit a PDF file with Preview, but you can leaf through its pages or print it, and you can select text and graphics from it, copy them to

What about QuickTime Pro?

If you've used QuickTime Player at all, you've surely noticed all the dimmed commands in its menus. The items preceded by the word *Pro* become available only if you purchase the QuickTime Pro upgrade, which is priced at $29.99 at this writing. I'm a big fan of QuickTime Pro and have purchased the upgrade for the past few versions of QuickTime. My favorite Pro feature is full-screen playback complete with a floating control. A lot of the movie trailers I download are in HD (high definition), which makes them look really cool at full size.

Another good Pro-only feature is the ability to easily share QuickTime content with my friends. I choose File⇨Share (⌘+Option+S), and QuickTime Pro does the rest, shrinking the movie to the appropriate size for e-mail or .Mac.

To purchase the upgrade, open the QuickTime System Preferences pane and click the Buy QuickTime Pro button in the Register pane.

the Clipboard, and paste them into documents in other applications. It's also the application that pops open when you click the Preview button in the Print dialog, as described in Chapter 14.

Actually, that's not entirely true. You can edit one certain type of PDF file: a form that has blank fields. Preview allows you to fill in the blanks and then resave the document. And although it's technically not editing, you can annotate a PDF document by using the Annotate tools on the toolbar.

One of the most useful things Preview can do is change a graphic file in one file format into one with a different file format. For example, you're signing up for a Web site and want to add a picture to your profile. The Web site requires pictures in the JPEG file format, but the picture file on your hard drive that you'd like to use is in the TIFF file format. Preview can handle the conversion for you:

1. **Just open the TIFF file with Preview by double-clicking the file. If another program (such as Adobe Photoshop) opens instead of Preview, drag the TIFF document onto the Preview icon or launch Preview and choose File⇨Open (shortcut: ⌘+O) to open the TIFF file.**

2. **Choose File⇨Save As (⌘+Shift+S).**

3. **Choose the appropriate file format — such as JPEG — from the pop-up Format menu, as shown in Figure 12-3.**

4. **If you want to make sure you don't confuse your original image with the one in the new format, change the name of your file in the Save As box, too.**

5. **Click Save.**

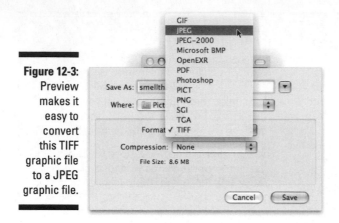

Figure 12-3:
Preview
makes it
easy to
convert
this TIFF
graphic file
to a JPEG
graphic file.

As you can see in Figure 12-3, Preview lets you convert any file it can open to any of the following file formats: Microsoft BMP, GIF, JPEG-2000, JPEG, PDF, Photoshop, PICT, PNG, SGI, TGA, and TIFF.

Chances are good that you'll never need to convert a file to most of these formats, but it's nice to know you could if you needed to.

Almost every OS X program with a Print command lets you save your document as a PDF file. Just click and hold the PDF button found in all Print dialogs and choose Save As PDF. Then, should you ever need to convert that PDF file in a different file format, you can do so by using the procedure described in the preceding steps.

Importing Media

Chances are good that you'll want to import pictures or video from your digital camera or DV camcorder someday. It's a piece of cake. So in the following sections, I show you how easy it is to get your digital photos into your Mac and help you get started with digital video (which is a bit more complex).

In the sections that follow, I focus on applications that are a part of Mac OS X. Technically, that doesn't include the iLife applications. What I mean is that if you bought a Mac OS X Leopard upgrade in a box at a store, it doesn't include iLife applications, such as iMovie and iPhoto. Your Mac almost certainly came with the iLife suite preinstalled, but depending upon how old your Mac is, you might not have the current versions, and the various versions all work differently. See the nearby sidebar for more details about iLife.

Downloading photos from a camera

This is the Mac I'm talking about, so of course, getting pictures from your digital camera onto your hard drive is a pretty simple task. Here's how to do it step by step using Image Capture:

1. **Turn on the camera and set it to review or playback mode.**

   This step might not be necessary for some cameras. It was for my old Olympus but isn't for my new Nikon P1.

2. **Connect the camera to your Mac with its USB cable.**

   At this point, Image Capture launches automatically as soon as the digital camera is detected. (But if you have iPhoto, it launches instead.)

   If you have both programs on your hard drive and the wrong one opens, you can change that behavior in Image Capture's preferences pane. Choose Image Capture⇨ Preferences and choose the appropriate application from the pop-up menu When a Camera Is Connected, Open Menu.

   Assuming you're using Image Capture, when you connect your camera, a window with your camera's name as its title (mine is Nikon DSC Coolpix P1) appears, as shown in Figure 12-4.

Figure 12-4:
You can download all the photos in your camera.

NIKON DSC COOLPIX P1

Download To: Pictures, Movies, and Music folders

Automatic Task: None
Occurs after downloading

Items to download: 1

Options...   Download Some...   Download All

3. **From that window, you can either Click Download All to download all the photos in your camera or click Download Some to choose which photos to download, as shown in Figure 12-5.**

   • *To choose contiguous photos* in the Download Some window, click the first photo you want to download, press Shift, and then click the last photo you want to download.

   • *To choose noncontiguous photos,* press ⌘ and click each photo you want to download. Either way, a blue highlight shows you which photos are going to be downloaded when you click the Download button (such as the first, fourth, and fifth photos in Figure 12-5).

Figure 12-5:
Click
Download
Some to
choose
which
photos to
download.

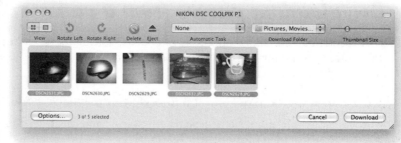

In Figures 12-4 and 12-5, the Download Folder pop-up menu is set to Pictures, Movies, and Music Folders. That's the default setting. If you click the Download button now, it downloads the photos in your camera to the Pictures folder inside your Home folder.

If you want to delete the photos from your camera after they're downloaded to your hard drive, select the photos you want to delete in the Download Some window and click the Delete button on the toolbar.

If a disk icon, often named No Name, appeared on your Desktop when you plugged in your camera, you have to eject that disk before you disconnect your camera, or you could lose or damage files in your camera. So try to remember. If you forget, Image Capture scolds you with a scary warning dialog, as shown in Figure 12-6.

Figure 12-6:
This
warning
means you
forgot to
eject your
camera's
disk icon.

Downloading DV video from a camcorder

Getting video from a DV camcorder to your hard drive is almost as easy as importing photos from your digital camera. Although it's beyond the scope of this book to explain how you download video, the following tips can help you get started:

✔ iMovie works well for downloading video from camcorders that include output via FireWire.

✔ If your camcorder records on mini-DVDs or uses USB to output its video, iMovie probably won't work.

✔ If you do plan to use iMovie, don't forget about the built-in Help system (⌘+Shift+?). Here, you find extensive assistance, as shown in Figure 12-7, which is the main Help page for iMovie HD.

Figure 12-7: Don't forget that help is just a click (or a keystroke) away.

Living the iLife

At under $100, the latest and greatest iLife suite is one of the fantastic bargains in software. If you had to buy all these programs from other vendors, I promise you'd pay a whole lot more. So if you don't have the latest version of iLife on your hard drive, take a look at the features and programs it includes (www.apple.com/ilife) and consider whether you'd benefit from all the new goodies you don't currently have.

In iPhoto, for example, after you download pictures to the iPhoto library, you can organize them into albums, edit them, create slide shows or books with them, use them in Web sites with iWeb, Photocast them, or whatever.

Chapter 13

Words and Letters

In This Chapter

- Processing words with TextEdit
- Finding out all about Leopard's fonts
- Managing fonts with Font Book

As I discuss in previous chapters, your Mac is well equipped for creating and managing media — music, movies, DVDs, and photos. But your Mac is also ready to handle more common tasks, such as typing a letter or writing an essay.

Furthermore, your Mac comes stocked with a wide variety of fonts (sometimes called *typefaces*), which allow you to change the way text looks on the screen and the printed page, as shown in Figure 13-1.

This is an example of the Times New Roman font, which is businesslike and stately.

This is an example of the Marker Felt font, which is casual and relaxed.

This is an example of the American Typewriter font, which looks like it was created on an old-fashioned typewriter.

Figure 13-1: Each of these fonts has its own unique look.

In this chapter, you look at the Mac OS X Leopard text-composition program, called TextEdit, and explore fonts and how to manage them.

Processing Words with TextEdit

TextEdit is a word processor/text editor that you can use to write letters, scribble notes, or open Read Me files. Although it's not as sophisticated as Microsoft Word (or AppleWorks or Pages, for that matter), you can definitely use it for light word processing and text editing. It's capable of doing some (but not much) text formatting and can even check your spelling.

TextEdit supports images, too. Just copy an image from another program and paste it into a TextEdit document. Or you can use drag-and-drop to put an image into a TextEdit document from many applications.

TextEdit can even open Microsoft Word documents (.doc files). This is fabulous if you don't happen to have a copy of Microsoft Word on your hard drive. Neat!

That's right — the free word processor that comes with Mac OS X can open Microsoft Word files, and it can modify and save them again, too. Why does this make me rave and marvel? Because now, even if you don't own a copy of Microsoft Word, you can open documents created by others using Word, edit, and resave them, all without having to buy your own copy of Word. Don't get me wrong — I use Word more than any other program, and I have no qualms. But for those of you who don't need a full-featured, professional-quality, relatively expensive writing environment, the freebie (TextEdit) may very well be all the word processor you'll ever need.

Here, take a closer look. . . .

Creating and composing a document

When you launch TextEdit, a blank, untitled document should appear on your screen. If one doesn't, choose File⇨New or use the shortcut ⌘+N. Before you begin work on any document, you should save it to your hard drive by choosing File⇨Save or using the shortcut ⌘+S. (If you're new to Mac OS Leopard Save sheets, flip to Chapter 6 for details.)

As you work with the document, it's a good idea to save it every few minutes, just in case. After you've named a file, all you need to do to save its current state is choose File⇨Save or use the shortcut ⌘+S.

Now begin typing your text. When you type text in a word processor, you should know a couple of things:

✔ **Press the Return (or Enter) key only when you reach the end of a paragraph.**

You don't need to press Return at the end of a line of text — the program automatically wraps your text to the next line, keeping things neat and tidy.

✔ **Type a single space after the punctuation mark at the end of a sentence, regardless of what your typing teacher might have told you.**

Word processors and typewriters aren't the same. With a typewriter, you want two spaces at the end of a sentence; with a word processor, you don't. (Typewriters use *fixed-width* fonts; computers mostly use fonts with variable widths. If you put two spaces at the end of a sentence in a computer-generated document, the gap looks too wide.) Trust me on this one.

✔ **Limit most documents to a maximum of two different fonts.**

Mac OS X offers you a wide selection of fonts, but that doesn't mean you have to use them all in one document.

To put certain characters in your TextEdit document, choose Edit⇔Special Characters (shortcut: ⌘+Option+T). This command opens the Character Palette, where you can choose special characters such as mathematical symbols, arrows, ornaments, stars, accented Latin characters, and so on. To insert a character into your document at the insertion point, simply click it and then click the Insert button.

And that's about all you need to know to create documents that don't scream, "I'm a computer newbie!"

Working with text

TextEdit operates on the "select, then operate" principle, as do most Macintosh programs, including the Finder. Before you can affect text in your document — change its font face, style, size, margins, and so on — you need to select the text you want to operate on.

You can use several methods to select text in a document:

✔ If you double-click a word, the word is selected.

✔ If you triple-click a word, the entire paragraph that contains the word is selected.

✔ You can click anywhere in the document, hold down the Shift key, and then click again somewhere else in the document, and everything between the two clicks will be selected.

✔ You can click anywhere in the document, hold down the Shift key, and use the arrow keys to extend the selection. Figure 13-2 shows some text that is selected.

Figure 13-2:
The last
sentence
in the first
paragraph is
highlighted,
showing
that it's
currently
selected.

Creating and Composing a Document

Styles | Spacing | Lists

Dear Reader,

This is the first sentence in a document called, "Creating and composing a document."
This is the second sentence in a document called, "Creating and composing a
document." This is the third sentence and it is currently selected.

This is the first sentence in the second paragraph of a document called, "Creating and
composing a document." This is the second sentence in the second paragraph of a
document called, "Creating and composing a document."

This is the first sentence of the third paragraph. And so on...

Regards,

Bob "Dr. Mac" LeVitus

Give all these methods of selecting text a try, decide which ones feel most comfortable, and then memorize them for future use.

When text is selected, you can operate on it. For example, you can use the Format menu's Font submenu to make text Bold, Italic, Underline, Outline, and so on, as shown in Figure 13-3.

TextEdit File Edit **Format** Window Help

Font	▶	Show Fonts	⌘T
Text	▶	✓ Bold	⌘B
Make Plain Text	⇧⌘T	Italic	⌘I
Prevent Editing		Underline	⌘U
Wrap to Page	⇧⌘W	Outline	
Allow Hyphenation		Styles...	
		Bigger	⌘+
		Smaller	⌘−
		Kern	▶
		Ligature	▶
		Baseline	▶
		Character Shape	▶
		Show Colors	⇧⌘C
		Copy Style	⌥⌘C
		Paste Style	⌥⌘V

Styles | Spacing | Lists

Dear Reader,

This is the first sentence in a document called, "Creatin
This is the second sentence in a document called, "Cre
document." **This is the third sentence and it is curren**

This is the first sentence in the second paragraph of a d
composing a document." This is the second sentence i
document called, "Creating and composing a document."

This is the first sentence of the third paragraph. And so on...

Regards,

Bob "Dr. Mac" LeVitus

Figure 13-3:
The
selected
sentence
is the only
part of the
document
affected
by these
formatting
commands.

The same idea applies to tabs and margins. In Figure 13-4, I've dragged the left margin markers from 0 inches to half an inch. Notice that the selected text is now indented by half an inch.

Margin markers

Select some text in your document and try all the items in the Format menu's Font and Text submenus. As you see, you have a great deal of control over the way your words appear on the screen. And because TextEdit, like most Macintosh software, is WYSIWYG (What You See Is What You Get), when you print the document (by choosing File➪Print), the printed version should look exactly like the version you see on the screen. For help with printing, see Chapter 14.

Before you print your masterpiece, however, you might want to check your spelling and grammar — something that TextEdit makes extremely simple. Merely choose Edit➪Spelling and Grammar➪Check Document Now or use the shortcut ⌘+; (semicolon). TextEdit highlights and underlines the mistakes in your document. Right-click (or Control+click) to correct the error, as shown in Figure 13-5.

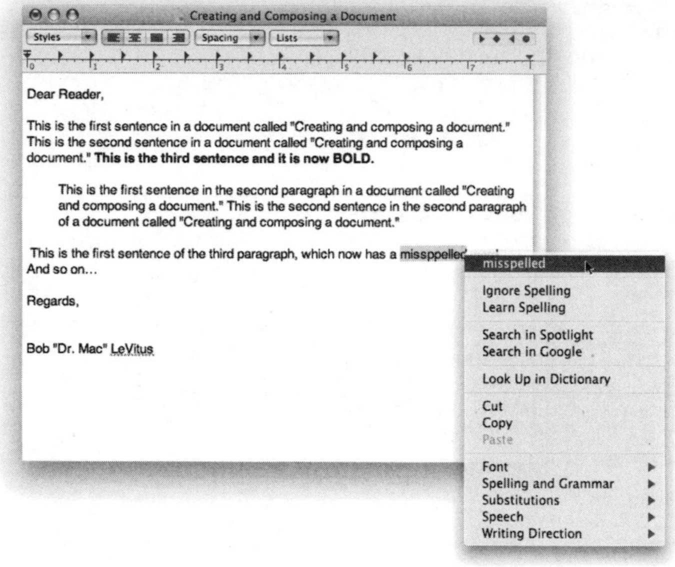

Figure 13-5:
Right-
click (or
Control+
click) to
correct a
spelling or
grammar
error.

Adding graphics to documents

Last but not least, you have a couple of ways to add pictures to a TextEdit document. The first works as follows:

1. **Copy a picture in another program — Preview, Safari, or whatever.**

2. **Put the cursor where you want the picture to appear in your TextEdit document.**

3. **Choose Edit⇨Paste.**

   The picture magically appears on the page.

Or you can drag a picture from the Finder or some applications (such as Safari or Mail) to a TextEdit document, as I did in Figure 13-6.

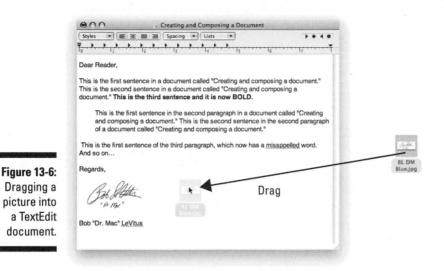

Figure 13-6:
Dragging a picture into a TextEdit document.

Font Mania

You can jazz up your documents — or make them a little more serious — with different fonts. To a computer user, *font* means *typeface* — what the characters look like. Although professional typographers will scream at my generalization, I'll go with that definition for now.

Tens of thousands of different fonts are available for the Macintosh. You don't want to use the same font for both a garage-sale flyer and a résumé, right? Luckily for you, Mac OS X comes with a bunch of fonts, as shown in Figure 13-7. Some are pretty predictable, such as Times New Roman (the font of this paragraph), but OS X gives you some artsy ones, too, such as Brush Script. If you *really* get into fonts, you can buy single fonts and font collections anywhere you can buy software. Plenty of shareware and public-domain fonts are also available from online services and user groups. Some people have *thousands* of fonts. (Maybe they need to get out more.)

The preinstalled fonts live in two different folders, both called Fonts. One is in the Library folder at root level on your hard drive; the other is in the Library subfolder within the System folder. Both are shown in Figure 13-7. (For an introduction to the Library folders, see Chapter 6.)

Figure 13-7:
Mac OS X
includes all
these fonts.

Mac OS X actually has four different Font folders. A third one, also called Fonts, is in the Library folder in your home directory. The upcoming section explains the subtle distinctions among those three locations. The fourth one is in the Network/Library folder, and you see it only when you're connected to a network server.

Installing new fonts

To install any new font, drag its icon into one of the two Fonts folders that you have access to, as follows:

- ✔ **If you want other users to be able to access the new font,** drag the font's icon to the Fonts subfolder inside the Library folder, which is at the root level of your hard drive. This Fonts folder has universal access.

- ✔ **If you want to limit access to the new font solely to yourself,** drag the font's icon to the Fonts subfolder located in the Library folder inside your Home folder — just keep digging, and you'll get there.

The Fonts folder on the right in Figure 13-7 — the one in the Library inside the System folder — is reserved for Mac OS X and can't be modified easily. If you try to remove a font from it — or add one, for that matter — you first have to authenticate yourself as an administrator. Do yourself a favor and never remove fonts from `/System/Library/Fonts`. You can really screw up your Leopard if you remove the wrong one.

If you've designated a Classic System Folder, OS X also loads any fonts in its Fonts folder, for a total of *five* different folders named Fonts. (Some applications — in particular, high-end design applications such as Adobe Illustrator and Adobe InDesign — add yet *another* Fonts folder to the mix:

the Application Support folder within the Library folder at the root level of your hard drive.) You can access any fonts in these out-of-the-way-places only when you're running the program that installed them.

Types of fonts

You can find many font formats with names like OpenType, Mac TrueType, Windows TrueType, PostScript Type 1, bitmap, and dfont. No problem — Mac OS X supports them all. In fact, the only font format I know of that Mac OS X *doesn't* support is PostScript Type 3.

That said, the three most common formats for Macs are TrueType, PostScript Type 1, and OpenType.

- ✔ **TrueType fonts:** These standard-issue Apple fonts come with Mac OS X. They're in common use on Macs as well as on Windows machines. That's partly because these fonts are *scaleable:* They use only a single outline per font, and your Mac can make their characters bigger or smaller when you choose a font size in a program.

- ✔ **Type 1 fonts:** These fonts are often referred to as *PostScript Type 1* fonts, and they're the standard for desktop publishing on the Mac (as well as Windows and UNIX). Tens of thousands of Type 1 fonts are available. (Not nearly as many high-quality TrueType fonts exist.)

  Type 1 fonts come in two pieces: a *suitcase* to hold the bitmap that tells the computer how to draw the font on your screen, and a second piece (called a *printer font*) that tells the printer how to print the font on a page. Some Type 1 fonts come with two, three, or four printer fonts, which usually have related names. Just toss all the parts in the appropriate Library folder, and you'll have those fonts available in every program you use.

- ✔ **OpenType fonts:** OpenType fonts are really TrueType fonts in which PostScript information is embedded. This gives you the greater typographic control that high-end typesetters require while keeping the one-file convenience of TrueType.

Manage your fonts with Font Book

Font Book lets you view your installed fonts, install new fonts, group your fonts into collections, and enable and disable installed fonts. If you've ever used the commercial program Extensis Suitcase, you can see that Font Book does much the same job.

The easiest way to install a new font is to double-click it in the Finder. Font Book opens and displays the font. Click the Install Font button to install the font.

Other ways you can install new fonts are to choose File➪Add Fonts or use the shortcut ⌘+O. A standard Open dialog allows you to select a font or fonts to be installed.

Note that by default new fonts are installed in your Home folder's Library➪ Fonts folder. You can change the default installation location in the Font Book preferences pane.

To view a font, click its name in the Font list. To change the size of the viewed font, choose a new size from the drop-down menu in the upper-right corner (it says *Fit* in Figure 13-8) or move the blue slider on the right side of the window up or down.

To disable a font so that it no longer appears in applications' Font menus, choose Edit➪Disable or click the Disable button (the check mark in a square button) at the bottom of the window.

To enable a previously disabled font, choose Edit➪Enable or click the Enable button (same as the Disable button) at the bottom of the window.

If you remove a font from the All Fonts collection, it disappears permanently. This action cannot be undone, so be careful when you remove fonts.

Figure 13-8:
Click a
font in the
Font list on
the left to
display it in
the pane on
the right.

Part IV
Making This Leopard Your Very Own

The 5th Wave   By Rich Tennant

AFTER INSTALLING OS X, NED AND LORETTA SELECT THE COMPUTER'S BACKGROUND

"Oh — I like this background much better than the basement."

In this part . . .

1 start this part by helping you decipher the myriad Print options so you can become a modern-day Gutenberg. Then, you look at all the different ways you can share data with others and access data other users have shared. Finally, you look at a bunch of other cool technologies included with Mac OS X Leopard to help you make your big cat look, feel, and act just the way you want her to.

There is something in this part for everyone, so don't touch that dial.

Chapter 14

Publish or Perish: The Fail-Safe Guide to Printing

. . . .

In This Chapter

▶ Connecting a printer

▶ Using Page Setup to prepare your document for printing

▶ Printing to most printers

▶ Mastering the printing process

. . . .

When you want to get what's on your screen onto paper, printing under Mac OS X should be as simple as pressing the keyboard shortcut ⌘+P and then pressing Return or Enter. Happily, that's usually just how easy printing something is; when it isn't, printing can turn into a raging nightmare. If you configure your printer and printing software properly, however, printing is as easy as can be. And that's pretty darn simple.

In this chapter, I scare away the bogeymen to help you avoid any printing nightmares. I walk you through the entire process as though you just unpacked a new printer and plugged it in.

Before Diving In . . .

Before I even start talking about hooking up printers, you should know a few essential things. So here's a little list that tells you just what those things are:

✔ **Read the documentation that came with your printer.** Hundreds of different printer makes and models are available for the Mac, so if I contradict something in your printer manual, follow your manual's instructions first. If that effort doesn't work, try it my way — use the techniques that you read about in the rest of this chapter.

✔ **The Print and Page Setup sheets differ slightly (or even greatly) from program to program and from printer to printer.** Although the examples I show you in this chapter are representative of what you'll probably encounter, you might come across sheets that look a bit different. For example, the Print and Page Setup sheets for Microsoft Word include choices I don't cover in this chapter (such as Even or Odd Pages Only, Print Hidden Text, and Print Selection Only). If you see commands in your Print or Page Setup sheet that I don't explain in this chapter, they're specific to that application; look within its documentation for an explanation. Similarly, Adobe Illustrator and Photoshop CS3 have added numerous gadgets, list boxes, radio buttons, and so forth to their Print dialogs, to the point where you might not even recognize them as Print dialogs.

✔ **Don't forget about Mac OS Help.** Many programs support this excellent Apple technology, which can be the fastest way to figure out a feature that has you stumped. So don't forget to check the Help menu before you panic. (I cover the Help menu way back in Chapter 1.)

So with those things in mind, get ready, set, print!

Ready: Connecting and Adding Your Printer

Before you can even think about printing something, you have to connect a printer to your Mac and then tell OS X that the printer exists. Here's how.

Connecting your printer

Once again, I must remind you that there are thousands of printer models that you could connect to your Mac, and each one is a little different from the next. In other words, if what you're about to read doesn't work with the printer you're trying to connect, I again implore you to RTFM (that's *Read the Fine Manual,* in case you're wondering). It should tell you how to load your ink or toner cartridges.

Remove all the packing material and little strips of tape, some of which you won't even see if you don't know where to look.

That said, here are some very general steps to connect a printer to your Mac:

1. **Connect the printer to your Mac with the cable snugly attached at both ends (printer and Mac).**

For your printer to work, you have to somehow connect it to a data source. (Think of your phone — you can't receive calls without some sort of connector between the caller and the callee.)

2. **Plug the printer's AC power cord into a power outlet.**

   Yup, I mean the regular kind of outlet in the wall; on a power strip; or best of all, on a UPS (Uninterruptible Power Supply).

   Some printers require you to plug one end of the AC power cord into the printer; others have the AC power cord attached permanently. The point is that your printer won't work if it's not connected to a power source.

3. **Turn on your printer. (Check out your manual if you can't find the switch.)**

4. **If your printer came with software, install it on your hard drive, following the instructions that came with the printer.**

5. **(Optional) Restart your Mac.**

   You need to do this only if you had to install software and the Installer told you to restart.

   That's it!

Any port on a Mac

Before you can print, you need to plug the printer cable into the appropriate port on the back of your Mac.

Therein lies the rub. Mac technology has changed dramatically since the previous editions of this book, when I used to say, "Begin by connecting the printer to the Printer port on the back of your Mac (with both the Mac and the printer turned off, of course — but you knew that, didn't you?)." Ah, nostalgia. Now I tell you, "You need to plug the printer cable into the appropriate port...." Why am I being so vague? Because I have to be. You see, these days, printers don't always connect to the same port:

✔ Some connect through the Universal Serial Bus (USB) port.

✔ Other printers connect to the Ethernet port or to an Ethernet hub (which is in turn connected to the back of your Mac).

✔ A few connect via the FireWire port.

So read the instructions that came with your printer, and plug your printer into the appropriate hole (port) for your Mac.

Typically, your printer connects to your machine via USB. Don't confuse the USB cable with your printer's AC power cord (the kind you find on everyday appliances). If your printer didn't come with a cable that fits into one of the ports on your Mac, contact your printer manufacturer and ask for one; it's cheesy not to provide the proper cable with a printer. Unfortunately, some manufacturers make printers with different kinds of connectors on the back (to sell to those poor souls stuck using Windows) and expect you to buy your own cable. Asking one of these manufacturers for a cable is an exercise in futility.

Setting up a printer for the first time

After you connect your computer and printer with a compatible cable, provide a power source for your printer, and install the software for your printer, you're ready . . . to configure your Mac. No rest for the weary. You have to do that so your Mac and your printer can talk to each other.

The Print & Fax System Preferences pane (which I am about to discuss) is the tool you use to tell your Mac what printers are available.

Many of the steps involving the Print & Fax System Preferences pane require that your printer be turned on and warmed up (that is, already run through its diagnostics and startup cycle) beforehand.

Follow these steps to set up a printer for the first time:

1. **Launch System Preferences, click the Print & Fax icon, and then click your printer's name in the Printer list.**

   You find System Preferences in the Applications folder. Click the Applications icon in the Sidebar of any Finder window or use the shortcut ⌘+Shift+A to open the Applications folder.

   Leopard is a pretty smart cat — it should have already recognized your new printer at this point, so your printer's name should appear in the Printer list of the Print & Fax System Preferences pane, as shown in Figure 14-1.

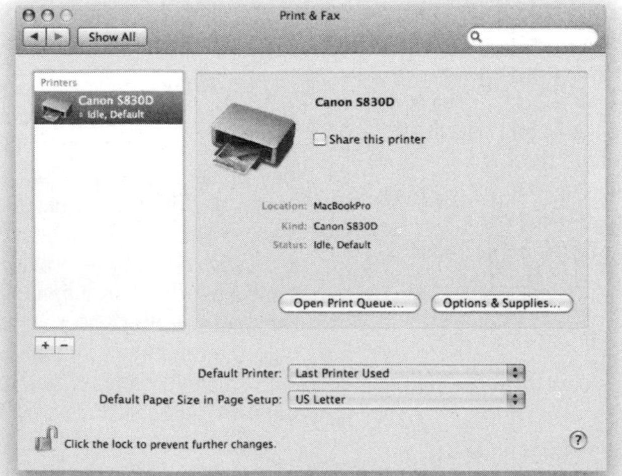

Figure 14-1:
Printers that Leopard recognizes appear in the Printer list.

Go for a driver

Many printer manufacturers introduce new drivers with enhanced functionality periodically. So the driver software on the CD in the box with your printer could be six months or even a year old when you buy that printer. It's always a good idea to determine whether the CD contains the latest version of the printer driver, so visit the printer manufacturer's Web site, check it out, and download a more recent version of the printer driver if necessary.

Apple includes a huge library of printer drivers on the Mac OS X Installer disk, which should cover most popular printer brands and models. These drivers are installed by default. If you chose *not* to install some or all of them when you installed Mac OS X Leopard, you will almost certainly need to install the appropriate printer driver before you can proceed.

My printer's name, as you can see, is Canon S830D.

If your printer *isn't* in the list, you need to install (or reinstall) its driver software, either from the CD that came with the printer or by downloading the latest driver software from your printer manufacturer's Web site. See the nearby sidebar for more on drivers.

2. **Select the printer you want selected by default in the Print dialog.**

3. **Select the default paper size you want to use with this printer (usually US Letter if you live in the United States).**

That's all there is to it. Close System Preferences, and you're ready to print your first document! Before you do, though, make sure you have the document set up to look just the way you want it to print. Read through the next section ("Set: Setting Up Your Document with Page Setup") for more info.

Set: Setting Up Your Document with Page Setup

After you set up your printer, the hard part is over. You should be able to print a document quickly and easily — right? Not so fast, bucko. Read here how the features in the Page Setup sheet can help you solve most basic printing problems.

Become familiar with Page Setup. You might not need to use it right this second, but it's a good friend to know.

Almost every program that can print a document has a Page Setup command on its File menu. Note that some programs use the name *Page Setup,* and others use *Print Setup.* (Print Setup is the quaint, old-fashioned term, more popular in the System 6 era and in Windows than on today's Macs.) Either way, this is the sheet where you can choose your target printer, paper size, page orientation, and scale (as shown in Figure 14-2).

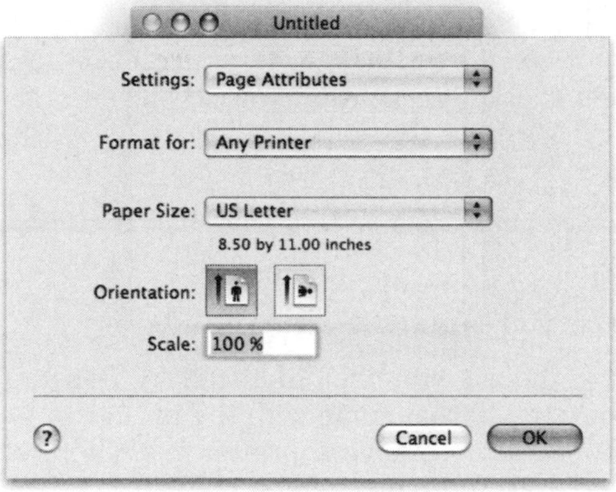

Figure 14-2:
The Page
Setup sheet
in TextEdit.

Users of network printers or PostScript printers might see slightly different versions of the Print and Page Setup sheet. The differences should be minor enough not to matter.

Click the little question mark in the lower-left corner at any time for additional help with the Page Setup sheet. If you do, Page Setup help opens immediately in the Help Viewer. (Okay, maybe not *immediately*, but Help Viewer in Leopard is much, much faster than in previous incarnations. . . .)

The options within the Page Setup sheet are as follows:

- **Settings:** When you have everything else in the Page Setup sheet configured just the way you want it to be for most documents, choose Save As Default to save the configuration as the default for Page Setup.

- **Format For:** In this pop-up menu, you find the name of the active printer. If you have several printers configured, you can choose any of them from this list.

   This menu usually defaults to Any Printer, which is the least effective setting. Unless the printer you want to use appears here, you might not get the full functionality that the printer offers.

- **Paper Size:** Use options in this pop-up menu to choose the type of paper currently in the paper tray of your printer or to choose the size of the paper that you want to feed manually. The dimensions of the paper that you can choose appear below its name.

Page Setup sheet settings (including Paper Size) remain in effect until you change them. For example, when you print an envelope, don't forget to change back to Letter before trying to print on letter-sized paper again.

✔ **Orientation:** Choose among options here to tell your printer whether the page you want to print should be *portrait-oriented* (like a letter, longer than it is wide) or *landscape-oriented* (sideways, wider than it is long).

Some programs offer additional Page Setup choices. If your program offers them, they usually appear in the Settings pop-up menu in the Page Setup sheet. (Adobe Photoshop and Microsoft Word have them; TextEdit doesn't.)

✔ **Scale:** To print your page at a larger or smaller size, change this option to a larger or smaller percentage.

Go: Printing with the Print Sheet

After you connect and configure your printer and then set up how you want your document to print, you come to the final steps before that joyous moment when your printed page pops out of the printer. Navigating the Print sheet is the last thing standing between you and your output.

Although most Print sheets that you see look like the figures I show in this chapter, others might differ slightly. The features in the Print sheet are strictly a function of the program with which you're printing. Many programs choose to use the standard-issue Apple sheet shown in this chapter, but not all do. If I don't explain a certain feature in this chapter, chances are good that the feature is specific to the application or printer you're using (in which case, the documentation for that program or printer should offer an explanation).

Printing a document

If everything has gone well so far, the actual act of printing a document is pretty simple. Just follow the steps here, and in a few minutes, pages should start popping out of your printer like magic. (In the sections that follow, I talk about some print options that you'll probably need someday.)

1. **Open a document that you want to print.**

2. **Choose File ⇨ Print (or use the keyboard shortcut ⌘+P).**

   You see the basic Print sheet, as shown in Figure 14-3.

3. **Click Print.**

   Wait a few minutes for the network to tell the printer what to do and then walk over to your printer to get your document.

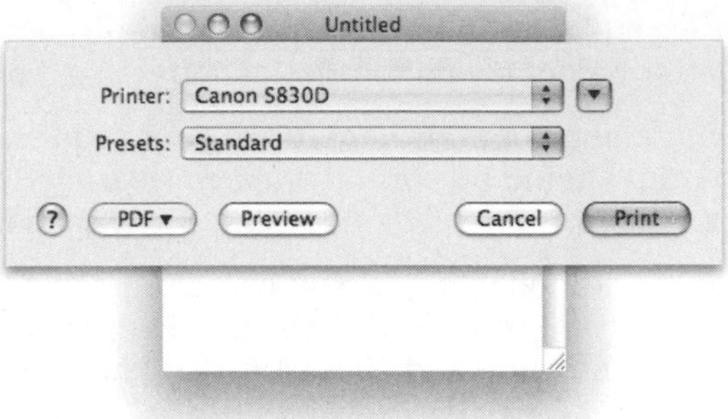

Figure 14-3:
Your basic
Print sheet.

Dictating perfection . . . sort of

The Print command appears on the File menu in the vast majority of the Mac programs you'll see and use. Every so often, you might come across a program that doesn't follow these conventions, but I would say *at least* 98 percent of commercial Mac programs put the Print command on the File menu and use ⌘+P for its keyboard shortcut.

One of the best things about the Mac is that Apple has published a set of guidelines that *all* Mac programs should use. Consistency among programs is one of the Mac's finest features. Notice how 98+ percent of all programs house the Open, Close, Save, Save As, Page Setup, and Print commands on their File menus and the Undo, Cut, Copy, and Paste commands on their Edit menus. That's the kind of convenience and consistency that the Macintosh Human Interface Guidelines recommend.

Macintosh Human Interface Guidelines also recommend that the keyboard shortcut ⌘+P be reserved for the command "plain text" unless it's used for Print, in which case ⌘+T should be used for Plain Text (which works much like the keyboard shortcuts ⌘+B and ⌘+I, used to format bold and italic text, respectively). Bottom line: ⌘+P is almost always the shortcut for the Print command in the File menu.

My point: Choosing File⇨Print (⌘+P) *won't* work for you if any one of the following is true for the software you're using:

- The Print command is on a different menu.

- There *is* no Print command. (Hey, it could happen.)

- The Print keyboard shortcut is anything but ⌘+P.

If any of the preceding is true for a program you're using, you just have to wing it. Look in all the menus and check out the product's documentation to try to get a handle on the Print command for that pesky program. You can also write the software company a brief note, mentioning that it could make things easier on everyone by putting the Print command in the proper place and using the generally agreed-upon keyboard shortcut.

Choosing among different printers

Just as you can in the Page Setup sheet, you can choose which printer you want to use from the Printer pop-up menu of the Print sheet.

You can choose only among the printers that you have added via the Print & Fax System Preferences pane, as I describe earlier in this chapter (in the section I lovingly refer to as "Setting up a printer for the first time").

Choosing custom settings

If you've created a custom group of settings previously, you can choose them from the Presets pop-up menu of the Print sheet. I touch more on this feature in the "Save custom settings" section later in this chapter.

By default, the Print sheet is displayed in its simple state. As such, just three menus are available — Printer, Presets, and PDF. To reveal the rest of the Print options, click the little triangle on the right side of the Printer menu. The expanded Print sheet then replaces the minimized one, as shown in Figure 14-4.

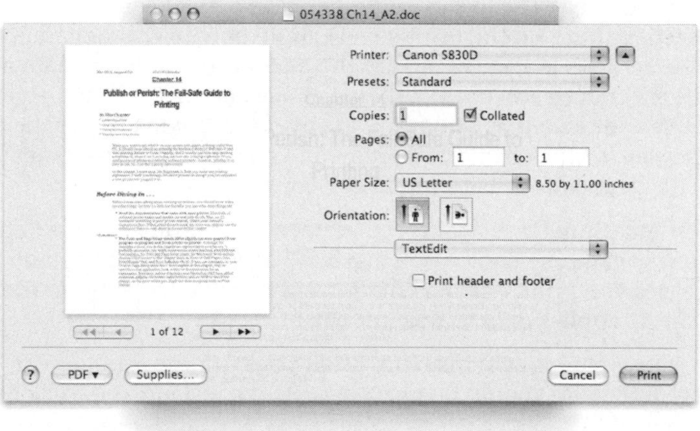

Figure 14-4:
Your
expanded
Print sheet.

Click in any of the fields and then press the Tab key. Your cursor jumps to the next text field in the sheet; likewise, press Shift+Tab to make the cursor jump to the previous field. By the way, this shortcut works in almost any program, window, dialog, or Web page that has text fields.

✔ **Copies:** In this text field, set how many copies you want to print. The Print sheet defaults to one copy (1) in most applications, so you probably see the numeral 1 in the Copies field when the Print sheet appears. Assuming that's the case, don't do anything if you want to print only one copy. If you want to print more than one copy of your document, highlight the 1 that appears in the Copies field and replace it by typing the number of copies you want.

✔ **Pages:** Here, you find two radio buttons: All and From. The default behavior is to print your entire document, so the All option is preselected. But if you want to print only a specific page or range of pages, mark the From radio button and then type the desired page numbers in the From and To text-entry boxes.

Suppose that you print a 10-page document — and then notice a typo on page 2. After you correct your error, you don't have to reprint the whole document — only the page with the correction. Reprint only page 2 by typing **2** in both the From and To fields. You can type any valid range of pages (um, you can't print page 20 if your document is only 15 pages long) in the From and To fields.

✔ **Paper Size:** Use options in this pop-up menu to choose the type of paper currently in your printer's paper tray or to choose the size of the paper that you want to feed manually. The dimensions of the paper appear below its name.

You've already seen this setting in Page Setup. The difference is that the settings here (in the Print sheet) apply only to this document, whereas the settings in Page Setup are the default for all documents and remain in effect until you change them in Page Setup. This can be very handy when, for example, you print an envelope. If you change the paper size setting for the envelope document, you don't have to remember to change it back to Letter in Page Setup.

✔ **Orientation:** Once again, you've seen this setting in Page Setup. And once again, the choice you make in Page Setup is the default for all pages you print, whereas the setting you choose here (in the Print sheet) applies only to this document.

Choose among options here to tell your printer whether the page you want to print should be portrait-oriented or landscape-oriented.

The following sections describe the features you can find in the unlabeled menu found in the expanded Print sheet (the one that says *TextEdit* in Figure 14-4). In addition to the TextEdit, Layout, and other options I cover in a moment, your pop-up menu might offer options such as Quality & Media, Color Options, Special Effects, Borderless Printing, and so on. (Whether you have these options depends on your printer model and its driver.) Check out these options if you have 'em — they usually offer useful features.

TextEdit

The only TextEdit–specific option is a check box that determines whether a header and footer will be printed for this document.

Layout

Choose Layout to set the number of pages per printed sheet, the layout direction, and whether you prefer a border. Here are your options for Layout:

- ✔ **Pages per Sheet:** Choose preset numbers from this pop-up menu to set the number of pages that you want to print on each sheet.

    Pages appear on-screen smaller than full size if you use this option.

- ✔ **Layout Direction:** Choose one of the four buttons that govern the way the small pages are laid out on the printed page.

- ✔ **Border:** Your choices from this pop-up menu are None, Single Hairline, Single Thin Line, Double Hairline, and Double Thin Line.

- ✔ **Two-Sided:** If your printer supports two-sided (known as *duplex*) printing, the three radio buttons allow you to specify whether you're going to use two-sided printing and, if so, whether you'll be binding (or stapling) along the long or short edge of the paper.

Color Matching

Choose Color Matching to choose a color-conversion method (usually either Apple's ColorSync or Vendor Matching technology). The idea here is to get the printed page to look as much like what's on your screen as possible.

Quartz filters include Black & White, Blue Tone, Gray Tone, Lightness Decrease, Lightness Increase, Reduce File Size, and Sepia Tone. They do pretty much what they say they do when you apply them to a print job.

Paper Handling

Choose Paper Handling if you want to reverse the order in which your pages print or to print only the odd- or even-numbered pages. You can also specify whether the document's paper size is to be used (in which case you might have lines that break across pages) or whether the output should be scaled to fit the chosen paper size.

Cover Page

Choose Cover Page to add a cover page to your print job.

Scheduler

The Scheduler lets you set a later time for printing (say, while you're asleep, at lunch, or in a meeting).

Summary

Select Summary to see the printing details for your document, as shown in Figure 14-5. Look here for one final check to verify your print-job settings — how many copies you want, whether you want them collated, the page range of your print job, your layout choice(s), plus any settings specific to your particular printer or the application you're printing from.

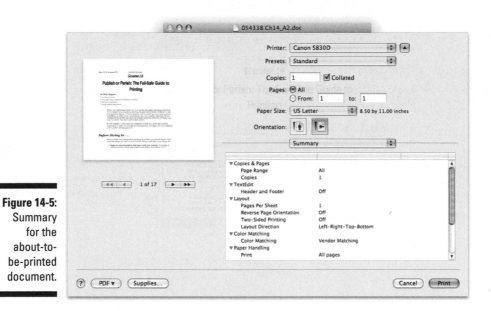

Figure 14-5:
Summary
for the
about-to-
be-printed
document.

Save custom settings

After you finalize the printer settings for Copies & Pages, Layout, Paper Handling, and any other options your printer driver provides, you can save them for future use. Just choose Save As from the Presets pop-up menu and name the settings; from then on, that setting appears as an option in the Presets pop-up menu. Just choose your saved set before you print any document, and all the individual settings associated with that preset are restored.

Preview and PDF Options

To see a preview of what your printed page will look like, choose Open PDF in Preview from the PDF button menu in the lower-left corner of the expanded Print sheet. When you do so, you see the page or pages that you're about to print, displayed by the Preview application, as shown in Figure 14-6.

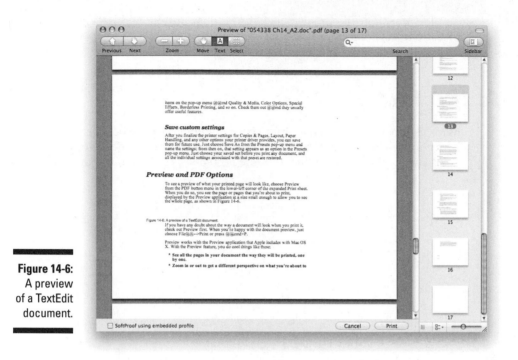

Figure 14-6:
A preview
of a TextEdit
document.

If you have any doubt about the way a document will look when you print it, check out Preview first. When you're happy with the document preview, just choose File⇨Print, press ⌘+P, or click the Print button at the bottom of the Preview window. Or, click the Cancel button to return to your application and make changes to the document.

Preview works with the Preview application that Apple includes with Mac OS X. With the Preview feature, you do cool things like these:

✔ **See all the pages in your document the way they will be printed, one by one.**

✔ **Zoom in or out to get a different perspective on what you're about to send to the printer (pretty cool!).**

✔ **Rotate the picture 90 degrees to the left or right.**

✔ **Spot errors before you commit to printing something.** A little up-front inspection can save you a lot of paper, ink (or toner), and frustration.

Check out the Preview program's View and Tools menus, as well as its toolbar. Here, you can zoom in or out, rotate your document, move forward or backward (through multipage documents), and do other stuff. So I urge you to pull down the View and Tools menus and check 'em out. If you have a multipage document (or multiple documents) open, a sidebar pops out of the side of the window to let you move through the pages, as shown in Figure 14-6.

To hide and show the drawer, click the Sidebar button, choose View➪Sidebar, or use the keyboard shortcut Shift+⌘+D.

Just the Fax . . .

Mac OS X includes the capability to fax a document right from the Print sheet. Just choose Fax PDF from the PDF pop-up menu button at the bottom of every Print sheet, and the sheet becomes the Fax sheet, as shown in Figure 14-7.

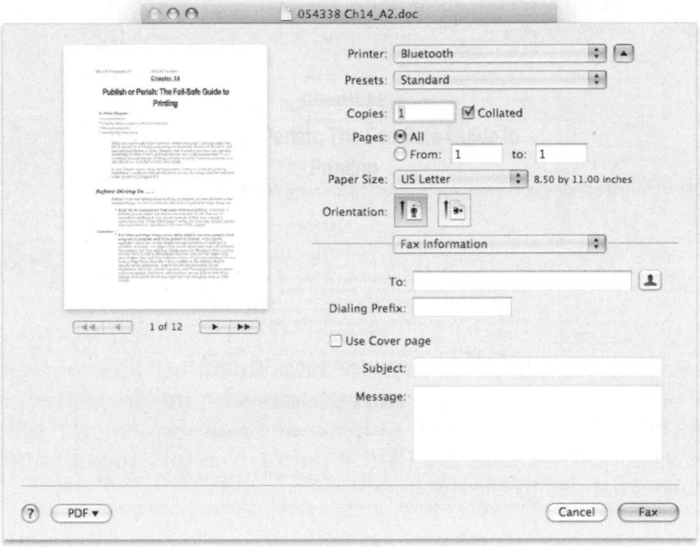

Figure 14-7:
In Leopard, faxing is just as easy as printing.

To fax a document, follow these steps:

1. **Choose Fax PDF from the menu that appears when you press and hold the PDF pop-up menu button on the Print sheet.**

2. **Type the fax phone number of the recipient in the To field.**

   If you click the button with the silhouette on the right of the To field, you can select a recipient from the Mac OS X Address Book.

3. **Add a dialing prefix if your phone requires one (such as 1, which most U.S. phones require to dial a ten-digit, long-distance phone number).**

4. **Click the Use Cover page check box if you want a cover page. If you do, you can type a subject in the Subject field and a brief message in the Message field, if you so desire.**

5. **Select your fax modem from the Printer pop-up menu, if it isn't already selected (as mine, named Bluetooth, is in Figure 14-7).**

   Everything else in the Fax sheet is just the same as in the Print sheet, which you can read all about in the previous sections.

6. **Click the Fax button.**

   Your fax is sent.

Before you try to fax something out into the world, make sure you have a functioning modem — and that it's configured, set up properly, connected to a phone line, and turned on. If you don't, this whole faxing process will (of course) fail. Note that most Macs sold in the past year or two, including all Intel-based models, don't include an analog modem, so they don't have built-in hardware fax support — you need to purchase a modem or other hardware to use this feature.

Faxing and Sharing Preferences

Earlier in this chapter, you work though the Printing features of the Print & Fax System Preferences pane. Now look at its other two functions:

- **Faxing:** First click the + button to add a fax machine to your Printers/Faxes list. Click the Fax machine's icon, and then type your fax number in the Fax Number field. Click the Receive Options button if you want to receive faxes on this Mac with this Fax machine. If so, you can set the number of rings you want the software to wait before answering a fax call in the Answer after __ Rings field. Select the Save To check box to enable a pop-up menu that lets you pick which folder incoming faxes will be saved to. Select the Print To check box to print incoming faxes automatically (to the printer you select in the pop-up menu next to the Print To check box). Or select the Email To check box to e-mail the fax to someone. You can type the person's email address into the Email To field or click the silhouette button on the right of the Email To field and select a recipient from your Address Book

- **Sharing:** To share a printer or fax machine, select the printer or fax you want to share in the list on the left. Then click the Share this Printer (or Share this fax) check box to allow printers (or fax machines) connected to this Mac to be available to other Macs on the local area network.

Chapter 15

Sharing Your Mac and Liking It

....

....

*H*ave you ever wanted to grab a file from your Mac while you were halfway around the world or even around the corner? If so, I have good news for you: It's not difficult with Mac OS X (believe it or not), even though computer networking in general has a well-deserved reputation for being complicated and nerve-wracking. The truth is that you won't encounter anything scary or complicated about sharing files, folders, and disks (and printers, for that matter) among computers as long as the computers are Macintoshes. And if some of the computers are running Windows, Mac OS X Leopard even makes that (almost) painless. Your Macintosh includes everything that you need to share files and printers — everything, that is, except the printers and the cables (and maybe a hub). So here's the deal: You supply the hardware, and this chapter supplies the rest. And when you're done hooking it all up, you can take a rest.

The first sections of this chapter provide an overview and tell you everything that you need to know to set up new user accounts and share files successfully. I don't show you how to actually share a file, folder, or disk until the "Connecting to a Shared Disk or Folder on a Remote Mac" section later in this chapter. Trust me, there's a method to my madness. If you try to share files without doing all the required prep work, the whole mess becomes confusing and complicated — kind of like networking Windows PCs.

One last thing: If you're the only one who uses your Mac, you don't intend to share it or its files with anyone else, and you never intend to access your Mac from another computer in a different location, you can safely skip this whole chapter if you like.

Introducing Networks and File Sharing

Macintosh file sharing enables you to use files, folders, and disks from other Macs on a network — any network, including the Internet — as easily as though they were on your own local hard drive. If you have more than one computer, file sharing is a blessing. It's easy and way better than SneakerNet.

Before diving in and actually sharing, allow me to introduce a few necessary terms:

- ✔ **Network:** For the purposes of this chapter, a *network* is two or more Macs connected by Ethernet cables, AirPort wireless networking, or FireWire cables (which are by far the least common type of network connection).

- ✔ **Ethernet:** A network protocol and cabling scheme that lets you connect two or more computers so they can share files, disks, printers, or whatever.

- ✔ **Ethernet ports:** Where you plug an Ethernet cable into your Mac.

- ✔ Be careful. On your Mac and printer, the Ethernet ports look a lot like phone jacks, and the connectors on each end of an Ethernet cable look a lot like phone cable connectors. But they aren't the same. Ethernet cables are typically thicker, and the connectors (RJ-45 connectors) are a bit larger than the RJ-11 connectors that you use with telephones. (See examples of both types of ports in the margin.) When you connect an Ethernet cable to your Mac, you can't put it into your RJ-11–friendly modem port (and you shouldn't try). Standard phone cables fit (very loosely) into Ethernet ports, but you shouldn't try that either — they'll probably fall out with the slightest vibration. It's unlikely that either mistake will cause any permanent damage, but it won't work and could frustrate you to no end.

- ✔ **Local devices:** Devices connected directly to your computers, such as hard or optical drives. Your internal hard drive, for example, is a local device.

- ✔ **Remote devices:** Devices you access (share) over the network. The hard drive of a computer in the next room, for example, is a remote device.

- ✔ **Protocols:** Kinds of languages that networks speak. When you read or hear about networks, you're likely to hear the words *AppleTalk, EtherTalk* (or *Ethernet*), *SMB,* and *TCP/IP* bandied about with great regularity. These are all protocols. Macs can speak several different protocols, but every device (Mac or printer) on a network needs to speak the same protocol at the same time to communicate.

Support for the TCP/IP protocol is built into every Mac. Your Mac includes all the software that you need to set up an TCP/IP network; the hardware that you need to provide comprises Ethernet cables and a hub (if you have more than two computers) or an AirPort base station. I'm using *hub* here generically — its more powerful cousins, switches and routers, also work. The AirPort base station, by the way, is a member of the router class.

Mac OS X Jaguar added support for a protocol called Bluetooth, and this support was enhanced in Mac OS X Panther and again in Mac OS X Tiger. Bluetooth offers wireless connectivity with devices such as cell phones in addition to other computers; however, it works only over very short ranges and at lower speeds than Ethernet or AirPort. Unlike TCP/IP, Bluetooth support isn't included with all Macs as standard equipment. You can order Bluetooth support as a build-to-order option on many Macs, or you can use a USB adapter, known as a *dongle,* on Macs that don't offer built-in Bluetooth support. The bottom line is that although you could use Bluetooth for networking Macs, due to its slower speed and shorter range, I limit the rest of this discussion to the protocol all Mac OS X users already have on their Macs — TCP/IP.

Portrait of home-office networking

A typical Mac home-office network consists of two Macintoshes, an Ethernet hub, and a network printer (usually a laser printer, although networked inkjet printers are becoming more common). Check out Figure 15-1 to see the configuration of a simple Ethernet network. In the figure, the black lines between the devices are Ethernet cables; the rectangular device with those cables going into it is a hub. (I tell you more about cables and hubs in the section "Three ways to build a network," later in this chapter.) You need enough Ethernet cable to run among all your devices.

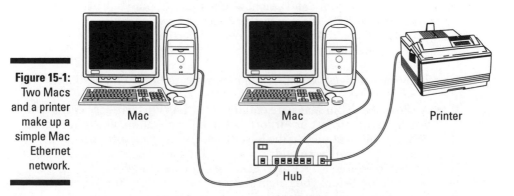

Figure 15-1:
Two Macs and a printer make up a simple Mac Ethernet network.

Mac   Mac   Printer

Hub

File sharing made easy with Bonjour

Perhaps all you want to do is share an occasional file (not necessarily a printer or a home Internet connection or a folder of music files or pictures). In that case, check out *Bonjour,* previously known as Rendezvous. It's a relatively new, zero-configuration network protocol that makes Mac networking simple. If two devices (and this includes all Macs running Mac OS X Jaguar or later) speak Bonjour, you don't have to do *any* configuration other than turning on the sharing capability, as I explain in "Setting Up File Sharing," later in this chapter. Bonjour queries the other available networked devices to see what services they support and then configures the connections for you automatically. Sweet!

With the setup shown in Figure 15-1, either Mac can use the other Mac's files, and both Macs can print to the same printer.

If you have a broadband Internet connection, you can also connect the cable or DSL modem to the hub so all Mac users on the network can share the Internet connection.

A network can — and often does — have dozens or hundreds of users. Regardless of whether your network has 2 nodes (machines) or 2,000, the principles and techniques in this chapter apply.

Three ways to build a network

In this chapter, I assume that you're working on a small network, the kind typically found in a home or small business. If you're part of a megamonstrous corporate network and you have questions about your particular network, talk to the PIC (*person in charge,* also known as your *network administrator*). If you're trying to build one of these meganetworks, you need a book a lot thicker and harder to understand than this one.

The following list gives you three common ways to build a modern network:

  ✔ **AirPort:** If all your Macs are equipped with AirPort wireless cards and you have the AirPort or AirPort Extreme Base Station, you don't need cables at all. Just plug in the base station, and Macs with AirPort cards can communicate with one another. If you use an Ethernet printer (connected to your Mac by Ethernet cable), you need to connect it to the base station before you can print from your wireless Macs. Both the Base Station and printer have Ethernet ports, so you can use a crossover cable to make the connection.

Although this setup is more expensive than Ethernet cables and a hub, it's also more flexible because you can move your devices anywhere. (Well, almost anywhere; you're limited to a maximum of 150–200 feet from each base station, and that's assuming that there's absolutely nothing in the way to block your signal. Your mileage may — and probably will — vary.)

For more information about wireless networking, check out the Apple AirPort Extreme Web page at www.apple.com/airportextreme. You can also check out *Airport and Mac Wireless Networking For Dummies,* by Michael E. Cohen (Wiley).

✔ **Small Ethernet:** If you have only two devices to network (two Macs or a Mac and an Ethernet printer, in most cases), you can use an Ethernet cable to connect them directly to each other via the Ethernet ports. You can purchase an Ethernet cable at your local electronics store. *Note:* Some older Macs might require you to use a special kind of Ethernet cable known as a crossover cable.

Plug one end of the Ethernet cable into one device and the other end into the other device. If it doesn't work and one of the Macs is more than a few years old, try a crossover cable.

An Ethernet crossover cable *won't* work with a hub (as explained in the sidebar "To cross over, or not?"). Therefore, if you buy a crossover cable, label it clearly as a crossover cable because it looks exactly like a regular Ethernet cable, and you don't want to become confused.

✔ **Traditional Ethernet:** All modern Macs have an Ethernet port. To connect your Mac to a network, you need Ethernet cables for each Mac and a little device called a *hub.* (A hub is like the center of a wagon wheel; the wires coming out of it are the "spokes.") A typical Ethernet hub includes two to eight Ethernet ports. You plug the hub into an electrical outlet and then connect Ethernet cables from each of your Macs and printers (from their Ethernet ports) to the hub. Voilà — instant network. Hubs are pretty cheap, starting below $10; cables start at a few bucks, increasing in price as the length and quality of the cable increase.

For each of these setups, if you have a cable modem or Digital Subscriber Line (DSL) as your Internet connection, you might need a router or switch instead of a hub. Routers and switches are similar to hubs but cost a bit more and have additional features that you might or might not need. Your ISP can tell you whether you're going to need one. For what it's worth, I have a DSL modem, but it works fine with a cheap hub.

To cross over, or not?

The type of Ethernet cable required to connect two Macs without a hub or other middle device has changed over time. In the old days, you absolutely had to have a crossover cable, or the Macs wouldn't be able to see each other.

The basic rule had always been that to connect two Macs, you had to use a crossover cable. And if you had a hub or router or other intermediary device, you had to use regular Ethernet cables.

That's less true today because many Macs built in the past few years — and all Macs sold today — have new and improved Ethernet that can determine what type of cable (regular or crossover) you're using and then automatically adjust itself so cable works properly.

These days, you might encounter one of three possibilities: If you want to connect two older Macs, you need a crossover cable. If you want to connect an older Mac to a newer Mac, you might or might not need a crossover cable. And if you want to connect *two* late-model Macs, you can use either a regular Ethernet cable or a crossover cable.

When in doubt, check Mac OS Help in the Help menu (press ⌘+Shift+?).

Setting Up File Sharing

Before you get into the nitty-gritty of sharing files, you must complete a few housekeeping tasks, such as enabling the appropriate type of file sharing.

Follow these steps to do so:

1. **From the menu, choose System Preferences and then click the Sharing icon.**

   The Sharing System Preferences pane appears. The long username of the first Admin account created on this computer appears in the Computer Name field by default.

2. **If you want to change the name of your computer from whatever Leopard decided to call it to something more personal, do that now in the Computer Name text field at the top of the Sharing pane.**

   In Figure 15-2, you can see that I named mine MacBookPro. You can name yours anything you like.

3. **Select the File Sharing check box.**

   Now other users on your network can access files and folders on your computer, as you see later in this chapter.

4. **Enable access for users by clicking the Folders or Users radio button, and then click the folder or user you want to work with.**

   In Figure 15-2, the folder I'm working with is my Home folder (bobl). I've used the pop-up menus to the right of each user's name to give myself

Read & Write access and to give everyone else Read Only access. So I can access my Home folder from any Mac on my local network, as you'll see shortly.

To choose a different user or folder to work with, click the user's name in the Shared Folders or Users lists. If the folder or person doesn't appear in the list, click the + button below the list and add the folder or person.

5. **(Optional) If you want remote users (that is, on the Internet, not your local area network) to be able to use a File Transfer Protocol (FTP), an Apple File Protocol (AFP), or a Server Message Block (Samba or SMB) client program (instead of using file sharing on another Mac) to upload and download files to and from this computer, click the Advanced button and then select any or all of the Share files and folders using AFP, FTP, or SMB check boxes.**

If you want to enable Windows or Linux users — or users of other operating systems — to share files with you, either the FTP or the SMB check box must be selected.

Other Mac users could use an FTP client to access your Mac, but they'll probably want to use file sharing instead, because it's easier.

Security risks are involved in allowing FTP access. I strongly suggest that you go to the Apple Web site (`www.apple.com`) and read about them before you enable this feature.

6. **(Optional) Windows users can also share files if you select the Windows File Sharing check box in the Sharing tab's Services pane.**

This feature takes most of the pain out of working with people using Microsoft Windows systems.

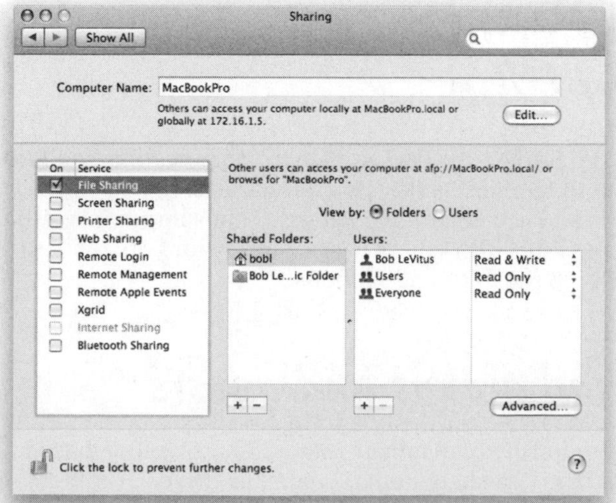

Figure 15-2:
Turning
personal file
sharing on
and off.

Sharing with TCP/IP

Although you don't need to know about TCP/IP to set up your network, when you select the FTP Access check box or the Windows File Sharing check box on the Services tab of the Sharing dialog, you're actually enabling TCP/IP access to this computer. *TCP/IP* is the network protocol used by Mac OS X Leopard for sharing files. It enables Macs, PCs, and other computers to communicate with one another (sometimes, but not always, via the Internet), even if they're running different operating systems. TCP/IP is always on, so you don't have to do anything further about it.

Computers connect to one another by using a number-based addressing system *(an IP address)*

that's standard all over the world. You can (and most big companies do) use this system to communicate in offices and over the Internet.

If you need to know more about using TCP/IP to connect to computers on your network than I've told you here, talk to the system administrator or the network geek in charge of these things where you work. Also, I touch more on TCP/IP in the "Connecting to a Shared Disk or Folder on a Remote Mac" section later in this chapter, where you can read how to use it to connect to a Mac or other server that's running it.

---

7. **Select the On check box (the leftmost column) for each account you want to enable to use these protocols to access your Mac.**

8. **Click the Close gumdrop button when you're done and then proceed to the section "Access and Permissions: Who Can Do What," later in this chapter, to continue setting up your network.**

Access and Permissions: Who Can Do What

After you set up file sharing (as I explain in the preceding section), your next step on the path to sharing files on a networks is telling your Mac who is allowed to see and access specific folders. That same info is also useful if you share your computer with others users. Luckily for you, this just happens to be what I cover in the following sections.

Users and groups and guests

Macintosh file sharing (and indeed, Mac OS X as well) is based on the concept of users. You can share items — such as drives or folders — with no users, one user, or many users, depending on your needs.

✔ **Users:** People who share folders and drives (or your Mac) are *users*. A user's access to items on your local hard drive is entirely at your discretion. You can configure your Mac so only you can access its folders and drives or so only one other person (or everyone) can share its folders and drives.

When you first set up your Mac, you created your first user. This user automatically has administrative powers, such as adding more users, changing preferences, and having the clearance to see all folders on the hard drive.

For the purposes of this book, I assume that some users for whom you create identities won't be folks who actually sit at your Mac, but rather those who connect to it only from a remote location when they need to give or get files. But they *could* use the same name and password to log in while sitting at your desk.

For all intents and purposes, a remote user and a local user are the same. In other words, after you create an account for a user, that user can log in to this Mac while sitting in your chair in your office, from anywhere on your local area network via Ethernet, or anywhere in the world via the Internet.

✔ **Administrative users:** Although a complete discussion of the special permissions that a user with administrator permissions has on a Mac running Mac OS X is far beyond the scope of this book, note two important things:

  • The first user created (usually when you install OS X for the first time) is automatically granted administrator (admin) powers.

  • Only an administrator can create new users, delete some (but not all) files from folders that aren't in his or her Home folder, lock and unlock System Preferences panes, and a bunch of other stuff. If you try something and it doesn't work, make sure you're logged in as a user with admin permissions.

You can give any user administrator permissions by selecting that user's account in the Accounts System Preferences pane, clicking the Password tab, and then selecting the Allow User to Administer This Computer check box. You can set this check box when creating the user account or subsequently.

✔ **Groups:** *Groups* are UNIX-level designations for privilege consolidation. For example, there are groups named `staff` and `wheel` (as well as a bunch of others). A user can be a member of multiple groups. For example, your main account is in the `wheel` and `admin` groups (and others, too). Don't worry — you find out more about groups shortly.

✔ **Guests:** Two kinds of guests exist. The first kind lets your friends log into your Mac while sitting at your desk without a user account or password. When they log out, all information and files in the guest account's Home folder are deleted automatically.

If you want this kind of guest account, you need to enable the Guest Account in the Accounts System Preferences pane.

The second kind of guest is people who access Public folders on your Mac via file sharing over your local area network or the Internet. They don't need a username or password. If they're on your local network, they can see and use your Public folder(s), unless you or the Public folder's owner has altered the permissions on one or more Public folders. If they're on the Internet and know your IP address, they can see and use your Public folder(s). Public folders are all that guests can access, luckily.

You don't have to do anything to enable this type of guest account.

Creating users

Before users can share folders and drives (or have their own accounts on your computer, for that matter), they must have an account on your Mac. You can create two different kinds of accounts for them — a User Account or a Sharing Account.

- ✔ **When you create a User Account** for a person (I call that person and account *User 1*), the account has its own Home folder (called — what else? — User 1), which is filled with User 1's files. Nobody but User 1 can access files in this Home folder unless, of course, User 1 has provided someone the account name and password.

- ✔ **When you create a Sharing Account** for a person (I call that person and account *Sharing 1*), the person using that account doesn't have a Home folder and can't access other users' Home folders. Sharing 1 can access only the Public folders inside all the Home folders on that Mac.

You can create a new User Account only in the Accounts System Preferences pane. You can create a Sharing Account in the Accounts or Sharing System Preference panes.

When you click the + button under the Users list in the Sharing System Preference pane and choose a contact in your Address Book (as opposed to choosing an existing user account), you create a Sharing account for that person.

Remote guests (LAN or Internet) can access your Public folder(s) — but no other folders — without having either type of user account.

To access files on your Mac remotely, a user needs a Sharing Account on your computer. In other words, giving a user access to certain folders on your system means that the user also has folders of his or her own on the Mac. When you add (create) a user, you need to tell your Mac who this person is. This is also the time to set passwords and administrative powers for this new user. Here's the drill:

1. **From the menu, choose System Preferences (or click the System Preferences icon in the Dock), click the Accounts icon, and then make sure that the Password tab is selected.**

   The Accounts System Preferences pane appears. In this pane (shown in Figure 15-3), you can see the name of the first user (Bob LeVitus) and the administrative control that this user is allowed. (Note that the Allow User to Administer This Computer check box is selected.)

   As I mention previously, the first user created (usually at the same time you installed OS X) always has administrator permissions.

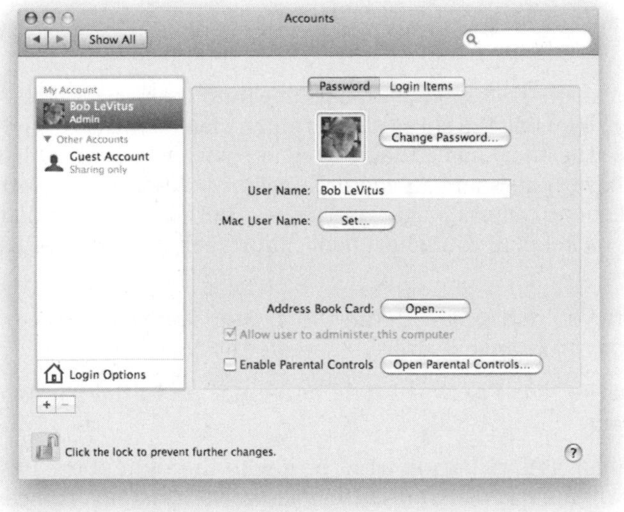

Figure 15-3:
The
Accounts
System
Preferences
pane shows
who can
use this
Mac.

2. **Click the + button beneath the list of users.**

   A sheet appears in which you enter the new user's information.

   If the + button is dimmed, you need to first click the lock (lower left), supply an administrator name and password in the resulting dialog, and then click OK.

3. **Choose Standard from the Type menu at the top of the sheet.**

4. **In the Name text box, type the full name of a user you want to add.**

   In the Short Name text box, your Mac inserts a suggested abbreviated name (or *short name,* as it's called). Check out Figure 15-4 to see both.

   In Figure 15-4, I added `Steven P. Jobs` as a user, typing the full name in the Name field. You don't really need to type the user's full name, but I do so in this example to show you the difference between a name and a short name.

5. **Press the Tab key to move to the next field.**

   Mac OS X suggests an abbreviated version of the name in the Short Name field (as shown in Figure 15-4).

   Because he's the only Steve who matters around here, I change the suggested Short Name from `stevenpjobs` to just plain `steve`, which is shorter than the short name recommended by Mac OS X. (In other words, I type **steve** in the Short Name field, replacing the suggested `stevenpjobs`.)

   The name of each user's folder (in the Users folder) is taken from the short name that you enter when you create a user.

   Users can connect to your Mac (or log in to their own Macs, for that matter) by using the short name, rather than having to type their full names. The short name is also used in environments in which usernames can't have spaces and are limited to eight or fewer characters. Although OS X Leopard allows longer usernames (but no spaces), you might be better off keeping your short name shorter than eight characters, just in case.

   Be sure you're happy with the short name you've chosen — there's no easy way to change it after you create the account.

6. **Tab to the New Password field and enter an initial password for this user.**

   The small, square button with the key to the right of the Password field, when clicked, displays the Password Assistant. You can use the Password Assistant to help generate a password that should be fairly easy for the user to remember but hard for a cracking program to guess or meet other requirements.

   To make your password even harder to guess or crack, choose Random or FIPS-181 compliant from the Password Assistant's Type pop-up menu.

7. **Press the Tab key to move your cursor to the Verify text field.**

8. **In the Verify text box, type the password again to verify it.**

9. **(Optional) To help remember a password, type something in the Password Hint text box to jog the user's memory.**

TIP

If a user forgets his or her password and asks for a hint, the text that you type in the Password Hint field pops up, hopefully causing the user to exclaim, "Oh, yeah . . . *now* I remember!" A password hint should be something simple enough to jog the user's memory but not so simple that an unauthorized person can guess. Perhaps something like "Your first teddy bear's name backward" would be a good hint.

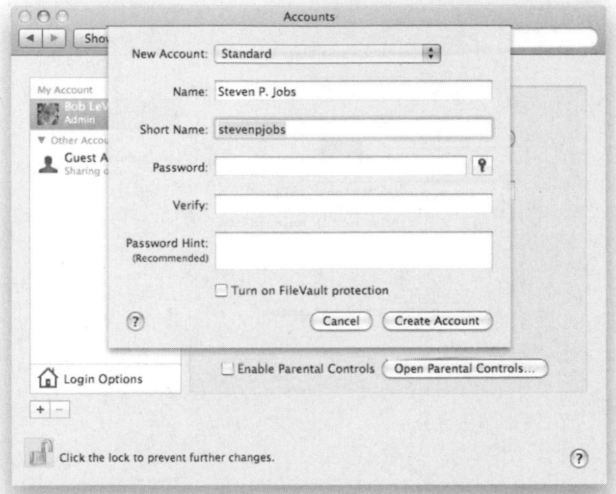

Figure 15-4:
Name the new user; your Mac suggests a short name.

10. **Click Create Account.**

The sheet closes, returning you to the Password pane.

11. **(Optional) Select the Turn on FileVault Protection check box if you want to encrypt this user's Home folder with FileVault.**

WARNING!

You can find out more about FileVault security in Chapter 17.

Several serious implications result from enabling FileVault. I strongly recommend that you read every word about FileVault in Chapter 17 before you even consider turning it on.

12. **Click the Create Account button to create the account.**

The sheet disappears, and the new user now appears in the Accounts System Preferences pane's Users list.

13. **(Optional) Click the account picture to the left of the Name and Short Name fields and choose a different one.**

Mac OS X suggests a picture from its default collection for each account, but you can select a different one from the pop-up mini-window shown in Figure 15-5, drag one in from the Finder (or iPhoto), or take a photo with an attached or built-in camera (such as an iSight) by choosing Edit Picture.

14. **(Optional) Type the user's .Mac user name.**

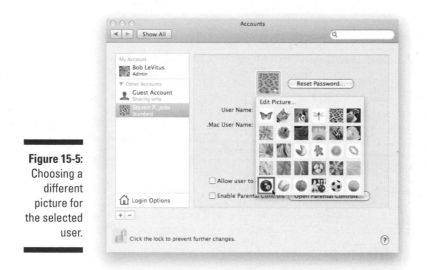

Figure 15-5:
Choosing a
different
picture for
the selected
user.

Changing a user

Circumstances might dictate that you need to change a user's identity, password, or accessibility, or perhaps delete a user. Follow these steps to change a user's name, password, or administration permissions:

1. **From the menu, choose System Preferences (or click the System Preferences icon in the Dock).**

   The System Preferences window appears.

2. **In the System Preferences window, click the Accounts icon.**

   The Accounts System Preferences pane appears.

3. **If the lock icon at the bottom of the window is locked, you have to click it and provide an administrator password before you can proceed.**

4. **Select the user's name in the accounts list.**

   The information for that person appears.

5. **Make your changes by selecting the existing username and then replacing the old with new text or a different setting.**

- If you want to change the password, click the Reset Password button and make your changes in the sheet that appears.

- To change the picture or other capabilities, click the Picture, Login Options, Allow User to Administer This Computer (to make this user an administrator on this Mac), or Enable Parental Control check box (more on this in a moment) and make the appropriate changes.

   To change a user, you must be logged in using an account that has administrator powers.

6. **Quit the System Preferences application or choose a different System Preferences pane.**

   Your changes are saved when you leave the Accounts pane.

Removing a user

To delete a user — in effect, to deny that user access to your Mac — select the user you want to delete in the list of accounts and then click the – button. You will be asked to confirm that you really want to delete the user. Click OK to delete the user but save the user's Home folder files in the Deleted Users folder, or click Delete Immediately to delete the user *and* his or her Home folder.

To remove a user from your Mac, you must be logged in using an account that has administrator permissions. When you delete the user, the files and folders that the user owned are stored in the Deleted Users folder in a Disk Image file.

Limiting a user's capabilities

Sometimes — especially with younger children or computerphobic family members — you want to limit what users can access. For example, you might want to make certain programs off limits. You do this by clicking the Parental Controls button in the Accounts System Preferences pane.

1. **From the menu, choose System Preferences (or click the System Preferences icon in the Dock).**

   The System Preferences window appears.

2. **In the System Preferences window, click the Accounts icon.**

   The Accounts System Preferences pane appears.

3. **Click the user's name to select it, click the Enable Parental Controls check box, and then click the Open Parental Controls button.**

   The Parental Controls tabs for that person appear, as shown in Figure 15-6.

   You can't apply Parental Controls to an account that has administrator permissions.

4. **Select the check box that corresponds to a user capability you want to restrict.**

- *System:* Determine which applications the user may access. Set whether she can print, burn optical discs, modify the Dock, or access System Preferences. Also determine whether she's restricted to a very limited and simplified Finder interface.

- *Content:* Hide profanity in the Dictionary and control access to Web sites.

- *Mail & iChat:* Provide a list of approved iChat and Mail communicants. This option also lets you notify someone (usually yourself) when the user tries to exchange e-mail with a contact not in the approved list.

- *Time Limits:* Set time limits for weekdays and weekends, and prevent access to this computer during specified hours on school nights and weekends.

- *Logs:* Monitor Web sites visited, Web sites blocked, applications used, and chat activity.

To change any of these items, you must be logged in using an account that has administrator powers, and the account you're modifying can't have administrator powers.

5. **Quit the System Preferences application or choose a different System Preferences pane.**

    Your changes are saved when you leave the Accounts pane.

    Another way to set or change Parental Controls is to click the Parental Controls icon in the System Preferences application (instead of Accounts).

Figure 15-6: You can control an account's access in five categories.

Mac OS X knows best: Folders shared by default

When you add users in the Accounts System Preferences pane as I describe earlier, Mac OS X automatically does two things behind the scenes to facilitate file sharing: It creates a set of folders, and it makes some of them available for sharing.

Each time you add a user, Mac OS X creates a Home folder hierarchy for that user on the Mac. The user can create more folders (if necessary) and also add, remove, or move anything inside these folders. Even if you create a user account solely to allow him or her to exchange files with you, your Mac automatically creates a Home folder for that user. Unless you, as the owner of your Mac, give permission, the user can't see inside or use folders outside the Home folder (which has the user's name), with only three exceptions: the Shared folder in the Users folder, the top level of other user account folders, and the Public and Shared folders in every other user's folder. A description of the latter follows:

- ✔ **Public:** A Public folder is located inside each user's folder. That folder is set up to be accessible (shared) by any user who can log in to the Mac. Furthermore, any user can log in (as a guest) and copy things out of this folder as long as he knows your Mac's IP address, even if he doesn't have an account on this Mac at all. Files put into the Public folder can be opened or copied freely.

  It's not hard for someone to obtain your IP address. For example, when you visit most Web pages, your IP address is saved to that site's log file. So be careful what you put in your Public folder, okay?

  Inside each user's Public folder is a Drop Box folder. Just like the name implies, this folder is where others can drop a file or folder for you. Only the owner can open the Drop Box to see what's inside or to move or copy the files that are in it. Imagine a street-corner mailbox — after you drop your letter in, it's gone, and you can't get it back out.

- ✔ **Shared:** In addition to a Public folder for each user, Mac OS X creates one Shared folder on every Mac for all users of this Mac. The Shared folder *isn't* available to guests, but it's available to all users who have an account on this machine. You find the Shared folder within the Users folder (the same folder where you find folders for each user). The Shared folder is the right place to put stuff that everyone with an account on this Mac might want to use. (If you haven't already, check out my introduction to the Mac OS Leopard folder structure in Chapter 6.)

Sharing a folder or disk by setting permissions

As you might expect, permissions control who can use a given folder or any disk (or partition) other than the startup disk.

Why can't you share the startup disk? Because Mac OS X won't let you. Why not? Because it contains the operating system and other stuff that nobody else should have access to.

Throughout the rest of this chapter, whenever I talk about *sharing a folder,* I also mean *sharing disks and disk partitions other than your startup disk* (which, when you think of it, are nothing more than big folders anyway). Why am I telling you this? Because it's awkward to keep typing "a folder or any disk (or partition) other than your startup disk." So anything that I say about sharing a folder also applies to sharing any disk (or partition) other than your startup disk. Got it?

You can set permissions for

- The folder's owner
- A subset of all the people who have accounts on the Mac (a group)
- Everyone who has the Mac's address, whether they have an account or not (guests)

To help you get a better handle on these relationships, a closer look at permissions, owners, and groups is coming right up.

Contemplating permissions

When you consider who can use which folders, three distinct kinds of users exist on the network. I describe each of them in this section. Then, in the "Useful settings for permissions" section, later in this chapter, I show you how to share folders with each type of user. Here's a quick introduction to the different user types:

- **Owner:** The owner of a folder or disk can change the permissions to that folder or disk at any time. The name you enter when you log in to your Mac — or the name of your Home folder — is the default owner of Shared folders and drives on that machine. Ownership can be given away (more on that in the "Useful settings for permissions" section, later in this chapter). Even if you own the Mac, you can't change permissions for a folder on it that belongs to another user (unless you get UNIX-y and do so as `root`). The owner must be logged in to change permissions on his or her folders.

Mac OS X is the owner of many folders outside the Users folder. If OS X owns it, you can see that system is its owner if you select the folder and choose File⇨Get Info (or use the shortcut, ⌘+I), as shown in Figure 15-7. Folders that aren't in the User directories generally belong to system; it's almost always a bad idea to change the permissions on any folder owned by system.

✔ **Group member:** In UNIX systems, all users belong to one or more *groups.* The group that includes everyone who has an account with administrator permissions on your Mac is called admin. Everyone in the admin group has access to Shared and Public folders over the network, as well as to any folder that the admin group has been granted access to by the folder's owner.

For the purposes of assigning permissions, you can create your own groups the same way you create a user account: Open the Accounts System Preferences pane, click the little plus sign, choose Group from the Type pop-up menu, type the name of the group, and then click the Create Group button.

The group appears in the list of users on the left, and eligible accounts appear with check boxes on the right, as shown in Figure 15-8.

✔ **Everyone:** This category is an easy way to set permissions for everyone with an account on your Mac at the same time. Unlike the admin group, which includes only users with administrative permissions, others includes, well, everyone (everyone with an account on this Mac, that is).

If you want people without an account on this Mac to have access to a file or folder, that file or folder needs to go in your Public folder, where the people you want to see it can log in as guests.

Figure 15-7:
Mac OS X (system) owns this folder, so you can't easily change its permissions.

Figure 15-8:
This group,
Outsiders,
contains my
Parrothead
and Steven
P. Jobs
accounts.

Sharing a folder

Suppose you have a folder you want to share, but it has slightly different rules than those set up for the Public folder, for the Drop Box folder within the Public folder, or for your personal folders. These rules are *permissions,* and they tell you how much access someone has to your stuff.

Actually, the rules governing Shared and Public folders are permissions, too, but they're set up for you when Mac OS X is installed.

I suggest that you share only folders located in your Home folder (or a folder within it). Because of the way Unix works, the Unix permissions of the enclosing folder can prevent access to a folder for which you *do* have permissions. Trust me, if you share only the folders in your Home folder, you'll never go wrong. If you don't take this advice, you could wind up having folders that other users can't access, even though you gave them the appropriate permissions.

By the way, you can set permissions for folders within your Public folder (like the Drop Box folder) that are different from those for the rest of the folder.

I said this before, but it bears repeating: Whenever I talk about sharing a folder, I also mean disks and disk partitions other than your startup disk (which you just can't share, period). So don't forget that anything I say about sharing a folder also applies to sharing any disk (or partition) other than your startup disk. Though you can't explicitly share your startup disk, anyone with administrator access can mount it for sharing from across the network (or Internet).

To share a folder with another user, follow these steps:

1. **From the menu, choose System Preferences (or click the System Preferences icon in the Dock).**

   The System Preferences window appears.

2. **In the System Preferences window, click the Sharing icon.**

   The Sharing System Preference pane appears.

3. **Click File Sharing in the list of services on the left.**

   The lists of shared folders and their users appear on the right, as shown in Figure 15-9.

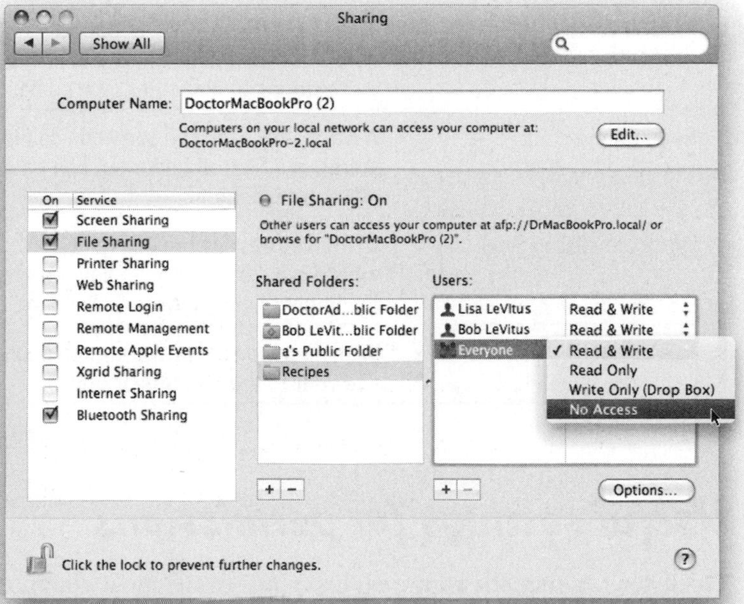

Figure 15-9: Set file sharing here.

4. **Click the + (plus) button under the Shared Folders column to add the folder you wish to share.**

5. **Click the + (plus) button under the Users column to add a user or group (if the user or group you desire isn't already showing in the Users column).**

6. **Click on the double-headed arrow to the right of a user or group name to change its privileges.**

   I'm changing the permission for Everyone from Read & Write to No Access in Figure 15-9.

   You can choose among three types of access for each user or group, as shown in Table 15-1.

   If you're the folder's owner (or have administrator access), you can click the padlock icon and change the owner and/or group for the file or folder.

Table 15-1	Privileges
Permission	*What It Allows*
Read & Write	A user with Read & Write access can see, add, delete, move, and edit files just as though they were stored on his or her own computer.
Read Only	A Read Only user can see and use files that are stored in a Shared folder but can't add, delete, move, or edit them.
Write Only (Drop Box)	Users can add files to this folder but can't see what's in it. The user must have read access to the folder containing a Write Only folder.
No Access	With no permissions, a user can neither see nor use your Shared folders or drives.

Useful settings for permissions

The following sections show you just some of the most common ways that you can combine permissions for a folder. You'll probably find one option that fits the way you work and the people you want to share with.

Owner permissions (single silhouette; bob1 (Me) in Figure 15-10) must be at least as expansive as Group permissions (double silhouette; admin in Figure 15-10) and Group permissions must be at least as expansive as Everyone's permissions (triple silhouette; everyone in Figure 15-10). So to set the Everyone privilege to Read & Write, the Group and Owner privileges must also be set to Read & Write.

Allow everyone access

In Figure 15-10, I configure settings that allow everyone on a network to access the Bob's Downloads folder. Everyone can open, read, and change the contents of this Shared folder. Do this by choosing Read & Write for Others from the Privilege pop-up menu in the Sharing & Permissions section of the folder's Get Info window.

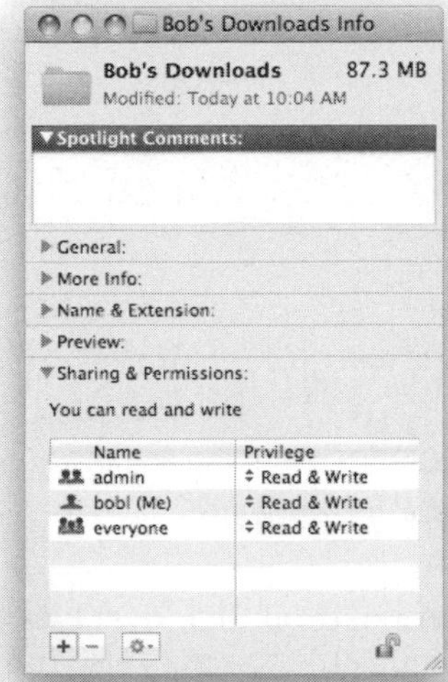

Figure 15-10:
Allow everyone access if you want.

Allow nobody but yourself access

The settings shown in Figure 15-11 reflect appropriate settings that allow owner-only access to the Bob's Downloads folder. No one but me can see or use the contents of this folder. Members of the Admin group can drop files and folders into this folder (see Drop Box section below). Choose Write Only (Drop Box) as the Admin privilege and No Access as the Everyone privilege.

Allow all administrative users of this Mac access

Check out Figure 15-12 to see settings that allow the group admin (in addition to the owner, bobl) access to see, use, or change the contents of the Bob's Downloads folder. Choose Read & Write for in the admin privilege pop-up menu.

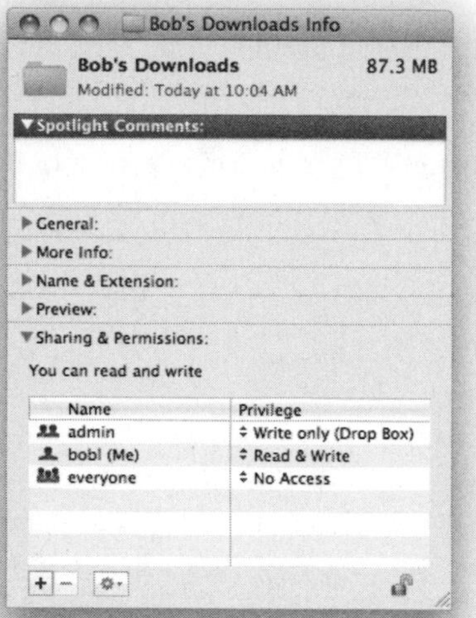

Figure 15-11:
Allow
access for
no one but
the folder's
owner.

Allow others to deposit files and folders without giving them access (a Drop Box)

The settings in Figure 15-13 enable users to drop their own files or folders in the Bob's Downloads folder without being able to see or use the contents of the Shared folder. After a file or folder is deposited in a drop folder, the dropper can't retrieve it because he or she doesn't have permission to see the items in the drop folder.

Read-only bulletin boards

If you want everyone to be able to open and read the files and folders in this Shared folder, choose Read Only from the Group and Others privilege pop-up menus. If you do this, however, only the owner can make changes to files in this folder.

One more privilege

The Apply to Enclosed Items button, at the bottom of the permissions section, does exactly what its name implies. This feature is a fast way to assign the same permissions to many subfolders at the same time. After you set permissions for the enclosing folder the way you like them, click this button to give these same permissions to all folders inside it.

Be careful — there is no Undo for this action.

Figure 15-12:
Allow
access to
one group:
admin.

Unsharing a folder

To unshare a folder that you own, change the Group Access and Others permissions to None. After you do, nobody but you will have access to that folder.

If you're not sure how to do this, see the "Sharing a folder" and "Useful settings for permissions" sections, earlier in this chapter.

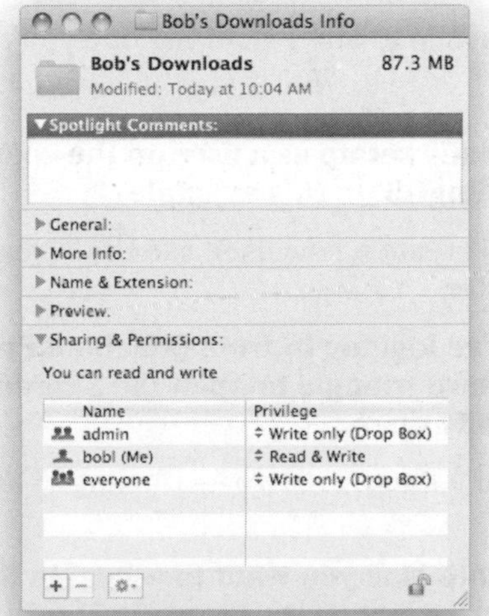

Figure 15-13:
Everyone
can drop
files into this
folder.

Connecting to a Shared Disk or Folder on a Remote Mac

After you set up sharing and assign permissions, you can access folders remotely from another computer. (Just make sure first that you have permissions to it.)

File sharing must be activated on the Mac where the shared files/folders reside; it doesn't have to be activated on the Mac that's accessing the files/folders. When file sharing is turned off, you can still use that Mac to access a remote Shared folder on another machine as long as its owner has granted you enough permissions and has file sharing enabled on his or her Mac.

If file sharing is turned off on *your* Mac, though, others won't be able to access your folders, even if you've assigned permissions to them previously.

If you're going to share files and you leave your Mac on and unattended for a long time, logging out before you leave it is a very good idea. This prevents anyone just walking up to your Mac from seeing your files, e-mail, applications, or anything else that's yours — unless you've given her a user account and granted her permissions for your files.

On to how to access your Home folder from a remote Mac — a supercool feature that's only bound to get more popular as the Internet continues to mature.

The following steps assume that you have an account on the remote Mac, which means you have your own Home folder on that Mac.

To connect to a Shared folder on a Mac other than the one you're currently on, follow these steps:

1. **Make sure that you're already set up as a user on the computer that you want to log in to (DuelingG5, in this example).**

   If you need to know how to create a new user, see the "Creating users" section, earlier in the chapter.

2. **On the computer that you're logging in from (MacBookPro, in this example), click the disclosure triangle to open the Shared section in the Sidebar if it's not already open.**

   All available servers appear. (There are two — DuelingG5 and Jacob eMac — in this example.)

3. **Click the name of the remote Mac you want to access in the Sidebar and then click the Connect As button, as shown in Figure 15-14.**

   A Connect to Server dialog appears with your username already in the Name field.

Figure 15-14:
Connecting to DuelingG5.

4. **Type your password and click the Connect button.**

   The Connect dialog appears. The name of the person logged in on MacBookPro automatically appears in the Name field (`Bob LeVitus` in Figure 15-15).

Figure 15-15:
The Connect to Server needs to know my password.

5. **If that's not you, type your username in the Name field.**

6. **Select the Guest radio button if you don't have an account on the remote computer and then click Connect. If you're logging in as a user, skip to Step 7.**

Pressing ⌘+G is the same as marking the Guest radio button, and pressing ⌘+R is the same as marking the Registered User radio button.

As a guest user, you see Drop Boxes for users who have accounts on DoctorMacBookPro, but nothing else. A registered user (somebody like me in this example) also sees his Home folder plus everyone else's Public folder.

7. **(Optional) If you select the Remember This Password in My Keychain check box in the Connect dialog, Mac OS X remembers your password for you the next time you connect to a server. Sweet!**

File sharing must be active on DuelingG5 (the Mac I'm accessing remotely in the example). If file sharing weren't active on DuelingG5, its name wouldn't have appeared in the first column, and I wouldn't have been able to connect to it. On the other hand, file sharing doesn't have to be active on the computer you're using (MacBookPro) for this to work.

8. **Type your password in the Password field and then click the Connect button.**

All available volumes on that computer appear in the second column below the Connect As button, as shown in Figure 15-16.

When you log in to a Mac on which you have a user account, you see a volume with your name representing your Home folder on the Mac you're logging into (bobl in Figure 15-16). If you have administrator permissions on that Mac (as I do), you might also see other hard drives connected to that Mac (such as BigBoy and Boots in Figure 15-16) or an iDisk if one is in use.

9. **Select the volume that you want to use (bobl in Figure 15-16).**

Figure 15-16:
Selecting
the volume I
want to
mount.

The contents of the remote volume (bob1 in Figure 15-16) appear in the third column. At the same time, an icon for the remote volume appears on your Desktop (the Desktop of MacBookPro). In my example, this icon represents the volume named bob1, which resides on the computer DuelingG5. Notice that the icon for your remote volume doesn't look like a drive or folder icon; it's more like sphere. This icon is what you see whenever a remote volume is mounted on your Desktop.

10. **When you finish using the shared volume, disconnect by using one of these methods:**

   - Drag the shared-volume icon to the Eject icon in the Dock.

     When a disk or volume is selected (highlighted), the Trash icon turns into a little arrow, which represents *eject.* Nice touch, eh?

   - Hold down the Control key, click the volume, and then choose Eject from the contextual menu that appears.

   - Select the icon and choose File⇨Eject.

   - Select the icon and press ⌘+E.

   - In a Finder window Sidebar, click the little Eject symbol to the right of the server's name or select the server and choose Eject from the Action pop-up menu.

   - If you've finished working for the day and don't leave your Mac on 24/7 as most folks do, choose Shut Down or Log Out from the menu. Shutting down or logging out automatically disconnects you from shared disks or folders. (Shut Down also turns off your Mac.)

Changing Your Password

You can change your password at any time. Changing your password is a good idea if you're concerned about security — for example, if there's a chance your password has been discovered by someone else.

You can change the password for your Mac, or you can change the password you use to connect to your account on a remote user's Mac. I show you how to do both in the following sections.

Changing your Mac's password

To change the password on your Mac, just follow these steps:

1. **Choose System Preferences from the menu on the Finder's menu bar or double click its icon in your Applications folder and then click the Accounts icon.**

   The Accounts System Preferences pane appears.

2. **Select your account in the list on the left.**

   Your account information appears in the area on the right.

3. **Click the Change Password button.**

   A sheet drops down.

4. **Type your current password in the Old Password field.**

   This demonstrates that you are who you're supposed to be and not someone who just walked up to your unattended Mac.

5. **Type your new password in the Password field in the Password pane.**

6. **Retype your password in the Verify field.**

7. **Click the Change Password button.**

   Assuming that you entered your old password correctly, the sheet disappears.

8. **Close the System Preferences window.**

Changing the password for your account on someone else's Mac

When you log in to a remote Mac, you can change your own password if you like. Follow these steps to do so:

1. **Log in to the remote computer on which you want to change your password.**

   See the "Connecting to a Shared Disk or Folder on a Remote Mac" section, earlier in this chapter, if you don't know how to log in to a remote computer.

   The Connect to Server dialog appears.

2. **Type your username in the Connect to Server dialog if it's not already there.**

3. **Click the Action button (the one that looks like a little gear) in the Connect to Server dialog and choose Change Password from the pop-up menu.**

   A sheet for changing your password appears.

   The other choice in the Actions pop-up is Options. The sheet that appears includes several options for encrypting your password, as it is sent over the network.

4. **Type your current password in the Old Password field.**

5. **Type your new password in the New Password and Verify fields.**

6. **Click OK.**

   Your password is changed, and you return to the Connect to Server dialog.

7. **(Optional) Type your new password and then click Connect to log in to the other Mac.**

   You can skip this step by clicking the Cancel button in the Connect to Server dialog if you don't need to use anything on the remote Mac at this time. Your password is still changed, and you need to use the new password the next time you log in to this Mac.

   Select the Add Password to Keychain check box in the Connect to Server dialog to store your passwords in a single place on the Mac, meaning that you don't have to retype them each time you access a Mac or other remote resource. (Read more about the Keychain in Chapter 18.)

Four More Types of Sharing

Several more types of sharing exist, and I'd like to at least mention a few in passing. All are found in (where else?) the Sharing System Preferences pane, which you can find by launching the System Preferences application (from the Applications folder, menu, or Dock) and clicking the Sharing icon.

Printer Sharing

This one's a snap. If you turn on Printer Sharing in the Sharing System Preferences pane, other people on your local network can use any printer connected to your computer.

Internet Sharing

If your Mac has an Internet connection and another Mac nearby doesn't, you can enable Internet Sharing, and that Mac will be able to share your Internet connection. The following steps show you how:

1. **Open the Sharing System Preferences pane by launching the System Preferences application (from the Applications folder,  menu, or Dock) and clicking the Sharing icon.**

2. **Choose the connection you want to share — Built-In FireWire, Bluetooth, AirPort, or Built-In Ethernet — from the pop-up Share Your Connection From menu.**

3. **Select the check box next to the connection the other computer will use — AirPort, Built-In Ethernet, or Built-In FireWire.**

   Figure 15-17 shows Internet Sharing configured to share my Ethernet Internet connection with another Mac using AirPort. That's it.

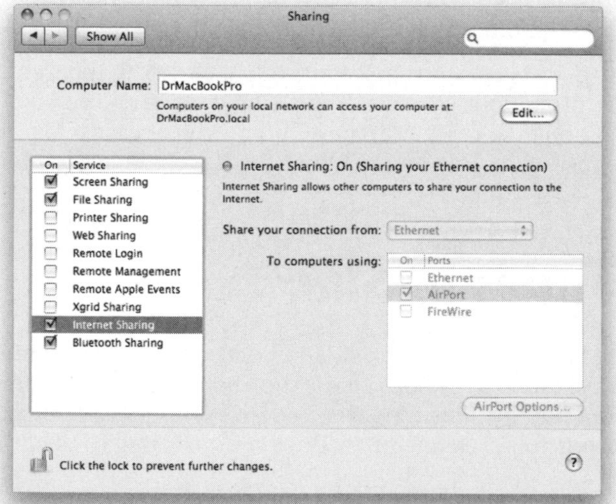

Figure 15-17:
Sharing my Ethernet Internet connection with another Mac using AirPort.

Web Sharing

Web Sharing enables others to share documents on your computer through the Web. You can set up a Web site just by adding HyperText Markup Language (HTML) pages and images to the Sites folder in your Home folder and then activating Web Sharing in the Sharing pane of System Preferences.

Web Sharing works only while your Mac is connected to the Internet or an internal network. In other words, if you use a modem and connect to the Internet by dialing up, this application won't be a lot of use to you.

Furthermore, even if you keep your modem connected to the Internet 24 hours a day with a Digital Subscriber Line (DSL) or cable-modem connection, using this feature could violate your agreement with your Internet service provider (ISP) because some ISPs prohibit you from running a Web site. Also, most cable and DSL connections use dynamic IP address assignment through Dynamic Host Configuration Protocol (DHCP), which means your IP address will change from time to time.

On the other hand, some ISPs don't care whether you run a Web site. Check with yours if you're concerned. I do turn on this feature occasionally, but (because I don't use it 24/7) I never bothered to check with my ISP. Do me a favor and don't rat me out.

Bluetooth Sharing

If you have a Bluetooth mobile phone or PDA and your Mac has Bluetooth, you can configure many of the default behaviors for transferring files to and from your Mac. A picture is worth a thousand words, so Figure 15-18 shows all the things Bluetooth Sharing lets you configure.

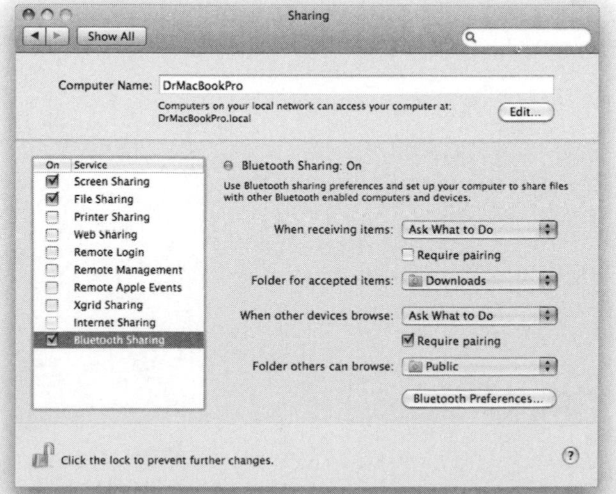

Figure 15-18:
You can configure items for Bluetooth file transfers between your Bluetooth phone or PDA and your Bluetooth-equipped Mac.

Chapter 16

Features for the Way You Work

This chapter delves into Mac OS X Leopard features that might very well improve the ways you interact with your computer. Unlike the more mainstream applications and utilities I discuss in Chapter 3 — Desktop, Screen Saver, Appearance, Keyboard, Mouse, and such — the items in this chapter are a little more esoteric. In other words, you don't *have* to use any of the technologies I'm about to show you. That said, many of these items can make you more productive and can make using your Mac even better. So I'd like to believe that at least some of you will *want* to use the cool features I'm about to introduce.

Talking and Listening to Your Mac

Your primary methods for interacting with your Mac are typing and reading text. But there's another way you can commune with your faithful computer — voice.

Whether you know it or not, your Mac has a lot of speech savvy up its sleeve (er . . . up its processor?) and can talk to you as well as listen and obey. In the following sections, you discover how to make your Mac do both.

Talking to your Mac

Speech Recognition enables your Mac to recognize and respond to human speech. The only thing you need to use it is a microphone, and all laptops and iMacs have a built-in mic these days.

Speech Recognition lets you issue verbal commands such as "Get my mail!" to your Mac and have it actually get your e-mail. You can also create AppleScripts and then trigger them by voice.

An *AppleScript* is a series of commands, using the AppleScript language, that tells the computer (and some applications) what to do. You find out more about AppleScript later in this chapter.

Setting up for Speech Recognition

To start using Speech Recognition, follow these steps:

1. **Open the Speech System Preferences pane.**

2. **Click the Speech Recognition tab and click the Settings sub-tab.**

3. **Click the On button for Speakable Items, as shown in Figure 16-1.**

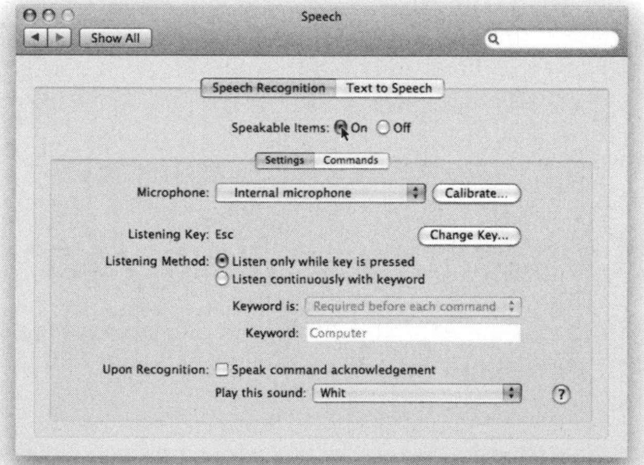

Figure 16-1:
Turn Speech
Recognition
on and off in
the Settings
sub-tab on
the Speech
System
Preferences
pane's
Speech
Recognition
tab.

4. **Now choose the microphone you want to use from the Microphone pop-up menu.**

If you have a laptop or an iMac, you can get better results from just about any third-party microphone. The one that's built into your Mac works, but it isn't a very good microphone.

5. **To test that microphone, click the Calibrate button and follow the on-screen instructions.**

   You have two ways to use Speech Recognition. The first is to press a particular key — Esc by default — when you want to talk to your Mac. The second is to have your Mac listen continuously for you to say a special keyword — Computer, by default — when you want to talk to your Mac.

6. **(Optional) You can have your commands acknowledged by your Mac, if you like, by selecting the Speak Command Acknowledgement check box and, optionally, choosing a sound from the Play This Sound pop-up menu.**

7. **Click the Commands sub-tab on the Speech System Preferences pane's Speech Recognition tab. Select the check box for each command set you want to enable.**

   I can't see any reason not to enable them all unless you don't use Apple's Address Book, in which case you don't need to enable it.

8. **Click the Helpful Tips button and read the tips.**

9. **Click each command set name, and if the Configure button is enabled, click it and follow the on-screen instructions.**

10. **If you create an AppleScript you want to be speakable, click the Open Speakable Items Folder.**

    The Speakable Items folder is opened for you.

11. **Place the script in the folder.**

    When you speak its name, the script is executed.

    If the Speech System Preferences pane isn't open and you want to open the Speakable Items folder, you can find it in your Home/Library/Speech folder.

12. **Close the Speech dialog when you're done.**

Using Speech Recognition

Here's how Speech Recognition works. For the sake of this discussion, I use the "Press Esc" listening method.

When Speech Recognition is turned on, a round feedback window appears on-screen, as shown in Figure 16-2.

I'm not pressing the Esc key in Figure 16-2, so the word *Esc* appears in the middle of the window to remind me which key to press before I speak a command.

Now, here's how to actually use Speech Recognition:

1. **To see what commands are available, click the little triangle at the bottom of the feedback window, and select Open Speech Commands Window, as shown in Figure 16-2.**

   As you might expect, selecting Speech Preferences from this menu opens the Speech System Preferences pane for you.

   The Speech Commands window appears on-screen, as shown in Figure 16-3.

Figure 16-2:
The round
Speech
Recognition
feedback
window.

Open Speech Commands window
Speech Preferences...

○○○	Speech Commands

Commands
▶ Address Book
▶ Front Window
▶ Menu Bar
▼ Speakable Items
    Cancel last command
    Close Speech Commands window
    Close this window
    Copy this to the clipboard
    Define a keyboard command
    Get my mail
    Hide this application
    Insert today's date
    Listen continuously
    Log me out
    Make new item
    Make this into a sticky note
    Make this speakable
    Minimize Speech Commands window
    Minimize Speech Feedback window
    Minimize this window
    Move page down
    Move page to bottom
    Move page to top
    Move page up
    Open a document
    Open my browser
    Open Speech Commands window
    Open Speech Feedback window
    Open the Speakable Items folder
    Open the Speech Preferences
    Open VoiceOver
    Paste the clipboard here
    Quit Speakable Items
    Quit this application
    Save this document
    Show me what to say
    Start screen saver
    Tell me a joke
    Turn on push to talk
    What day is it?
    What time is it?
▶ Application Switching

Figure 16-3:
The Speech
Commands
window.

2. **Peruse the Speech Commands window and find a command you'd like to execute by speaking its name.**

3. **Speak that command exactly as written.**

   In this example, I press the Esc key and say to my Mac, "Tell me a joke."

   At this point, several things happen:

   - The microphone in the Feedback window changes to a speaker.

   - The command and my Mac's response appear in little boxes above and below the Feedback window.

   - The Speech Commands window changes to reflect the command I've spoken.

   My Mac then says, "Knock knock," and the lower part of the Speech Commands window displays the commands I can speak in response.

   You can see all this in Figure 16-4. And that's pretty much it for Speech Recognition.

Figure 16-4:
Here's what happened when I pressed Esc and said, "Tell me a joke."

This technology is clever and kind of fun, but it can also be somewhat slow on all but the fastest Macs. And it requires a microphone — something not all Macs have. The bottom line is that I've never been able to get Speech Recognition to work well enough to continue using it beyond a few hours at best. Still, it's kind of cool (and it's a freebie), and I've heard more than one user profess love for it. Which is why it's included here.

Listening to your Mac read for you

The camera pans back — a voice tells you what you've just seen, and suddenly it all makes sense. Return with me now to those thrilling days of the off-camera narrator. . . . Wouldn't it be nice if your Mac had a narrator to provide a blow-by-blow account of what's happening on your screen?

Or . . .

Your eyes are tired from a long day staring at the monitor, but you still have a lengthy document to read. Wouldn't it be sweet if you could sit back, close your eyes, and let your Mac read the document to you in a (somewhat) natural voice? The good news is that both are possible with Mac OS X Leopard — the former with VoiceOver and the latter with Text to Speech.

VoiceOver

Leopard's VoiceOver technology is designed primarily for the visually impaired, but you might find it useful even if your vision is 20/20. VoiceOver not only reads what's on the screen to you, but also integrates with your keyboard so you can navigate around the screen until you *hear* the item you're looking for. When you're there, you can use Keyboard Access to select list items, select check boxes and radio buttons, move scroll bars and sliders, resize windows, and so on — with a simple keypress or two.

To check it out, launch the System Preferences application (from the Applications folder, ★ menu, or Dock), click the Universal Access icon, and then click the Seeing tab or use the keyboard shortcut ⌘+F5 (⌘+Fn+F5 on notebook/laptop models).

After VoiceOver is enabled, you turn it on and off in the Seeing tab of the Universal Access System Preferences pane. When it's turned on (keyboard shortcut: ⌘+F5), your Mac talks to you about what is on your screen. For example, if you clicked the Desktop, your Mac might say something along the lines of, "Application, Finder; Column View; selected folder, Desktop, contains 8 items." It's quite slick. Here's another example: When you click a menu or item on a menu, you hear its name spoken at once, and when you close a menu, you hear the words "Closing menu." You even hear the spoken feedback in the Print, Open, and Save (and other) dialogs.

VoiceOver is kind of cool (talking alerts are fun), but having dialogs actually produce spoken text becomes annoying really fast for most folks. Still, I urge you to check it out. You might like it and find times when you want your Mac to narrate the action for you.

The VoiceOver Utility

The VoiceOver Utility lets you specify almost every possible option the VoiceOver technology uses. You can adjust its verbosity; specify how it deals with your mouse and keyboard; change its voice, rate, pitch, and/or volume; and more.

You can open the VoiceOver Utility by clicking the Open VoiceOver Utility button on the Seeing tab of the Universal Access System Preferences pane or the usual way, by double-clicking its icon (which you find in your Applications/ Utilities folder).

There's actually a third way, too. Because Apple considers the VoiceOver Utility so important, Apple assigned it a canned keyboard shortcut: ⌘+F5 (⌘+F5+fn on laptops).

Of course, you might get the machines-are-taking-over willies when your Mac starts to talk to you or make sounds — but if you give it a try, it could change your mind.

I wish I had the space to explain further, but I don't. That's the bad news. The good news is that VoiceOver Help is extensive and clear, and it helps you harness all the power of VoiceOver and the VoiceOver Utility.

Text to Speech

The second way your Mac can speak to you is using Text to Speech, which converts on-screen text to spoken words. If you've used Text to Speech in earlier versions of Mac OS X, you'll find that it's pretty much unchanged.

The only real change to Text to Speech in Leopard is a new voice called Alex, which happens to be the best and most natural-sounding voice ever included with any version of Mac OS.

Why might you need Text to Speech? Because sometimes hearing is better than reading. For example, I sometimes use Text to Speech to read a column or page to me before I submit it. If something doesn't sound quite right, I give it another polish before sending it off to my editor.

You can configure this feature in the Speech System Preferences pane:

1. **Open System Preferences (from the Applications folder or menu) and click the Text to Speech tab to check it out.**

2. **Choose from the list of voices in the System Voice pop-up menu to set the voice your Mac uses when it reads to you.**

3. **Click the Play button to hear a sample of the voice you selected.**

4. **Use the Speaking Rate slider to speed up or slow down the voice. Click the Play button to hear the voice at its new speed.**

   I really like the new guy, Alex, who says, "Hi, I'm a new voice for Leopard." My second favorite is Fred, who says, "I sure like being inside this fancy computer."

5. **Select the Announce When Alerts Are Displayed check box if you want to make your Mac speak the text in alert boxes and dialogs.**

You might hear such alerts as "The application Microsoft Word has quit unexpectedly" or "Paper out or not loaded correctly."

6. **Click the Set Alert Options button to choose a different voice to announce your alerts; the phrase your Mac speaks ("Alert," "Attention," "Excuse me," and the like) when alerting you; and the delay between the time the alert appears and when it's spoken to you.**

7. **(Optional) If you like, select either of the two check boxes: Announce When an Application Requires Your Attention and Speak Selected Text When the Key Is Pressed.**

   They both do what they say they'll do. In the case of the latter, you assign the key you want to press by clicking the Set Key button.

8. **(Optional) If you want to have the clock announce the time, click the Open Date & Time Preferences button, and you're whisked to that System Preferences pane. Then click the Clock tab and select the Announce the Time check box.**

   That's it for your preferences.

Now, to use Text to Speech to read text to you, copy the text to the Clipboard, launch TextEdit, paste the text into the empty untitled document, click where you want your Mac to begin reading to you, and then choose Edit⇨Speech⇨ Start Speaking. To make it stop, choose Edit⇨Speech⇨Stop Speaking.

Automatic Automation

Mac OS X Leopard offers a pair of technologies — AppleScript and Automator — that make it possible to automate repetitive actions on your Mac.

AppleScript is "programming for the rest of us." It can record and play back things that you do (if the application was written to allow the recording — Finder, for example, was), such as opening an application or clicking a button. You can use it to record a script for tasks that you often perform and then have your Mac perform those tasks for you later. You can write your own AppleScripts, use those that come with your Mac, or download still others from the Web.

Automator is "programming without writing code." With Automator, you string together prefabricated activities (known as *actions*) to automate repetitive or scheduled tasks. How cool is that?

Automation isn't for everyone. Some users can't live without it; others could go their whole lives without ever automating anything. So the following sections are designed to help you figure out how much — or how little — you care about AppleScript and Automator.

AppleScript

Describing AppleScript to a Mac beginner is a bit like three blind men describing an elephant. One man might describe it as the Macintosh's built-in automation tool. Another might describe it as an interesting but often-overlooked piece of enabling technology. The third might liken it to a cassette recorder, recording and playing back your actions at the keyboard. A fourth (if there were a fourth in the story) would assure you that it looked like computer code written in a high-level language.

They would all be correct. AppleScript, a built-in Mac automation tool, is a little-known (at least until recently) enabling technology that works like a cassette recorder for programs that support AppleScript recording. And scripts do look like computer programs. (Could that be because they *are* computer programs? Hmm . . .).

If you're the kind of person who likes to automate as many things as possible, you might just love AppleScript because it's a simple programming language that you can use to create programs that give instructions to your Mac and the applications running on your Mac. For example, you can create an AppleScript that launches Mail, checks for new messages, and then quits Mail. The script could even transfer your mail to a folder of your choice. Of course, Tiger also introduced Automator, which includes a whole lot of preprogrammed actions that makes a task like the one just described even easier.

I call AppleScript a time-and-effort enhancer. If you just spend the time and effort it takes to understand it, using AppleScript will save you oodles of time and effort down the road.

Therein lies the rub. This stuff is far from simple — entire books have been written on the subject. So it's far beyond the purview of *Mac OS X Leopard For Dummies.* Still, it's worth finding out about if you'd like to script repetitive actions for future use. To start, check out *AppleScript For Dummies,* 2nd Edition, by Tom Trinko. Also, check out the following tips:

- **You can put frequently used AppleScripts in the Dock or on your Desktop for easy access.**

- **Apple provides a script menu extra that you can install on your menu bar by double-clicking the AppleScript Utility** — along with a number of free scripts to automate common tasks, many of which are in the Example Scripts folder. (An alias to that folder is present in the AppleScript folder.) Furthermore, you can always download additional scripts from www.apple.com/applescript.

- **Many AppleScripts are designed for use in the toolbar of Finder windows,** where you can drag and drop items onto them quickly and easily.

- **Other scripts can enhance your use of iTunes, iPhoto, and iDVD.**

- ✔ **The Applications folder contains an AppleScript folder, which in turn contains the Script Editor program** (plus an alias that takes you to a folder full of sample AppleScripts).

- ✔ **Script Editor is the application you use to view and edit AppleScripts.** Although more information on Script Editor is beyond the scope of this book, it's a lot of fun. And the cool thing is that you can create many AppleScripts without knowing a thing about programming. Just record a series of actions you want to repeat and use Script Editor to save them as a script. If you save your script as an application (by choosing Application from the Format menu in the Save sheet), you can run that script by just double-clicking its icon.

- ✔ **If the concept of scripting intrigues you, I suggest that you open the Example Scripts folder.** Rummage through it to check out the scripts available at `www.apple.com/applescript`. When you find a script that looks interesting, double-click it to launch the Script Editor program, where you can examine it more closely.

Automator

Automator does just what you'd expect: It enables you to automate many common tasks on your Mac. If it sounds a little like AppleScript to you (which I discuss in the preceding section), you're not mistaken — the two share a common heritage. But this relatively new tool (introduced in Mac OS X Tiger) is a lot simpler to use, albeit somewhat less flexible, than AppleScript.

For example, in AppleScript, you can have *conditionals* (if this is true, do that; otherwise, do something else), but Automator is purely *sequential* (take this, do that, then do the next thing, and then . . .).

The big difference is that conditionals allow AppleScripts to do things involving *decision-making* and *iteration* (while this is true, do these things); Automator workflows can't make decisions or iterate.

The upsides to Automator are that you don't have to know anything about programming, and you don't have to type any archaic code. Instead, if you understand the process you want to automate, you can just drag and drop Automator's prefab Actions into place and build a *workflow* (Automator's name for a series of Actions).

An *Action* is nothing more than an item that performs a single specific task. In other words, an Action is a single step in a process; such a process is known as a workflow in Automator.

You do need to know one thing about programming (or computers), though: Computers are stupid! You heard me right — even your top-of-the-line dual processor MacBook Pro is dumb as a post. Computers do only what you tell them to do, though they can do it faster and more precisely than you can. But all computers run on the GIGO principle — garbage in/garbage out — so if your instructions are flawed, you're almost certain to get flawed results.

Another similarity between Automator and AppleScript is that it's up to the developers of the applications you want to automate to provide you the actions or with scripting support. Not all developers do so. For example, in Apple's wonderful iLife suite of multimedia applications, iTunes, iPhoto, and iDVD are all AppleScript-able — and they've supplied Actions for Automator users. Neither iMovie nor GarageBand, however, supports AppleScript or Automator at this time.

When you launch the Automator application, you see the window in Figure 16-5. Choose one of the starting points if you want Automator to assist you in constructing a new workflow or choose Custom to start building a workflow from scratch.

Figure 16-5:
Choose a
starting
point and
Automator
will assist
you; choose
Custom to
start a
workflow
from
scratch.

I choose Custom for the sake of this demonstration. When I do, I see the window shown in Figure 16-6.

The Library window on the left contains all the applications Automator knows about which have actions defined for them. Select an application in the top part of the Library window, and its related actions appear below it. When you select an action, the pane at the bottom of the Library window (Get Text from Webpage in Figure 16-6) explains what that action does, what input it expects, and what result it produces. Just drag actions from the Action list into the window on the right to build your workflow.

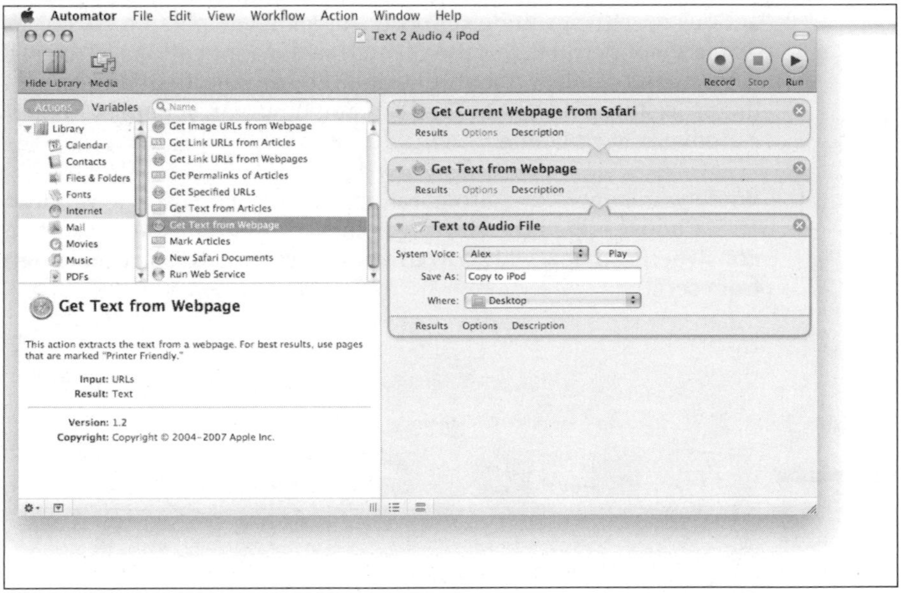

Figure 16-6: Build workflows from the Actions you specify in Automator.

This particular workflow, which took me around ten minutes of trial and error to get working, is quite useful. It takes text from a Web page and uses Mac OS X Text to Speech to convert the text to an audio file, which I can then listen to in iTunes or on my iPod in the car or on a plane. Sweet!

Automator is a very useful addition to Mac OS X; it's deep, powerful, and expandable, yet relatively easy to use and master. Do yourself a favor and spend some time experimenting with ways Automator can save you time and keystrokes. You won't regret it.

A Few More Useful Goodies

Even more neat and useful technologies are built into Leopard, but I'm running out of space. So here are, at least in my humble opinion, the best of the rest.

Universal Access

 Universal Access is mostly designed for users with disabilities or who have difficulty handling the keyboard or mouse. The Universal Access System Preferences pane has a check box and four tabs.

Select the Enable Access for Assistive Devices check box at the bottom of the window to use special equipment to control your computer.

The Seeing tab

On the Seeing tab, you can turn on a terrific feature called *hardware zoom.* Toggle it on and off with the shortcut ⌘+Option+8. Zoom in and out using the shortcuts ⌘+Option+= (the equals key) and ⌘+Option+– (the minus key), respectively. Try this feature even if you're not disabled or challenged in any way; it's actually a great feature for everyone.

You can also display the screen as white on black (like a photographic negative), as shown in Figure 16-7. The shortcut is ⌘+Option+Control+8; use the same keyboard shortcut to toggle back to normal. If you're in the normal black-on-white mode, you can desaturate your screen into a *grayscale display* (so it works like a black-and-white TV).

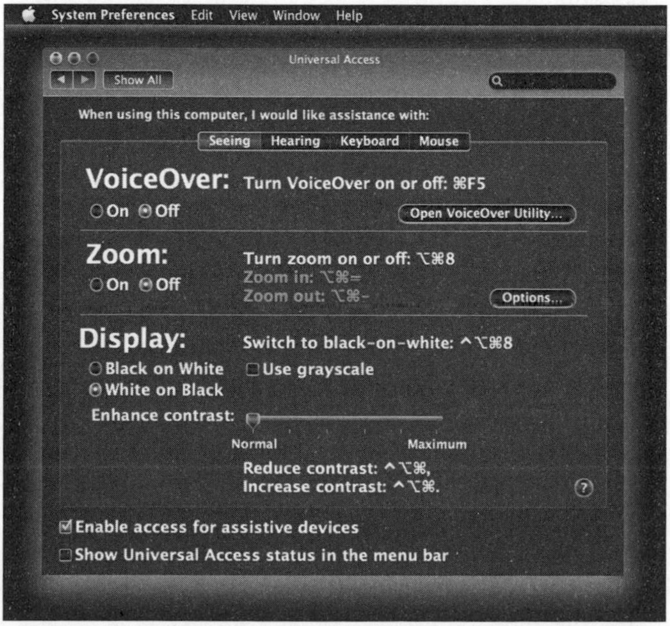

Figure 16-7:
The White
on Black
option
reverses
what you
see on-
screen, like
this.

Finally, the Options button lets you specify minimum and maximum zoom levels, display a preview rectangle when zoomed out, and toggle image smoothing on or off.

The Hearing tab

The Hearing tab lets you choose to flash the screen whenever an alert sound occurs.

This feature, created for those with impaired hearing, is quite useful if you have a PowerBook or iBook and want to use it where ambient noise levels are high.

The Keyboard tab

The Keyboard tab offers two types of assistance:

- The **Sticky Keys** application treats a *sequence* of modifier keys as a key combination. In other words, you don't have to simultaneously hold down ⌘ while pressing another key. For example, with Sticky Keys enabled, you can do a standard keyboard shortcut by pressing ⌘, releasing it, and then pressing the other key. You can select check boxes to tell you (with a beep and/or an on-screen display) what modifier keys have been pressed.

  As useful as Sticky Keys can be, they're really awkward in applications like Adobe Photoshop that toggle a tool's state when you press a modifier key. So if you're a big Photoshop user, you probably don't want Sticky Keys enabled.

- **Slow Keys** lets you adjust the delay between when a key is pressed and when that keypress is accepted.

The Mouse tab

Finally, the Mouse tab lets you specify that you want to use the keys on the numeric keypad instead of the mouse. In this situation, everything centers on the numeric keypad's 5 key (which means clicking the mouse): 8 is up; 2 is down; 4 is left; 6 is right; and 1, 3, 7, and 9 are diagonal movements. Pressing 0 (zero) is the same as holding down the mouse button so the other numeric keys can now drag in the indicated directions. You can also increase the cursor size from the normal setting (16×16) to about 64×64.

Energy Saver

All Macs are Energy Star–compliant (and have been for years), allowing you to preset your machine to turn itself off at a specific time or after a specified idle period. It offers two tabs — Sleep and Options — and a Schedule button.

Sleep

To enable Sleep mode, move the slider to the desired amount of time. You can choose any number between 1 minute and 3 hours, or turn off Sleep entirely by moving the slider all the way to the right to Never.

You can also set separate sleep times for your Mac and your display. And you can choose whether to let your hard drive go to sleep if it supports sleep mode. Setting the display to sleep might come in handy if you want your Mac to keep doing what it's doing and you don't need to use the monitor. The hard drive's sleep option is less useful unless you have a laptop. Selecting this option forces your hard drive to sleep after a few minutes of inactivity, which saves you some battery power.

To activate display sleep, select the Put the Display to Sleep When Computer Is Inactive for check box and then drag the slider to the idle-time interval you want.

To wake up your Mac from its sleep, merely move your mouse or press any key.

Drag the slider to 30 or 45 minutes for sleep; remember to turn off your Mac manually when you're not going to need it for a couple of days or more.

Options

The Options tab is home to a small collection of useful settings. On this tab, you find check boxes telling the Mac to wake up automatically for Ethernet network administrative access (handy in a corporate setting where an IT person maintains system configurations) and to restart automatically after a power failure.

Laptop users get additional Energy Saver options, including the following:

- ✔ A check box to show the battery-status indicator on the menu bar
- ✔ A Settings pop-up menu that lets you choose specific settings for when your Mac is plugged in (Power Adapter) and when it's running on battery power
- ✔ An Optimization pop-up menu that offers three options: Better Energy Savings, Normal, and Better Performance

  Choose Better Performance when AC power is connected and choose Better Energy Savings when you need to conserve battery power.

Schedule

To start up, shut down, or put your Mac to sleep at a predetermined time, select the appropriate check box and choose the appropriate options from the Schedule tab's pop-up menus.

Bluetooth

Bluetooth is wireless networking for low-bandwidth peripherals, including mice, keyboards, and mobile phones. If your Mac has Bluetooth built in or is equipped with a USB Bluetooth adapter, you can synchronize wirelessly with phones and Palm devices, print wirelessly to Bluetooth printers, and use Bluetooth mice and keyboards.

Bluetooth is designed to work with iSync — Apple's synchronization technology — to let you synchronize your Address Book, calendar, and bookmarks wirelessly with Bluetooth phones, such as the Motorola L2 I use.

Ink

Ink is the Mac OS X built-in handwriting-recognition engine. If you have a stylus and tablet connected to your Mac, just turn it on in this pane, and you can write anywhere you can type with the keyboard.

The Ink pane is another one you see only if you have one of the handful of tablets that Ink supports connected to your Mac.

All currently supported tablets come from Wacom (www.wacom.com), with prices starting under $100 for a small, wireless stylus and tablet.

Automatic Login (Accounts System Preferences pane)

Some users don't care for the fact that Mac OS X Leopard is a multiuser operating system and dislike having to log in when they start up their Mac. For those users, here's a way to disable the login screen:

1. **Open the Accounts System Preferences pane, select yourself from the list of users, and click the Login Options button below the list.**

2. **Select the Log In Automatically As check box and then choose your account from the pop-up menu.**

   To disable the logging-in requirement, you have to be an administrator, and you might need to unlock the Accounts System Preferences.

When you disable logging in, you also affect all the preferences set by anyone else who shares your Mac. (Yikes.) So if your Desktop pattern, keyboard settings, and so forth are different from those of someone else who uses your machine, those preferences won't be properly reflected unless each of you has a separate, individual login account. Even if you're not worried about security, consider keeping logging in enabled if any other users have accounts on your machine or you don't want just anyone to be able to turn on your Mac and see your personal stuff.

Note that only one account is allowed to use autologin. If another user wants to use this Mac, you need to choose Log Out from the menu, press ⌘+Shift+Q, or have Fast User Switching enabled. And if you've disabled automatic login in the Security System Preferences pane, you can't enable it here.

Boot Camp

Boot Camp is Leopard's built-in technology that allows you to run Microsoft Windows XP or Vista on any Intel-based Mac. If your Mac meets the following requirements, you can run Windows on your Mac (if you so desire):

- An Intel-based Mac
- At least 10GB of free hard drive space
- A hard drive that isn't partitioned
- A blank recordable CD
- A printer (for printing the instructions, which you'll want to do)
- A full install copy of Microsoft Windows XP Service Pack 2 or Vista

You really do need a full install copy of Windows. If your copy came with your Dell or HP, you probably won't be able to install it under Boot Camp.

To install Windows on your Mac, here are the basic steps you need to follow:

1. **Launch the Boot Camp Assistant application, which is in your Applications/Utilities folder.**

   This step creates a partition on your hard drive for Windows and then burns a special CD with all the drivers you'll need to use Windows on your Mac.

2. **Install Windows on the new partition.**

3. **Install the drivers from the CD you just burned.**

From now on, you can hold down Option during startup and choose to start up from either the Mac OS X Leopard disk partition or the Windows partition.

It's that simple. However, if these installation steps seem beyond your comfort level, just ask your favorite Mac geek for help.

If running Windows on your Mac appeals to you, you might want to check out Parallels Desktop, an $80 program that not only allows you to run Windows on your Mac, but also lets you do so without partitioning your hard drive or restarting every time you want to use Windows. In fact, you can run Mac and Windows programs simultaneously with Parallels Desktop. For more information, visit www.parallels.com.

Part V

The Care and Feeding of Your Leopard

The 5th Wave   By Rich Tennant

"Brad! That's not your modem we're hearing! It's Buddy!! He's out of his cage and in the iMac!!"

In this part . . .

Here I get into the nitty-gritty underbelly of Mac OS X. In this part, I cover topics like protecting your valuable data by backing it up, and I discuss everything you need to know about Macintosh security (which, thankfully, isn't much). Next you look at some utilities that might or might not be useful but that you should know about anyway. Finally, you find out what to do when things go wonky (which also, thankfully, doesn't happen very much) and experience a quick run-through of Dr. Mac's (okay, Dr. Bob's) top troubleshooting tips for those infrequent times when a good Leopard goes bad.

This material is a little geekier than the first four parts, but it could very well be the most important information in the book. Don't miss out!

Chapter 17

Safety First: Backups and Other Security Issues

Although Macs are generally reliable beasts (especially Macs running Mac OS X), someday your hard drive will die. I promise. They *all* do. And if you don't back up your hard drive (or at least back up any files that you can't afford to lose) before that day comes, chances are good that you'll never see your files again. And if you do see them again, it will be only after paying someone like Scott Gaidano of DriveSavers Data Recovery Service a king's ransom, with no guarantee of success.

DriveSavers is the premier recoverer of lost data on hard drives. The people there understand Mac hard drives quite well, do excellent work, and can often recover stuff that nobody else could. (Ask the producers of *The Simpsons* about the almost-lost episodes.) Understandably, DriveSavers charges accordingly. Here are some phone numbers for DriveSavers: 800-440-1904 toll free and 415-382-2000.

Now pray that you never need those numbers — and if you back up often, you won't. But if, somehow, none of this sinks in, tell Scott that I said, "Hi."

In other words, you absolutely, positively, without question *must back up* your files if you don't want to risk losing them. Just as you adopt the Shut Down command and make it a habit before turning off your machine, you must remember to back up important files on your hard drive to another disk or device, and back them up often.

How often is often? That depends on you. How much work can you afford to lose? If your answer is that losing everything you did yesterday would put you out of business, you need to back up daily or possibly twice a day. If you would lose only a few unimportant letters, you can back up less frequently.

Following the comprehensive coverage of backup options, I look at the possible threat to your data from viruses and other icky things, as well as how you can protect against them.

Finally, I look at what you can do to keep other people from looking at your stuff.

Backing Up Is (Not) Hard to Do

You can back up your hard drive in basically three ways: the superpainless way with Leopard's excellent new Time Machine, the ugly way using the brute-force method, or the comprehensive way with specialized third-party backup software. Read on and find out more about all three. . . .

Backing up with Leopard's excellent new Time Machine

Time Machine is a brand-new backup system introduced with Mac OS X Leopard. I say it's a system because it consists of two parts — the Time Machine System Preferences pane, shown in Figure 17-1, and the Time Machine application, shown in Figure 17-2.

To use Time Machine to back up your data automatically, the first thing you need is another hard drive that's the same size or larger than your startup disk. It can be a FireWire hard drive, USB 2 hard drive, another internal hard drive if you have a Mac that supports it like the Mac Pro or Power Mac G5, or even a wireless AirPort Disk. The first time that new disk is connected to your Mac, Time Machine automatically asks whether you'd like to back up your main drive to that drive. If you say yes, the Time Machine System Preferences pane opens automatically with the new disk already chosen as the backup disk.

If that doesn't happen or you want to use an already-connected hard drive with Time Machine, open the Time Machine System Preferences pane and click the big On/Off switch to On. Now click the Choose Disk button (which may or may not say Change Disk instead of Choose Disk) and select the proper hard drive. Mine is called Time in Figure 17-1.

Figure 17-1:
The Time
Machine
System
Preferences
pane.

The only other consideration is this: If you have other hard disks connected to your Mac, you should click the Options button to reveal the Do Not Back Up list, which tells Time Machine which volumes (disks) not to back up. To add a volume to this list, click the little + button; to remove a volume from the list, select it and click the – button.

The Options sheet also has a check box for warning you when old backups are deleted; check it if you want to be warned.

For the record, Time Machine stores your backups for the following lengths of time:

✔ Hourly backups for the past 24 hours.

✔ Daily backups for the past month.

✔ Weekly backups until your backup disk is full.

When your backup disk gets full, the oldest backups on it are deleted and replaced by the newest.

When does it run? Glad you asked—it runs when you're not doing other things with your Mac.

If you enable and set up Time Machine as I've just described you'll never forget to back up your stuff, so just do it.

What does Time Machine back up?

Time Machine backs up your whole hard disk the first time it runs, and then backs up files and folders that have been modified since your last backup. That's what backup systems do. But Time Machine does more — it also backs up things like contacts in your Address Book, pictures in your iPhoto Library, and events in your iCal calendars. That makes it unlike other backup systems and is a sweet feature indeed.

How do I restore a file (or a contact, a photo, an event, and so on)?

To restore a file or any other information, follow these steps:

1. **Launch the appropriate program — the one that contains the information you want to restore.**

   If what you want to restore happens to be a file, that program is the Finder, which, as you know, is always running. So to restore an individual file, you don't actually need to launch anything. But to restore a contact, a photo, or an event, for example, you need to launch Address Book, iPhoto, or iCal, respectively.

2. **With the appropriate application running, launch the Time Machine application, as shown in Figure 17-2.**

3. **Click one of the bars in the lower-right corner of the screen or click the big "forward" and "back" arrows next to them to choose the backup you want to restore from (Tuesday, March 27, 2007 8:14AM in Figure 17-2).**

Figure 17-2:
The Time Machine application is ready to restore a file in the Finder.

Backing up by using the manual, brute-force method

If you're too cheap to buy a second hard drive, the most rudimentary way to back up is to do it manually. You would accomplish this by dragging said files a few at a time to another volume — a CD-R, CD-RW, DVD-R, or DVD-RW. (If you use an optical disc, don't forget to actually *burn the disc;* merely dragging those files onto the optical-disc icon won't do the trick.)

By doing this, you're making a copy of each file that you want to protect. (See Chapter 7 for more info on removable storage.)

Yuck! If doing a manual backup sounds pretty awful, trust me — it is. This method can take a long, long time; you can't really tell whether you've copied every file that needs to be backed up; and you can't really copy only the files that have been modified since your last backup. Almost nobody in his right mind sticks with this method for long.

Of course, if you're careful to save files only in your Documents folder, as I suggest several times in this book, you can probably get away with backing up only that. Or if you save files in other folders within your Home folder or have any files in your Movies, Music, Pictures, or Sites folders (which often contain files you didn't specifically save in those folders, like your iPhoto photos and iTunes songs), you should probably consider backing up your entire Home folder.

As you read in the following section, that's even easier if you use special backup software.

Backing up by using commercial backup software

Another way to back up your files is with a third-party backup program. Backup software automates the task of backing up, remembering what's on each backup disc (if your backup uses more than one disc) and backing up only files that have been modified since your last backup.

Furthermore, you can instruct your backup software to back up only a certain folder (Home or Documents) and to ignore the hundreds of megabytes of stuff that make up Mac OS X, all of which you can easily reinstall from the Mac OS X Install DVD.

Your first backup with commercial software might take anywhere from a few minutes to several hours and use one or more optical discs — CD-R, CD-RW,

DVD-R, DVD-RW, magneto-optical disc — or non-optical media, such as another hard drive or any kind of tape backup. Subsequent backups, called *incremental backups* in backup-software parlance, should take only a few minutes.

If you do incremental backups, be sure to label all the discs you use during that operation — if you use multiple discs, number them. Your backup software may prompt you with a message such as `Please insert backup disk 7.` If you haven't labeled your media clearly, you could have a problem figuring out which disc *is* disc 7 or which disc 7 belongs to that particular backup set.

Fortunately, plenty of very good backup programs are available for well under $150, including the excellent Retrospect family of backup solutions from EMC/Dantz Development (`www.emcinsignia.com`).

Retrospect Desktop protects up to two networked desktops or notebooks for around $129. If you need to protect more than two computers, additional client licenses are available at reasonable prices.

Here's a nice touch: The Retrospect network client runs on Windows Vista, Windows XP, Windows 2000 Professional, Windows NT 4.0 Workstation, Windows 95/98/Me, Red Hat Linux (versions 6.2, 7.1, 7.2, 7.3, and 8), and, of course, Mac OS 9 or Mac OS X. So if you have any non-Mac computers, chances are good that Retrospect can back them up over your local area network at no additional expense.

Other backup offerings include SilverKeeper (free) from LaCie (`www.lacie.com`); Data Backup (around $60) from Prosoft Engineering (`www.prosofteng.com`); and so-called *synchronizer* programs such as ChronoSync ($20) from Econ Technologies (`www.econtechnologies.com`) and SuperDuper ($28) from ShirtPocket Software (`www.shirt-pocket.com`).

If you want the most flexible, top-of-the-line backup software, spend a little more and pop for Retrospect. It can do everything the others can do — and more. It's the only backup software you'll ever need.

One of the best things about good backup software is that you can set it up to automate your backups and perform them even if you forget. And although Time Machine is a step in the right direction and might be sufficient for your needs, it's not good enough for me. I use four FireWire hard drives as my backup media of choice, and Retrospect backs up all the important stuff on my main hard drive four times each day, each time to a different backup set and hard drive. At night, my entire boot drive is duplicated to another hard drive, giving me a bootable backup I can use in emergencies. (Where my data is concerned, I sleep pretty well, thanks.)

Why You Need Two Sets of Backups

You're a good soldier. You back up regularly. You think you're immune to file loss or damage.

Now picture yourself in the following scenario:

1. One day you take a DVD or your portable FireWire hard drive to QuicKopyLazerPrintz to print your résumé on the high-resolution laser printer there. You make a few changes while at QuicKopyLazerPrintz and then take the disk home and stick it into your Mac (or connect it if it's a FireWire drive). Unbeknownst to you, the disk or document became infected with a computer virus at QuicKopyLazerPrintz. (I discuss viruses in the section "All about viruses," later in this chapter.)

2. When you insert or connect the disk, the infection spreads to your boot drive like wildfire.

3. Then you do a backup. Your backup software, believing that all the infected files have been recently modified (well, they *have* been — they were infected with a virus!), proceeds to back them up. You notice that the backup takes a little longer than usual, but otherwise things seem to be okay.

4. A few days later, your Mac starts acting strangely. You borrow a copy of an excellent virus-detection software, such as Virus Barrier or Norton AntiVirus (formerly Symantec Anti-Virus), and discover that your hard drive is infected. "A-ha!" you exclaim. "I've been a good little Mac user, backing up regularly. I'll just restore everything from my backup disks."

   Not so fast, bucko. The files on your backup disks are also infected!

This scenario is totally fictitious. As the upcoming "All about viruses" section explains, there are few (if any) malicious viruses that affect Mac OS X. But it does demonstrate why you need multiple backups. If you have several sets of backup disks, chances are pretty good that one of the sets will work even if the others are infected (or lost, stolen, or destroyed).

I always keep at least three current sets of backup disks going at any one time. I use one set on even-numbered days and another on odd-numbered days, and I update the third set once a week and store it somewhere other than my office (such as a neighbor's house or a safe deposit box). This scheme ensures that no matter what happens — even if my office burns, is flooded, is destroyed by a tornado or a hurricane, or is robbed — I won't lose more than a few days' worth of work. I can live with that.

Nonbackup Security Concerns

As you've probably surmised by now, backing up your files is critical unless you won't mind losing all your data someday. And although backing up is by far your most important security concern, several other things could imperil your data — things like viruses, worms, malware, spyware, and intruder attacks. That's the bad news. The good news is that all those things are far more likely to affect Windows users than Mac users. In fact, I'd venture to say that viruses, worms, malware, spyware, and intruder attacks are rarer than hens' teeth for Mac users.

That said, here are a few precautions Mac users should consider, just in case.

All about viruses

A computer *virus,* in case you missed it in *Time* or *Newsweek,* is a nasty little piece of computer code that replicates and spreads from disk to disk. Most viruses cause your Mac to misbehave; some viruses can destroy files or erase disks with no warning.

The good news is that most virus scares that you hear and read about won't affect you (O, lucky Mac user!) because they are specific to users of Windows systems. Most viruses are specific to an operating system — Mac viruses won't affect Windows users, Windows viruses won't affect Mac users, and so forth. The one real exception here is a "gift" from the wonderful world of Microsoft Office (Word and Excel, for example) users: the dreaded *macro viruses* that are spread with Word and Excel documents containing macros written in Microsoft's VBA (Visual BASIC for Applications) language. But you're safe even from those if you practice safe computing as I describe.

As it happens, so far almost all the viral activity affecting Mac OS X involved various Windows macro viruses. In fact, at the time of this writing, I know of no OS X–specific viruses or of any that attack Mac OS X exclusively — and (at least so far) none that cause damage. Still, the advice in this chapter is sound — one never knows when the little boys out there will decide to attack the Mac. OS X viruses aren't impossible or nonexistent; they just don't exist in known examples at this moment in time. But they could someday; better safe than sorry.

If you use disks that have been inserted into other computers, you need some form of virus-detection software. If you download and use files from Web and File Transfer Protocol (FTP) sites on the Internet, you need some form of virus detection as well.

You don't have too much to worry about if

- ✔ You download files only from commercial online services, such as AOL, which is very conscientious about viral infections.
- ✔ You use only commercial software and don't download files from Web sites with strange names.

You should definitely worry about virus infection if

- ✔ An unsavory friend told you about a Web site called `Dan'sDenOfPiratedIllegalStolenBootlegSoftware.com` — and you actually visited it.
- ✔ You swap disks with friends regularly.
- ✔ You shuttle disks back and forth to other Macs.
- ✔ You use your disks at service bureaus or copy shops.
- ✔ You download files from various and sundry places on the Internet, even ones that don't sound as slimy as `Dan'sDenOfPiratedIllegalStolenBootlegSoftware.com`.
- ✔ You receive e-mail with attachments (and open them).

If you're at risk, do yourself a favor and buy a commercial antivirus program. Although you can choose among many shareware and freeware antivirus solutions, none that I know of are as trustworthy as Virus Barrier and Norton. The big advantage of buying a commercial antivirus program is that the publisher contacts you each time a virus is discovered and provides you a software update to protect you against the new strain. (Or, for a fee, the publisher can send you a new version of the software every time a new virus is found. But that can get expensive; new viruses appear every day.)

On the commercial front, two leading virus-detection utilities are Virus Barrier and Norton AntiVirus (NAV; formerly Symantec Anti-Virus). Each has its advocates. I've used Virus Barrier for a couple of years and have never been infected with a virus.

Firewall: Yea or nay?

According to the Mac OS X built-in Oxford American Dictionary, a firewall is

> *Part of a computer system or network that is designed to block unauthorized access while permitting outward communication.*

Using a firewall protects your computer from malicious users on other networks or the Internet and keeps them from gaining access to your Mac.

Unlike older versions of Windows, Mac OS X is quite difficult to crack. There have been few (if any) reports of outsiders gaining access to Macintosh computers running Mac OS X. One of the reasons for that might be that Mac OS X has a built-in firewall. That's the good news. The bad news is that said firewall is disabled by default. You'll need to activate it if you want to be protected against unauthorized access to your computer.

To activate your firewall, follow these steps:

1. **Open the System Preferences application (from the Applications folder, menu, or Dock).**

2. **Click the Security icon and then click the Firewall tab.**

   The default setting is Allow All Incoming Connections, which is the least secure option.

3. **For the highest level of protection for your Mac, select the Block All Incoming Connections radio button, as shown in Figure 17-3. Or if you need to allow some connections for any of the reasons outlined in the following list, use the alternative solution I recommend instead.**

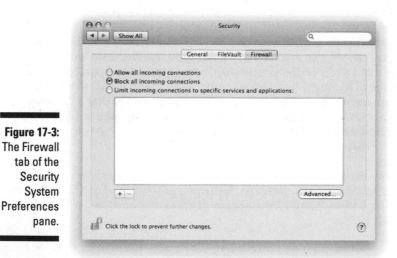

Figure 17-3:
The Firewall tab of the Security System Preferences pane.

Sometimes it's desirable to allow incoming connections from outside computers. The following list outlines the most common scenarios and explains how to set up your firewall accordingly:

✔ **You want to host a Web site on your Mac using the Mac OS X built-in Personal Web Sharing feature.** If you've selected the firewall's Block All Incoming Connections setting, nobody can access your Web site — access is blocked by the firewall.

Solution: When you enable a service in the Sharing System Preference pane, the Firewall automatically allows incoming connections for it. So click the Show All button and then click the Sharing icon. Enable Web Sharing, and you're good to go. I've enabled both File Sharing and Web Sharing in the Sharing System Preference pane, as reflected in the Security System Preference pane shown in Figure 17-4. The firewall magically figures out that it should allow others to share files and view personal Web sites on this Mac.

✔ **A third-party application needs you to allow outside connections to it in order to function.** How would you know? Check the user manual, Read Me file, or application Help. If a program requires you to open your firewall, you can almost certainly find some information in one (or more) of these places.

Note: Your firewall already knows about Mac OS X applications and services such as iTunes Music Sharing and iPhoto Photo Sharing, so you don't need to apply any special configurations for those.

Solution: If you're using the Limit Incoming Connections to Specific Services and Applications setting (as described in the preceding bullet) and need to open your firewall for a third-party application, click the little + button on the left near the bottom of the window. A standard Open File sheet drops down over the window; select the appropriate program, click the Add button, and then choose Allow All Connections from its pop-up menu.

That's how I enabled incoming connections for QuickTime Player in Figure 17-4.

✔ **You encounter problems with a network-related activity and suspect your firewall may be the problem**.

Solution: Click the Allow All Incoming Connections radio button temporarily to see whether that resolves the issue. If it does, follow the instructions above to add the program to your firewall's list of applications and then choose Allow All Connections from its pop-up menu. If it doesn't resolve the issue, don't forget to reselect your previous setting — either Block All Incoming Connections or Limit Incoming Connections to Specific Services and Applications.

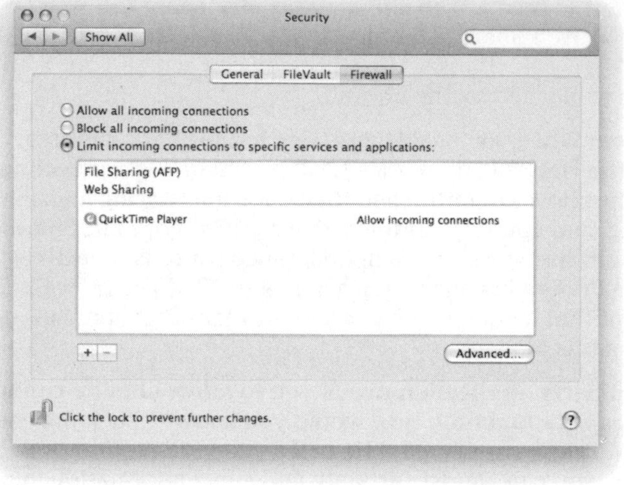

Figure 17-4:
I enabled
File Sharing
and Web
Sharing in
the Sharing
System
Preference
pane.

Install recommended software updates

Every so often, your Mac informs you that a new Software Update is available and asks whether you'd like to install it. In almost all cases, you do. Apple issues Software Updates only to fix newly discovered security concerns or to fix serious bugs in Mac OS X or its bundled applications.

Every so often, one of these Software Updates has an unintended side effect, and while fixing one problem, it introduces a different problem. Apple is generally pretty careful, and this doesn't happen very often, but if you want to be safe, don't install a Software Update until you've visited MacFixIt (www.macfixit.com) or MacInTouch (www.macintouch.com) and looked at their reports on the update. If there *are* widespread issues with a particular Software Update, these two sites will have the most comprehensive coverage (and possible workarounds).

Protecting Your Data from Prying Eyes

The last kind of security I look at in this chapter is protecting your files from other users on your local area network and users with physical access to your Mac. If you don't want anyone messing with your files, check out the security measures I describe in the following sections.

Blocking or limiting connections

The first thing you might want to do is open the Sharing System Preferences pane by launching the System Preferences application (from the Applications folder, ❖ menu, or Dock) and clicking the Sharing icon. Nobody can access your Mac over the network if all the services in the Sharing pane are disabled and your firewall is set to either Block All Incoming Connections or Limit Incoming Connections to Specific Services and Applications. See the section "Firewall: Yea or nay?" earlier in this chapter for details on these settings.

Locking down files with FileVault

If you absolutely, positively don't ever want anyone to be able to access the files in your Home folder, FileVault allows you to encrypt your entire Home folder and its contents. It protects your data with the latest government-approved encryption standard — Advanced Encryption Standard with 128-bit keys (AES-128).

When you turn on FileVault, you're asked to set a *master password* for the computer. After you do, you or any other administrator can use that master password if you forget your regular account login password.

If you turn on FileVault and then forget both your login password and your master password, you can't log in to your account, and your data is lost forever. Really. Not even DriveSavers has a hope of recovering it. So don't forget both passwords, okay?

FileVault is useful primarily if you store sensitive information on your Mac. If you're logged out of your user account and someone gets access to your Mac, there is no way they can access your data. Period.

Because FileVault encrypts your Home folder, some tasks that normally access your Home folder might be prevented. For one thing, some backup programs choke if FileVault is enabled. Also, if you're not logged in to your user account, other users can't access your Shared folder(s).

And because FileVault is always encrypting and decrypting files, it often slows down your Mac when you add or save new files, and it takes extra time before it lets you log out, restart, or shut down.

To turn on FileVault, follow these steps:

1. **Open the Security System Preferences pane and select the FileVault tab.**

2. **Click the Set Master Password button and set a master password for your computer.**

3. **Click the Turn on FileVault button to enable FileVault.**

To turn off FileVault, click the Turn off FileVault button.

The last time I tested this feature (with Mac OS X Tiger), when I tried to turn off FileVault, I got an error message and was unable to disable FileVault. I tried every trick I know (and I know a lot) and contacted Apple's support group, too. The issue was never resolved. I ended up having to erase the hard drive and restore files from backups (yet another reason multiple backups are a good thing).

Setting other options for security

The System tab of the Security System Preferences pane offers several more options that can help keep your data safe. They are

- **Require Password to Wake This Computer from Sleep or Screen Saver:** Enable this option if you want your Mac lock itself up and require a password after the screen saver kicks in or it goes to sleep. It can become a pain in the butt, having to type your password all the time. But if you have nosy co-workers, family members, or other individuals you'd like to keep from rooting around in your stuff, you should probably enable this option.

- **Disable Automatic Login:** One of the login options in the Accounts System Preferences pane is automatic login. With automatic login enabled, you don't have to choose an account or type a password when you start up this Mac. Instead, it bypasses all that login stuff and goes directly to the Desktop of the designated account. If you want to disable this feature for all accounts, so that every user of this Mac sees the login screen and is required to choose an account and type a password, you should enable this option.

- **Require Password to Unlock Each System Preference Pane:** If you prefer that nonadministrator users be prevented from changing the settings in any System Preferences pane, enable this option.

- **Log Out after X Minutes of Inactivity:** This feature does what it says — it logs out the current user after a specified length of idle time.

- **Use Secure Virtual Memory:** It is remotely possible that a motivated hacker could recover data you've recently read or written from one of Mac OS X's virtual-memory swap files. Because it might have an adverse effect on your Mac's performance, you probably want to keep this option disabled unless you're extremely paranoid about anyone seeing any data on your Mac.

- **Disable Remote Control Infrared Receiver:** Most Macs come with an Apple Remote control device these days. To disable it for all users, enable this option.

Chapter 18

Utility Chest

Mac OS X Leopard comes with a plethora of useful utilities that make using your computer more pleasant and/or make you more productive when you use your computer. In this chapter, I give you a glimpse of the ones that aren't covered elsewhere in this book.

The first item, Calculator, is in your Applications folder; all the other items in this chapter are in your Utilities folder, inside your Applications folder.

Calculator

Need to do some quick math? The Calculator application gives you a simple calculator with all the basic number-crunching functions that your pocket calculator has. To use it, you can either click the keys with the mouse or use your numeric keypad on your keyboard to type numbers and operators (math symbols such as +, –, and =). Calculator also offers a paper tape (Window➪Show Paper Tape) to track your computations and, if you want, provide a printed record. It can even speak numbers aloud (Speech➪Speak Button Pressed and Speech➪Speak).

Check out the Calculator in Figure 18-1.

Figure 18-1:
The
Calculator
(left),
Convert
menu
(middle),
and Paper
Tape (right).

| Calculator | File | Edit | View | Convert | Speech | Window | Help |

Calculator   17486

MC	M+	M−	MR
C	±	÷	×
7	8	9	−
4	5	6	+
1	2	3	
0	.	=	

Recent Conversions ▶

Area...
Currency...
Energy or Work...
Length...
Power...
Pressure...
Speed...
Temperature...
Time...
Volume...
Weights and Masses...

Paper Tape

1492 + 1776 + 2525 + 1969 +
1941 + 1918 + 1955 + 1955 +
1955
= 17486

Clear

In my humble opinion, the most useful feature in the Calculator (after the paper tape) is the Convert menu — more specifically, the Currency conversion feature. It actually checks the Internet for the exchange rate before calculating the conversion for you. That's very cool.

Beyond that, Calculator has three modes: Basic, Scientific, and Programmer. Basic is the default, and you access the other two modes as follows:

✔ Pressing ⌘+2 (View➪Scientific) turns the formerly anemic calculator into a powerful scientific calculator.

✔ View➪Programmer (⌘+3) turns it into the programmer's friend, letting you display your data in binary, octal, hexadecimal, ASCII, and Unicode. It also performs programming operations like shifts and byte-swaps. (If you're a programmer, you know what all that means; if you aren't, it really doesn't matter.)

Activity Monitor

In Unix, the underlying operating system that powers Mac OS X, applications and other things going on behind the scenes are called *processes.* Each application and the operating system itself can run a number of processes at the same time.

In Figure 18-2, you see 51 different processes running, most of them behind the scenes. Note that when this picture was taken only three applications were actually running (the Finder, Dashboard, and Activity Monitor itself).

To display the three CPU Monitor windows below the Activity Monitor window as shown in Figure 18-2, choose Window➪CPU Usage (keyboard shortcut ⌘+2), CPU History (keyboard shortcut ⌘+3), and/or Floating CPU Window (no keyboard shortcut).

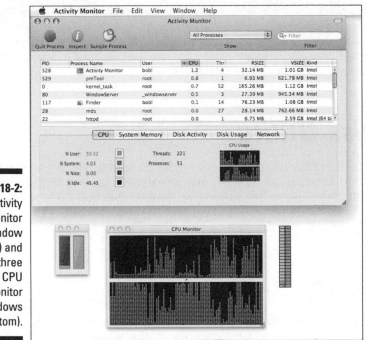

Figure 18-2:
The Activity Monitor window (top) and the three little CPU Monitor windows (bottom).

You also select what appears in the Activity Monitor's Dock icon — CPU Usage, CPU History, Network Usage, Disk Activity, Memory Usage, or the Activity Monitor icon — by choosing View➪Dock Icon. All but the Activity Monitor icon appear *live,* meaning that they update every few seconds to reflect the current state of affairs.

To choose how often these updates occur, choose View➪Update Frequency.

But be careful — shorter durations cause Activity Monitor itself to use more CPU cycles, which can decrease overall performance.

Finally, the bottom portion of the Activity Monitor window can display one of five different monitors. Just click the appropriate tab — CPU, System Memory, Disk Activity, Disk Usage, or Network — to see that particular monitor.

Geeks and troubleshooters can use Activity Monitor to identify what processes are running, which user owns the process, and how much CPU capacity and memory the process is using. You can even quit or force quit a process that you think might be causing problems for you.

Messing around in Activity Monitor isn't a good idea for most users. If you're having problems with an application or with Mac OS X, try quitting open applications; force-quitting applications (press ⌘+Option+Esc — the Mac "three-finger salute"); or logging out and then logging back in again before you start mucking around with processes.

AirPort Disk Utility

You use AirPort Disk Utility to discover USB 2.0 hard drives connected to your AirPort Extreme Base Station. You also use it to add an AirPort Disks menu item to your menu bar so you can see available USB 2.0 hard drives on your AirPort wireless network and connect to them manually. Find out more about sharing and networking with AirPort in Chapter 15.

AirPort Utility

You use AirPort Utility to set up an AirPort Base Station and configure its individual settings, such as base-station and wireless-network passwords, network name, Internet connection type, and so on.

When you first open AirPort Utility, select the AirPort Base Station you want to work with by clicking its icon on the left side of the window.

If you want assistance with setting up your base station, just click the Continue button in the bottom-right corner of the AirPort Utility window. You're asked a series of questions, and your base station will be configured accordingly. If you know what you're doing and want to change your base station's settings manually, choose Base Station➪Manual Setup (⌘+L) instead.

Audio MIDI Setup

This program is the control center for any MIDI devices built into or connected to your Mac.

Bluetooth File Exchange

If you have a Bluetooth device and your Mac has a Bluetooth adapter connected to a USB port (or has Bluetooth built in, although no Mac has it at the time of this writing), you can copy files from your Mac to the Bluetooth

Whither Bluetooth?

Bluetooth is the de facto standard for wireless communication between intelligent devices over short distances. At least that's my definition. One such intelligent device is the Motorola L2 wireless phone I've been using.

Bluetooth is a smart protocol. When two Bluetooth devices have been prepared (actually, paired), they recognize each other when they're within range — 20–30 feet — and then they automatically perform whatever task they were instructed to perform when they were paired.

My phone can receive calendar items, contacts, and little pictures from my Mac. I can back up the phone's memory to my Mac's hard drive, as well. And because my MacBook Pro has Bluetooth built into it, I can use the phone as a wireless modem and surf the Internet or check my e-mail from the beach if I want to, just like on TV.

What AirPort is to wireless networking, Bluetooth is to intelligent wireless peripheral connections.

Alas, Bluetooth isn't very fast and has a limited range (around 20–30 feet from your Mac). But it's swell for sending small amounts of data back and forth between devices. Watch for devices that you currently use via USB (digital cameras, printers, and such) to offer Bluetooth connectivity soon.

Warning: If your Mac doesn't have Bluetooth built in (or a Bluetooth adapter connected to it) and you try to launch Bluetooth File Exchange, it alerts you that your Mac doesn't have the proper Bluetooth hardware connected to it — and refuse to launch.

device — wirelessly — via Bluetooth. To do so, simply drag icons for Address Book items (vCard files), iCal items (vCal files), and pictures (.gif files) onto the Bluetooth File Exchange icon.

ColorSync Utility

ColorSync helps ensure color consistency when you're scanning, printing, and working with color images. This package includes ColorSync software as well as premade ColorSync profiles for a variety of monitors, scanners, and printers. And the ColorSync Utility has a bunch of tools designed to make working with ColorSync profiles and devices easier. You'll probably never need it, but I wanted to let you know it's there, just in case.

A *ColorSync profile* is a set of instructions for a monitor, scanner, or printer, which tells the device how to deal with colors and white so the device's output is consistent with that of other devices, as determined by the ColorSync profiles of the other devices. In theory, if two devices have ColorSync profiles, their output (on-screen, on a printed page, or in a scanned image) should match perfectly. Put another way, the color that you see on-screen should be exactly the same shade of color that you see on a printed page or in a scanned image.

If you're not a graphics artist working with color files and calibrating monitors and printers to achieve accurate color matching, you probably don't need the ColorSync Utility (unless you've gotten hooked on iPhoto and want your printed inkjet color pictures to match up correctly).

If you're compelled to do whatever it takes to get accurate color on your monitor and printer, check out *Color Management For Digital Photographers For Dummies,* by Ted Padova and Don Mason (Wiley).

DigitalColor Meter

The DigitalColor Meter program displays what's on your screen as numerical color values, according to two different systems: RGB (red-green-blue) or CIE (the abbreviation for a chromaticity coordinate system developed by the Commission Internationale de l'Eclairage, the international commission on illumination). If you're not a graphic artist or otherwise involved in the production of high-end color documents, you'll almost certainly never need it.

To calibrate or not to calibrate?

One thing you might want to try, even if you never plan to use ColorSync, is calibrating your monitor. This process adjusts the red, green, blue, and white levels and could make what you see on your screen look better than it does now.

To calibrate your monitor, follow these steps:

1. **Open the Displays System Preferences pane.**

2. **Click the Color tab and then write down the Display Profile that your Mac is currently using (it's highlighted in the Display Profile list).**

3. **Click the Calibrate button.**

   The Display Calibrator Assistant appears.

4. **Follow the simple on-screen instructions to calibrate your monitor and create a custom display profile.**

5. **Give your profile a name; then click the Continue button.**

If you decide that you don't like the results of your calibration, just select the Display Profile that you wrote down in Step 2 from the Display Profile list in the Displays System Preferences pane. Your monitor goes back the way it was before you calibrated it.

Disk Utility

If you're having problems with your hard drive or need to make changes to it, Disk Utility is a good place to start. This application has five active components: First Aid, Erase, Partition, RAID, and Restore.

First Aid

If you suspect something's not quite right with your Mac, the First Aid portion of Disk Utility should be among your first stops. Use First Aid to verify and (if necessary) repair an ailing drive. To use it, click the First Aid button on the left side of the Disk Utility window. Click a volume's icon and then click Verify. You get information about any problems that the software finds. If First Aid doesn't find any problems, you can go on your merry way, secure in the knowledge that your Mac is A-okay. If verification turns up trouble, click Repair to have the problem fixed. You can also use First Aid to fix disk permission problems.

You won't be able to use the copy of Disk Utility in your Applications/Utilities folder to repair your Mac OS X boot disk. To do that, you must reboot from a Mac OS X installation CD or DVD and run the copy of Disk Utility on that CD or DVD.

You can't use Disk Utility First Aid to fix a CD or DVD; neither can you use it to fix most disk image files. These disks are read only and can't be altered. You *can* fix Zip disks, SuperDisks, DVD-RAM discs, or any other writeable media that can be mounted by your Mac.

Erase

Use Erase to format (completely erase) a disk. You can't do this to the startup disk — the one with Mac OS X on it.

When you format a disk, you erase all information on it permanently. Formatting can't be undone — unless you're absolutely sure this is what you want to do, don't do it. Unless you have no use for whatever's currently on the disk, make a complete backup of the disk before you format it. If the data is critical, you should have at least two (or even three) known-to-be-valid backup copies of that disk before you reformat.

Partition

Use this tab to create disk partitions (multiple volumes on a single disk), each of which is treated as a separate disk by OS X.

RAID

By using Redundant Array of Individual Disks (RAID), you can treat multiple disks as a single volume, which is sort of the opposite of partitioning.

Restore

Use the Restore tab to restore your Mac to factory-fresh condition from a CD-ROM or disk-image file.

Speaking of disk images (and I will be in a minute), Disk Utility contains the functionality formerly found in the now-discontinued Disk Copy program.

Of partitions and volumes

Partitioning a drive lets you create multiple volumes. A *volume* is a storage space that (from the Mac's point of view) looks and acts just like a hard drive; a *partition* is simply a designated volume on a drive, completely separate from all other partitions (volumes). You can create any number of partitions, but it's a good idea to limit yourself to no more than a small handful. Lots of people, including me, use one partition for Mac OS X and another for Mac OS 9.

You can create drive partitions only on a newly formatted drive. So to partition a drive, first format it in Drive Setup and then create partitions. Before you do that, give some thought to how large a partition you want to create. You won't be able to change your mind about it later.

I think that partitions should be no smaller than 5GB. You can get away with 2GB if you have a smaller drive, but you don't need to create a lot of little partitions just to store your stuff.

Instead, use folders: They work just great for organizing things the way you like. The one exception to this rule is if you burn a lot of CDs with your CD-RW drive. In that case, a 650MB or 700MB (if you use that size CD) partition lets you *prototype* your CDs before you burn them — set up the content and check to see just how much stuff *will* fit on a single 650MB or 700MB disc. Of course, creating disk-image files of those sizes would leave the space free for other uses when you aren't prototyping.

By the same token, it's not necessary to use partitions. Many users never partition a hard drive and get along just fine. If you do choose to partition, you should probably limit the number of partitions you create. An iMac with a 120GB drive will do just fine with one or two (or maybe three) partitions — there's no need to create more.

In most cases, you install new software on your Mac from a CD-ROM or DVD-ROM, or by downloading it from the Internet. Software vendors typically use an installer program that decompresses and copies files to their proper places on your hard drive. After you've installed the software, you're back in business.

Apple's variation on this theme is a humongous file called the *disk image* — everything you'd normally find on a disk, without the disk. These days, more developers are adopting the disk-image format for their downloadable installers and updaters. When mounted on your Desktop (more on what *mounting* means in a minute), a disk image looks and acts just like a real disk. You can open it and see its contents in a Finder window, copy files from its window to another disk, drag it to the Eject button to remove it from your Desktop — go wild. To make a disk image appear on your Desktop, you double-click the image file. At that point, the Disk Utility application takes over and puts an icon (which for all intents and purposes looks like a disk) on your Desktop.

Disk Utility not only mounts images when you double-click them, but also lets you create your own disk-image files and burn them onto CD-ROMs and DVD-ROMs.

Because you can transfer disk images via the Internet — and because they act just like disks — they're a great substitute for a CD-ROM or other disk-based software installer. A software maker can create both a CD version of an installer and a disk image that can be downloaded.

By the way, you find out more about Disk Utility (mostly how to use it for troubleshooting) in Chapter 19.

Grab

Want to take a picture of your screen? I used to do this a lot so that I could bring you the screen shots in this book's figures. You can use Grab to take a picture of all or part of the screen and then save that file for printing or sending around (say, to all your screaming fans who want to see your Desktop pattern or how you've organized your windows). The first edition of this book used Grab, but I used the superb Snapz Pro X utility (Ambrosia Software; www.ambrosiasw.com) for the figures in subsequent editions. It's definitely worth the shareware fee.

Grab's best feature is its capability to do a timed screen capture. Like those cameras that let you start the timer and then run to get into the shot, Grab gives you ten seconds to bring the window you want to the front, pull down a menu, get the cursor out of the way, or whatever you need to do to get the screen just right.

Grab's default behavior is to display no cursor. If you want to show a cursor in your screen shots, choose Grab⇨Preferences and then select a pointer from the ten choices in the Preference dialog. To have no cursor, click the topmost, leftmost item, which is an empty box that indicates *no cursor*.

Grapher

Grapher is a venerable piece of eye candy that shows off your CPU's computational power. A quick, visual math instructor, Grapher can graph equations in two or three dimensions and speaks hexadecimal, octal, base ten, and binary to boot. You can even graph curves, surfaces, inequalities, differential equations, discrete series, and vector and scalar fields . . . whatever that means. (I found all that information in Apple Help.)

Installer

Installer is an application that you'll never need to open yourself. But don't get rid of it — software developers, including Apple, write installer scripts that automate the process of putting software on your Mac (that's what all those .pkg and .mpkg file extensions are about). These scripts know where everything should go and in what order — and to run, those installer scripts need to find this little program. If you simply leave this critter alone to snooze in peace, everything will be hunky-dory.

Java

This folder contains three tools for using the versatile and powerful Java language with your Mac:

✔ **Input Method Hot Key:** Use this tool to designate a hot key that allows you to choose among multiple input methods in a pop-up menu.

The hot key is available only while a Java application is the active application.

✔ **Java Preference:** This is a control panel for Java and plug-ins that you may run in your Web browser.

✔ **Java Web Start:** This nifty little tool lets you launch full-featured applications written in the Java language with a single click from within your Web browser. One big advantage of an application written in Java is that you don't have to wait for the publisher to create a Mac OS X version. The same Java code that runs on Windows or Linux or Solaris (Sun's version of Unix) will run on Mac OS X and inherit the Mac OS X interface.

Keychain Access

A *keychain* is a way to consolidate all your passwords — the one you use to log into your Mac, your e-mail password, and passwords required by any Web sites. Here's how it works: You use a single password to unlock your keychain (which holds your various passwords) and then you don't have to remember all your other passwords. Rest assured that your passwords are secure because only a user who has your keychain password can reach the other password-protected applications.

The Keychain Access utility is particularly cool if you have multiple e-mail accounts, and each one has a different password. Just add them all to your keychain, and you can get all your mail at the same time with one password.

A keychain known as the login keychain is automatically created for you when you install Mac OS X Leopard (or buy a new Mac with Leopard preinstalled).

Here's how to add passwords to your login keychain:

✔ **To add passwords for applications,** just open Mail or another application that supports the keychain. When the program asks for your password, supply it and choose Yes to add the password to the keychain.

How do you know which programs support the Keychain Access utility? You don't until you're prompted to save your password in a keychain in that Open dialog, connect window, or so forth. If a program supports Keychain Access, it offers a check box for it in the user ID/password dialog or window.

✔ **To add a Web site password to a keychain,** open the Keychain Access application and click the Password button. In the New Password Item window that opens, type the URL of the page (or copy and paste it) in the Keychain Item Name text field; type your username in the Account Name field; and then type your password in the Password text field, as shown in Figure 18-3.

Figure 18-3:
Add a URL
to the
keychain in
Keychain
Access.

> **Keychain Access**
>
> Keychain Item Name:
>
> https://www.banking.wellsfargo.com
>
> Enter a name for this keychain item. If you are adding an Internet password item, enter its URL (for example: http://www.apple.com)
>
> Account Name:
>
> 71077345
>
> Enter the account name associated with this keychain item.
>
> Password:
>
> yoke1[wish
>
> Enter the password to be stored in the keychain.
>
> Password Strength: Weak
>
> ☑ Show Typing
>
> Cancel   Add

To use the new URL password, use Safari to open the URL. If the account name and password aren't filled in for you automatically, choose Edit⇨AutoFill Form (⌘+Shift+A), and they will be. Now just click the appropriate button on the Web page to log in.

TIP

If you select the User Names and Passwords check box on the AutoFill tab of Safari's Preferences window (Safari⇨Preferences or ⌘+,), you don't have to add sites, accounts, or passwords manually. Instead, the first time you visit a site that requires an account name and password, when you log in, Safari asks whether you would like to save your password, as shown in Figure 18-4.

Figure 18-4:
The easy
way to add
to your
keychain.

> **Would you like to save this password?**
>
> To review passwords you have saved and remove them, open the AutoFill pane of Safari preferences.
>
> Never for this Website   Not Now   Yes

Migration Assistant

This is pretty much a one-trick pony, but that pony is a prizewinner. You use the Migration Assistant to transfer your account and other user information from another Mac or another volume on the current Mac to this one. You need to authenticate as an administrator to use it, but it's a pretty handy way to transfer an account without having to re-create all the preferences and other settings. When you first installed Leopard (or when you booted your nice new Leopard-based Mac for the first time), the setup utility asked you whether you wanted to transfer your information from another Mac — if you answered in the affirmative, it ran the Migration Assistant.

System Profiler

System Profiler is a little program that is launched when you click the More Info button in the About This Mac window (⌘⇨ About This Mac). It provides information about your Mac. (What a concept!) If you're curious about arcane questions such as what processor your Mac has or what devices are stashed inside it or are connected to it, give the Profiler a try. Click various items in the Contents list on the left side of the window, and information about the item appears on the right side of the window. Feel free to poke around this little puppy as much as you like — it's benign and can't hurt anything.

If you ever have occasion to call for technical support for your Mac, software, or peripherals, you're probably going to be asked to provide information from System Profiler. So don't get rid of it just because you don't care about this kind of stuff.

Terminal

Mac OS X is based on Unix. If you need proof — or if you actually want to operate your Mac as the Unix machine that it is — Terminal is the place to start.

Because Unix is a command-line-based operating system, you use Terminal to type your commands. You can issue commands that show a directory listing, copy and move files, search for filenames or contents, or establish or change passwords. In short, if you know what you're doing, you can do everything on the command line that you can do in Mac OS X. For most folks, that's not a desirable alternative to the windows-and-icons of the Finder window. But take my word for it; true geeks who are also Mac lovers get all misty-eyed about the combination of a command line *and* a graphical user interface.

You can wreck havoc upon your poor operating system with Terminal. You can harm your Leopard in many ways that just aren't possible using windows and icons and clicks. Before you type a single command in Terminal, think seriously about what I just said. And if you're not 100 percent certain about the command you've just typed, don't even think about pressing Return or Enter.

Chapter 19

Troubleshooting Mac OS X

In This Chapter

▶ Facing the dreaded Sad Mac

▶ Dealing with the flashing question mark

▶ Recovering from startup crashes

As a bleeding-edge Mac enthusiast with over 20 years of Mac experience under my belt, I've had more than my share of Mac troubles. Over those years, I've developed an arsenal of surefire tips and tricks that I believe can resolve more than 90 percent of Mac OS X problems without a trip to the repair shop.

Alas, if your hardware is dead, then, sadly, neither you nor I can do anything about it because it is now a job for your friendly Mac repairman and your fat checkbook or high-limit credit card.

But if your hardware is okay, you have a fighting chance of using the suggestions in this chapter to get your machine up and running.

Dem Ol' Sad Mac Chimes of Doom Blues

Although you usually see a stylish Apple logo when you turn on your computer, once in a blue moon, you might see the dreaded Sad Mac icon (shown in the left margin) and hear that melancholy arpeggio in G minor (better known as the *Chimes of Doom*), the sound of breaking glass, a car wreck, or any of the other horrible sounds that Macs make when they're dying.

The Sad Mac usually indicates that something very bad has happened to your Mac; often, some hardware component has bitten the dust. But Sad Macs are rather uncommon — many Mac users go an entire lifetime without seeing one. If you ever have a Sad Mac experience, don't despair immediately. Before you diagnose your Mac as terminally ill, try the following:

✔ Disconnect any external FireWire and USB devices (everything except your keyboard and mouse) and try booting from DVD-ROM to bring it back to life.

✔ If you've installed third-party memory (RAM from a vendor other than Apple), remove all non-Apple RAM chips and try booting from DVD-ROM to bring it back to life.

When I talk about *booting,* I mean starting up your Mac from a particular disk or disc. If you have your OS X installation DVD-ROM ready, you can skip to the section "Booting from a DVD-ROM," later in this chapter. If you're not sure about your Mac OS X installation DVD-ROM, see the next section.

The ultimate startup disk: The Mac OS X installation DVD

I bet you have a copy of the ultimate startup disk right there on your computer table — the installation DVD that came with your computer or (if you purchased a boxed retail copy of Leopard) Install Disk 1.

You see, in addition to the system software that you need to make your Mac work, all Mac OS X installation discs are bootable and include a working copy of Disk Utility, which I discuss in the section "Step 1: Run First Aid," later in this chapter.

If you see a flashing question-mark-on-a-folder sign (top left in Figure 19-1), prohibitory sign (top center), spinning-disc cursor (top right), or kernel panic alert (the text below the three top images) that doesn't go away when you start up your Mac, the first thing to do is attempt to repair hidden damage to your hard drive with the Apple Disk Utility program's First Aid feature.

Figure 19-1: These mean it's troubleshooting time.

Another of Disk Utility's features lets you verify and repair disk permissions, which is a handy thing to do if your Mac is telling you that you don't have the correct permission to do things that you *used* to be able to do, such as move a file or folder into the Applications (or other) folder or move an icon to the Trash.

You get a brass-tacks view of using these utilities throughout the rest of this chapter.

If you don't have a bootable DVD-ROM, preferably a Mac OS X Install DVD-ROM, you can't do most of the rest of the stuff in this chapter. So if you don't have it handy, go find it now. If you really can't find one, consider calling Apple or your Apple dealer to arrange for a replacement — you really shouldn't be without it.

Booting from a DVD-ROM

To boot your Mac from a DVD-ROM installation disc, follow these steps:

1. **Insert a bootable DVD-ROM (the Mac OS X Install DVD is a good choice).**

   If your Mac uses a tray to hold the DVD, make sure that it retracts and that the disc is in.

Better safe than Macless

The bootable Mac OS X Install DVD-ROM is soooo important — try to have more than one copy around. That way, if one gets misplaced, damaged, eaten by the dog, scuffed, scratched, or otherwise rendered useless, you won't be out of luck. I keep the Mac OS X Install DVD in my middle desk drawer and several other bootable CDs and DVDs on the bookshelf. An older version of Mac OS and the CD or DVD that came with your computer are examples of extra bootable discs that you might have hanging around. The Mac OS X Install DVD is bootable, as well. All these can boot your Mac in an emergency, which is why they're so important to have handy.

One thing I'd do — if I had only one of these valuable discs — is use Apple's Disk Utility (in Applications/Utilities) to create a disk image of the disc and then burn a copy or two as spares. Don't forget to test the burned discs to ensure that they work and are bootable.

Note: Mac OS X Leopard comes on a dual-layer DVD. That means that unless your Mac is relatively new you won't be able to burn a copy of it. If that's the case, find a friend or relative with a newer Mac and use it to copy the DVD. Trust me — it'll be worth the time and trouble if your original disc gets lost or damaged.

If you have a tray-loading DVD-ROM drive and it's closed, you can get it to open by restarting (or starting up) your Mac while pressing the mouse button. Continue pressing until the drive tray pops out; then release.

2. **Shut down or restart your Mac.**

   If you shut it down, wait a few seconds and then start it up the usual way.

3. **Press and hold down the C key immediately and keep it pressed until your Mac either boots from the DVD or doesn't. At this point, if it does boot from the DVD-ROM, skip to the section called, um, "If you can boot from DVD-ROM." If it doesn't boot, try Step 4.**

   If it boots, you see a Welcome screen; if it doesn't, you see a flashing question mark, prohibitory sign, or spinning wheel of death . . . anything but the first screen of the Mac OS X Installer, the login window, or the Finder.

4. **If your Mac doesn't boot after Step 3, hold down the Option key while booting to display the built-in Startup Manager (see Figure 19-2).**

   It displays icons for any bootable discs that it sees and allows you to select one (including the installation DVD).

Figure 19-2: The built-in Startup Manager.

5. **Click the DVD-ROM icon to select it (on the right in Figure 19-2), and then press Return or Enter to boot from it.**

   This technique is quite useful if your usual boot disk is damaged or having an identity crisis during startup. If it doesn't work, however, skip to the "If you can't boot from DVD-ROM" section.

If you can boot from DVD-ROM . . .

If you see the Mac OS X startup Welcome screen when you boot from your DVD-ROM, hope flickers for your Mac. The fact that you can boot from another disc (a DVD-ROM, in this case) indicates that the problem lies in one of two places: your hard drive and/or Mac OS X itself. Regardless of what the cause is, your Mac will probably respond to one of the techniques I discuss throughout the rest of this chapter.

So your Mac boots from the installation DVD-ROM, but you still have this little problem: You prefer that your Mac boot from your (much faster) hard drive than from the Install DVD-ROM. Not to worry. All you need to do is reinstall Mac OS X (as described in the appendix at the end of this book).

If you can't boot from DVD-ROM . . .

If the techniques in this chapter don't correct your Mac problem or you still see the Sad Mac icon when you start up with the DVD, either you just installed something new that's aggravating your Mac, or your Mac is probably toasted and needs to go in for repairs (usually to an Apple dealer).

To get your Mac up and running again, you can try any of the following:

- ✓ **Call the tech-support hotline.** Before you drag it down to the shop, try calling 1-800-SOS-APPL, the Apple Tech Support hotline. The service representatives there may be able to suggest something else that you can try. If your Mac is still under warranty, it's even free.

- ✓ **Ask a local user group for help.** Another thing you might consider is contacting your local Macintosh user group. You can find a group of Mac users near you by visiting Apple's User Group Web pages at www.apple.com/usergroups.

- ✓ **Try Dr. Mac Consulting.** Shameless plug alert! You can check out my consulting services at www.boblevitus.com or call 408-627-7577. My team of expert troubleshooters does nothing but provide technical help and training to Mac users, via telephone, e-mail, and/or our unique Internet-enabled remote control software, which allows us to see and control your Mac no matter where in the world you are.

- ✓ **Check whether you have RAM issues.** Here's a common problem: If you get the Sad Mac immediately after installing random-access memory (RAM) — or any new hardware, for that matter — double-check that the RAM chips are properly seated in their sockets. (*Warning:* Don't forget to shut down your Mac first.) With the power off and your Mac unplugged, remove and reinsert the RAM chips to make sure that they're seated properly. If you still have problems, remove the RAM chips temporarily and see whether the problem still exists.

  Follow the installation instructions that came with the RAM chips or the ones in the booklet that came with your Mac. But even if they don't say to, you should get rid of the spark, either by using an antistatic strap (available from most RAM sellers) or by touching an appropriate surface (such as the power-supply case inside your Mac) before you handle RAM chips.

Question Mark and the Mysterians

When you turn on your Mac, the first thing that it does (after the hardware tests) is check for a startup disk with Mac OS X on it. If your system doesn't find such a disk on your internal hard drive, it begins looking elsewhere — on a FireWire or Universal Serial Bus (USB) disk (Intel-based Macs only) or on a CD or DVD.

If you have more than one startup disk attached to your Mac, as many users do, you can choose which one your Mac boots from in the Startup Disk System Preferences pane.

At this point, your Mac usually finds your hard drive, which contains your operating system, and the startup process continues on its merry way with the happy Mac and all the rest. If your Mac can't find your hard drive (or doesn't find on it what it needs to boot Mac OS X), you encounter a flashing-question-mark icon or the prohibitory sign.

Don't go cryin' *96 Tears*. Those icons just mean that your Mac can't find a startup disk, a hard drive, or bootable CD-ROM or DVD-ROM with valid system software (either Mac OS X or a previous version supported by your particular Mac).

Think of the flashing question mark or prohibitory sign as your Mac's way of saying, "Please provide me a startup disk."

If Apple can figure out a way to put a flashing question mark or prohibitory sign on the screen, why the heck can't the software engineers find a way to put the words `Please insert a startup disk` on the screen, as well? The curtness of these icons is one of my pet peeves about the Macintosh. I know — you're clever and smart (because, of course, you're smart enough to find help reading *Mac OS X Leopard For Dummies*), so you know that a flashing question mark or prohibitory sign means you should insert a startup disk. But what about everyone else?

If you encounter any of these warning icons, go through the steps I outline next in this chapter. You can try different options, such as using Disk Tools and First Aid, zapping the parameter RAM (PRAM), and performing a Safe Boot. Try them in the order listed, starting with Step 1. Then, if one doesn't work, move on to the next.

Step 1: Run First Aid

In most cases, after you've booted successfully from the Mac OS X DVD, the first logical troubleshooting step is to use the First Aid option in the Disk Utility application.

Every drive has several strangely named components such as B-trees, extent files, catalog files, and other creatively named invisible files. They're all involved in managing the data on your drives. Disk Utility's First Aid feature checks all those files and repairs the damaged ones.

Here's how to make First Aid do its thing:

1. **Boot from your Mac OS X DVD by inserting the DVD and restarting your Mac while holding down the C key.**

   The Mac OS X Installer appears on your screen.

2. **Choose Installer⇨Open Disk Utility to launch the Disk Utility application that's on the DVD.**

3. **When the Disk Utility window appears, click the First Aid tab to select that function of Disk Utility.**

4. **Click the icon for your boot hard drive at the left of the Disk Utility window (*Macintosh HD* in Figure 19-3).**

   Your boot drive is the one with Mac OS X and your Home folder on it. I call this one *Macintosh HD*.

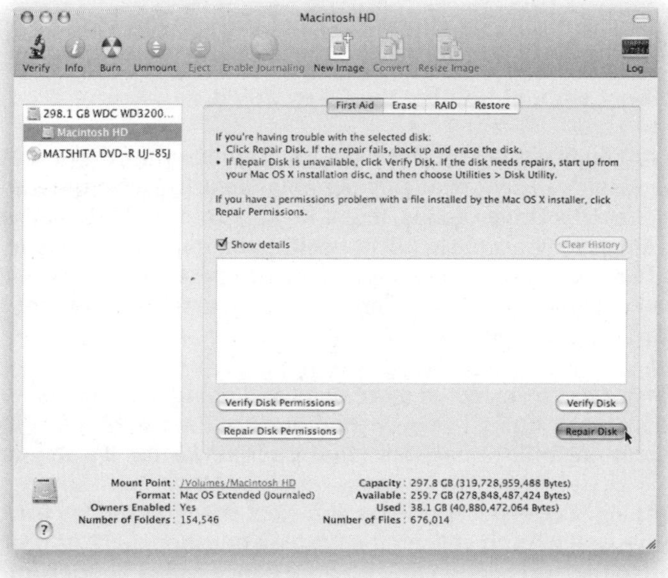

Figure 19-3:
First Aid, ready to perform its magic on the disk named Macintosh HD.

5. **Click the Repair Disk button.**

   Your Mac whirs and hums for a few minutes, and the results window tells you what's going on. Ultimately, First Aid tells you (you hope) that the drive has been repaired and is now okay, as shown in Figure 19-4. If so, go back to work.

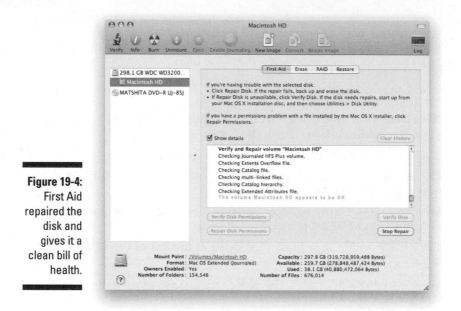

Figure 19-4:
First Aid
repaired the
disk and
gives it a
clean bill of
health.

6. **Quit Disk Utility by choosing Disk Utility⇨Quit Disk Utility or by pressing ⌘+Q.**

7. **Reboot without holding the C key down.**

If First Aid finds damage that it can't fix, a commercial disk-recovery tool, such as Alsoft's DiskWarrior (my personal favorite), MicroMat's TechTool Pro, or Prosoft's Drive Genius, might be able to repair the damage. And even if First Aid gave you a clean bill of health, you might want to run DiskWarrior or another third-party utility anyway, just to have a second opinion. Make sure you're running a current version; older versions might not be compatible with Mac OS X Leopard.

DiskWarrior has resurrected more dead and dying hard drives for me than any other disk-repair utility I've ever tried or all of them combined. If you're going to buy only one utility, make sure that it's DiskWarrior. It's almost like magic.

If everything checks out with First Aid, eject the DVD and try to boot from your hard drive again. If you still get the flashing question mark or prohibitory sign, proceed to the next section to try a little dance called booting into Safe Mode.

Step 2: Safe Boot into Safe Mode

Booting your Mac in Safe Mode might help you resolve your startup issue by not loading nonessential (and non–Mac OS X) software at boot time. You do it by holding down the Shift key during startup, as shown in Figure 19-5.

Figure 19-5:
You see
Safe Boot in
the startup
screen.

Keep holding down Shift until the Finder loads completely. If your Mac is set up so you don't have to log in, keep pressing the Shift key until the Finder loads completely. If you do log in to your Mac, type your password as usual, but before clicking the Log In button, press the Shift key again and hold it until the Finder loads completely.

You know you held the Shift key long enough if your Startup Items don't load (assuming that you have Startup Items; you can create them in the Accounts System Preferences pane, although some programs create them for you).

Booting in Safe Mode does three things to help you with troubleshooting:

- ✔ It forces a directory check of the startup (boot) volume.

- ✔ It loads only required kernel extensions (some of the items in /System/Library/Extensions).

- ✔ It runs only Apple-installed startup items (some of the items in /Library/Startup Items and /System/Library/Startup Items). Note that the startup items in the Library folders are different from the Startup Items in the Accounts System Preferences pane.

Taken together, normally these changes can work around issues caused by software or directory damage on the startup volume.

Some features don't work in Safe Mode. Among them are DVD Player, capturing video (in iMovie or other video-editing software), using an AirPort card, using some audio input or output devices, or using an internal or external USB modem. Use Safe Mode only if you need to troubleshoot a startup issue.

If your Mac boots in Safe Mode, you might be able to determine what's causing the issue by moving your Preferences folder (in Home/Library) to the Desktop temporarily or by disabling Startup Items (in the Accounts System Preferences pane). If either of these things works, you can put preferences files back in Home/Library/Preferences a few at a time, or you can re-enable Startup Items one at a time until you figure out which one is causing your problems.

If your Mac still has problems, try Step 3.

Step 3: Zapping the PRAM

Sometimes your *parameter RAM* (PRAM) becomes scrambled and needs to be reset. PRAM is a small piece of memory that's not erased or forgotten when you shut down; it keeps track of things such as:

- Time-zone setting
- Startup volume choice
- Speaker volume
- Recent kernel-panic information, if any
- DVD region setting

To reset (often called *zapping*) your PRAM, restart your Mac and press ⌘+ Option+P+R (that's four keys — good luck; it's okay to use your nose) until your Mac restarts itself. It's kind of like a hiccup. You might see the flashing question mark or spinning-disc cursor for a minute or two while your Mac thinks about it — then the icon disappears, and your Mac chimes again and restarts. Most power users believe you should zap it more than once, letting it chime two, three, or even four times before releasing the keys and allowing the startup process to proceed.

Now restart your Mac without holding down any keys.

If the PRAM zap didn't fix your Mac, move on to "Step 4: Reinstalling Mac OS X."

Remember that your chosen startup disk, time zone, and sound volume are reset to their default values when you zap your PRAM. So after zapping, open the System Preferences application to reselect your usual boot disk and time zone, and set the sound volume the way you like it.

Unlike previous versions of the Mac OS, Mac OS X doesn't store display or network settings in PRAM. If you're having problems with video or networking, resetting PRAM won't help.

Step 4: Reinstalling Mac OS X

I present the procedure to reinstall the system software as a second-to-last resort when your Mac won't boot correctly, because it takes the longest and is the biggest hassle. I detail this procedure at great length in the appendix.

Read the appendix and follow the instructions. If you're still unsuccessful after that point, you have no choice but to consider Step 5. . . .

Step 5: Take your Mac in for repair

If none of my suggestions works for you and you're still seeing anything you shouldn't when you start up your Mac, you have big trouble.

You could have any one of the following problems:

✔ Your hard drive is dead.

✔ You have some other type of hardware failure.

✔ All your startup disks and your system software DVDs are defective (unlikely).

The bottom line: If you still can't start up normally after trying all the cures I list in this chapter, you almost certainly need to have your Mac serviced by a qualified technician.

If Your Mac Crashes at Startup

Startup crashes are another bad thing that can happen to your Mac. These crashes can be more of a hassle to resolve than flashing-question-mark problems but are rarely fatal.

You know that a *crash* has happened when you see a System Error dialog, a frozen cursor, a frozen screen, or any other disabling event. A *startup crash* happens when your system shows a crash symptom any time between your flicking the power key or switch (or restarting) and having full use of the Desktop.

Try all the steps in the previous sections before you panic. The easiest way to fix startup crashes (in most cases) is to just reinstall Mac OS X from the DVD, using the Archive and Install option. I detail this procedure at great length in the appendix. Read the appendix and follow the instructions. If you're still unsuccessful after that point, come back and reread the "Step 5: Take your Mac in for repair" section.

Part VI
The Part of Tens

The 5th Wave   By Rich Tennant

"I tell you, it looks like Danny, it sounds like Danny, but it's <u>NOT</u> Danny!! I think the Mac has created an alias of Danny! You can see it in his eyes — little wrist watch icons!"

In this part . . .

These last chapters are a little different — they're kind of like long top-ten lists. Although I'd like for you to believe I included them because I'm a big fan of Dave Letterman, the truth is that Wiley always includes The Part of Tens section in its *For Dummies* books. This book continues the tradition. And because Wiley pays me, I do these chapters how I'm asked. (Actually, it's kind of fun.)

First, I tell you how to speed up your Mac experience. I then move on to a subject near and dear to my heart — awesome things for your Mac that are worth spending money on. Last but not least is a collection of great Mac-related Web sites.

Chapter 20

Ten Ways to Speed Up Your Mac Experience

● ●

*T*his chapter is for speed demons only. At some time in their Mac lives, most users have wished that their machines would work faster — even those with new Macs with multiple processors. I can't help you make your processors any faster, but here, I cover some ways to make your Mac at least *seem* faster. Better still, most of these tips won't cost you one red cent.

Use Those Keyboard Shortcuts

Keyboard shortcuts (see Table 20-1 for a way-groovy list of the most useful ones) can make navigating your Mac a much faster experience compared with constantly using the mouse, offering these benefits:

✔ If you use keyboard shortcuts, your hands stay focused on the keyboard, reducing the amount of time that you remove your hand from the keyboard to fiddle with the mouse.

✔ If you memorize keyboard shortcuts with your head, your fingers will memorize them, too.

✔ The more keyboard shortcuts you use, the faster you can do what you're doing.

Trust me when I say that using the keyboard shortcuts for commands that you use often will save you a ton of effort and hours upon hours of time.

Make a list of keyboard shortcuts you want to memorize and tape it to your monitor or somewhere where you'll see it all the time when using your Mac. (Heck, make a photocopy of Table 20-1!)

Table 20-1	Great Keyboard Shortcuts	
Keyboard Shortcut	*What It's Called*	*What It Does*
⌘+O	Open	Opens the selected item.
⌘+. (period)	Cancel	Cancels the current operation in many programs, including the Finder. The Esc key often does the same thing as Cancel.
⌘+P	Print	Brings up a dialog that enables you to print the active window's contents. (See Chapter 14 for info on printing.)
⌘+X	Cut	Cuts whatever you select and places it on the Clipboard. (I cover the Clipboard in Chapter 6.)
⌘+C	Copy	Copies whatever you select and places it on the Clipboard.
⌘+V	Paste	Pastes the contents of the Clipboard at the spot where your cursor is.
⌘+F	Find	Brings up a Find window in the Finder; brings up a Find dialog in most programs.
⌘+A	Select All	Selects the entire contents of the active window in many programs, including the Finder.
⌘+Z	Undo	Undoes the last thing you did in many programs, including the Finder.
⌘+Shift+?	Help	Brings up the Mac Help window in the Finder; usually, the shortcut to summon Help in other programs.
⌘+Q	Quit	Perhaps the most useful keyboard shortcut of all — quits the current application (but not the Finder because the Finder is always running).
⌘+Shift+Q	Log Out	Logs out the current user. The login window appears on-screen until a user logs in.
⌘+Delete	Move to Trash	Moves the selected item to the Trash.

Improve Your Typing Skills

One way to make your Mac seem faster is to make your fingers move faster. The quicker you finish a task, the quicker you're on to something else. Keyboard shortcuts are nifty tools, and improving your typing speed and accuracy *will* save you time. Plus you'll get stuff done faster if you're not always looking down at the keys when you type.

As your typing skills improve, you also spend less time correcting errors or editing your work.

The speed and accuracy that you gain has an added bonus: When you're a decent touch typist, your fingers fly even faster when you use those nifty keyboard shortcuts. (I list a gaggle of these in the preceding section, in Table 20-1.)

An easy way to improve your keyboarding skills is by using a typing tutor program such as Ten Thumbs Typing Tutor ($25 at www.tenthumbstyping tutor.com) or TypeTrainer4Mac (free at http://homepage.mac.com/ typetrainer4mac/Menu1.html).

Resolution: It's Not Just for New Year's Anymore

A setting that you can change to potentially improve your Mac's performance is the resolution of your monitor. Most modern monitors and video cards (or onboard video circuitry, depending on which Mac model you use) can display multiple degrees of screen resolution. You change your monitor's display resolution in the same place where you choose the number of colors you want: the Display System Preferences pane. Select your resolution choice from the Resolutions list on the left side of this tab.

In Displays System Preferences, select the Show Displays in Menu Bar check box to change resolutions and color depth without opening System Preferences. You can then select your resolution from the Displays menu that appears near the right end of your menu bar, as shown in Figure 20-1.

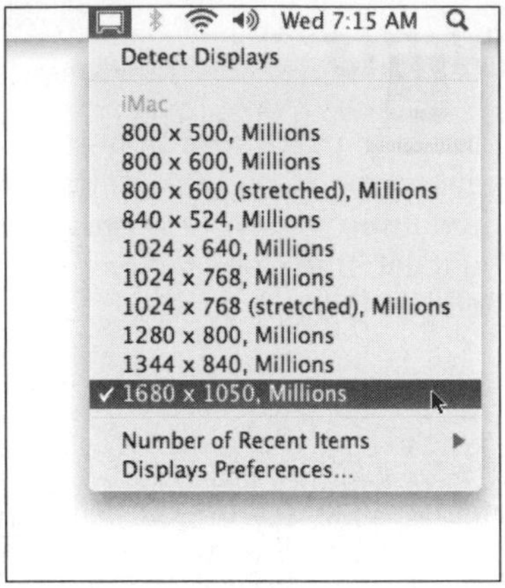

Detect Displays

iMac
800 x 500, Millions
800 x 600, Millions
800 x 600 (stretched), Millions
840 x 524, Millions
1024 x 640, Millions
1024 x 768, Millions
1024 x 768 (stretched), Millions
1280 x 800, Millions
1344 x 840, Millions
✓ 1680 x 1050, Millions

Number of Recent Items ▶
Displays Preferences...

Figure 20-1:
The handy
Displays
menu.

Here's the deal on display resolution: The first number is the number of pixels (color dots) that run horizontally, and the second number is the number of lines running vertically. It used to be that fewer pixels refreshed faster. But with LCD (flat-panel) monitors and notebooks, this isn't always true. I have to admit that the speed difference among resolutions these days is a lot less Z that you have to do and lets you display more open windows on-screen. Therefore, you could say that higher resolutions can speed up your Mac, as well.

Bottom line: Choose a resolution based on what looks best and works best for you. That said, if your Mac seems slow at its current resolution, try a lower resolution and see whether it feels faster.

Although you can use Mac OS X at resolutions of less than 1,024 x 768, Apple has designed the OS X windows and dialogs on the assumption that your resolution will be at least 1,024 x 768. So if you choose a resolution lower than that, some interface elements in some windows or programs may be drawn partially or completely off-screen. Just keep that in mind if you choose a resolution below 1,024 x 768.

A Mac with a View — and Preferences, Too

The type of icon display and the Desktop background that you choose affect how quickly your screen updates in the Finder. You can set and change these choices in the View Options window. From the Finder, choose View➪Show View Options (or use the keyboard shortcut ⌘+J).

The View Options window, like our old friend the contextual menu, is . . . well, contextual. Depending on what's active when you choose it from the View menu, you see one of four similar versions (shown in Figure 20-2). From left to right, the figure shows folders in Icon view, folders in List view, folders in Column view, folders in Cover Flow view, and the Desktop.

Figure 20-2:
Your
choices
in the View
Options
windows for
Icon view,
List view,
Column
view, Cover
Flow view,
and the
Desktop.

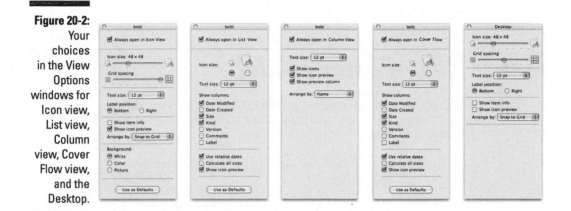

A handful of settings can impact the speed of your Mac or your ability to see what you want quickly:

- ✔ **Icon size:** The smaller the icon, the faster the screen updates, especially if the folder has many graphic files with *thumbnails* (those little icon pictures that represent the big picture the file contains).

  In the Icon view of the View Options window, moving the Icon Size slider to the left makes icons smaller and faster; moving it to the right makes them bigger and slower. In List view, select one of the two Icon Size radio buttons to choose smaller (faster) or larger (slower) icons. The difference is greater if you have an older Mac.

- ✔ **Calculate All Sizes:** I recommend that you deselect the Calculate All Sizes check box in the View Options window for List view. If you activate this option, the Finder calculates the size of every folder of every open window in List view and displays that number in the Size column. At least to me, the screen feels as though it redraws faster with this feature turned off. If you want to know how big a folder is, you can always just click it and choose File➪Get Info (or use the keyboard shortcut, ⌘+I).

- ✔ **Show Columns:** When it comes to speed, don't worry about the Show Columns check boxes in the View Options window for List view — Date Modified, Date Created, Size, Kind, Version, and Comments. The effect of these items on screen updating is pretty small these days, so your choice should probably be made according to the specific information you want to see in Finder windows, not on whether choosing them slows down your Mac.

The Use As Defaults buttons at the bottom of the Icon and List View Options windows set the default appearance for *all* Finder windows of that type. If you don't click the Use As Defaults button, any changes you make apply only to the active window (bobl in Figure 20-2). Note that Column windows and the Desktop don't have a Use As Defaults button; in both cases, any changes you make automatically become the default.

Get a New, Faster Model

Apple keeps putting out faster and faster Macs at lower and lower prices. But some Mac models still ship with a paltry 1GB of RAM — not enough to run Leopard at its best.

Check out the latest iMacs and Mac minis — they're excellent values. Or if you crave portability, MacBooks and MacBook Pros are rocking good computers and have never been less expensive. You might even consider a used Mac that's faster than yours. The big-time honcho of auction Web sites, eBay (`www.ebay.com`), has hundreds of used Macs up for auction at any given time. Shopping on eBay might just get you a better Mac at an outstanding price. Give it a try!

Another excellent option is to visit the Apple Web site and search for refurbished equipment. You can frequently save hundreds of dollars by purchasing a slightly used Mac that has been refurbished to factory specifications by Apple. Another advantage to refurbs is that they come with an Apple warranty. If you're on a tight budget, definitely check it out.

You Can Never Have Too Much RAM!

You get a lot of bang for your buck when you upgrade your Mac's RAM. Get an additional 512MB, 768MB, heck, even a gigabyte or two — you can never have too much. Your Mac will run better with at least 2GB of RAM, which will cost you around $100 in most cases and can be installed by anyone. Yes, anyone — the instructions are right there in your User Guide booklet, or you can find them at the Apple Technical Support pages (`www.apple.com/support`; search for *RAM upgrade* and your Mac model).

Unless, that is, you own a Mac mini. The Mac mini, you see, is exceedingly difficult to open without the proper and very specialized tool (a putty knife). And Apple frowns upon mere mortals applying such a tool to said Mac mini. Therefore, if you have a Mac mini, you might want to opt for the services of an authorized, certified Mac cracker-opener to perform your RAM upgrade. Or not.

Get a CPU Upgrade

In some cases, you can replace the processor (CPU) in your Mac with a faster one. CPU upgrades are rare for Apple's notebook models, but you might very well be able to upgrade your desktop Mac with a faster processor.

Before you plunk down the cash for an upgrade, be sure that it's compatible with Mac OS X Leopard. Some upgrades work only with older versions of Mac OS — and those won't help you.

Visit www.macworld.com for information on the various upgrade options available and how they compare with one another. Another great resource is Other World Computing at www.macsales.com, which offers a wide selection of CPU upgrades.

Upgrades start at a couple of hundred dollars and go up to more than a thousand clams. The older your Mac is, the more bang you can get for your CPU upgrade buck and the closer in price replacing your Mac gets to upgrading, especially when it comes to RAM speed. The slower RAM in many older Mac models imparts a severe bottleneck with most processor upgrades.

Get an Accelerated Graphics Card

An *accelerated graphics card* is designed to speed up one thing: the screen-update rate. They're extremely popular with graphic-arts professionals and gamers. Accelerated graphics cards blast pixels onto your screen at amazing speeds. And because the OS X Quartz Extreme imaging architecture hands off part of its load to the processor on an accelerated graphics card, it might even make other tasks faster because it does some of the work that your Mac's main processor (CPU) used to do.

That's the good news.

The bad news is that you can use a graphics accelerator only if your Mac has an accelerated PCI slot for it, which is where you install these suckers. Currently, only the PowerMac G4 or G5 and Mac Pro models are capable of graphics card upgrades.

Again, visit www.macworld.com for information on the various graphics cards available and how they compare with one another. Cards start at around a hundred dollars and go up from there. And remember, the older your Mac, the greater the performance boost you'll see.

Get a New Hard Drive

Depending on how old your Mac is, a faster hard drive could provide a substantial speedup. If you have a relatively new Mac — any Mac with a G5 or Intel processor — the internal hard drive that came with it is pretty fast already. Unless you also need more storage space, a new hard drive probably isn't the best way to spend your bucks. On the other hand, if you have an older G3 or G4 model, a faster (and larger) FireWire or USB 2 (if your Mac supports it) hard drive could be just the ticket.

FireWire and USB 2 are the fastest *busses* (or data pathways) you can use for external devices on most Macs.

FireWire, the current state of the art in connecting devices that need fast transfer speeds, is used to connect devices that require high-speed communication with your Mac — hard drives, CD burners, scanners, camcorders, and such.

FireWire is the fastest, easiest way to add storage to Macs that include it.

If you must use USB, make sure you get USB 2 and not plain ol' USB (Universal Serial Bus). Plain old USB works, of course, but it's as slow as molasses by comparison. (Plain old USB runs at about 3 percent of the speed of FireWire.)

USB 2, on the other hand, transfers data at roughly the same speed as FireWire. So if you have the need for speed, be sure you opt for a FireWire or USB 2 hard drive model and not a plain ol' USB model.

The good news is that whatever you choose, you can usually just plug it in and start using it. Ninety-nine percent of the time, there's nothing more to it!

If you have a Power PC processor (a G3, G4, or G5), note that you cannot use a USB 2 hard drive as your startup drive. Macs with Intel processors can boot from a USB 2 hard drive, but Macs with PowerPC processors cannot.

Chapter 21

Ten Ways to Make Your Mac Better by Throwing Money at It

● ●

*T*his is one of my favorite chapters. I love souping up my Macs. I live to find ways of working smarter, saving time or hand motion, and coaxing my Mac to do more work in less time. So it gives me great pleasure to share in this chapter my favorite top ten things that you can buy for your Mac to tweak it and make it faster, easier to use, and (I hope) more fun.

The items listed in this chapter are things I have, use every day, love dearly, and would (and probably will!) buy again.

RAM

RAM, or *random-access memory,* is your computer's primary working memory. The more you have, the smoother your Mac runs — period. If you have anything less than 1GB in your Mac, you'll like your Mac *a lot* better if you upgrade to 1GB or more. If you like to do more than a few things at the same time, more RAM will make you a much happier camper. (For what it's worth, RAM has never been cheaper than it is today — it's worth every penny.)

I know I mention it in the previous chapter, but in addition to speeding up your Mac, more RAM makes using your Mac better in other ways. For example, when you have plenty of RAM, you can open many programs at the same time without a performance penalty. I have 2GB of RAM in my desktop Mac and 3GB in my MacBook Pro. I almost always have the 15 or 20 programs I use most open at all times. Then, all my favorite applications are available instantly, and I don't have wait while a program launches.

It's also easy as pie to install RAM in most Macs made this decade. Chances are good that the manual for your Mac includes step-by-step instructions simple enough for a 9-year-old to follow. I know, because I once asked my (then) 9-year-old son to do it. Which he did — and with no trouble, either.

Backup Software and/or Hardware

Only two kinds of Mac users exist: those who have lost data and those who are going to. If your work means anything to you, you had better back it up before it's too late. If you have a spare hard drive, by all means use the cool new Time Machine software that comes with Mac OS X Leopard. If you want to create multiple backups to several different devices or types of media (DVD-R, CD-R, Tape, and so on), invest in the appropriate hardware and software.

In case you missed it, you can find a lot of info about backup software and hardware in Chapter 17.

A Better Monitor (Or a Second One)

If you have a tiny monitor, get a bigger one. With a larger monitor, you spend less time scrolling and rearranging windows and more time getting actual work done — which is a good thing, right?

The best thing about it is that most Macs let you use two monitors as though they were a single display. For example, my main computer setup includes two monitors: a 22-inch Apple Cinema flat-panel LCD display and an old-fashioned CRT display, a 24-inch NEC MultiSync. It's an awesome setup — one that I highly recommend. With two big monitors, I have the menu bar and Finder windows on the first monitor and document(s) that I'm working on displayed on the second. Or, when using a program such as Adobe Photoshop (which has lots of floating palettes), I can put the palettes on one monitor and documents I'm using on the other. And so on.

Another thing most Macs can do with two monitors is mirror what's on one display on the second one. So you can work with one display facing you and point the other one (or a projector) at the audience so they can see what you're doing, too.

Flat-panel LCD displays, such as the Apple Cinema Displays, have come down dramatically in price over the past year. In my humble opinion, LCD displays are brighter and easier on the eyes than traditional CRT (glass picture tube) monitors. Apple must agree, because it no longer sells any CRTs. If you can afford one, that's what you really want. Alas, owners of older iMacs, as well as most iBook owners, are out of luck on this tip — it's not possible to add a second monitor to those models. If you have a more recent iMac that includes a video port, however, you can get a bigger second monitor.

A Fast Internet Connection

High-bandwidth (that is, fast-Internet-access) connections just *rock.* If you add a high-speed Internet connection, such as digital subscriber line (DSL) or cable modem, your capacity to communicate electronically increases tenfold. With this add-on, you can join an online service, surf the Internet, e-mail your friends, and do much, much more, at speeds ten or more times faster than dial-up service with an analog modem. Web pages that took minutes to load with dial-up appears on-screen almost instantly. And broadband is fast enough for you to listen to streaming audio or watch streaming video without (many) hiccups.

If you can afford cable/DSL ($25–50/month in most places) and live in an area where you can get cable modem or DSL (not all places can yet), it will change the way you view the Internet. For more on setting up an Internet connection, see Chapter 9.

A DVD Burner

Most Macs come with an internal SuperDrive — Apple's name for a CD and DVD reader/writer. If your Mac *doesn't* have a SuperDrive, and you want to back up or archive a lot of data, consider adding an external CD/DVD burner.

Another reason you might want an external DVD burner is that many Macs now come with a slot-loading drive, which means you can't use mini-DVDs that many cameras and camcorders now employ. Most external DVD burners are tray-loading, making them more useful to mini-DVD camera and camcorder users. And having two DVD burners makes duplicating your iDVD offerings and the like faster and easier.

External DVD burners are available from many manufacturers and connect to your Mac via either FireWire or USB 2. These external devices have the same capabilities as a built-in Apple SuperDrive — they burn CD-Rs or CD-RWs that can hold up to 700MB of data, and DVD-Rs or DVD-RWs that can hold up to 8.5GB of data. The only difference between an Apple SuperDrive and a third-party CD/DVD burner is that the latter is external. And because it's not made by Apple, it isn't called a "SuperDrive."

If you don't already have a DVD burner, an external CD/DVD burner is the way to go. If you're getting a new Mac soon, pop for a SuperDrive — I promise you won't regret it.

If you have a SuperDrive (or an external CD/DVD burner), for goodness' sake — use it to back up your stuff!

Games

Gaming on the Mac has never been better, and the game developers are getting better and better at coaxing even more performance out of Mac OS X.

Some of the games I love include *Prey, Unreal Tournament,* and every pinball game LittleWing (`www.littlewingpinball.com`) has ever created. Try one — you'll be amazed at how far computer gaming has come.

Multimedia Titles

Many great games, references, and educational titles come on CD-ROM or DVD-ROM these days. My favorite is *World Book,* which makes use of many Mac features to deliver an encyclopedia that's both authoritative and fun to use. You'll love it, and so will your kids. Remember, your Mac is more than just a computer — it's a full-blown multimedia player. Enjoy it.

Don't forget that most Macs can also play video DVDs like those you rent at Blockbuster or NetFlix.

Some Big Honking Speakers with a Subwoofer

Face it: Most Macs have crummy speakers (or, worse, only one crummy speaker). With a decent set of speakers, games are more fun, music sounds like music instead of AM radio, and the voiceovers in your multimedia titles suddenly become intelligible. If you're into sound, you'll enjoy your Mac much more if you add a set of window-rattling speakers, preferably with a massive subwoofer to provide that booming bass that sound lovers crave. So crank it up! I'm partial to Blue Sky's EXO 2.1 Stereo Monitoring Speaker System (`www.abluesky.com`), which is totally awesome but not cheap (around $350). But any good speakers kick the stuffing out of the speakers built into any Mac.

If you have a DVD-ROM drive, a killer set of speakers makes watching movies on your Mac a zillion times better.

A New Mouse and/or Keyboard

If you're still using that crummy one-button mouse that came with your iMac, G3, or G4, do yourself a favor and beat it to death with a hammer. Then buy a real mouse. You'll be so much happier if you upgrade to a mouse that's easier to move around, more comfortable to use, and maybe even has two or more buttons and/or a scroll wheel. You'll be amazed at how much easier it is to work with a mouse that fits your hand. OS X knows all about multibutton mice and scroll wheels. And with a two-button mouse, you no longer have to hold down the Control key while clicking to display a contextual menu — you can just right-click.

Also consider ditching the silly little keyboard that came with your iMac, eMac, Power Mac, Mac Pro, or whatever. Third-party Mac keyboards on the market today are a huge improvement over what probably came with your Mac.

Although I'm partial to third-party keyboards, even I have to admit that the standard Apple Pro keyboard is an excellent product.

I'm partial to so-called ergonomic keyboards, which I find more comfortable for prolonged writing sessions. I also think I type faster with this kind of keyboard. My current axe is a Microsoft Natural Ergonomic Keyboard 4000. Even though it's a Windows keyboard and the modifier keys are mislabeled (the ⌘ key says *Alt,* and the Option key says *Start* and has a Windows logo on it), Microsoft offers excellent Mac OS X drivers for it.

A MacBook or MacBook Pro

You need a laptop because one Mac is never enough. With a portable Mac, you can go anywhere and continue to compute. And both MacBooks and MacBook Pros come with Apple AirPort Extreme wireless networking, so you can surf the Net, print, and share files from the couch, pool, the airport (the kind with airplanes and a lowercase *a* and *p*) — or Starbucks, for that matter.

Chapter 22

Ten (Or So) Great Web Sites for Mac Freaks

• •

As much as I would love to think that this book tells you everything you need to know about using your Mac, I know better. You have a lot more to discover about using your Mac, and new tools and products come out every single day.

The best way to gather more information than you could ever possibly soak up about all things Macintosh is to hop onto the Web. There, you can find news, *freeware* and *shareware* (try-before-you-buy software) to download, troubleshooting sites, tons of news and information about your new favorite OS, and lots of places to shop. So make sure that you read Chapter 9 to get set up for the Internet — because this chapter is all about finding cool stuff on the Web to help you use your Mac better (and have lots of fun doing it).

The sites in this chapter are the best, most chock-full-o'-stuff places on the Web for Mac users. By the time you finish checking out these Web sites, you'll know so much about your Mac and Mac OS X Leopard that you'll feel like your brain is in danger of exploding. On the other hand, you might just feel a whole lot smarter. Happy surfing!

MacFixIt

www.macfixit.com

Frequent *Macworld* contributor and consultant Ted Landau put together an excellent troubleshooting site to help users solve common problems and keep current on compatibility issues with new system software and third-party products.

Alas, Ted has taken a less active role in the site of late, and there is now a surcharge to search the archives. This site isn't quite as useful as it once was if you don't purchase a Pro membership (currently $25 a year). But even without paying, it's worth checking this site when you have any problem with your Mac. Chances are good that MacFixIt has a solution.

If you're serious about Mac troubleshooting, though, I encourage you to pop for a Pro subscription at just over $2 a month. It's worth more than that to have unlimited access to MacFixIt's extensive, searchable troubleshooting archives and special reports.

I use it so much that I'd consider it a bargain at twice the price.

VersionTracker

www.versiontracker.com

For free software or shareware, check out VersionTracker. It's one of the best sites in the world for software to use with Leopard (or any version of Mac OS, for that matter). It's also terrific for getting the latest version of any kind of software: commercial, shareware, and/or freeware. VersionTracker is a virtual treasure trove of software and updates, and it's worth visiting even when you aren't looking for anything in particular.

You can also purchase a subscription to VersionTracker Pro (which is offered in combination with a MacFixIt Pro subscription at a reduced price and is what I have). Your subscription gets you special Version Tracker software that searches your hard drive for applications and can notify you when any program you own has been updated. If you own or download a lot of programs, a VersionTracker Pro subscription is a wonderful thing indeed. So check it out and download something useful, interesting, fun, or all three.

I love this site and sometimes visit it several times a day. (I know — I should get a life.)

MacInTouch

www.macintouch.com

For the latest in Mac news, updated every single day, check out MacInTouch. com. Authored by longtime *MacWeek* columnist Ric Ford and his staff of newshounds and knowledgeable readers, this site keeps you on the bleeding edge of Mac news, including software updates, virus alerts, and Apple happenings. It also offers extensive and unbiased reviews of most Apple hardware and software soon after its release.

I consider MacInTouch essential for keeping up with what's new and cool for your Mac.

MacMinute

www.macminute.com

Here's another great source of up-to-the-minute Macintosh news. It's a great site, updated many times a day with lots of useful stories, links, and other Mac info.

Apple Support and Knowledge Base

www.apple.com/support

Do you have a technical question about any version of Mac OS or any Apple product — including Mac OS X Leopard? March your question right over to the Apple Support and Knowledge Base page, where you can find searchable archives of tech notes, software update information, and documentation. The Knowledge Base is especially useful if you need info about your old Mac — Apple archives all its info here. Choose among a preset list of topics or products and type a keyword to research. You're rewarded with a list of helpful documents. Clicking any one of these entries (they're all links) takes you right to the info you seek. The site even has tools that can help narrow your search.

The site also offers a section with user discussions of Apple-related topics. Although not officially sanctioned or monitored by Apple, it's often the best place to gain insights, especially on slightly esoteric or obscure issues not covered in the Knowledge Base.

The Mac OS X Home Page

www.apple.com/macosx/leopard

Part of the main Apple Web site, this section is all about Mac OS X Leopard, its cool features, how to get the most from it, what applications are available for it, and so on. Check in here to see what Apple has cooking; think of it as one-stop shopping for your Mac.

ramseeker

www.macseek.com

One of the best ways to make your Mac better is to buy more random-access memory (RAM). *RAM* is the readily available memory that your computer uses; the more you have, the smoother programs run. Although Mac OS X might run on a Mac with less than 512MB of RAM, it works much better and faster with more than that — at least 1GB, in my opinion. As cheap as RAM is today, the price that you pay for it can still vary quite a bit. The best way I know to get the lowdown on RAM prices is to use the ramseeker feature of this site, which surveys multiple vendors daily and then organizes current memory prices by Mac type.

Other World Computing

www.macsales.com

Other World Computing has become the "go to" place for Mac peripherals. Whether you need RAM, hard drives, optical drives, video cards, processor upgrades, or anything else you can think of, Other World Computing probably has it at a reasonable price. Because of its inexpensive and reliable delivery and a solid guarantee of every item, you can't go wrong buying from OWC.

EveryMac.com

www.everymac.com

The author of this site claims that it's "the complete guide of every Macintosh, Mac Compatible, and upgrade card in the world." You can't argue with that (unless you've done a staggering amount of research). Check out the Forum and Q&A sections for answers to Mac-related questions.

The Mac Observer

www.macobserver.com

The Mac Observer gives you Mac news, views, reviews, and much more. I write a column — "Dr. Mac's Rants & Raves" — for it twice a month, but I loved this site long before it hired me.

Inside Mac Games

www.imgmagazine.com

Inside Mac Games is the best of the Mac gaming sites on the Web (at least in my humble opinion). Order CDs of game demos, download shareware, check out game preview movies, or shop for editors and emulators. Find forum camaraderie and troubleshoot gaming problems, too.

dealmac

www.dealmac.com

Shopping for Mac stuff? Go to dealmac ("How to go broke saving money," this site boasts) first to find out about sale prices, rebates, and other bargain opportunities on upgrades, software, peripherals, and more.

Dr. Mac Consulting

www.boblevitus.com

Dr. Mac Consulting is (in all due modesty) my cool new troubleshooting, training, and technical-support site, designed just for Mac users. With several expert technicians on staff, Dr. Mac Consulting provides jargon-free expert technical help at a fair price, regardless of your physical location — and usually on the same day. Let one of our experts (or even me) provide high-quality Macintosh troubleshooting, technical support, software or system training, prepurchase advice, and more! We do our thing via phone; e-mail; iChat; and/or our unique Web-enabled, remote-control software (or Leopard Screen Sharing), which lets us fix many common Mac ailments in less than an hour, controlling your mouse and keyboard remotely as we explain everything we're doing to you on the phone.

The next time you need help and none of the aforementioned sites does the trick, why not let Dr. Mac Consulting make the mouse call? (So to squeak.)

Note: This crass commercial message is the only time in the whole book where I blather on about my "day job." So if there's something you want to know about your Mac or something you would like examined or fixed, we can probably help you in less than an hour. I hope you'll give it a try.

And now, back to your regularly scheduled programming.

Appendix

Installing or Reinstalling Mac OS X Leopard (Only If You Have To)

*I*f Mac OS X Leopard came preinstalled on a new Mac, you'll probably never need this appendix.

If you're thinking about reinstalling because something has gone wrong with your Mac, know that a Mac OS X reinstallation is a pain-in-the-buttocks final step. Be sure you've tried all the stuff in Chapter 19 before even thinking about reinstalling OS X. If nothing else fixes your Mac, reinstalling Mac OS X could well be your final option before invasive surgery (that is, trundling your Mac to a repair shop). You don't *want* to reinstall OS X if something easier can correct the problem. So if you have to do a reinstallation, realize that this is more or less your last hope (this side of the dreaded screwdriver, anyway).

In this appendix, you discover all you need to know to install or reinstall OS X, if you should have to. I say reinstalling is a hassle because although you won't lose the contents of your Home folder, applications you've installed, or the stuff in your Documents folder (unless something goes horribly wrong or you have to reformat your hard drive), you might lose the settings for some System Preferences, which means you'll have to reconfigure those panes manually after you reinstall. And you might have to reinstall drivers for third-party hardware such as mice, keyboards, tablets, and the like.

It's not the end of the world, but it's almost always inconvenient. That said, reinstalling OS X almost always corrects all but the most horrifying and malignant of problems. And as you soon see, the process is (compared with root-canal work or income taxes) relatively painless.

I stay with you through it all, though; don't you worry about a thing.

How to Install (or Reinstall) Mac OS X

In theory, you should have to install Mac OS X only once. And in a perfect world, that would be the case. But you might find occasions when you have to install/reinstall it, such as

- ✔ If you get a Mac that didn't come with Mac OS X Leopard preinstalled
- ✔ If you have a catastrophic hard-drive crash that requires you to initialize (format) your boot drive
- ✔ If you buy an external hard drive and want it to be bootable
- ✔ If any essential Mac OS X files become damaged or corrupted, or are deleted or renamed

The following instructions do double duty: They're what you do to install OS X for the first time on a Mac, and they're also what you do if something happens to the copy of OS X that you boot your Mac from. That is, the following describes both the process for installing and the process for *re*installing OS X. The only difference is the choice you make in the Options window in Step 4.

If you've backed up or duplicated your entire hard drive, you might prefer to reinstall from your backup disks, CDs, DVDs, or tapes rather than reinstalling OS X from the Install Mac OS X DVD. That way, you can be certain that anything you've tweaked on your Mac will be just the way you left it — your System Preferences will be the way you like them, and you won't have to bother with reinstalling drivers for your third-party hardware.

Here's how to install (or reinstall) OS X, step by step:

1. **Boot from your Install Mac OS X DVD by inserting the DVD into your machine's DVD drive and then restarting your Mac while holding down the C key.**

   When Mac OS X has finished booting your Mac, the Install program launches automatically. Here's where you begin the process of installing or reinstalling Mac OS X.

2. **Unless you want to use a language other than English for the main language of Mac OS X, click the Continue button (a blue arrow pointing to the right) in the first screen you see.**

   If you do want to use another language, select the language by clicking its name and then click the Continue button.

3. **Read the Welcome and Software License Agreement screens, clicking Continue after each.**

A sheet drops down, asking whether you agree to the terms of the license agreement. If you don't, you can't go any farther, so I advise you to go ahead and click the Agree button.

4. **Choose the disk on which you want to install (or reinstall) Mac OS X by clicking its icon once in the Select a Destination screen. Then select an option from the Options button.**

   At the bottom of the Select a Destination screen is the Options button, which offers three mutually exclusive choices:

   - *Upgrade Mac OS X:* Choose this option to upgrade an earlier version of OS X installed on the disk you choose in this step. Your Home and other files are left undisturbed; after the upgrade, things will be (more or less) as they were before, except you'll be running a redone installation of OS X.

   - *Archive and Install:* Choose this option to move all the System components from your existing OS X installation into a folder named Previous System and then install a fresh new copy of OS X. The Previous System folder cannot be used to boot — but it does contain any and all files that were in any of the OS X folders before you upgraded.

     If you select this option, a check box for a second option — Preserve Users and Network Settings — becomes available. Select it if you want to import all the existing users of this Mac, their Home folders, and their network settings — but still archive all the old System stuff in the Previous System folder.

     If you choose this option, you skip the Setup Assistant discussed later in this appendix.

   - *Erase and Install:* Choose this option if you want to completely erase the disk that you selected in Step 4, starting completely from scratch — which gives you a factory-fresh installation.

     If you choose the Erase and Install option, the disk you selected in Step 4 will be erased — and all your files will be deleted immediately! You should choose this option only if you've backed up all your documents and applications. In most cases, erasing the startup disk isn't necessary.

     If you select this option, the Format Disk As pop-up menu appears. Your choices are Mac OS Extended (Journaled), which is the one you want, and Unix File System (the one you don't want).

     Unix File System isn't a good choice for most Mac OS X users. Suffice it to say that 99.9 percent of people should absolutely and positively *avoid* Unix File System like the proverbial plague (the 0.1 percent know who they are — and why they need a UFS disk). 'Nuff said.

5. **Click OK to return to the Select a Destination screen and then click Continue.**

6. **Select which installation to perform — easy or customized:**

    • *Easy Install* copies all Mac OS X onto your chosen hard drive (which you choose in Step 4).

    • *Custom Install* (click the Customize button at the bottom of the screen) enables you choose to install only the items that you want to install.

In almost all cases, whether you're either doing a complete installation or reinstallation, Easy Install is the easy way to go — so that's what I assume you'll choose for the rest of these steps.

7. **To begin the installation, click the Install button.**

    The operating system takes 10 to 30 minutes to install, so now might be a good time to take a coffee break. When it's done installing, your Mac restarts itself, and you can begin using Mac OS X . . . hopefully trouble-free.

    After your Mac reboots, the Setup Assistant appears — *unless* you've chosen Archive and Install and also selected the Preserve Users and Network Settings option, which would obviate the need for the Setup Assistant. (Your settings from before the installation would be intact.)

8. **Work your way through all the Setup Assistant screens.**

    You have to do that housekeeping before you can begin working in OS X, and I show you how in the next section.

Getting Set Up with Setup Assistant

Assuming that your installation (or reinstallation) process goes well and your Mac restarts itself, the next thing you should see (and hear) is a short, colorful movie that ends by transforming into the first Setup Assistant screen, fetchingly named *Welcome*.

To tiptoe through the Setup Assistant, follow these steps:

1. **When the Welcome screen appears, choose your country from the list by clicking it once and then click the Continue button.**

    If your country doesn't appear in the list, select the Show All check box, which causes a bunch of additional countries to appear in this list.

    After you click Continue, the Personalize Settings screen appears.

2. **Choose a keyboard layout from the list by clicking it once; then click Continue.**

   If you're an American (or want to use an American keyboard setup), click the U.S. listing. If you prefer a different country's keyboard layout, select the Show All check box, and a bunch of additional countries (as well as a pair of Dvorak keyboard layouts) appears in the list. Choose the one you prefer by clicking it — and *then* click Continue.

   The Migration Assistant screen will appear next. If this is a brand-new Mac or you're installing Mac OS X Leopard on a Mac and have an older Mac nearby, you can transfer all your important files and settings by following the on-screen instructions and connecting the new and old Macs via FireWire cable. Just follow the instructions given by the Migration Assistant and then chill for a while — it'll probably take an hour or more to transfer your files and settings from the old Mac to the new one.

   The Your Apple ID screen appears.

3. **Click the appropriate radio button: My Apple ID Is, Create an Apple ID for Me, or Don't Create an Apple ID for Me. If you have an Apple ID, type your username and password in the appropriate fields. Now click Continue.**

   Click the Learn More button to find out more about an Apple ID and what it can do for you. In a nutshell, it lets you make one-click purchases at the iTunes Store, iPhoto, or the Apple Store. If you get one now, you also get a free, limited 60-day trial account with .Mac. When you're finished reading, click OK and then click Continue.

   The Registration Information screen appears.

4. **Fill out the fields (name, address, phone number, and so on) and then click Continue.**

   If you're interested in what Apple will and won't do with this information, click the Privacy button on this screen and read the Privacy Policy.

   The Thank You screen appears.

5. **Click Continue.**

   The Create Your Account screen appears.

6. **Fill in the Name, Short Name, Password, Verify, and Password Hint fields; then click Continue.**

   This first account that you create will automatically have administrator privileges for this Mac. You can't easily delete or change the name you choose for this account, so think it through before you click Continue.

   Each of these fields has an explanation below it.

   You can't click the Continue button until you've filled in all five fields.

   The Get Internet Ready screen appears.

7. **Select one of these four radio buttons and then click Continue:**

   • I'd Like a Free Trial Account with EarthLink

   • I Have a Code for a Special Offer from EarthLink

   • I'll Use My Existing Internet Service

   • I'm Not Ready to Connect to the Internet

If you choose to use your existing Internet service, you see another series of screens in which you provide specific information about how you connect to the Internet, your IP address (if you have one), what kind of connection you have, and so on. If you don't know one or more of the items in this series of screens, don't worry — just leave them blank and keep clicking the Continue button. Later, after the Setup Assistant finishes and you're up and running with OS X, you can ask your ISP (Internet service provider) about any empty fields, get any needed information, and add information in the appropriate places (the Network and/or Internet System Preference panes).

When you've completed this selection, the Set Up Mail screen appears.

8. **If you want to set up the Mail program now, click the appropriate radio button — Use My Mac.com Account Only or Add My Existing Email Account. Fill in the blanks and then click Continue.**

   The Select Time Zone screen appears.

9. **Click your part of the world on the map, choose a city from the pop-up menu, and then click Continue.**

   The Set the Date and Time screen appears.

10. **Set today's date and the current time, and then click Continue.**

11. **When the next screen appears, click Done.**

   The assistant quits, and in a few moments, the Mac OS X Desktop appears. That's it. You're done.

Index

SPORTS, FITNESS, PARENTING, RELIGION & SPIRITUALITY

0-471-76871-5

0-7645-7841-3

Also available:
- Catholicism For Dummies
  0-7645-5391-7
- Exercise Balls For Dummies
  0-7645-5623-1
- Fitness For Dummies
  0-7645-7851-0
- Football For Dummies
  0-7645-3936-1
- Judaism For Dummies
  0-7645-5299-6
- Potty Training For Dummies
  0-7645-5417-4
- Buddhism For Dummies
  0-7645-5359-3

- Pregnancy For Dummies
  0-7645-4483-7 †
- Ten Minute Tone-Ups For Dummies
  0-7645-7207-5
- NASCAR For Dummies
  0-7645-7681-X
- Religion For Dummies
  0-7645-5264-3
- Soccer For Dummies
  0-7645-5229-5
- Women in the Bible For Dummies
  0-7645-8475-8

TRAVEL

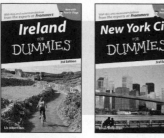

0-7645-7749-2

0-7645-6945-7

Also available:
- Alaska For Dummies
  0-7645-7746-8
- Cruise Vacations For Dummies
  0-7645-6941-4
- England For Dummies
  0-7645-4276-1
- Europe For Dummies
  0-7645-7529-5
- Germany For Dummies
  0-7645-7823-5
- Hawaii For Dummies
  0-7645-7402-7

- Italy For Dummies
  0-7645-7386-1
- Las Vegas For Dummies
  0-7645-7382-9
- London For Dummies
  0-7645-4277-X
- Paris For Dummies
  0-7645-7630-5
- RV Vacations For Dummies
  0-7645-4442-X
- Walt Disney World & Orlando
  For Dummies
  0-7645-9660-8

GRAPHICS, DESIGN & WEB DEVELOPMENT

0-7645-8815-X

0-7645-9571-7

Also available:
- 3D Game Animation For Dummies
  0-7645-8789-7
- AutoCAD 2006 For Dummies
  0-7645-8925-3
- Building a Web Site For Dummies
  0-7645-7144-3
- Creating Web Pages For Dummies
  0-470-08030-2
- Creating Web Pages All-in-One Desk
  Reference For Dummies
  0-7645-4345-8
- Dreamweaver 8 For Dummies
  0-7645-9649-7

- InDesign CS2 For Dummies
  0-7645-9572-5
- Macromedia Flash 8 For Dummies
  0-7645-9691-8
- Photoshop CS2 and Digital
  Photography For Dummies
  0-7645-9580-6
- Photoshop Elements 4 For Dummies
  0-471-77483-9
- Syndicating Web Sites with RSS Feeds
  For Dummies
  0-7645-8848-6
- Yahoo! SiteBuilder For Dummies
  0-7645-9800-7

NETWORKING, SECURITY, PROGRAMMING & DATABASES

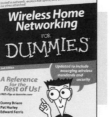

0-7645-7728-X

0-471-74940-0

Also available:
- Access 2007 For Dummies
  0-470-04612-0
- ASP.NET 2 For Dummies
  0-7645-7907-X
- C# 2005 For Dummies
  0-7645-9704-3
- Hacking For Dummies
  0-470-05235-X
- Hacking Wireless Networks
  For Dummies
  0-7645-9730-2
- Java For Dummies
  0-470-08716-1

- Microsoft SQL Server 2005 For Dummies
  0-7645-7755-7
- Networking All-in-One Desk Reference
  For Dummies
  0-7645-9939-9
- Preventing Identity Theft For Dummies
  0-7645-7336-5
- Telecom For Dummies
  0-471-77085-X
- Visual Studio 2005 All-in-One Desk
  Reference For Dummies
  0-7645-9775-2
- XML For Dummies
  0-7645-8845-1